Ius Gentium: Comparative Perspectives on Law and Justice

Volume 109

Ius Gentium is a book series which discusses the central questions of law and justice from a comparative perspective. The books in this series collect the contrasting and overlapping perspectives of lawyers, judges, philosophers and scholars of law from the world's many different jurisdictions for the purposes of comparison, harmonisation, and the progressive development of law and legal institutions. Each volume makes a new comparative study of an important area of law. This book series continues the work of the well-known journal of the same name and provides the basis for a better understanding of all areas of legal science.

The *Ius Gentium* series provides a valuable resource for lawyers, judges, legislators, scholars, and both graduate students and researchers in globalisation, comparative law, legal theory and legal practice. The series has a special focus on the development of international legal standards and transnational legal cooperation.

Sohail Aftab

Comparative Perspectives on the Right to Privacy

Pakistani and European Experiences

Springer

Sohail Aftab
Ministry of Information and Broadcasting
Government of Pakistan
Islamabad, Pakistan

ISSN 1534-6781 ISSN 2214-9902 (electronic)
Ius Gentium: Comparative Perspectives on Law and Justice
ISBN 978-3-031-45574-2 ISBN 978-3-031-45575-9 (eBook)
https://doi.org/10.1007/978-3-031-45575-9

This Springer imprint is published by the registered company Springer Nature Switzerland AG
The registered company address is: Gewerbestrasse 11, 6330 Cham, Switzerland

*I dedicate this book to **Qandeel Baloch**, whom I consider a symbol of privacy infringement. Her life and tragic demise serve as a poignant case study that vividly illustrates the delicate connection between the right to live freely and exercise one's right to free expression with an anonymous or pseudonymous identity, and the severe consequences that ensue when that shield of privacy is relentlessly pierced by the media.*

Qandeel Baloch's story also sheds light on a critical legal perspective. Infringement of privacy, as outlined under Article 14(1) of the Constitution of Pakistan, not only encroaches upon an individual's personal space and dignity but also poses a profound threat to the right to one's life, as protected under Article 9 of the same Constitution.

Foreword

In the modern onli*fe* world, which is characterized by new media, increasing surveillance, profiling, or datafication of many aspects of life, privacy is anything but an outdated construct. On the contrary, it is a valuable concept that has important functions in modern societies. As normative safeguards, rights to privacy are enshrined in international documents and human rights codifications as well as in the Charter of Fundamental Rights of the European Union and in the constitutions of a considerable number of nation states.

In view of the finding that there is a lack of appropriate privacy protection in Pakistan, among other things against intrusive activities of the media, the study of Sohail Aftab aims to comprehensively provide the foundations for such protection. He illustrates his starting point with numerous cases from selected fields: media coverage of sexual violence that is sensationalistic, hassling and trauma-reinforcing, media exposure of women that has the potential to become a life threat or of children that affects their wellbeing, or inappropriate media coverage of private matters of public figures or of crimes and legal proceedings. His in-depth analysis of the theoretical approaches to privacy substantiates the richness and suitability of this concept. The Constitution of Pakistan provides merely limited normative anchors for the protection of privacy; however, their understanding has been broadened in landmark decisions of the Supreme Court of Pakistan and several higher courts. To "bring privacy principles out of the closet," Sohail Aftab presents detailed comparative law analyses, which include the ECHR and the case law of the ECtHR as well as privacy protection in Germany and in the UK. The outcomes prove to be fruitful for his recommendations on how to develop a basic legal framework to protect privacy in Pakistan.

Sohail Aftab's insights and results are timely, crucial, and of high practical relevance. His book will enrich the further development of the overarching discussions and the legal situation.

University of Hamburg, Faculty of Law,
Hamburg, Germany
October 2023

Marion Albers

Acknowledgment

In the culmination of this academic journey, I find myself humbled and profoundly grateful to many individuals and institutions who have contributed to the realization of this work, "Comparative Perspectives on the Right to Privacy: Pakistani and European Experiences."

First and foremost, I extend my deepest gratitude to my supervisor, Professor Dr. Marion Albers. Her wholehearted support throughout this long expedition has been the cornerstone upon which this research rests. Her guidance has not only enabled me to navigate the intricate concept of privacy but has also empowered me to unravel its multifaceted dimensions and complete this extensive research. Her expertise in information and privacy law, coupled with her reasoned encouragement, has enriched my understanding and made my research insightful and practically applicable.

My heartfelt thanks go to Professor Dr. Markus Kotzur, my second supervisor, for his scholarly comments and encouraging remarks, which have been instrumental in shaping this work.

I would like to acknowledge Professor Ingo Wolfgang Sarlet (Pontifícia Universidade Católica do Rio Grande do Sul—PUCRS, Brazil) for his invaluable support during my research stay in both Porto Alegre and Rio De Janeiro. His hospitality, guidance, and comparative law insights greatly enhanced my learning experience during my stay in Brazil.

I extend my appreciation to my father, Abdul Aziz Khan, whose unwavering love for education and learning has been a continuous source of inspiration. To my son, Azlan Aftab (8 years old), and my wife, Habiba Aftab, I owe a debt of compassion for their consistent support and patience throughout this demanding process. Their presence in Hamburg, Germany, enabled me to stay on track and persevere.

To all my esteemed colleagues and the members of Professor Albers' Chair, your support and mentorship have been invaluable. Special thanks to Anna Schimke and Dr. Raoul Veit for their mentoring roles and their patience in explaining complex German philosophical, constitutional, and legal concepts, such as Allgemeines Personlichkeitsrecht, dogmatics, and landmark German cases. Kelly Dhru deserves special mention for her motivating role, which kept me inspired throughout this endeavor. Stefanie Porath-Walsh, the secretary of Professor Albers, efficiently handled logistical matters and coordination, facilitating the smooth progression of various aspects of this research.

I extend my thanks to my friend, Dr. Ikramullah, Assistant Professor at the International Islamic University Islamabad, who initially planted the seed of the idea to pursue a Ph.D. His steadfast support and guidance were instrumental in overcoming moments of self-doubt and writer's block.

My heartfelt thanks also go to my friend, Misbah Ul Mustafa, Advocate at the Supreme Court of Pakistan, who was always available to provide clarity on various aspects of Pakistani law in practice.

I am grateful to Dr. Khurram Shehzad, who consistently made his time and dormitory near Hamburg University available, facilitating my research endeavors.

Dr. Muhammad Abid, a noble sole, deserves my thanks for his support and guidance in learning various research tools.

Acknowledgment is also due to the German Academic Exchange Service (DAAD) for their outstanding execution of the scholarship, as well as the Higher Education Commission of Pakistan (HEC) for funding my Ph.D. studies.

I would like to express my sincere appreciation to Springer Nature, the publisher of this book, and its dedicated editors, including Laura Hofmann (Associate Editor Law), Pradeep Kuttysankaran (Project Coordinator), and Leonie Sittner (Editorial Assistant). Their prompt responses, invaluable guidance, and commitment to the culmination of this publishing process have been truly commendable. Their contributions have played a pivotal role in bringing this work to fruition.

This book would not have been possible without the collective support, guidance, and encouragement of these individuals and organizations. Your contributions have been invaluable, and I am deeply grateful for your trust and belief in this project.

Islamabad, Pakistan Sohail Aftab

Contents

Chapter 1
Introduction

This research presents a legal analysis of the problem of media intrusion into people's private lives in Pakistan and suggests measures for an effective protection of the right to privacy. Media intrudes in private lives through its non-consensual, surreptitious and deceptive newsgathering practices. The images and private information gathered through such intrusive means are disseminated to a large audience through all mediums. However, the victims of privacy violation do not have an effective remedy under the existing legal framework of Pakistan. The courts have never attempted to intervene into the matter in such a way in order to explore the possibility of a comprehensive protective mechanism against the blatant infringements of the right to privacy. There is no statutory or common law tool in Pakistan which directly empowers the victims to claim remedy for violation of her right to privacy. The existing civil laws related to torts and damages have never been invoked by the victims to get remedy for a breach of their right to privacy. Therefore, this study develops a comprehensive case for legal reform in Pakistan and suggests legislation which expressly provides the general right to privacy and whereby its infringement is recognized as an actionable wrong. It relies on the insight gained from an extensive review of the theoretical approaches of privacy at one hand and from the actual adjudication of "media and privacy" type of cases in the selected European jurisdictions.

An analysis of media content of private television programs in Pakistan presents ample empirical evidence regarding the gravity and enormity of the problem of invasive practices. Private television channels cover for hours the incidents of sexual crimes. The identity of victims is disclosed along with the details regarding their relatives and their addresses in a routine manner. Media ignores the fact that women face many challenges in the patriarchal society of Pakistan. They are faced with decisional subordination and even honor killing in the case of minor parental disobedience or slight aberration from tribal norms. Still media exposes their private affairs with impunity. Media disregards the wellbeing and developmental requirements of minors. Journalists interview children directly or their family members in

S. Aftab, *Comparative Perspectives on the Right to Privacy*, Ius Gentium: Comparative Perspectives on Law and Justice 109,
https://doi.org/10.1007/978-3-031-45575-9_1

the aftermath of personal and familial tragedies. Traumatic footages of crying children and family grieves are broadcasted to sensationalize the programs and thereby attract more and more audience by dramatizing the actual tragedies.

Pakistani media covers public figures as if they have 'zero privacy'. It covers everybody across the board having any kind of connection to the public life. No distinction is being made to isolate and differentiate their subjects on the basis of the level of involvement in the public life. Media does not consider as to what extent some revelation or dissemination of facts could contribute to the public interest. Rather it presents sensational content in order to generate interest of the public and thereby to attract large number of viewers.

Television channels owned by private entities broadcast special programs which are based on the typical pattern of "grief journalism". These programs are dramatized with an overwhelming sensational theme. The voiceovers, video footages as well as the overall content are designed in a way to depict a 'doom and gloom' scenario.

A favorite area of media is the news related to crimes and punishments. Full-fledge coverage is given to cases of different nature in high courts and in the Supreme Court of Pakistan. These cases may range from family disputes of celebrates, politicians and ordinary people to multi-million corruption scams.

The broadcasting pattern of Pakistani media is not only *per se* against the fundamental right of the people such as privacy and dignity but it also damages many other aspects of human lives. The problems related to psychological health, personality development and the opportunity of rehabilitation in the case of criminals are closely associated with media-related privacy infringements. Despite the immense importance of the right to privacy, the existing media regulatory mechanism has been miserably failed to ensure its protection. Neither self-regulatory bodies cater for the privacy related needs of the public nor does the national regulator has any mechanism to effectively enforce privacy standards on the media. Pakistan Electronic Media Regulatory Authority (PEMRA) devised an ethical code of conduct in 2015 but it has failed to draw a visible impact on media's intrusive and invasive practices.

No doubt, freedom of speech and freedom of the press is an essential pillar of every democratic society. However, this freedom is not absolute and there are corresponding responsibilities attached to it. A prime responsibility of the press is to pay attention to people's right to privacy and conduct its newsgathering and publication business in a way as to uphold its own freedom at one hand and respect people's right to privacy on the other hand. If press transgresses its limits, various legal systems and approaches are in place internationally to provide the necessary relief to the aggrieved party.

The Constitution of Pakistan provides for the protection of the right to privacy, inviolability of human dignity and freedom of speech. It also imposes limitations on the free speech based on societal interests such as glory of Islam, national security and contempt of court. However, the legislature or the courts have not articulated these provisions for the sake of protecting the concrete areas in a substantive manner. As a result, no appropriate balancing mechanism has been established in Pakistan to reconcile the important rights of free speech and privacy and thus no comprehensive and effective legal dispensation is available to any person whose right to privacy is infringed.

The main question this research deals with is that how the infringements of such an important value and a crucial fundamental right to privacy could be brought from a lawless scenario into a legally protective enforcement regime where the victims have access to legal norms. These norms should be able to provide them the required legal dispensation and remedy in a court of law. Starting with this generic premise, the book delves deep into further subsidiary but important questions that need answers in order to address the main problem. Firstly, what are the privacy-related interests that are most vulnerable to violation in the course of media practices? Secondly, what are the existing legal frameworks and judicial principles in Pakistan that can provide the required normative foundation for prescribing an effective legal protection? Thirdly, before prescribing the legal protection of the right to privacy, this study explores dominant theoretical approaches to the concept of privacy and its moral and philosophical origin as well as its interaction with the right to free speech. These insights are instrumental to find out the value of privacy against other countervailing interests. Fourthly, the European approach towards legal treatment of the right to privacy as well as its reconciliation with the freedom of speech is analyzed with a comparative perspective. Finally, the book proposes a law reform through enacting a statute which recognizes and protects the general right to privacy, on the basis of guiding principles devised as a result of lessons learnt from an extensive doctrinal and comparative study.

To answer the above questions, the book, after presenting an empirical evidence of different intrusive practices of electronic media in Pakistan as well as publication of information about private lives, makes a survey of existing protection mechanism with a view to find out whether there is a gap in the enforcement of existing laws or there is an actual absence of law. For this purpose, it explains the general catalogue of fundamental rights, and specifically the scope and enforcement of both the rights of free speech and privacy, in order to look for guidance in answering the primary research questions. For any preliminary study with a normative dimension, it is required that the philosophical and sociological underpinnings of the related concepts are clear. Particularly, the concept of privacy is very much nascent not only for the lawmakers but also for many lawyers and academicians in Pakistan. It needs a detailed descriptive and analytical treatment. Due to this reason, significant space is dedicated to elaborate the concept of privacy in a detailed manner. The prominent theoretical approaches to the understanding of "privacy", such as its meaning, its types, the protected areas attached to it, its inherent and instrumental value, as well as the critical perspectives about its scope shall be illuminated.

For any law reform work, it is an established approach to undertake a comparative law methodology in order to obtain knowledge about diverse jurisprudence and enforcement measures. With that objective at its heart, the research looks outside

Pakistan.[1] Privacy is a universal human right protected by international law instruments such as Universal Declaration of Human Rights and European Convention on Human Rights (ECHR),. Therefore, the selection of the ECHR which binds 47 nation states and is the fundament of an elaborated human rights jurisprudence of the European Court of Human Rights (ECtHR), spanning six decades with decisions committing a population of more than three hundred million people, is something that must never be missed in any discussion of human rights' scope and interpretation. The jurisprudence developed by ECtHR through interpretation of the Convention provides useful guidelines for protection of the right to privacy. Particularly, the jurisprudence regarding the balancing of freedom of expression with the right to respect for private life comprises principles and guidelines, are much valuable for comparative studies. As the ECtHR is an international law court, the actual reception of these principles within the member states' legal regimes provides more concrete insights. For that purpose, two high contracting parties, Germany and the United Kingdom, are examined more closely. As for the German jurisdiction, the somewhat unique but comprehensive constitutional concept of the general right to the development of personality in combination with the inviolability of dignity provides a very effective mechanism for protection of the right to privacy. Beyond that, the German principles of proportionality and the balancing of free speech with the right to privacy are worthy for a comparative study. The book highlights several leading decisions of the selected jurisdictions that illustrate relevant factors in the balancing exercise. In the United Kingdom, privacy law and principles are so far in the developing phase. The tort of "breach of confidence" is the main tool to protect the misuse of private information. After the promulgation of the Human Rights Act of 1998, which has made unlawful for public bodies to disregard the Convention, the chances of remedies for the victims of privacy intrusions are much increased despite the fact that United Kingdom is hesitant to recognize a full-fledge general right of privacy either through case law or by way of enacting a statute.

The results of a comprehensive-theoretical and comparative- analysis under this book are orchestrated in the form of guiding principles for the proposed privacy law. On theoretical front, this work will have some contribution to the body of knowledge related to the concept of privacy as well as to the comparative law and approaches to the legal protection of the right to privacy. At a practical front, this research initiates a fundamental and multidimensional law reform debate for legal protection of the right to privacy in Pakistan.

[1] Van Hoecke (2015), p. 01: "[t]he wording of the research question will be the main criterion for the choice of legal systems to be compared."

1.1 An Overview of the Media Landscape in Pakistan[2]

Some of independent media and journalists organizations describe Pakistani media landscape as dynamic and vibrant.[3] However, it was only after 2002 when private television channels were allowed to operate. Prior to that, there was only a single government-owned television channel with the name of Pakistan Television (PTV). On the other hand, print media existed even before 1947- the year in which the country came into being. Muhammad Ali Jinnah, the founder of Pakistan, established the English language daily newspaper called Dawn as early as in 1941. There were also Urdu language newspapers, mostly representing the parties struggling against the British rule on the Indian Subcontinent. The post-independence history of Pakistani media is full of legal sanctions and censures, particularly during various military rules. The freedom of journalists was curtailed through pre-speech censors and post-speech censures. Thus, owing to military dictatorships and civilian authoritarian rule, Pakistan has a baggage of checkered history of press freedom.[4] Ironically, media also got its so-called freedom in the era of the last military dictator who permitted to issue licenses to private television channels. The motive behind it is said to be the realization on the part of the then military leadership that they could not win "media war" from its traditional foe (India) unless private television channels were allowed to operate and compete with Indian channels in their counter propaganda.[5]

The liberalization policy of General Musharraf changed the entire media landscape dramatically. Now there are around 89 TV channels broadcasting news and entertainment 24/7. Initially, these channels were allowed without making any kind

---

[2] See for details, Najam U Din, 'Pakistan-Media Landscape' https://medialandscapes.org/country/pakistan . Accessed 26 August 2023.

[3] International Media Support, 'Media in Pakistan: Between radicalization and democratization in an unfolding conflict' (Media Assessment Report 2009) https://www.mediasupport.org/publication/pakistan-between-radicalisation-and-democratisation-in-an-unfolding-conflict/. Accessed 26 August 2023.

[4] There were three military coups in Pakistan (General Ayub Khan 1958–1971, General Zia ul Haq 1977–1988, General Pervez Musharraf 1999–2008). The total span of direct military rule is more than thirty years after Pakistan was granted independence in 1947 by the then British rule. The Press and Publication Ordinance promulgated by General Ayub Khan in 1963 is considered as a 'black law. The said ordinance granted immense powers to the administration, for instance, any newspaper or printing press could be confiscated in the event of any news item that was supposed to 'bring into hatred the Government'. Further stringent provisions were added to press law in 1980 by General Zia UlHaq, where a journalist could be prosecuted for writing anything not liked by the then military establishment. Lashing and other corporal punishments awarded to well-known journalists during that period is still remembered as a dark chapter of the history of media development in Pakistan. Ironically, these laws were repealed by another military ruler- General Pervez Musharraf- through Press, Newspapers, News Agencies and Books Registration Ordinance, 2002.

[5] International Media Support, 'Media in Pakistan: Between radicalization and democratization in an unfolding conflict' (Media Assessment Report 2009) https://www.mediasupport.org/publication/pakistan-between-radicalisation-and-democratisation-in-an-unfolding-conflict/. Accessed 26 August 2023.

of homework for adopting an effective regulatory approach. A complete deregulatory approach was adopted by the Government of Pakistan and it awarded licenses to private television channels *en bloc*. This deregulatory approach was not representative of a coherent media policy. Rather, it showed a complete absence of policy-objectives with respect to the new broadcasting milieu. To date, no long term media policy goals have ever been set to instill a balance between the right to freedom of speech and other corresponding constitutional rights which is a prerequisite for an enlightened citizenry. Resultantly, the media broadcast and newsgathering practices evolved in a directionless manner and ultimately culminated at present to a very unfavorable situation. This situation calls for an immediate legal and regulatory redressal.

An abrupt privatization of electronic media brought about many legal and ethical problems. Journalists having no prior experience of electronic media, lack of professional personnel such as camera crew, editors and directors in television stations, obvious leaning of opinions in news and talk shows to one or the other party due to political affiliations of media owners, and agenda setting are some of the problems that generate serious ethical questions on the conduct of journalists for their lack of social responsibility.[6]

Most of these channels are owned by the people who were owners of newspapers prior to the commencement of private television channels, and they extended their print media business to electronic media. This tendency resulted into an extreme form of cross media ownership which now poses another regulatory challenge as a few big companies have monopolized different sources of information and communication. Furthermore, the technological convergence is also a challenge for the current regulatory scheme because of the fact that there are separate regulators for all the three mediums of print (Press Council of Pakistan), Television (PEMRA) and online media (PTA).

The television became a dominant source of news and entertainment and private channels not only diverted the readers of newspapers but also a great sum of advertisement revenue. Now, on average, a Pakistani television viewer spends two hours a day watching television.[7] Similarly, television grabbed not less than 50% share of the total advertisement revenue from all other mediums.[8] The extreme reliance on advertisement revenue started a cutthroat competition for high Television Rating Points (TRP) between the private channels in order to attract more and more commercial advertisements. The rate per second and frequency of advertisements are also directly proportional to the size of viewership. This tendency has jeopardized not only ethical values but sensationalism and a war for breaking and spicy news has brought Pakistani media to a point where it needs a serious soul-searching. Pakistani

---

[6]Malik Muhammad Ashraf, 'Media landscape in Pakistan' The nation (Islamabad, 27 April 2018).

[7]Najam U Din, 'Pakistan-Media Landscape' https://medialandscapes.org/country/pakistan. Accessed 26 August 2023.

[8]Najam U Din, 'Pakistan-Media Landscape' https://medialandscapes.org/country/pakistan. Accessed 26 August 2023.

media practices are presenting typical examples of the abuse of the sacred rights of access to information and the right to freedom of speech.

The broadcasting patterns have no respect for constitutional principles, socio-cultural values and for the limits prescribed by international covenants. Rather than to highlight issues related to the enforcement of human rights, media practices are infringing citizens' right to privacy as a norm and not as an exception. As will be demonstrated in the next section of this book, the media persons are not only committing tortuous acts, some of their practices amount to serious felonies. Lady Justice Arden has rightly pointed out the "untold damage" of privacy violation by the press of the modern internet era. According to her,

> If the press intrudes into someone's private life and publishes things that the public are not entitled to know, there is a huge problem of containing damage. The material can be republished on the Internet and Twitter, and it may thus not be able to recall all the material. This can lead to untold damage to an individual whose privacy is wrongly breached.[9]

The advent of internet technology and social media provide virtual permanency to publications in online newspapers as well as to footages of television broadcasts uploaded to video sharing websites and social media. The present ICT scenario makes the deletion of videos and images almost impossible. This virtual permanency of the damage accrues irreparable loss to the victims of privacy violation.

1.2 Justification of the Study, Its Scope and Practical Constraints

A survey of Pakistani laws and jurisprudence shows that no guiding principles are available which can provide a foundation to the policy makers in enforcing the protection of the right to privacy, mentioned in Article 14 (1) of the Constitution of Pakistan. Therefore, a comparative analysis is made here for the purpose of learning lessons from foreign jurisdictions. The scope of the current research study covers general principles of privacy protection in the selected jurisdictions. The general principles of privacy jurisprudence provide standard parameters for enactment and enforcement of privacy laws in such jurisdictions where there is a legal lacuna (mainly in the form of absence of privacy law) and thereby lack effective enforcement of various privacy rights.

As for the media laws and regulations in Pakistan, no doubt, many problems and loopholes are well known such as cross media ownership, no regulatory response to media convergence and other technological advancements, absence of self-regulatory mechanism, and so on. However, this research follows a human rights approach and aims at the best possible protection of constitutional values.

---

[9] Lady Justice Arden, 'Media intrusion and human rights: striking the balance' (public lecture at Cardiff Law School 2012).

For the purpose of this research, it is important to explain what "media" mean. Media convergence has, in fact blurred the boundaries between various mediums of mass communication. It is no more important to focus on any particular form of media as same reporters usually create content for the entire three major sources, i.e. television, print and websites. Although, there are separate regulators for the electronic, print and online media, yet the problem of privacy violation identified here is beyond the ambit of enforcement and lies at the legislative level. It is believed that whatever the regulatory framework might be, it will enforce the norm once a statutory remedy is provided. Similarly, the rights holders shall have the right to file suits against public bodies for the failure to protect their right to privacy.

A clarification of the scope of research with respect to the concept of privacy under consideration is also essential. It is a fact that privacy is a vast concept, and the challenges to the right to privacy are also of a very diverse nature. At a practical level too, this right faces plethora of challenges in Pakistan. For example, no comprehensive protection mechanisms are available for the health data, or financial data; there are scores of issues related to surveillance of citizens and problems of privacy with respect to investigation techniques used by police against the accused person (e.g. polygraph test or the use of so-called lie detector is commonly used by police in Pakistan). Each one of these issues needs a full-fledged research project and it is not possible to investigate *all* these legal issues in a single book. In this research, only those privacy aspects are covered that are directly or indirectly related to the media and communication, such as when privacy infringement is made with the purpose of dissemination to an audience, or in the course of journalistic activities. The emphasis on media intrusions should not be viewed as disregarding the remaining privacy issues. Other areas of privacy have equal importance and the interests attached as such need equal protection. It is believed that the present work may prove to be a starting point for the protection of every possible facet of the cherished right to privacy.

The scope of the study extends from elaborating the problem with an empirical evidence and doctrinal analysis of the Pakistani legal regime to the consideration of foreign jurisdictions in order to look for best possible solution of the problem. This approach may be questioned for its relevancy and usefulness for the purpose of applying it in a different socio-legal setting. Any comparative approach should be conscious of both internal and external context that influences the ultimate value of particular constitutional rights. For example, the possibility of suspension or abrogation of fundamental rights through amendment might be different in different jurisdictions.[10] Keeping in view this criticism, the study restrains itself to the consideration of constitutional principles having a potential to be universally applied. These principles have been developed mainly through diverse jurisprudence of privacy related cases. Thus the research does not delve deep into the administrative structures or institutional arrangements in place in foreign jurisdictions for the protection of the right to privacy. This exercise is based on the belief that whatever

[10] Barak (2015), p. 379.

might be the structure of enforcement mechanisms, the enforcement of a statute based on the derived general guidelines could make a difference.

It is important to submit that this book does not propose any kind of curbs on the media in a unidirectional manner. The bleak situation of the right to free speech and freedom of expression is acknowledged and the shabby history of press freedom is all the way in the canvass while this study is being conducted. Due to these considerations, other model jurisdictions are selected with an understanding of the fact that they give immense importance to free speech as well and regard it as a pillar of modern democracy. Therefore, the focus is on the *reconciling* of both privacy right and freedom of speech, in the interest of common people in upholding their fundamental rights.

1.3 Research Methodology

For an extensive monograph, it is neither possible nor desirable to stick to a single research methodology at every point of discussion. Different methods of research are used in a complementary manner, as these methods are not mutually exclusive.[11] For example, the chapter elaborating the problems of privacy in Pakistan uses empirical evidence in the shape of random examples of media's most flagrant intrusions into personal privacies.[12] Similarly, the exploration of the meaning and value of "privacy" has been done in an analytical and conceptual manner, while the analysis of a legal regime for privacy right enforcement follows a doctrinal approach. In order to arrive at a legal solution of the problems and at a convincing proposal, the dominant methodology used here is the comparative law methodology.

Some scholars do not agree with the requirement to justify the utility of legal comparison and the insight gained through this process of one's own legal system is a sufficient justification for comparison.[13] To ask from comparatist the question of utility has been equated to asking an astronomer about the objective behind his exploration, where mere curiosity can be a valid justification.[14] Nevertheless, there are sufficient reasons to justify the comparison in this work as it goes beyond mere curiosity and actually has an applicable purpose and practical utility. The objective

[11] Van Hoecke (2015), p. 01.

[12] Similar approach could be found in law reform exercises. See Law Reform Commission of Hong Kong, 'Privacy and Media Intrusions' (December 2004) https://www.hkreform.gov.hk/en/docs/rmedia-e.pdf. Accessed 26 August 2023.

[13] Sacco (1991), p. 4: "Like other sciences, comparative law remains a science as long as it acquires knowledge and regardless of whether or not the knowledge is put to any further use. It remains a science when the jurist does make use of it to borrow the rules or institutions of foreign legal systems. Indeed, it then becomes a science with exciting practical potential. When the legislator borrows from a foreign legal system aided by the sophisticated analysis of a jurist, they earn the respect we accord to enlightened practical activity. "

[14] Cremer (2010), pp. 7–10.

of comparison is, apart from the primary aim of knowledge,[15] to suggest law reform in the area of privacy right's enforcement in Pakistan in line with the guiding principles we have in the shape of, in particular, ECtHR and German jurisprudence. The consideration of "comparative law as a tool of law reform" is a well-established practice with a long history where legal developments abroad have been taken into consideration for new ideas and techniques by lawmakers.[16] The comparative methodology as a comparison of different legal systems has a history of more than a hundred years, passed through different phases and by now it is considered as a useful method and sometimes a necessary exercise.[17] Basel Markesinis, an eminent scholar of German law and comparative law is a strong supporter of looking to the outside world for "learning lessons" and applying the knowledge acquired as such to the local problems. To him, those who reject foreign law in spite of the fact that they could find valuable ideas are "timorous souls".[18]

Zweigert et al. divide the scales of legal comparisons into large scale (macro comparison) and small scale (micro comparison). The general legal approaches such as techniques of law making or styles of judicial opinions are compared during macro comparison, while the small scale or micro comparison focuses on the method of resolution of specific problems.[19] This research uses both micro and macro comparison as the boundary between these methods is "admittedly flexible".[20] Comparative law is not merely to "state" foreign law or laws just like various international reports on different legal systems accumulate a variety of legal information. Comparative law must have *comparative reflections* on the legal problem at hand. According to Zweigert et al., comparative law "is best done if the author first lays out the essentials of the relevant foreign law-country by country-, then uses this material as a basis for critical comparison, ending up with conclusions about the proper policy for the law to adopt, which may involve a reinterpretation of his own system".[21]

After justification of adopting the comparative law methodology, the question arises which foreign solution can be a valuable guide for resolution of the local

[15] Zweigert and Kötz (1998), p. 15: "The primary aim of comparative law, as of all sciences, is knowledge."

[16] Kahn-Freund (1974), pp. 1–2: "[L]egal ideas are now moving freely around the world so as to influence legislation and pending law reform." (citation omitted)

[17] Zweigert and Kötz (1998), pp. 1–2.

[18] Markesinis (1999), p. 63. See also: Zweigert and Kötz (1998), p. 16. "Legislators all the world have found that on many matters good laws cannot be produced without the assistance of comparative law, whether in the form of general studies or of reports specially prepared on the topic in question." Van Hoecke (2015), p. 03: "When one tries to improve one's own legal system, be it as a legislator or as a scholar, it has become obvious to look other side of the borders."

[19] Zweigert and Kötz (1998), p. 04.

[20] Zweigert and Kötz (1998), p. 05: "Indeed, one must often do both at the same time, for often one has to study the *procedures* by which the rules are in fact applied in order to understand why a foreign system solves a particular problem in the way it does."

[21] Zweigert and Kötz (1998), p. 06.

problems of legal dispensation. According to Zweigert et al., for any proposed solution to be superior, it must be proved satisfactory in the country of origin and secondly, its workability in the adopting country must be considered after necessary modification.[22] This approach is based on the assumption that almost all societies undergo similar social problems at one or the other point in their history and the legal responses to those problems can vary from society to society. The comparative study of those responses and of their respective "functions" is most probably a valuable enterprise. Zweigert el al. opine thus, "[i]f law is seen functionally as a regulator of social facts, the legal problems of all countries are similar. Every legal system in the world is open to the same questions and subject to the same standards, even countries of different social structures or different stages of development. "[23]

These insights bring us to the point to consider *functionality* as the fundamental methodological principle of all comparative law. "From this basic principle stem all the other rules which determine the choice of laws to compare, the scope of the undertaking, the creation of a system of comparative law, and so on. Incomparables cannot usefully be compared, and in law the only things which are comparable are those which fulfill the same function", Zweigert *et al.* declare.[24] It is a fact that comparative method does not mean to compare only "black-letter-law". There must be a consideration for the legal system, particularly, how the law as practiced and applied through judicial decisions is highly important.[25] According to Reitz, a good comparative study should explore the degree to which "functional equivalents" could be found in the legal systems, which require consideration of the overall working of these systems.[26] The differences, which can affect the outcome in one way or the other, should be highlighted in a good quality research.[27] Furthermore, comparative law should also consider "the gap between the law on the books and the law in action."[28] The research by no means suggests merely a "copying of foreign law", as it denotes the absence of comparative law method rather than to be taken as a "method".[29]

While undertaking the comparative analysis, the criticism on the use and misuse of comparative law methodology is well considered because the use of comparative law approach as a tool of law reform is not without criticism.[30] The main thrust of the scholars who reject this method as a useful tool for legal research is on the peculiarities of legal systems and the diversity in socio-cultural value systems. The

[22]Zweigert and Kötz (1998), p. 17.

[23]Zweigert and Kötz (1998), p. 46

[24]Zweigert and Kötz (1998), p. 34.

[25]Zweigert and Kötz (1998), p. 16: "The functional method refers already by definition to a context: which societal problem is solved with what kind of legal construction?"

[26]Reitz (1998), p. 621.

[27]Reitz (1998), p. 622.

[28]Reitz (1998), pp. 628–630.

[29]Van Hoecke (2015), pp. 01, 30.

[30]For a detailed analysis see: Kahn-Freund (1974), p. 1.

criticism has focused more on the type of legal comparison, which aims at a hard-core legal transplant without taking into consideration the prerequisites of foreign legal and institutional transplant. To propose any solution for local problems that has been chosen in foreign systems, the risks and chances of adoption need to be carefully weighed.[31] The factors such as environmental as well as political systems are crucial to be taken into consideration before suggesting legal transplantations, which are dependent on these systems such as water related laws or labour laws respectively.[32] Relying on the criteria for transplantation as well as on the arguments put forward by Montesquieu, Kahn-Freund suggests that the suitable geographical, social and political environment in the borrowing jurisdiction can minimize the risk of rejection of legal transplant.[33] All these risks and condition have been considered in the comparative methodology of this book and the factors which may affect the privacy law proposal are not out of sight.

The research in hand does not prescribe a transplant of a foreign system or institution or statute, but is looking for broad constitutional principles of which can help Pakistani jurisdiction dealing with its problem of reconciling privacy and free speech. It does, by no means, suggest hard-core transplantation of a legislative instrument, court system, media regulatory mechanism or privacy protection commissioner's office. What it suggests is to formulate a local law, passed by Pakistani Parliament according to its own socio-political and legal system. The proposed local privacy law must reflect the principles derived from European jurisprudence. The book builds a case for these principles by establishing that these are the most valuable guidelines which will help fulfilling the objective of privacy protection in Pakistan. These guiding principles are not unique to a particular jurisdiction but have been evolved as a reaction to the sort of problems of privacy in Pakistan elaborated in this research. Furthermore, the jurisprudence of ECtHR has a universal dimensi1on and an inherent capacity to be adopted by a variety of legal systems of the parties to the Convention. However, this research does not count on merely the exposition of the principles developed under an International law treaty and considers it important to ensure the impact of such principles on the national jurisdictions also.

The selection of one or the other country does not entail hard and fast rules and many factors can lead to the adoption of one or the other jurisdiction such as the level of interest on the part of researcher about a particular country or the consideration of legal families; but the actual objective of law comparison mostly plays a decisive role.[34] An obvious criticism can be that both Germany and Pakistan belong to different legal systems of civil and common law respectively. At the outset, the

---

[31] Reitz (1998), p. 623.

[32] Kahn-Freund (1974), p. 1.

[33] Kahn-Freund (1974), p. 27: "All I have wanted to suggest is that its use requires a knowledge not only of the foreign law, but also of its social, and above all its political, context. The use of comparative law for practical purposes becomes an abuse only if it is informed by a legalistic spirit which ignores this context of the law."

[34] Pieters (2009), pp. 15–16. According to Van Hoecke (2015), p. 05: "The wording of the research question will be the main criterion for the choice of legal systems to be compared."

critique may sound valid when one thinks that how it would be possible to make comparison for a law reform purpose, where both the jurisdictions belong to completely different legal cultures. A major difference between both systems is that Civil law countries have detailed codes to follow, while the common law countries mostly have binding case law and authoritative precedents for the lower courts to abide by. However, a detailed look into the privacy law in Germany shows, on the one hand, that case law and not codes has contributed into its development. On the other hand, there is no case law or precedents in Pakistan, which can provide a base to codification of privacy law. The German approach in the area of privacy and data protection is regarded as nearer to the "ideal" of protection of these values, and suggestions are, therefore, made to consider it as a model jurisdiction for law reform even in common law countries such as Australia.[35]

1.4 Structure of the Book

To set the stage, this Chapter introduces the research problem in a contextual manner. It offers justification of the study, demarcates the scope of the book and elaborates the relevancy and suitability of the adopted research methodology.

Chapter 2 systematically unfolds the problem under research in a detailed manner. It shows different kinds of privacy violations committed by media in Pakistan at one hand as well as the inability of media regulatory framework to contain the damage to the crucial right to privacy on the other hand.

Chapter 3 delves deep into the concept of privacy with a meta-theoretical perspective. It describes the richness of privacy value with the help of its philosophical underpinnings. Expounding the inherent and instrumental value of privacy, this chapter enumerates the linkages of privacy with negative liberty in the form of right to be let alone, concealment of one's secrets and limitation on the access to oneself. This discussion however expands to encircle positive dimension of privacy as well as its fundamental role in the promotion of human relations, individuality and human dignity. Chapter 3 also analyses modern approaches to the conceptualization of privacy and their usefulness for resolution of the modern day problems requiring theoretical sophistication, all-inclusiveness as well as open-to-change cataloging of different facets of privacy. Afterwards, critical perspectives which either view privacy as detrimental to society or doubt on its conceptual coherence are being highlighted with an attempt to respond to major criticism. At the end of this chapter, the concept of free speech as a countervailing right against privacy right has been analyzed.

Chapter 4 provides a doctrinal analysis of the constitutional law and the legal framework of fundamental rights in Pakistan. It draws on legal provisions and jurisprudential principles in order to explore the existing legal and constitutional

[35] For more details see: Webb (2003).

position of the right to privacy in Pakistan. Especially focusing on the analysis of privacy and free speech case law, it intends to find out as to what extent the constitutional system is conducive to the protection of different aspects of the right to privacy.

Chapter 5 turns to the prime model jurisdiction of this comparative study and extensively explains as how privacy right is protected under Article 8 of the European Convention on Human Rights (ECHR) in the light of the judgments of the European Court of Human Rights (ECtHR). This chapter attempts to articulate the principles devised by the ECtHR for the balancing of countervailing values of free speech and the right to privacy.

Chapter 6 undertakes the exercise of finding privacy law and its interaction with free speech in Germany and United Kingdom with a focus as how much privacy protection was enhanced by the application of the ECtHR's principles.

The book concludes with the concrete recommendations in Chap. 7. It looks again into Pakistani laws with the intent to find existing legal tools and analyze their effective applicability on the cases of privacy infringements. This chapter not only proposes legislation, but it also formulates the principles for the proposed privacy law in the light of privacy conceptualization and comparative analysis of ECtHR, Germany and United Kingdom.

References

Barak A (2015) Human dignity: the constitutional value and the constitutional right. Cambridge University Press

Cremer HJ (2010) Human rights and the protection of privacy in tort law: a comparison between English and German law. Routledge-Cavendish

International Media Support, 'Media in Pakistan: Between radicalization and democratization in an unfolding conflict' (Media Assessment Report 2009). https://www.mediasupport.org/publication/pakistan-between-radicalisation-and-democratisation-in-an-unfolding-conflict/. Accessed 27 Aug 2023

Kahn-Freund O (1974) On uses and misuses of comparative law. Mod Law Rev 37:1

Markesinis B (1999) Privacy, freedom of expression, and the horizontal effect of the human rights bill: lessons from Germany. Law Quart Rev 47

Najam U Din, 'Pakistan-Media Landscape' https://medialandscapes.org/country/pakistan. Accessed 14 Aug 2023

Pieters D (2009) Functions of comparative law and practical methodology of comparing. Syllabus Research Master in Law

Reitz JC (1998) How to do comparative law. Am J Comp Law 46:617

Sacco R (1991) Legal formants: a dynamic approach to comparative law (Installment I of II) Am J Comp Law 39(1):1

Van Hoecke M (2015) Methodology of comparative legal research, Law and method

Webb P (2003) A comparative analysis of data protection laws in Australia and Germany. J Inform Law Technol 2

Zweigert K, Kötz H (1998) An Introduction to comparative law. Tony Weir tr, 3rd edn. Oxford University Press

Chapter 2
The Problem and Its Scale: Privacy Invasions of Pakistani Media

> The press is overstepping in every direction the obvious bounds of propriety and of decency. Gossip is no longer the resource of the idle and of the vicious, but has become a trade, which is pursued with industry as well as effrontery. To satisfy a prurient taste the details of sexual relations are spread broadcast in the columns of the daily papers. To occupy the indolent, column upon column is filled with idle gossip, which can only be procured by intrusion upon the domestic circle. The intensity and complexity of life, attendant upon advancing civilization, have rendered necessary some retreat from the world, and man, under the refining influence of culture, has become more sensitive to publicity, so that solitude and privacy have become more essential to the individual; but modern enterprise and invention have, through invasions upon his privacy, subjected him to mental pain and distress, far greater than could be inflicted by mere bodily injury.[1]

Thirteen decades ago, Warren and Brandeis wrote this remarkable passage. There cannot be a better than this elaboration of the current media scenario in Pakistan where the *overstepping* of media into individuals' privacy has become a rampant problem and only the recourse to legal solution can protect such an important right. This chapter will present the empirical evidence in the form of actual illustrations of media intrusions into the private sphere of the people. It aims at establishing the seriousness of the problem of unwarranted media intrusion which affects the most vulnerable sections of society. The explanation of selected instances of media intrusions will support the hypothesis that media intrusions have reached to a point which needs an urgent legal response. This chapter will also explore the options of an effective regulatory approach. After determining the extent to which the prescribed law reform is necessitated by the absence of any other remedy, this section highlights the need for formulating an effective legal mechanism for privacy protection.

[1] Warren and Brandeis (1890), p. 196.

S. Aftab, *Comparative Perspectives on the Right to Privacy*, Ius Gentium: Comparative Perspectives on Law and Justice 109,
https://doi.org/10.1007/978-3-031-45575-9_2

2.1 Invasive Media Practices

Media in Pakistan offers one of the best case studies, illustrating the abuse of free speech and freedom of the press. Due to the mushroom growth of private television channels, there is a cutthroat competition for advertisements, which is directly dependent on the rating of a particular channel. The number of audience of a television channel mainly determines the frequency and rate of advertisement. In their struggle to win over their competitors, almost all channels resort to sensationalistic newsgathering and broadcasting. Reporters of television channels look for stories which revolve around sexual violence, exposure of intimate affairs of women, exposing children to the general public, disclosure of private information of public figures, filming and dramatizing tragedies and interviewing accused/under-trial persons in the custody of police. Some of these invasive practices, their elaboration and empirical evidence are elaborated in the following sections.

2.1.1 Media Coverage of Sexual Violence

According to official figures, the number of reported rape cases was more than 14,000 in the last four years (2018–2021).[2] These incidents usually make breaking news in the media and all the sordid details of these events are disseminated without the consideration to conceal identities of victims. The heinousness of criminality as well as age and gender vary considerably in these incidents. Many of these cases go unreported, in particular, where the victim survives and is an adult. In any event, such news is given a prominent space by private television channels. If the victim could not survive, which happens in most cases of minor victims, the family members of the deceased are interviewed and they remain on-screen for hours and hours due to the high number of news channels. In case of the survival of the victim, media gets access to victims by hook or by crook and interviews the victim.

One of their tools is that journalists indoctrinate the victim or her family by pretending that dissemination of the event to the public at large would help them in getting sympathy or that through media, they can reach to higher judiciary and relevant authorities for a speedy justice. In societies like Pakistan, these are attractive incentives because of the social power imbalance, weak state institutions and corrupt police system. The victims are so vulnerable and helpless that they are compelled to tradeoff their dignity and privacy against the hope of getting noticed by authorities at the helm of the legal system. Secondly, most of the victims and their family are not educated enough to foresee the harmful implications of media disclosures due to the

[2] Gurmani, 'More than 14,000 rape cases reported over last four years, NA told' *Daily Dawn*, 24 December 2021, https://www.dawn.com/news/1665575/more-than-14000-rape-cases-reported-over-last-four-years-na-told. Accessed 26 August 2023.

low literacy rate of female population in Pakistan.[3] Even if they are educated, the traumatic situation is not conducive for undertaking an informed judgment. Thus, policy makers have greater responsibility to formulate very strict criteria for giving consent because most of the people are not unaware about the repercussions of media intruding their private sphere.[4] A psychological tendency also obliges victims to share the details of the event and their feelings about it. It is the thinking that hesitation to share all the relevant (or irrelevant) information or refusal to talk to the media may make them suspicious in the eyes of public and authorities and people would start doubting on the veracity of their allegations. Such mistrust on the law enforcement institutions of Pakistan has made it a trend to bring every case to the media rather than to report the crime to the police and fight it in the court of law.

In 2018, Nazia Iqbal, a famous Pashto language singer, accused her brother of raping her two minor daughters.[5] Before reporting the matter to the police, she turned to the media for seeking justice. She narrated the story in a very detailed manner, among other things, how she discovered and witnessed that her brother was sexually abusing her daughters for a long time. After the incident, she was interviewed by many channels. In some interviews, her minor daughters were also sitting beside her, apparently to forcefully pursue her case in the media. In 2019, the court concluded the trial and awarded death sentence to the rapist.[6] Again her video messages made rounds on the internet regarding her response to the court judgment in which she expressed her satisfaction and thanked the electronic and social media for supporting her and highlighting the matter.

It is not always the case that social media users or the commenters on online news portals make sensible remarks. In the case of Nazia Iqbal too, all the social media users were not supportive or sympathetic. Some users blamed her for showing carelessness in the looking after of her daughters. Others pointed fingers at her 'immoral career'. Media illustrated itself as being the proverbial double-edged sword. In the wake of such a traumatic episode, Nazia Iqbal left the country for good with the hope to start a new life in the United Kingdom.[7] Though her case was concluded in a court of law, still dozens of her news reports, children video footages,

---

[3] See for details: Rehman et al. (2015), pp. 240–144. According to this research, Pakistan is one of the countries having lowest literacy rate and in certain areas, female literacy rate is not more than 9%.

[4] See for a detailed account of the traumatic situation of the victims of the biggest child abuse scandal: Shah, 'Grim lessons from Kasur: A tragic legacy of child sexual abuse' (Geo TV) https://www.geo.tv/latest/178431-grim-lessons-a-tragic-legacy-of-kasurs-2015-child-abuse-scandal. Accessed 26 August 2023.

[5] Naseer, 'Pashto singer Nazia Iqbal accuses brother of raping her daughters' *Daily Dawn*, 25 April 2018, https://www.dawn.com/news/1403804. Accessed 26 August 2023.

[6] Naseer, 'Man who raped his two nieces sentenced to death by court in Rawalpindi' *Daily Dawn*, 8 March 2019 https://www.dawn.com/news/1472232. Accessed 26 August 2023.

[7] See for details: Nazia Iqbal interview to BBC Pashto, https://www.youtube.com/watch?v=hGRnr2ZDqI4&t=767s. Accessed 26 August 2023.

and her interviews are available on YouTube. These images might haunt her virtually forever.

One lesson from this incident is that though media exposed Nazia Iqbal, the whole episode exposed the media as well. There is a very dark side of resorting to media publicity and making some issue *viral* as things in the online media never remain in control. An expedite administration of justice is always cherished for such brutal offences; however, using media for that purpose could bring more harm than good.

Pakistani media's sensationalistic coverage of sexual violence touched a high mark in January 2018. A six year-old girl was abducted and her dead body was found near a garbage disposal site in the district of *Kasur*. The forensic report verified that the child was raped and strangled to death. There was hardly any channel left that did not interview her father. The coverage continued non-stop for weeks unless the police arrested the accused with the help of CCTV footage and confirmed his involvement after they conducted his DNA test. According to content analysis during a case study, the coverage of the incident by print and electronic media was not only out of proportion but it was also extremely sensationalistic, showing photos and videos of the victim and her family, and in violation of all the available ethical codes.[8] The subject research study concludes:

> Instead of highlighting the real issues at play — the socio-cultural reasons of child sexual abuse, what kind of and how much sensitisation is needed for children and their families, how to teach children the notions of good touch and bad touch, among others — the media gets caught in a vicious cycle of ratings, glamourising a crime and getting carried away while writing, reporting or anchoring something on this issue. This has its negative effects, as it was reported that there was a rise in drop-outs in young school-going girls as parents didn't want them to become victims.
>
> A new repertoire is needed, which reflects both public rage at savage crimes, and indeed, how to build safeguards in the system that prevent sexual violence of any sort.[9]

In general, there is a rich legal and scholarly debate which analyses various dimensions of the issue of rape victims' identity and the prevailing newsworthiness value of such incidents. The disclosure of names of rape victims has many adverse impacts on the victims and their families. The publicity of such incidents discourages the victims to report the crime to police and some of them simply deny that they were being assaulted so as to save themselves from a lifetime stigma.[10] Studies show that even in the developed countries such as the United States, many rape victims do not report the crime due to identity-related problems.[11] The uncertainty regarding the

---

[8] See for research and content analysis: Uks, 'Media and the Kasur child rape case' *Daily Dawn* (01 April 2018) https://www.dawn.com/news/1398484. Accessed 26 August 2023.

[9] Uks, 'Media and the Kasur child rape case' *Daily Dawn* (01 April 2018) https://www.dawn.com/news/1398484. Accessed 26 August 2023.

[10] See for example: Imtiaz, 'Media circus: Rape victim frightened into withdrawing FIR' *Daily Express Tribune* (21 December 2021) http://tribune.com.pk/story/92275/clifton-gang-rape-case-sindh-governor-takes-notice/. Accessed 26 August 2023.

[11] See for detailed analysis of the problem: Marcus and McMahon (1990).

protection of their privacy is one of the prime causes for rape victims who do not report the tragedy.[12]

The normative debate about the disclosure of rape victims' identity predominantly supports the privacy protection of rape victims and rejects the justification of disclosure under the guise of newsworthiness. The arguments that 'disclosure will reduce stigma' or that 'it will add credibility to the news story' and that 'the editor is capable enough to determine the newsworthiness' do not apply to the traditional society of Pakistan.[13] Beyond that, burdening the victim with the additional responsibility of contributing to the presumed good of society is not justified as she has already been through a very traumatic situation.[14]

News media do not care much about objectivity and credibility. The news related to sexual crimes are broadcasted in a highly exaggerated and sensationalistic manner, overloaded with the use of emotional cliché. Editorial decision making is not made on the basis of genuine newsworthiness or public interest. Rather, the consideration of how much the news would serve the morbid curiosity of a large number of audience plays a decisive role. The high level of sensation in a news story is what is behind the story's way onto the television screen.

However, in Pakistan, the media coverage of a minor girl's rape incident in 2012 was considered only once in a court of law, where the Lahore High Court merely expressed its satisfaction that a regulatory advice had been issued to television channels. The Court said that the advice sufficiently protects the right to dignity and privacy provided by Article 14 of the Constitutional of Pakistan. The Court made the advice as part of the order and directed the Pakistan Electronic media Regulatory Authority (PEMRA) to enforce that. The advice reads:

> The marathon coverage of minor rape victims, revealing their identities, and of their parents and barging into their four walls with cameras and mikes to seek the comments of family who are already in state of shock is no service to the cause of providing information to the viewers within the limits of commonly accepted cultural norms. It is unfortunate that TV channels do not even realize that an irresponsible coverage could have far-reaching adverse consequences for victims or their family. Merely labeling 'PG' does not dissipate the suffering that media inflicts upon the unfortunate victims or their families.[15]

---

[12] Marcus and McMahon (1990).

[13] See for different perspectives: Denno (1992), pp. 1123–1131.

[14] Marcus and McMahon (1990).

[15] Staff Reporter, 'LHC directs media to follow PEMRA instructions' *Daily Dawn*, October 26 2013 http://www.dawn.com/news/1052205/lhc-directs-media-to-follow-pemra-instructions. Accessed 26 August 2023. According to the report, Justice Syed Mansoor Ali shah granted interim direction for enforcement of the said advice terming it as supporting Article 14, which is related with the protection of privacy and human dignity.

2.1.2 Media Exposure of Women

The protection of women against certain misogynistic biases and sexual crimes needs particular attention. In Pakistani society, the causes of vulnerability of women have a special context. The culture in Pakistan is predominantly paternalistic and most women have a traditional role of housekeeping and looking after children. Woman is considered as the sole harbinger of tribal honor and her minor cultural deviancy can put into question the 'honor' of all the adherents. This makes rampant the problem of honor killing of women to such a big scale that, according to Honor Based Awareness Network, 1000 killings out of 5000 worldwide killings are committed in Pakistan.[16] In other words, every fifth of the global honor killing crime is committed in Pakistan. Perhaps due to the advent of mobile phones and online platforms which facilitate the disclosure of intimate affairs of women, last decade has witnessed a surge in the honor killing in Pakistan.[17] A total of 470 offences have been reported to the police in 2021 in spite of the fact that majority of cases go unreported. [18] Similarly, Pakistan ranked 153 out 156 countries on the World Economic Forum's Global Gender Gap index in 2021.[19]

Honor killing is a homicide that is carried out by the family members of the victim with a belief (or even suspicion in many cases) that some action of the deceased has brought ill repute or shame to the family or tribe. Most of the honor killings revolve around extra marital relations. The allegations leveled by the offenders against their targeted family members range from involvement in the adultery to any kind of act that has the potential to bring 'shame' and 'bad name' to the family. In some cases, a mere refusal of an offer already assented by family elders to get her married to a particular person may result into grievous hurts or even murder. A marriage against the wishes of parents or elders of the family or tribe can also result into dire consequences for a female.[20] Therefore, dating between opposite genders is the most secretive affair and any 'leakage' of footage evidencing meetups could bring

[16]'Statistics and Data', Honour Based Violence Awareness Network, http://hbv-awareness.com/statistics-data/. Accessed 26 August 2023.

[17]'Shocking: Surge of Honor Killings in Pakistan', (Amnesty International, 2 July 2014) https://www.amnestyusa.org/shocking-surge-of-honor-killings-in-pakistan/. Accessed 26 August 2023.

[18]'Getting away with murder in Pakistan', (France 24, 26 May, 2022) https://www.france24.com/en/live-news/20220525-getting-away-with-murder-in-pakistan. Accessed 26 August 2023.

[19]'Getting away with murder in Pakistan', (France 24, 26 May 2022) https://www.france24.com/en/live-news/20220525-getting-away-with-murder-in-pakistan. Accessed 26 August 2023.

[20]'Pakistani family murder newlyweds over free-will marriage in 'honour' killing' *Independent UK*, 28 November 2017 https://www.independent.co.uk/news/world/asia/honour-killings-newlyweds-murdered-abdul-hadi-hasina-bibi-karachi-pakistan-a8079411.html. Accessed 26 August 2023.). This report is a single instance, while it is not a singular incidence as majority of marriages are solemnized by parents called "arrange marriage". The extramarital relations (even if not based on sexual intimacy) of couples or ending up in marriage (called love marriage and is mostly discouraged) without prior consent of parents (usually father, or in his absence, elder brother or any other male member of the family) have always the chances of violence of varying degree i.e. from social boycott or ostracism to homicide of the female or both partners.

lethal consequences. In this vein, the female inhabitants of rural areas of Pakistan have to observe immense care in using social media and online communication applications. An email, WhatsApp message, or an SMS have a great potential to become a life threat. In such circumstances, it becomes imperative upon the individuals to take extra measures to conceal their personal data such as identity, location,[21] communication recipients as well as the content of their communication.

The family honor is not connected only to the issues of dating, love affairs, marrying without permission, or disregarding the family commitments in the affairs of *arranged marriage*. It is customary and a matter of common observation that women of rural areas in Pakistan remain inside the house and whenever they have to go outside of the house they observe veil. The observance of veil is sometimes so strict that women even do not disclose their face. In some tribal communities, the rules of the so-called morality and decency are so rigid that women are supposed to remain inside the house, unnoticeable by any male outside of the instant family. Under such circumstances, the publication of images or videos of women is regarded as a very serious matter that may amount to animosity and armed conflicts. Many instances from the recent past confirm the fact that how the disclosure of images or videos of Pakistani women ended up in assassinations of females.

In 2012, an ultraconservative family killed three women in Kohistan region of Pakistan just because of a video footage showing them singing a folk song.[22] These women were allegedly killed after a decree of their killing was issued by the local tribal elders in a *Jirga*.[23] Soon after the news came to light, it became an issue of national as well as international concern. The Chief Justice of Pakistan took *Suo Moto* notice and directed the relevant authorities for investigating the matter. The tribal members denied the allegations; however, the authorities have failed to verify aliveness of the ladies by making them appear before the court or the media. No media persons or government investigators were given access to the village by the tribal council or *jirga*. In an interview, the imam judged the act as 'dishonorable' but refused the issuance of killing orders.[24] Subsequent enquiry revealed that the girls

[21] 'Policeman kills niece in the name of honor' *BBC Urdu*, 4 May, 2017 http://www.bbc.com/urdu/pakistan-39800820. Accessed 26 August 2023.

[22] Vice News, 'The Kohistan Story: Killing for Honor' https://www.youtube.com/watch?v=xoPXW8Qm8U8. Accessed 26 August 2023.

[23] Jirga is a form of informal dispute settlement mechanism which is based upon tribal rules and procedures. It decides upon issues pertaining to a variety of subjects including civil as well as criminal matters. Jirga members assemble and adjudicate upon any question of local significance. Jirga is a very controversial tribal practice and its legality is questioned every time it issues illegal decrees. Many honour killing in Pakistan are usually followed by jirga's decrees issued to that effect. The Economist has termed the whole process as *barbaric* and myogenic. See for details: https://www.economist.com/news/asia/21730202-it-fast-and-cheap-if-not-always-edifying-pakistan-mainstreaming-misogynist-tribal-justice. Accessed 26 August 2023.

[24] Vice News, 'The Kohistan Story: Killing for Honor' https://www.youtube.com/watch?v=xoPXW8Qm8U8. Accessed 26 August 2023.

were murdered.[25] The local freelance journalist who broke the story was also shot dead in March, 2019.

In another incident, Qandeel Baloch, a social media celebrity with a pseudonymous identity was killed in 2016 after her actual data was revealed by a local newspaper.[26] Her only 'fault' was that she would post her bizarre videos and pictures on social media and would comment and gossip about different public figures. She was killed 'in the name of honor' by her brother.

In January, 2012, a television program called The Maya Khan[27] show which had based its theme on the so-called moral policing of media persons got much popularity. In that program, the anchor assumed the role of a media vigilante.[28] As in Pakistani society, it is socially and religiously prohibited for opposite genders, who are not related by blood relationship or wedlock to mingle with each other. The disclosure of such *objectionable* associations is regarded as highly offensive to the victims and may have very drastic implications for their reputation. This could even endanger their lives in some cases depending on the nature of their family ethos. The format of the show was that, in an outdoor broadcast, the host would "catch" some young couples, alleging them for dating in a public park. Maya Khan was shown as running and chasing the escaping couples.[29] Most of the couples tried to shy away from TV camera. If they succeeded to escape, they were still identifiable in video footages. The dilemma for the captured ones was even more severe as they were asked stringent personal questions about the nature of their relationship and that whether their parents knew what they were doing in the park.

Commentators belonging to different walks of life criticized the show with immense abhorrence.[30] Much was written against the type of 'moral policing' by the national media and its dangerous fallout in a traditional society which is well known for its obscurantist values.[31] The jerk of the event to the national regulator was only to the extent of issuing 'warning' to Samaa TV.[32] However, The *Maya Khan Show* is not a deviation from the otherwise ethical broadcast patterns of the rest

---

[25] Bhatti, 'Girls in 2011 Kohistan video were killed, Supreme Court told' *Daily Dawn,* 2 January 2019 https://www.dawn.com/news/1455038. Accessed 26 August 2023.

[26] For details see blog: Aftab, 'Online anonymity as a guaranty to the right to life (part 2)' *Recht und Netz University of Hamburg,* 24 July 2017 http://rechtundnetz.com/online-anonymity-as-a-guaranty-to-the-right-to-life-part-2/. Accessed 26 August 2023.

[27] The TV program was named after its host name Maya Khan.

[28] 'Media's moral policing' http://www.dawn.com/news/691258/media-s-moral-policing. Accessed 26 August 2023.

[29] The video is still available on a popular online video streaming platform.

[30] See for details: Abbas, 'Why 'vigil aunty' caused Pakistan media storm' *BBC News,* 2 February 2012 https://www.bbc.com/news/world-asia-16809139. Accessed 26 August 2023.

[31] See for example: Zakaria, 'Public spaces, private lives' Daily Dawn 01 February 2012 http://www.dawn.com/news/692321/public-spaces-private-lives. Accessed 26 August 2023.).

[32] Press Release dated 28 January 2013, issued by General Manager (Media and PR) Pakistan Electronic Media Authority.

of the media; rather, it is an emblematic feature of a much deteriorated scenario.[33] One can find many such programs uploaded to YouTube which have been broadcasted on the mainstream or regional television channels.

From a theoretical point of view, the value of privacy for women in Pakistan makes a strong case to choose a more differentiated approach than the so-called 'feminist critique' on privacy right which surrounds around the premise that it is a male's right *"to be let alone"* in order to oppress women with impunity.[34] The protection of privacy rights of women, to protect them from becoming a subject of media sensationalism and prurience, is urgently required as the consequences of women's privacy violation are dangerous as compared to permissive societies. The prevailing social inequality and the vulnerability of women in Pakistan call for state intervention so that to actively prevent all the practices which lead to the violation of women's right to life. Mackinnon aptly writes, "if inequality is socially pervasive and enforced, equality will require intervention, not abdication, to be meaningful."[35]

The Constitution of Pakistan provides for measures to ensure women participation in all walks of national life.[36] For that purpose, special quota has been reserved for women in both National and Provincial legislative assemblies. A number of legal provisions especially provide for the protection of women, exhibiting seriousness of the state regarding the special challenges faced by women in Pakistan.[37] The sensitivity of modesty of women and her bodily privacy is so crucial that the penal law provides capital punishment for the person who assaults a woman and uses criminal force to strip her clothes, exposing her to public view.[38] Through these stringent measures, the legislature intends to provide extra-protection to the marginalized women. In the similar manner, the State is required to take into account the threat posed by media to women's privacy.

---

[33] See for details: Siddiqui, 'Its not just Maya' *Daily Dawn*, 20 March 2012 http://www.dawn.com/news/704081/its-not-just-maya. Accessed 26 August 2023.

[34] See for introduction to this concept: MacKinnon (1989). We will analyze the feminist critique more closely in Sect. 3.5.2.3.

[35] MacKinnon (1989), p. 191. She presents this argument against the American abortion choice in the context of decisional privacy and power imbalance between male and female in the determination of sexual relationship. She is of the view that the existing status quo will be protected if an 'intimate sphere' is given protection from government interference under the right to privacy.

[36] Article 34 Constitution of Pakistan 1973.

[37] For example, Pakistan Penal Code (PPC) Section 354 (Assault or criminal force to woman with intent to outrage her modesty).

[38] PPC Section 354 provides: "Whoever assaults or uses criminal force to any woman and strips her of her clothes and in that condition, exposes her to the public view, shall be punished with death or with imprisonment for life, and shall also be liable to fine."

2.1.3 *Pakistani Media and Children Wellbeing*

Children are vulnerable to different kinds of abuses because they lack the capacity to make decisions for their wellbeing. When it comes to media coverage whether they are the subject of news as victims or interviewed as juveniles and when media is publishing their actual images and disclosing their identities, children should be treated keeping in view their vulnerabilities.

In Pakistan, however, the broadcasts of electronic media show no sign of respect for the protection of privacy, dignity and the wellbeing of children.[39] Due to the low literacy level in Pakistan, parents are usually unaware of the social and psychological effects of television programs. Media persons also disregard the right of privacy of children during news gathering. It is a common media practice that reporters interview the children who are subjected to a traumatic situation, either due to the loss of their father, mother or any other close relative.[40] Journalists pose 'how-do-you-feel' sort of questions to children undergoing a traumatic situation apparently to sympathize with them. It is just another way to sensationalize the broadcast which resultantly causes immense secondary victimization of the children.[41] Even if journalists talk to their parents, the presence of children watching their parents narrating some tragic accident has also grave effects on their psychological wellbeing and it adversely affects their personality development.

In principle, children have a right to privacy even against everybody else including their parents, which may *be qualified according to the child's age and evolving capacities*.[42] Society has a collective responsibility to ensure a foolproof protection of their basic rights. Most countries have special legal and institutional arrangements for socialization, personality development, and guardianship. International human rights instruments as well as national constitutions and bills of rights expressly protect the rights of children including their right to privacy. The Constitution of Pakistan obliges the state for protection of children in general terms.[43] Additionally, Pakistan is a party to the United Nation Convention on the rights of the Child 1989. This Convention states: "No child shall be subjected to arbitrary or unlawful interference with his or her privacy, family, home or correspondence, nor to unlawful attacks on his or her honor and reputation*;*" and "[T]he child has the right to the protection of the law against such interference or attacks".[44] The Ethical Code of Conduct devised by Pakistan Electronic Media Regulatory Authority (PEMRA)

[39] There are hundreds of such TV programs uploaded to the internet as well.

[40] See for instance: Khalil, 'Pakistan Taliban: Peshawar school attack leaves 141 dead' http://www.bbc.com/news/world-asia-30491435. Accessed 26 August 2023.

[41] See for details regarding media's disregard for children's privacy: Tandon (2007). This report primarily focuses on India, but the findings could be reasonably correlated to Pakistan media scenario.

[42] Shmueli and Blecher-Prigat (2010), p. 763.

[43] Article 35: "the State shall protect the marriage, the family, the mother and the child".

[44] Article 16 (1) and (2) The United Nations Convention on the rights of the Child 1989.

provides for the protection of children in advertisement as well as in editorial programs.[45] The code obliges TV channels to refrain from broadcasts that disturb the wellbeing of children and which are based on violence or deceit. More importantly, it requires a careful consideration of physical and emotional wellbeing as well as the dignity of persons less than eighteen years of age, *irrespective of any consent given by the participant or by a parent, guardian or other person over the age of eighteen years in loco parentis.*[46]

However, the issue is bigger than media ethics. No 'show cause notice' issued by PEMRA can ameliorate the damage accrued to some aspect of personality development. Children need proper legislative protection against any harm to their right to privacy. As a result, the legal protection of children against media exposure must be strengthened because the media practices ignore basic protection requirements.

2.1.4 Reporting Private Matters of Public Figures

Public figures are the favorite subjects of media across the globe. People are believed to have great interest in the private lives, habits and daily activities of politician, sports persons, and media celebrities. The stories related to their love affairs, holiday destinations, luxurious life styles, and marriages are sold by the media like hot cake. Their breakups, sicknesses, insolvencies, and divorces are equally attractive enterprises. From journalists' bodies to the justices of higher courts, there subsists a conviction that only a very miniscule zone of privacy exists for public figures. During balancing of privacy with free speech, the tilt of scale shifts towards protection of free speech in most cases where the complainant is a public figure. The justification put forward by the believers of 'zero privacy' for public figures is that public figures have an existential interest to retain their celebrity status in the media because their success in professional life is directly proportional to the extent of media coverage they get. Another line of arguments is related to the public interest in bringing them into media focus. A common argument is that public has a legitimate interest to know about most of the aspects of their life because people follow celebrities from sports and entertainment industry and consume time and money to appreciate their performance. In order to enable people to make decisions regarding becoming or not becoming members of such 'fan clubs', they must know as much as possible regarding their 'heroes' and so-called 'role models'. In the case of politicians and public officeholders, people want their leaders to be exposed before them and they think themselves entitled to 'keep an eye' on them. Such watchful eye enables the public to make an informed decision at the time of elections.

[45] Section 12 PEMRA Code of Conduct 2015.

[46] Section 12 (3) PEMRA Code of Conduct 2015.

These justifications might be convincing at least to some extent, however the matter is not that straight forward. The problem arises with the categorization of public figures and the criteria of how to differentiate the public sphere from the private sphere of their lives. It is wrong to presume that all the subjects of media attention actually seek publicity. The lives of many people become NEWS accidently, for instance victims of accidents and emergencies. Many people become part of some news story without their conscious effort or intention to grab media attention.[47] They may not like presence in the media even if people want to watch or listen to them or to know about them. These people can be enumerated as temporary public figures even if they are in the public places, because privacy cannot be viewed in a 'binary way' of either public or private.[48] Even celebrities or famous people may have the status of public figure against their will or assumed such position by virtue of their family or descent. The problem of extra interest of tabloid press in celebrity's life has been an issue very long debated in the ethics and law of media. Internationally, the conduct and misdemeanors of journalist came to the limelight after the death of Princess Diana who died in a car accident in an attempt to escape from paparazzi in France. It sparked a debate of how to regulate media behavior vis-à-vis public figures, particularly when such behavior amounts to harassment and has the potential to serious mental harm or even bodily injury.[49]

The coverage of Pakistani television channels shows that electronic media in Pakistan do not recognize any boundary with respect to the dignity and privacy of public figures. Salacious details of private lives of the celebrities and politicians are broadcasted without any ethical and moral considerations. The example of a Pakistani public figure, the Prime Minister of Pakistan, Imran Khan can provide a good case study for an illustrative elaboration of the problem. He has enjoyed a first class celebrity status long before he came to politics due to his heroic performance as a captain of the Pakistani national cricket team, which ultimately became a winner in the World Cup championship of 1992 during his captaincy. At that time he was well known to the British tabloid press as a 'playboy of the Western world'.[50] His popularity further boosted after he married Jamima Goldsmith, daughter of business

[47] See for instance: Henig (2005).

[48] Solove (2007), p. 07: "Under existing notions, privacy is often thought of in a binary way—something is either private or public. According to the general rule, if something occurs in a public place, it is not private. But a more nuanced view of privacy suggests that this case involved taking an event that occurred in one context and significantly altering its nature—by making it permanent and widespread." See Introduction of the book for a detailed analysis of the "Dog poop girl" incident in the context of public/private dichotomy of privacy right.

[49] See for instance this debate in the American context: Halperin (1999).

[50] Adams, 'Playboy of the Western World' (2016) https://www.independent.ie/woman/celeb-news/playboy-of-the-western-world-26414288.html. Accessed 26 August 2023.

tycoon, Sir James Goldsmith.[51] Their nine-year married life and subsequent divorce got an immense media coverage.[52]

Imran Khan's second marriage with a BBC weather news presenter, Reham Khan, who is a British citizen of Pakistani descent, lasted only for a few months.[53] Imran Khan was the chairman of a mainstream political party and an opposition leader at that time. Their divorce became a flashpoint for Pakistani media which gave a disproportional coverage to minute details of actual and concocted facts. Many stories were narrated regarding the possible causes of divorce. The journalist and media anchors tried their level best to spread speculative version of the events, to make the issue perverted and sensational. Media unearthed and reported varying causes of divorce - from a dispute over dog's presence in their bedroom to connecting Reham Khan to a foreign spying agency. Imran Khan in his tweet appealed to the media to respect their privacy,[54] and condemned the reports about settlements as "false and shameful."[55] The media drama around his personal life did not end here. It reached its real climax when some portions of Reham Khan's transcript of a book to be published leaked and made rounds in the media. The content of the book is a typical revengeful 'kiss and tell' type biography. It is full of salacious narration of fact, judgments and conjectures, which touched almost everybody near to Imran Khan, including his former wife, children, friends and family members.[56] Jemima Goldsmith threatened to sue Reham Khan for libel and breach

[51] See for Jamima Khan Biography: *Hello!,* https://www.hellomagazine.com/profiles/jemima-khan/ . Accessed 26 August 2023.

[52] Watch a small footage from Associated Press Archives on YouTube as a reference to how International media has been giving him coverage for decades: https://www.youtube.com/watch?v=cJrdl9FVXZo. Accessed 26 August 2023.

[53] Abbas, 'Imran Khan, Reham divorce with mutual consent', *Daily Dawn,* 30 October 2015 https://www.dawn.com/news/1216377 . Accessed 26 August 2023.

[54] See Imran Khan's Tweet: 'This is a painful time for me & Reham & our families. I would request everyone to respect our privacy.' 30 October 2019, https://twitter.com/ImranKhanPTI/status/660011225154265089. Accessed 26 August 2023.

[55] See Imran Khan's Tweet: 'Reports & speculation about financial settlements are absolutely false and shameful.' 30 October 2015 https://twitter.com/ImranKhanPTI/status/660012355905044480. Reham Khan also expressed her privacy concerns many times. For instance see: 'Reham Khan: Marrying Imran Khan meant everyone in Pakistan got involved in my private affairs' *The Guardian,* 17 November 2015 https://www.theguardian.com/lifeandstyle/2015/nov/17/reham-khan-imran-khan-pakistan-politics-marriage-divorce . Accessed 26 August 2023.

[56] A reviewer summarizes the revelations as: "It all unravelled spectacularly. Reham Khan accuses the great man of a plethora of minor flaws: he is callous to animals; he is embarrassed about his hair implants; he tells the same boring stories over and over; he is superstitious enough to slather his whole body in "dal"—cooked lentils—to ward off envy, on the advice of a quack healer; he is callow; he is venal; he thrives on gossip; he is duplicitous; he is so lazy that his typical working day is barely three hours long; he "pleasures himself" while watching gay porn; he is not at all as well-endowed as people assume (she quotes a Bollywood star whom Khan is said to have bedded saying he was "big talk and small delivery"." Max Rodenbeck, 'Imran Khan: Captain Pakistan's wild ride.' *Financial Review*, 13 December 2018 https://www.afr.com/life-and-luxury/arts-and-culture/imran-khan-captain-pakistans-wild-ride-20181128-h18h74. Accessed 26 August 2023.).

of privacy of her 16 year old son, if the book was published in the United Kingdom.[57] The leaked portions and its subsequent formal publication brought a storm of discussions, analysis, debates and rebuttals as the contents of the book contained every abuse of free speech, that is, from libelous accusations to privacy violation of the most intimate sphere and sensitive information. The publication of the book was taken as something Pakistani media had longing for. They gave full coverage to the book as well as to its detailed contents. They also interviewed the people about whom the book contained accusations of immorality. In such a conservative society, it is causes more shame if someone asks such questions as whether or not he had intimate relations with Imran Khan.[58]

The death of a public figure is a newsworthy matter. The eventuality of dying, coffins, graves and funeral processions naturally attracts the curiosity of people. Media around the world covers the death news of famous people. In Pakistan too, media has an extreme interest in the news involving dead bodies and it is not an exaggeration to say that even the graves and dead bodies of public figures are shown in the media. The death of a public figure is broadcasted in every possible sensationalistic way. The news stories are packaged with all the visual and sound effects that add a dramatic character to these broadcasts. In one of such attempts, while providing a live coverage to the funeral services of a renowned philanthropist Abdul Sattar Edhi, a field journalist of a private television channel (Express News), was shown reporting from inside the grave of the deceased. This action was highly criticized nationally, internationally as well as on social media.[59] The faces of dead bodies are shown normally by the media. Similarly, another channel showed the video of Edhi's dead body without blurring the image. This type of journalism and media reports cannot be justified anywhere in a civilized world. Dead bodies are entitled to be treated with respect and there cannot be any public interest in showing the grave of a popular person. However, there is no precedent in the legal system of Pakistan where the heirs of the deceased person could have found a relief for the disparagement of dead. In other countries, the ethical codes of self-regulation set the limits for the publishing or broadcasting of images of dead bodies. For example, in Germany, the right to image has been recognized by the courts where the heirs can claim for any kind of unauthorized publication.

---

[57] She tweeted, "'I've been assured that it's too libellous to be published in the UK,' Jemima claimed on social media. 'But, if it is published here, I will be suing for defamation and breach of privacy on behalf of my [then] 16-year-old son and in relation to the moronic, re-hashed Zionist conspiracy theories. Sigh." See Daily Mail Report (07 June, 2018) as her tweet on Twitter is no longer available, 'Battle of Imran Khan's exes: Jemima Goldsmith threatens to sue retired cricketer's second wife – a former BBC weathergirl – over tell-all book which threatens to derail his campaign to become Pakistan PM.' https://www.dailymail.co.uk/news/article-5816927/Battle-Imran-Khans-exes-Jemima-Goldsmith-threatens-sue-retired-cricketers-second-wife.html Accessed 26 August 2023.

[58] Many such talk shows of Pakistani television channels are available online.

[59] Saleem A (2017) Poor journalistic practice in Pakistan. https://www.dw.com/en/whats-causing-poor-journalistic-practice-in-pakistan/a-38212788 Accessed 23 September 2023.

Mubashir Luqman, a popular anchor who has been hosting different talk shows is notorious for his scathing and blunt style. One of his shows *Kharri Baat* (means straight talk) on ARY News channel broadcasted footages, showing a number of men and women, arrested by police allegedly from a brothel house.[60] A political leader of the ruling party is particularly shown, making him prominent through a red circle around his face.

This is an unending story of media in Pakistan transgressing every boundary of laws, ethical principles, and humanely concerns. No theory of free speech or the right to privacy can justify such journalistic behavior. Public figures, particularly politicians, have zero privacy in the very literal sense of the term when it comes to their portrayal in the media. It makes no difference whether they are in their house, at parliament, at office, at hospital[61] or even on the deathbed. They are humiliated in the name of satirical programs, where the subject of parody revolves more around the physical features, pitch of voices, paunch, color of skin and so on, and little around political themes. Their private lives are brought into public light as a matter of routine.

2.1.5 Grief Journalism

Tragedies, calamities and emergencies such as road accidents, plane crashes, bomb blasts and fire events make headline news. People have a legitimate interest to be informed regarding such tragedies.[62] The victims of these tragedies, however, happen to attract media attention and they become involuntary or accidental public figures. The victims of such events undergo the moments of personal sorrows and grief. In such situations, people usually want to be left alone as grief is not shared with strangers. Particularly, they are not in the position to express an informed consent for the media coverage. The decision to allow publicity of their tragedies may not be the same had they not been subjected to such traumatic situation.

When covering such events, journalists often try their best to scratch them as much as possible in order to extract information about every detail of the incident. Media gives full coverage to calamities, emergencies and tragic events such as road accidents, earth quacks or fire incidents. A simple search on YouTube would reveal Pakistani media's handling of such events. Enough empirical evidence of video

---

[60] Footage has been publically available on Facebook.

[61] A noteworthy example involves the dissemination of sensitive medical information in the media as a routine practice. For instance, a high-rated television channel like Geo TV, with a substantial viewership in Pakistan, publicly showed on screen a medical lab-test report containing sensitive information. This report pertained to an individual of significant political stature, Shahbaz Sharif, a three-time Chief Minister of Pakistan's largest province and the current opposition leader.

[62] See: Martinson, 'Are journalists prying too far into grief?' *The Guardian*, 25 May 2017 https://www.theguardian.com/commentisfree/2017/may/25/journalists-grief-media-manchester-attack . Accessed 26 August 2023.

footages and photos show the height of sensationalism and undue hype of the media. In one of such videos of a fire incident in a factory, people are shown jumping down from high rise buildings in a struggle to rescue themselves from fire. In other videos a statement just before dying is broadcasted, which was recorded through mobile camera. A medical College student was shot in an apparent case of 'jealous lover turns murderer'. She succumbed to injuries and died. Before her death, her family recorded a small video in which she can be heard naming the person who was behind her attack. All the channels broadcasted the video for hours and it is still available online.

Grief journalism is a dominant feature of television channels in Pakistan and there are specific shows dedicated to such programs. The anchors of these shows conduct interviews of families, children and relatives of victims whose death has newsworthiness due to the cause of death as in road accidents, electrocuted, or during robbery.

The depiction of grief is a common phenomenon around the world. However, the practice of bringing the victims, affectees and members of bereaved families to the media lime-light, interviewing them, asking them to narrate the events and express their sorrows is at the next level in Pakistan. Researchers have shown that the intense media attention and recounting their traumatic stress in the aftermath of tragedy cause immense harm of at least five categories; firstly, *fear and loss of physical security;* secondly, *loss of emotional equilibrium due to 'fear, indignation, anger and exhaustion*; thirdly, *being treated as means to an end and not an end in itself*; fourthly, *loss of autonomy and control;* and fifthly, *impending recovery due to insufficient emotional expression and not being capable to retreat with certain other to build relationship.*[63]

2.1.6 *Reporting in the Course of Legal Proceedings: Public Shaming, Investigative Journalism and Sting Operations*

Press always shows deep interest in the news related to law and order scenarios as well as *sub judice* matters. Most of the newspapers, tabloids in particular, contain news related to crimes, stories of deviance, police arrests, and accounts from the witness box of the local courts. In Pakistan, newspapers have special "crime and punishment" corners, where the target audience is facilitated with an easy access. Similarly, television channels have also dedicated time slots for crime reports and they maintain an updated version of crime reporters' diaries and submissions.

Giving intensive coverage to issues connected to law and order by the print and electronic media in Pakistan has become a normal exercise that has never become the subject of any normative debate. Disclosure of full name of the accused, publishing

[63] See for details: Moreham and Tinsley (2018).

his picture, and also finding out his whereabouts and interviewing the local people who know him is order of the day. There is no consideration of any other individual or societal interest. 'Unearthing' the crime and bringing the wrongdoer to the forefront is a sufficient public interest that media thinks it can legitimately undertake.

A common practice of media journalists is that they approach the alleged criminals in the police station and their confessional statements are recorded for broadcasting. The evidentiary value of those confessional footages is a debate outside the scope of this book. However, it is argued that such coverage undermines the due process and the fundamental right to justice and fair trial.[64] Additionally, the privacy of individuals is protected even if they are in a public place because of their reasonable and justified expectations of privacy. It is the 'context' of a particular situation that demands protection from outside intrusion.[65]

During the content analysis of private media in Pakistan, several instances come to light. For instance, one anchor focused her program on the topic of homosexuality, specifically delving into how some men engage in same-gender relationships while adopting a female guise to conceal their identity. Regrettably, it appears that the media personality behind this program may not fully comprehend the severe implications of these actions, as evident in the video footage. Engaging in such behavior could place these individuals in extremely perilous situations, given that homosexuality constitutes a serious offense under the Pakistan Penal Code.[66] Beyond legal repercussions, this activity could lead to far more dire consequences, including the risk of honor killings.

In another program, a journalist sends his colleague to a CD rental shop. His colleague asks for a pornographic film, while the anchor secretly records the whole episode. A pornographic film is allegedly provided by the sales men at the CD shop, and then the anchor and his crew appears. They catch the salesmen by surprise and start asking embarrassing questions. The salesman alleges that the person, who helped the media men in trapping him, himself supplies such CD's to CD shops.[67]

Last but not least, the investigative program titled *Sar-e-Aam* (means bluntly) is regularly broadcasted on ARY News. Although this program is very popular in the Pakistani audience yet, the main plot of almost all the programs is based on disguised tactics with hidden microphones and cameras. This program is being broadcasted since many years with hundreds of 'successful' episodes.

[64] See for a strong case against media coverage of court proceedings: Phillipson (2008).

[65] For the detailed elaboration of public/private dichotomy, reasonable expectations of privacy and the concept of contextual integrity see: Nissenbaum (2009).

[66] Section 377 of Pakistan Penal Code provides for definition and punishment of homosexual activity with a title, "Unnatural offences" in such words as, "Whoever voluntarily has carnal intercourse against the order of nature with any man, woman or animal, shall be punished with imprisonment for life, or with imprisonment of either description for a term which shall not be less than two years nor more than ten years, and shall also be liable to fine."

[67] The video footage is available on some online platforms but could not be retrieved here due to privacy concerns.

Reporting crimes, punishments and court proceeding legitimately make use of a public interest under the right to access to information and the media and press enjoy immense respect due to their association with the right to freedom of speech. However, this is not an absolute right and media does not have absolute freedom to use every means of newsgathering or dissemination of true information. The right to free speech must be weighed against dignitarian interests of those involved in the committal of crimes and against the societal interests related to rehabilitation of criminals as well as fair administration of justice. The media also has an additional responsibility as opinion leader to educate readers and viewers.

Against this background, a tug of war is common between media and privacy advocates to make their respective points as whether upholding speech right is more valuable or that there should be a consideration for human privacy and personality rights as well. In order to find out how Pakistan deals with these practical paradoxes, the following sections will elaborate its media regulatory setup as it operates in the general legal and constitutional regime.

2.2 The State of Media Regulatory Affairs

Due to the prevalence of diverse interests, the formulation of rules and regulations for a useful and an effective mass communication exercise is a universally known phenomenon. There are regulatory mechanisms, self-regulatory codes, private law protections, common law torts and many other legal and quasi legal instruments available that try to balance free speech with other rights and interest. In this scenario, the case of Pakistani media is a curios one. The problem of infringements of privacy in the wake of media practices, the disregard of people's privacy right, as illustrated above, right and the lack of legal mechanism to enforce that right properly need an urgent consideration.

As we have seen in our overview, there is a galore of TV programs in which media-men enter into private premises forcibly and without any intimation to the inmates for 'capturing' people inside allegedly involved in so-called 'immoral activities'. Apart from this *moral-policing*, media persons visit police stations and lockups for recording confessional interviews of the alleged criminals or those under custody for being suspicious. The footages of such programs are broadcasted without any venture to keep secret the identities of subjects. Many times, it has been observed that the repeated requests and imploring to stop recording are ignored with an antipathetic manner, subjecting human beings to a very deplorable situation. Since the start of their broadcasts, private TV channels have recorded and broadcasted hundreds of programs with thousands of privacy violations. A permanency to the harm is being granted automatically when the video clips of such television programs are uploaded on video-sharing websites after their broadcast on television channels. One can find hundreds of such videos as an evidence of media persons' transgressions into the sacred bounds of private lives and premises. In many cases, the newsgathering and recordings' modus operandi amount to criminal intrusion into privacy. Against this background, the right to privacy of citizens and the dignity of man has long been observed as a defenseless victim, violated as a rule and not exception during the collection of news stories and their dissemination on audio-visual mass media.

Pakistan Electronic Media Regulatory Authority (PEMRA) is the official watch-dog, established to regulate both the administrative and content-related issues of private television channels.[68] All TV and radio channels are legally required to get a license from PEMRA before going on-air.[69] However, an overview of PEMRA Ordinance, rules, regulations, system of complaints and an analysis of the *sub judice* matters either in the regular courts or before the "Authority" suggest that its main focus is to deal with the financial aspects of electronic media and FM radio channels. The lenient and lackluster attitude towards content regulation is evident from the fact that in spite of the fact where Section 19 (5) of PEMRA Ordinance provides for a code of conduct, it took almost twelve years to formulate one. It has only become possible after the Supreme Court of Pakistan intervened and directed the federal government to notify the draft code.[70] The Supreme Court of Pakistan also directed all media channels to obey the code which provided the teeth to the otherwise benign ethical instrument.

A thorough analysis of the recent Code of Conduct reveals the self-contradictory nature of this document. It gives a privacy right to citizens at one hand but takes away the same at the other. Several articles of the Electronic Media (Programs and Advertisement) Code of Conduct of 2015 lay down basic principles for TV content and address the licensees to ensure that private aspects of individual's life should not be intruded upon or made public.[71] Similarly, there is an exclusive article titled "privacy and personal data protection" defining door stepping and prohibiting it along with forced interviews.[72] The irony with all these provisions is that the proviso of 'public interest' is attached to each one. These provisions categorically permit intrusion into private lives where violation of privacy is outweighed", "justified" or "warranted" by public interest. Regrettably, Article 21 defines public interest in such a broad manner that it would include almost everything under the sun and no media

[68] The regulatory authority was established in 2002, through PEMRA Ordinance. See for a detailed profile: www.pemra.gov.pk. Accessed 26 August 2023.

[69] Section 19 (2) of PEMRA Ordinance 2002 (amended) says: "no person shall engage in any broadcast media or distribution service [footnote omitted] except after obtaining a license issued under this Ordinance". The ordinance also gives powers to make rules, code of conduct and prescribe terms and conditions for licensees.

[70] Ministry of Information and Broadcasting notified the Code of Conduct on 20th of August 2015 after Supreme Court of Pakistan issued directions.

[71] Articles 3(4) and 4(7)(d) of Electronic Media (Programs and Advertisement) Code of Conduct 2015.

[72] Article No 11 of Electronic Media (Programs and Advertisement) Code of Conduct 2015.

intrusion could ever be labeled as in contravention to the so-called code of conduct. According to Article 21, "a program may be considered in the public interest if it:

(i) *exposes or detects crime;*
(ii) *exposes significant anti-social behavior;*
(iii) *exposes corruption or injustice;*
(iv) *protects people's health and safety; prevents people from being misled by any statement or an individual or organization; or discloses information that assists people to better comprehend or make decisions on matters of public importance."*

In our analysis of media practices, it has become clear why the determination of public interest cannot be left to media in general and especially in the peculiar media environment of Pakistan. Any media coverage under the guise of exposing crime or anti-social behavior and for the so-called protection of people's health cannot be categorized as public interest and a pretext for privacy rights violation. The current code of conduct reveals the unfortunate reality that policy makers in Pakistan are neither abreast of the general importance of privacy nor the specific sensitivities of Pakistani society are given any consideration in the legal and administrative scheme devised for media regulation.

Apart from state regulation, self-regulation works satisfactorily in many countries of the world as an acceptable alternative to the former. In Pakistan, however, not a single effective measure has been taken by representative entities of media houses. Pakistan Broadcasters' Association (PBA) is active in protecting their commercial rights such as initiation of campaign and legal proceedings against import and broadcast foreign media content. The lack of interest in human rights' related aspects is evident from the fact that its 'ethical code of conduct' is still a 'proposed' document. Moreover, the enforcement mechanism for the code has never been established so far.[73] Similarly, Pakistan Federal Union of Journalists (PFUJ) is another organization that represents the journalists' community. The main objective of PFUJ is to safeguard the rights and 'interests' of journalists. Its constitution is, therefore, silent about liabilities of journalists and does not have any reference to ethical practices.[74] However, there is a thirteen-point 'code of conduct', which has some good words about ethics and commits that journalists would not cause 'humiliation" to "innocent persons" and that that they should acquire news with

[73] For details see proposed self-regulatory ethical code and its enforcement mechanism: http://pba.org.pk/psr.asp. Accessed 26 August 2023. The proposed document provide for an enforcement mechanism for the code of conduct in the shape of a "Media Council", to be comprised of an Eleven-member Governing body and a complaint redressal committee, etc.

[74] Constitution of PFUJ is available at: http://pfuj.pk/archive/constitution/ . Accessed 26 August 2023.

[75] For details see: http://pfuj.pk/code-2/. Accessed 26 August 2023.

"honest methods".[75] The problem with the code of conduct provided by PFUJ is that it does not have any enforcement mechanism and is just a piece of advice.

In the nutshell, no legal instrument is available that should have sharpened the broad concept of the right to privacy enshrined by constitution, religious injunctions and case law. Legislature has not capitalized the strong foundation provided to privacy as such and, to date, no attempt has been made to bridge the legal gap through an enabling privacy law. Likewise, PEMRA Act, which has created a national regulator for electronic media, has failed to safeguard the right to privacy from sensational overtures of private television channels. Self-regulatory mechanisms have very little effect, because media houses themselves are neither interested in privacy right's protection nor does it suit their commercial interests. In such a situation, the buck stops at national policy makers.

2.3 Conclusion: Privacy Law for Pakistan?

The illustrations of media's intrusive practices sufficiently explain the width and breadth of the violation of the right to privacy in Pakistan. The prevalence of intrusion at a widespread level, without being subject to any regulatory, executive or judicial prevention, reveals that such mode of broadcasting and publication has got a silent acceptance in the society. However, the universality of privacy rights and the drastic effects on human personality demand state's attention. In many countries of the world there are either sector-specific privacy statutes or comprehensive legal instruments that cover most of privacy violations. The legal system in Pakistan, however, has left a lacunae and no effective statutory protection has been made available for safeguarding the constitutional rights of dignity and privacy. As privacy protection demands more than what is provided by trespass law and Defamation Ordinance, the State of Pakistan has to establish a comprehensive privacy law statute which is oriented to the principles laid down by constitution, social and religious norms and courts' judgments. Legislating adequate legal rules and their enforcement in an effective manner would work as an instrument for social change. The proposed privacy law should be capable of extending to all the possible infringements of the right to privacy irrespective of the platform used for dissemination of private information and images.

In order to bring privacy as value and interest under the protection of statutory cause of action and to draft a privacy statute, the conceptual and philosophical underpinnings of privacy must be sufficiently explored. This is all the more important as apart from the absence of privacy law in Pakistan, one cannot find any kind of academic or jurisprudential debate on the nature, meaning, scope, or effective legal protection of privacy. Similarly, the right to free speech, its justification, its extent and limitations must also be subject of closer exploration since this right is often invoked as a defense and justification for privacy violations by media. The overarching goal has to be a balanced legal regime which supports all the fundamental rights and which does not upheld one right at the cost of another one.

Thus, the next section aims at establishing a conceptual framework, which will work as a touch stone in the subsequent analysis of legal principles.

References

Abbas N (2012) 'Why 'vigil aunty' caused Pakistan media storm' BBC News, 2 February 2012 https://www.bbc.com/news/world-asia-16809139. Accessed 16 Aug 2023

Adams T (2016) Playboy of the Western World. https://www.independent.ie/woman/celeb-news/playboy-of-the-western-world-26414288.html. Accessed 17 Aug 2023

Aftab S (2017) Online anonymity as a guaranty to the right to life (part 2). Recht und Netz University of Hamburg, 24 July 2017 http://rechtundnetz.com/online-anonymity-as-a-guaranty-to-the-right-to-life-part-2/ . Accessed 27 Aug 2023

Bhatti (2019) Girls in 2011 Kohistan video were killed, Supreme Court told. Daily Dawn, 2 January 2019 https://www.dawn.com/news/1455038. Accessed 27 Aug 2023

Denno DW (1992) Perspectives on disclosing rape victims. Fordham Law Rev 61:1113

Gurmani N (2021) More than 14,000 rape cases reported over last four years, NA told. Daily Dawn, 24 December 2021, https://www.dawn.com/news/1665575/more-than-14000-rape-cases-reported-over-last-four-years-na-told. Accessed 26 Aug 2023

Halperin AE (1999) Newsgathering after the death of a princess: do American laws adequately punish and deter newsgathering conduct that places individuals in fear or at risk of bodily harm. Vill Sports Ent Law J 6:171

Henig S (2005) The tale of dog poop girl is not so funny after all. Columb J Rev 7

Imtiaz S (2021) Media circus: Rape victim frightened into withdrawing FIR. Daily Express Tribune, 21 December 2021 http://tribune.com.pk/story/92275/clifton-gang-rape-case-sindh-governor-takes-notice/. Accessed 25 Aug 2023

MacKinnon CA (1989) Toward a feminist theory of the state. Harvard University Press

Marcus P, McMahon TL (1990) Limiting disclosure of Rape Victim's identities. Southern Calif Law Rev 64:1019

Martinson J (2017) Are journalists prying too far into grief? The Guardian, 25 May 2017 https://www.theguardian.com/commentisfree/2017/may/25/journalists-grief-media-manchester-attack. Accessed 25 Aug 2023

Moreham NA, Tinsley Y (2018) The impact of grief journalism on its subjects: lessons from the Pike River mining disaster. J Media Law 10(2):189–218

Naseer T (2018) Pashto singer Nazia Iqbal accuses brother of raping her daughters. Daily Dawn, 25 April 2018 https://www.dawn.com/news/1403804. Accessed 25 Aug 2023

Naseer T (2019) Man who raped his two nieces sentenced to death by court in Rawalpindi. Daily Dawn, 8 March 2019 https://www.dawn.com/news/1472232. Accessed 25 Aug 2023

Nissenbaum H (2009) Privacy in context technology, policy, and the integrity of social life. Stanford Law Books

Phillipson G (2008) Trial by media: the betrayal of the First Amendment's purpose. Law Contemp Probl 71(4):15–29

Rehman A, Jingdong L, Hussain I (2015) The province-wise literacy rate in Pakistan and its impact on the economy. Pac Sci Rev B Human Soc Sci 1(3):140

Shmueli B, Blecher-Prigat A (2010) Privacy for children. Colum Human Rights Law Rev 42:759

Siddiqui Q (2012) Its not just Maya. Daily Dawn, 20 March 2012 http://www.dawn.com/news/704081/its-not-just-maya. Accessed 25 Aug 2023

Solove D (2007) The future of reputation: gossip, rumor, and privacy on the internet. Yale University Press

Staff Reporter (2013) LHC directs media to follow PEMRA instructions. Daily Dawn, October 26 2013 http://www.dawn.com/news/1052205/lhc-directs-media-to-follow-pemra-instructions. Accessed 27 Aug 2023

Tandon N (2007) Secondary victimization of children by the media: an analysis of perceptions of victims and journalists. Int J Crim Just Sci 2(2):119–135

Warren SD, Brandeis LD (1890) The right to privacy. Harv Law Rev 15:193–220

Chapter 3
The Concept of the Right to Privacy

3.1 The Need for Conceptualization

> To begin to solve some of the problems of privacy, we must develop an approach to conceptualizing privacy to guide policymaking and legal interpretation.[1]

An effective legal protection of important values depends on their adequate conceptualization. Articulation of the right to privacy, of its content, substance as well as of its inherent and instrumental value is a prerequisite for seeking relief against its violation. On the other hand, an inadequate conceptualization of privacy can potentially obstruct its effective protection through constitutional and legal means.

Therefore, this chapter provides an extensive account of the prevalent concepts of privacy and elucidates theoretical dimensions of the right to privacy. Skeptical theories of privacy which either reject *privacy* as a coherent concept or consider its legal enforcement detrimental to other important values are also addressed. The description of major theories of privacy, their critique and counter-critique would help in chalking out a theoretical framework for this study. This framework is supplemented by reflections on the value and importance of free speech which is considered as a countervailing right. As the book focuses on the right to privacy, the concept of free speech is discussed only briefly by mentioning its main justifications.

The outcomes of this chapter will provide the basis for a comparative analysis of major legal approaches to privacy protection. The results of the conceptual considerations and of the comparative law study in the form of general legal insights as well as concrete principles will work as guidelines for the resolution of privacy problems discussed in the previous chapter.

[1] Solove (2002), p. 1089.

S. Aftab, *Comparative Perspectives on the Right to Privacy*, Ius Gentium: Comparative Perspectives on Law and Justice 109,
https://doi.org/10.1007/978-3-031-45575-9_3

3.2 Richness of the Concept

Whether it is a judgment of a court of law or an academic piece, almost every discussion on the topic of privacy contains a lamenting acknowledgment of the difficulty to formulate an exhaustive and precise definition. With such a dismal starting point, the demarcation of boundaries as to the scope of privacy as well as its countervailing value in the balancing exercise poses a subsequent challenge. Judges, commentators and scholars have approached the concept of privacy by using varied methodologies, which is one of the main reasons for the prevalence of a variety of conceptualizations of privacy. This seems to be a natural consequence as the concept of privacy has its underpinnings in different disciplines of philosophical, legal, psychological, cultural and sociological studies. The concept has been approached under all these disciplines, using their respective research and heuristic methodologies. Rather, interdisciplinary approaches to explore the concept of privacy have offered more enlightened insights. This is due to the nature of privacy and its value, which cannot be precisely determined in a linear manner. The concept of privacy is so complex and rich in its nature and content that it is at odds with every descriptive circumference. Scholars have not always appreciated this definitional dilemma and some of them have expressed this intricacy of privacy concepts in the following words:

- "there are serious problems of defining the essence and scope of this right."[2] "Protean capacity to be all things to all lawyers";[3] "The subject is just too difficult, too important and too controversial."[4] "[A]llas there are numerous competing conceptions of privacy."[5]
- "Privacy is too complicated a concept to be boiled down to a single essence. [.....] "Privacy is a concept in disarray. Nobody can articulate what it means. [.....] Privacy seems to be about everything, and therefore it appears to be nothing"[6]
- "The more we look into the concept of privacy, the more we realize how little we understand it."[7]
- "Privacy is a notoriously elastic and equivocal notion" and it is "intuitively coherent but definitionally elusive"[8]
- "Privacy is a notoriously protean concept"[9]

[2]Beaney (1966), p. 255.

[3]Gerety (1977), p. 233.

[4]Hallborg (1986), p. 176.

[5]Moore (2003), p. 215.

[6]Solove (2006), p. 477.

[7]Birnhack (2011), p. 51.

[8]Carolan (2011).

[9]Krotoszynski (2016), p. xi.

The review of the main scholarly literature on the concept of privacy reveals the variation in approaches towards formulation of a definition. One can find an identical trend in their line of arguments. Starting from the need to conceptualize privacy, most of authors criticize the narrowness or ambiguity in the existing definitions and so they attempt to coin their own definition, which is then subjected to similar criticism other scholars. Hence, *privacy* is lucky that it is a central theme and focus of attention for a never-ending intellectual and academic discourse. In this background, everybody is right, yet nobody is impeccable.

The existence of enormous literature on the topic of privacy and the diversity of approaches to conceptualize privacy has resulted into some skeptic viewpoints as well. Theoretical skepticism, which mainly draws on the difference of opinions between scholars, infers that privacy is a vague concept and that the conceptual discourse is full of confusing conclusions. This skeptic approach to the concept of privacy does not restrain itself to theoretical discourse only; rather, it rules out any attempt to a legal or regulatory dispensation for the protection of privacy rights.

Against this background, an inadequate conceptualization of privacy can potentially obstruct its effective protection through constitutional and legal means. For example, Daniel Solove considers American privacy law as "ineffective and blind to the larger purposes for which it must serve" because of the difficulty in articulating, "what privacy is and why it is important". He contends,

> Judges, politicians, and scholars have often failed to adequately conceptualize the problems that privacy law is asked to redress. Privacy problems are often not well articulated, and as a result, we frequently do not have a compelling account of what is at stake when privacy is threatened and what precisely the law must do to solve these problems. Thus, the need to conceptualize privacy is significant; yet the discourse about conceptualizing privacy remains deeply dissatisfying.[10]

Anita Allen has rightly observed that the *type* of definition for privacy "will determine the plausibility of claims about what protecting privacy [. . . .] and privacy-related interests."[11]

In the following sections, we will elucidate the insight that the enormous amount of writings should not be viewed as a *confusion* of the concept of privacy. Rather, it is an evidence of the theoretical *richness* of this concept, which is duly capable of providing the required theoretical foundation to the proposed legal protection of the right to privacy.

---

[10] Solove (2002), p. 1090.

[11] Allen (1988), p. 04.

3.3 Meta-Theoretical Analysis of the Concepts of Privacy

Every academic discourse on privacy has attempted to explore one or the other dimension of its concept. One can find some common features among various theories which make their categorization possible.[12] Yet, there is a lot of overlap and some definitions fall simultaneously in more than one category.[13] Some of these definitions follow a normative approach and consider privacy as a *right, claim, or interest* worthy of legal protection, while others view privacy as a *state* or *condition*, which is value neutral in itself and merely describe a situation on the basis of which further normative analysis could be made.

3.3.1 Privacy as a Negative Liberty to Remain Secluded

A number of theorists define privacy in terms of either complete or limited seclusion from outside interference. People want to impose some level of restriction on the access to the very *person* and to substances they consider secret, confidential or private. Resultantly, any physical or technological interference in their seclusion as well as publication of their private facts are regarded as intrusion into privacy. This is a classic approach to conceptualizing privacy as it reflects the differentiation between public and private spheres. Privacy as a right to be let alone, concealment of secrets and control over access to oneself shall be discussed under this broad category.

3.3.1.1 Privacy as a Right to be Let Alone

The concept of privacy As a "right to be let alone" has its origin in the seminal article of Louis D. Warren and Samuel D. Brandeis, which was published in Harvard Law Review in 1890.[14] The purpose of their article was to consider whether the prevailing law offered such principles which could be invoked for the protection of individual privacy and also to explore the nature and extent of such legal protection.[15] The reverberation of this groundbreaking article could be heard in

---

[12] For example, Solove has categorized the concepts of privacy into six groups.

[13] For instance, Solove has explained Warren and Brandeis approach under the "right to be alone" heading, while Judith Decew has explained it under Informational Privacy in her piece, "Privacy (Stanford Encyclopaedia of Philosophy), saying: "Warren and Brandeis thus laid the foundation for a concept of privacy that has come to be known as control over information about oneself." and "Narrow views of privacy focusing on control over information about oneself that were defended by Warren and Brandeis."

[14] Warren and Brandeis (1890), p. 196.

[15] Warren and Brandeis (1890), p. 197.

almost all succeeding theoretical debates and the "right to be let alone" marked its footprints in many judgments of the Supreme Court of the United States. According to a research study on the most-cited law review articles, "The Right to Privacy" is the second most-cited article of all time.[16]

Warren and Brandeis started from the urgency of defining new dimensions of human life worthy of legal protection, based on the justification that corporeal property generates associated incorporeal rights. Appreciating the development of human civilization where the value of sensations was termed as more than the tangible sphere of life, they proposed the "next step" protection of associated values. This protection was sought from "instantaneous photographs and newspaper enterprise [that had] invaded the sacred precinct of private and domestic life."[17]

Warren and Brandeis described human sensitivity to publicity as prompting people to opt for solitude and privacy. They lamented that people could not exercise their choice to remain secluded due to intrusion into their privacy, and so they are prone to psychological issues such as depression and mental stress. Excessive media focus on celebrities, small talk and gossips potentially divert the attention away from important issues towards trivial matters.

Injury to the feelings is a valid ground for legal redress in the fields of law other than privacy. This fact led Warren and Brandeis to advocate the recognition of the right to privacy by common law on similar grounds. They analyzed the case law and found that the interests protected by the courts were not created solely by contractual relationships or property law principles. Rather many rights in the cases they studied were available against the world at large without any private law obligation. "If the invasion of privacy constitutes a legal *injuria*, the elements for demanding redress exist, since already the value of mental suffering, caused by an act wrongful in itself, is recognized as a basis for compensation", they asserted.[18] Therefore,

> The principle which protects personal writings and any other productions of the intellect or of the emotions, is the right to privacy, and the law has no new principle to formulate when it extends this protection to the personal appearance, sayings, acts, and to personal relation, domestic or otherwise.[19]

Warren and Brandeis presented a list of private matters which should not be susceptible to publication. These matters are,

> those which concern the private life, habits, acts, and relations of an individual, and have no legitimate connection with his fitness for a public office which he seeks or for which he is suggested, or for any public or quasi public position which he seeks or for which he is suggested, and have no legitimate relation to or bearing upon any act done by him in a public or quasi public capacity. The foregoing is not designed as a wholly accurate or exhaustive definition, since that which must ultimately in a vast number of cases become a question of individual judgment and opinion is incapable of such definition; but it is an attempt to

---

[16] See Table 1: Shapiro and Pearse (2012), p. 1489.

[17] Warren and Brandeis (1890), p. 195.

[18] Warren and Brandeis (1890), p. 213.

[19] Warren and Brandeis (1890), p. 205.

> indicate broadly the class of matters referred to. Some things all men alike are entitled to keep from popular curiosity, whether in public life or not, while others are only private because the persons concerned have not assumed a position which makes their doings legitimate matters of public investigation.[20]

Warren and Brandeis clarified the non-absolute nature of this right and explained the possibility that various countervailing interests could delimit the right to privacy. Accordingly, public interest, privileged communication, and publication *at will* could work as valid limitations on privacy. However, they expressed their doubt regarding legal protection against oral publication in the absence of special damages. The truth of the matter and the absence of actual malice were clearly declared as insufficient defenses.[21]

They suggested that the remedies available to plaintiffs in defamation cases, which are damages and injunctions, could be extended to privacy wrongs as well. Furthermore, they expressed the desirability for legislation in order to get legal protection against extreme kinds of intrusion under criminal law.[22]

After 38 years of the Harvard Law Review article, Loius D. Brandeis made another significant contribution to constitutional protection of privacy, and that too, from a strong position of US Supreme Court justice. He registered a well-articulated dissent in Olmstead v United States, where the majority of the jury condoned telephone taping of the accused by the government officials as admissible evidence.[23] Defending the 'right to be let alone' against the government's ability *to obtain disclosure in court of what is whispered in the closet,* he wrote,

> The protection guaranteed by the Amendments is much broader in scope. The makers of our Constitution undertook to secure conditions favorable to the pursuit of happiness. They recognized the significance of man's spiritual nature, of his feelings, and of his intellect. They knew that only a part of the pain, pleasure and satisfactions of life are to be found in material things. They sought to protect Americans in their beliefs, their thoughts, their emotions and their sensations. They conferred, as against the Government, the right to be let alone -- the most comprehensive of rights, and the right most valued by civilized men. To protect that right, every unjustifiable intrusion by the Government upon the privacy of the individual, whatever the means employed, must be deemed a violation of the Fourth Amendment. And the use, as evidence in a criminal proceeding, of facts ascertained by such intrusion must be deemed a violation of the Fifth.[24]

In the subsequent para, Justice Brandeis rejected the notion that only physical access to the premises qualifies the intrusion for a legal claim. He also asserted that the objective of law enforcement cannot be an absolute justification for intrusion into

---

[20] Warren and Brandeis (1890), p. 216. (Footnote omitted).

[21] Warren and Brandeis (1890), pp. 217–218.

[22] Warren and Brandeis (1890), pp. 193, 219.

[23] Olmstead v. United States 277 U.S. 438 (1928) (Justice Brandeis registered his dissent which should be considered as an important appendix to his article, covering intrusion this time, which was not comprehensively discussed. The article primarily focused on the publication of private information.)

[24] Olmstead v. United States 277 U.S. 438 (1928) 479–478

individual's privacy. The categorical assertion of Justice Brandeis' dissent provided a ground for legal protection against surreptitious and high-tech intrusions in the seclusion of others. He thus presented a very strong case for a "comprehensive" right to privacy and defended it against the government interference on the basis of constitutional provisions.[25]

The contribution of Warren and Brandeis in the form of "The right to privacy" was acknowledged worldwide and it remained an influential scholarship of American privacy law. Roscoe Pound appreciated its contribution as "nothing less than add a chapter to our law".[26] William Prosser, who wrote a kind of rebuttal of "the right to be let alone" in 1960, also commended the work as, "the outstanding example of the influence of legal periodicals upon the American law."[27] Solove states that the concept of right to be let alone was "far ahead of time" and has been "a profound beginning" of privacy law.

However, the concept has also been criticized on various grounds. According to Solove, "the right to be let alone" is only an "attribute" of privacy but it does not give any idea about the actual "matters" where we want to be left alone. Richard Posner opines that it is "wholly unsatisfactory", "narrowly directed" and based on "unsupported propositions", because "very few people want to be let alone. They want to manipulate the world around them by selective disclosure of facts about themselves".[28] In James H. Moor's view, the article is "ground breaking and insightful", yet the authors failed to provide a "clear and explicit account of privacy".[29] He also considers their definition as either too broad or too narrow. Judith Jarvis Thomson, who has a reductionist view about privacy, presents her own hypothetical situations to support her argument that the right to be let alone is both narrow and broad at the same time.[30] William Parent seconds the view of J.J. Thomson and laments the over-broadness of the right to be let alone. With the help of almost similar examples, he asserts that the definition of privacy as freedom

[25] Olmstead v. United States 277 U.S. 438 (1928) P. 483: ("Decency, security and liberty alike demand that government officials shall be subjected to the same rules of conduct that are commands to the citizen. In a government of laws, existence of the government will be imperiled if it fails to observe the law scrupulously. Our Government is the potent, the omnipresent teacher. For good or for ill, it teaches the whole people by its example. Crime is contagious. If the Government becomes a lawbreaker, it breeds contempt for law; it invites every man to become a law unto himself; it invites anarchy. To declare that, in the administration of the criminal law, the end justifies the means -- to declare that the Government may commit crimes in order to secure the conviction of a private criminal -- would bring terrible retribution. Against that pernicious doctrine this Court should resolutely set its face.")

[26] Letter from Roscoe Pound to William Chilton (1916) quoted in: Brandeis A Mason, 'A Free Man's Life' 70 (1956), cited in: Glancy (1979). See also: Kramer (1989).

[27] Prosser (1960), p. 384.

[28] Posner (1978), p. 400.

[29] See for details: Moor (1990), pp. 69–82.

[30] Thomson (1975), p. 4. According to her approach, X-ray device does not interfere with seclusion yet capable of getting private information. On the other hand, physical assault on somebody is tantamount to not letting him alone yet this is not a privacy violation.

from intrusion is "so broad that it totally obscures the conceptual core of privacy."[31] There are "innumerable ways of failing to let a person alone which have nothing to do with his privacy" and in Parent's view, the concept cannot deal with the situation where, for instance, if A clubs B on the head or repeatedly insults him; such actions are not a problem of not letting somebody alone, but described under concepts like violence or harassment.[32]

A thorough look at the Warren and Brandeis article reveals the answers to most of the questions raised by its critiques. For instance, the authors have never claimed to offer a 'clear and explicit account of privacy'. Rather, they have accepted that privacy is incapable of an exhaustive definition due to its dependency on individual judgments and opinions. It does not mean that they have left private matters completely undefined. They have asserted that private life, habits, acts and relations which has no legitimate connection with someone's qualification for a public office should be protected from undue publicity. The article also gives valuable hints for the later evolution of privacy law and concept such as accepting its broad nature and mentioning the interests related to a general right to personality.

However, in spite of the fact that "The right to privacy" has a pioneering position in the conceptual discourse of privacy, its presentation of the right to privacy as a negative liberty falls short. Privacy is not only a right to be let alone. It also enables the right holder to fully participate in society and still exercise the right to privacy. Its essence does not lie in an absolute seclusion from rest of the world; rather, privacy empowers protected persons to decide who may have access to one's private spaces and who is not allowed to such spaces. As a result, the concept of privacy as a "right to be let alone" fails to fathom other dimensions of privacy.

3.3.1.2 Privacy and Concealment of Secrets

As the right to be let alone does not fully articulate the types of facts and information which need to be kept private from outsiders, some scholars have tried to further develop the concept of privacy by articulating privacy in terms of concealment of secrets so as to focus on the things and matters which people want to keep private. Concealment of secret information regarding certain matters is one of the common understandings of privacy.[33] Some English language dictionaries also define privacy as secrecy or concealment.[34] This concept may be viewed as an extension of the right to be let alone, as one of the shortcomings mentioned by critiques was that people do not want to be let alone just in vein but actually they do not want their secrecies to be disclosed to others. The concept of privacy as concealment of secrecies is viewed as either complete seclusion or restricted access of outsiders. Scholars who have a

[31] Parent (1983b), p. 342.

[32] Parent (1983a), p. 269.

[33] Solove (2002), p. 1105.

[34] DeCew (1986), pp. 154–155.

skeptic view of the positive value of privacy, such as Judge Posner and Amitai Etzioni, usually consider privacy as concealment of secrets.

Judge Richard Posner considers the concealment of information as an aspect of privacy, a concept upon which he centers his economic critique. He opines that withholding of "discreditable facts" about oneself is one of the main interests privacy attempts to safeguard. According to Posner, when people demand privacy, they do not want complete seclusion; rather, they want the concealment of such information which has the potential to be used for their disadvantage. The secrecy related definition is used by Posner to support his thesis that privacy is not conducive to economic efficiency. He asserts that the *actual* picture of someone can be obtained through intrusive means such as prying.[35]

Under his *communitarian treatment*, Amitai Etzioni suggests a secrecy based definition for privacy. In his view, is, "a societal license that exempts a category of acts (including thoughts and emotions) from communal, public, and governmental scrutiny".[36]

According to Solove, "the view of privacy as secrecy often leads to the conclusion that once a fact is divulged in public, no matter how limited or narrow the disclosure, it can no longer remain private. Privacy is thus viewed as coextensive with the total secrecy of information."[37] Complete concealment of information is desired when it belongs to the secret "zone of privacy". Thus, this concept is also related to the understanding of privacy in a zonal categorization, whereby a person has a great expectation of privacy if the information is related to a secret zone.

This conception of privacy tries to sharpen the substantive issues of privacy. However, it does not cover many dimensions of privacy. Even though it is true that—provided that further clarifications are made—secrecy can be one of the areas privacy attempts to protect, privacy protection needs to extend to many other areas beyond secret zones. Moreover, the problem of 'everything is private or nothing is private' envisages that once the secret is out by any legal or illegal means, it permanently deprives the holder of the privacy right of any subsequent relief. Metaphorically, disclosure does to a secret what a needle does to a balloon. If someone's secret is disclosed even to a limited extent, he loses the expectation of privacy with respect to that secret. Last but not least, secrecy and privacy may overlap but these concepts are not "coextensional". Something may be secret but not essentially private (e.g. secret treaties and military plans); on the other hand, privacy does not always require secrecy (e.g. one's debts might not be concealed but these still remain private matters).[38]

The shortcomings of the above definitions of privacy do not mean that they might not be helpful to a certain extent. In some cases, the right of privacy in terms of a negative right to remain secluded personally or to desire restrictions on the access to

[35]Posner (1978), p. 393.

[36]Etzioni (2005), p. 196.

[37]Solove (2002), p. 1107.

[38]DeCew (1986), pp. 154–155.

one's person or secret information can still provide an important tool to determine the nature and extent of intrusion. The concepts of private spheres or zones can be useful where some of the areas have been granted constitutional protection from intrusion such as the inviolability of home and correspondence. However, privacy is more than an individual's negative right and demands more than the protection from divulgence of personal secrecies. Privacy requires more nuanced approaches than an "all or none" approach. It is also exercising a choice in the selection of a person with whom even deep secrets could be shared. Selective disclosure of secrets does not deprive the person from a subsequent right to privacy regarding those secrets with respect to someone else. Therefore, we need to explore further concepts and theories of privacy which are more abstract than merely restricted to secret information and which confer a right of control to dissemination of one's own information rather than obliging one to absolutely conceal one's secrets or lose any legitimate expectation of privacy.

3.3.1.3 Privacy as Relative Inaccessibility to Oneself

The conceptualization of privacy as a control over access to oneself is a broader abstraction which attempts to overcome the narrowness of previous concepts of privacy as right to be let alone and the desire to conceal one's secret information. It broadens the concept of privacy and views it far from complete seclusion of oneself or hiding one's private information.

Ernest Van Den Haag defines privacy as,

> the exclusive access of a person (or other legal entity) to a realm of his own. The right to privacy entitles one to exclude others from (a) watching, (b) utilizing, (c) invading (intruding upon, or in other ways affecting) his private realm.[39]

James Rachel[40] who draws on the definition provided by Thomas Scanlon, considers privacy rights as having "a common foundation in the special interests that we have in being able to be free from certain kinds of intrusions".[41] Elaborating the importance of privacy in terms of creating and maintaining social relationships, Rachel states that it is closely connected to "our ability to control who has access to us and to information about us."[42]

Ruth Gavison approaches privacy by combining the idea of (in)accessibility with reflections on the value and the functions of privacy whereby privacy promotes liberty, autonomy, and freedom. This approach avoids the problem of demarcating the form and extent of both "access" and "control".[43] According to Gavison:

---

[39] Haag (1971), p. 149.

[40] Rachels (1975), p. 323.

[41] Scanlon (1975), p. 315.

[42] Rachels (1975), p. 326.

[43] Solove (2002), p. 1104.

> Our interest in privacy, [. . . .] is related to our concern over our accessibility to others: the extent to which we are known to others, the extent to which others have physical access to us, and the extent to which we are the subject of others' attention. This concept of privacy as a concern for limited accessibility enables us to identify when losses of privacy occur. Furthermore, the reasons for which we claim privacy in different situations are similar. They are related to the functions privacy has in our lives: the promotion of liberty, autonomy, selfhood, and human relations, and furthering the existence of a free society.[44]

Privacy violation happens with the change in any of the "three independent and irreducible elements: secrecy, anonymity, and solitude".[45] From a normative point of view, Gavison supports a neutral concept of privacy due to the fact that there should not be pre-conceived notions regarding the sanctity of one value against the other.

Legal theorist Anita Allen already relies on what can be called "restricted access" class of definitions.[46] She views that privacy "denotes a degree of inaccessibility of persons, of their mental states, and of information about them to the senses and surveillance devices of others. She links privacy to conditions like seclusion, secrecy, and anonymity. To her, "privacy is a parent concept, the broadest of a family of narrower concepts. The concepts of seclusion, secrecy, confidentiality, and anonymity are included in the privacy family."[47] She also supports a neutral concept of privacy stating that privacy denotes "conditions that are neither always desirable and praiseworthy, nor always undesirable and unpraiseworthy."[48]

Last but not least, Sissela Bok chooses an access-oriented, yet quite abstract definition. She describes privacy as,

> the condition of being protected from unwanted access by others - either physical access, personal information, or attention. Claims to privacy are claims to control access to what one takes [. . .] to be one's personal domain.[49]

She thinks that human beings are capable of getting control over access to them "even under conditions of near-constant physical proximity to others".[50] This conception provides much autonomy to the individual. She or he is not compelled to remain secluded from rest of his or her fellows and still entitled to exercise control to her or his personal sphere.

Although these concepts seek to achieve flexibility compared to the original approach of the "right to be let alone" and are increasingly abstract in their definitions, there are fundamental objections to them as well. William Parent criticizes the access based conception under the separate headings of "control of access to oneself" and "limitation of access to oneself". Regarding controlling the access to oneself, Parent says that it is tantamount to giving sovereign powers to the right's

---

[44] Gavison (1980), p. 423. Footnote omitted.

[45] Gavison (1980), p. 423.

[46] Allen (1988), p. 03.

[47] Allen (1988), p. 3.

[48] Allen (1988), p. 3.

[49] Bok (1989), pp. 10–11.

[50] Bok (1989), p. 12.

holder as only she can unilaterally control and set the terms of relationship, while the "liberal ideals of relationships founded on mutual accord and respect". Parent holds the view that all control based definitions substitute privacy for liberty and attempt to "perform a plethora of alien roles." Regarding the conception of privacy in terms of limitation of access to the self, he explains that either causal access (access through physical contact) or interpretative access (access through obtaining knowledge) can be exercised and in both cases, access based conceptions have interpretative difficulties when applied to various counter-examples.[51] Solove offers a differentiated critique with a view to the various approaches.[52] He highlights the lack of clarity. The approaches declare 'limited access' as the core value but often omit the clarification of "private sphere" to which the right holder actually wants to be inaccessible to others. "The substantive matters for which access would implicate privacy" and the "degree of access" are not given or at least not sufficiently clear. Most of the conceptions are thus narrow, as they reduce privacy to solitude and secrecy.[53] The result of the criticism is once again that privacy requires a conception which is "a richer and more flexible" one.[54]

The theories of privacy which explain it as a negative liberty focus on either complete seclusion of oneself, concealment of one's secret facts and information, or limited accessibility of oneself to the outside world. Among these theories, Warren and Brandeis assertion has been a starting point which has many useful insights. It led the theory of privacy to evolve into a much sophisticated area of legal science. That concept was further concretized when other theorists explained that people specifically want to be left alone when they want to conceal their secrets from outside world. Similarly, access-oriented theories elaborated privacy in a more abstract manner and explained that people do not want to be left alone absolutely nor do they desire complete concealment of secrets. Rather, privacy is their ability or entitlement to impose restrictions on the accessibility to their personal domains.

All these insights are very important when viewed from a meta-theoretical perspective. All the theories mention important aspects and dimensions of privacy and enable us to appreciate abstract descriptions for privacy interests as well as concrete private items (e.g. secret facts). However, the seclusion requirement, obligation to conceal secrets and limitation on accessibility understand privacy as a negative liberty, which means that privacy offers protection when people do not want to be interfered in all these manners. However, this does not cover, for example, situations where once public information becomes private as a result of subsequent development. A more abstract view of privacy is when it is understood in

---

[51] Parent (1983b), pp. 344–346.

[52] He terms Gavison's approach as a unique and "the most compelling" definition that addresses some shortcomings.

[53] Solove (2002), p. 1104.

[54] Biehler et al. (2008), pp. 8–9: "It envisages privacy as an original state of secret inaccessibility. It can either be preserved in this pristine state or destroyed. Once access is allowed, the privacy interest is lost."

terms of exercising control rather than non-interference. This notion can already be found to some extent in the access-oriented approaches and will be analyzed more closely in the following section.

3.3.2 *Privacy and Control Over Personal Information*

The conception of privacy as a control over private information is relevant to the internet communication and mainly focuses on the justification of the right to informational privacy. At the end of 1960's, a number of prominent scholars emphasize the informational dimension of privacy, mainly due to new developments in communication technologies. Alan Westin is a popular name, who defines privacy as,

> the claim of individuals, groups, or institutions to determine for themselves when, how, and to what extent information about them is communicated to others.[55]

He also regards anonymity as an important state of privacy which is acquired when a person feels free from identification and surveillance despite his presence in a public place. Therefore, the core of many anonymous actions is human desire for "public privacy".[56] Among many virtues of such informational self-determination, fundamental is the human capability to take important decisions for oneself without external strains. According to Westin,

> The basic point is that each individual must, within the larger context of his culture, his status, and his personal situation, make a continuous adjustment between his need for solitude and companionship; for intimacy and general social intercourse; for anonymity and responsible participation in society; for reserve and disclosure. A free society leaves this choice to the individual, for this is the core of the "right of individual privacy" - the right of the individual to decide for himself, with only extraordinary exceptions in the interests of society, when and on what terms his acts should be revealed to the general public.[57]

Charles Fried contributes to the concept of privacy in both ways, through defining what it means and also through elaborating what it protects. According to him, the initial estimation of privacy which relates it to secrecy or "limiting the knowledge of others about oneself" needs to be refined, because "privacy is not simply an absence of information about us in the minds of others, rather it is the control we have over information about ourselves".[58] The control over information about ourselves gives us the power to decide, as a matter of right, about when and how much revelation of information is made.[59]

---

[55] Westin (1067), p. 05.

[56] Westin (1067), pp. 4–5.

[57] Westin (1067), p. 46.

[58] Fried (1968), p. 482.

[59] See: E L Beardsley, 'Privacy: Autonomy and selective disclosure' in J Ronald Pennock & J V Chapman eds Privacy (Nomos XIII 1971) 56–70) as cited in: Moor (1990), p. 74.

In the 1970's and 1980's, the definition of privacy coined by Alan Westin has got so much popularly associated with the control over information conception that William Parent calls it "a dogma of contemporary Jurisprudence".[60]

In spite of its influence on privacy scholarship, Westin's work has still some prominent critiques. For instance, Louis Lusky gives a detailed critique of Alan Westin and his 'disciple' Arthur Miller's approach,[61] prior to presenting his own version of privacy conception.[62] Lusky argues in detail against a unitary definition of privacy which presupposes privacy as a *right* or *claim*. He illustrates his objection with the help of explaining two possibilities; firstly sometimes incomplete information is more harmful than a complete disclosure, and secondly complete disclosure maximizes the harm in many cases. To Lusky,

> Westin and his disciples offer no useful conceptual basis for distinguishing between these two situations. Both are said to involve violation of "the" right of privacy. The unfortunate result is that development of comprehensive remedies is hampered, because a remedy suitable to the one case is wholly inappropriate to the other; and remedial action is therefore devised, instead, on an atomistic basis (if at all) - a separate legislative proposal for each separate type of fact-situation.[63]

Therefore, Lusky declares that the approach adopted by Alan Westin in his seminal book, *Privacy and Freedom* is flawed due to its "failure to recognize the importance of the difference between too much truth and too little truth".[64] In fact, Lusky rejects every conceptualization of privacy which considers it as a *right* and declares such approach as biased and "enemy of just balance". He claims that such biases "distort by loading the scale in favor of the value for which recognition is asserted as a broad proposition, subject only to occasional exceptions".[65] He seems to be against any kind of normative connotations used by scholars which assume the need for protecting privacy right. He proposes to avoid *judgmental* approach in favor of privacy as "to whether, how, and to what extent it should be accorded legal protection".[66]

---

[60] Parent (1983a).

[61] Miller (1971). Miller defines privacy as: "the basic of an effective right to privacy is the individual's ability to control the circulation of information relating to him."

[62] Lusky (1972), p. 693.

[63] Lusky (1972), p. 697.

[64] Lusky (1972), pp. 699–700. Likewise, Lusky also criticizes the courts for following the *Westinian* approach in balancing other values vis-à-vis privacy. To Lusky, balancing is not a judicial function rather it is a legislative function. The ordinary function of the courts is not to engage in balancing exercise but to "interpret and apply the legislative (or constitutional) rules that embody the results of "balancing" in the broader, non-Westinian sense".

[65] Lusky (1972), p. 706.

[66] Lusky (1972), p. 693. According to Lusky (1972), p. 708: "Is it better, for our purpose, to describe our problems by use of a term connoting the underlying human value that is the object of our concern (privacy)-deferring judgment as to whether, how, and to what extent it should be accorded legal protection or should we take a short cut and adopt, as our basic term, a phrase that assumes legal protection or the need for it (right of privacy)?"

Lusky presents his own definition as, "privacy is the condition enjoyed by one who can control the communication of information about himself".[67] Elaborating this definition, Lusky says that the condition is either absolute or contingent depending upon the degree of control a person can exercise upon the communication of information relating to him or her. If somebody has a control over communication of information, privacy is absolute, otherwise, privacy is contingent and exists under particular circumstances only.[68]

William Parent suggests that control based definitions should be 'jettisoned' because of their failure to accommodate voluntary disclosure of information.[69] He claims that this confusion is due to the mistake of considering privacy as a part of liberty. In another essay, Parent attacks "control based definitions" with the help of counter examples. To him, the comatose patient has no control over information relating to him, but still, has privacy, while merely the development of an X-ray device capable of intrusion is not a violation of privacy in itself until it is actually used.[70]

Richard B. Parker points out different shortcomings in the definitions, specifically mentioning Fried, Miller,[71] and Westin, before he presents his own control-based definition of privacy with a detailed methodology for devising it. [72] He presents his criteria which must be fulfilled by a definition of privacy and weighs the existing popular definitions of privacy against those criteria. To Parker, a definition must satisfy three tests; (a) it should fit to the data, which means that it should work according to our shared intuitions about the gain or loss of privacy; (b) it should be simple, which means that it should enlist some of the common 'evils' or characteristics of various kind of violations; (c) it should be useful and capable of applying in legal processes. Parker buys the *control* portion of these definitions but criticizes another part which is related to *information.* To him, "it is tempting to try and limit the definition of privacy to control over *certain* items of information".[73] It is both overbroad as to loose control over *all information* does not constitute privacy violation; and too narrow because it ignores many privacy harms that may not be strictly connected to *information.*[74] After setting a detailed framework, Parker presents his own control based definition in a detailed fashion. According to him:

> [P]rivacy is control over when and by whom the various parts of us can be sensed by others. By "sensed," is meant simply seen, heard, touched, smelled, or tasted. By "parts of us," is meant the parts of our bodies, our voices, and the products of our bodies. "Parts of us" also includes objects very closely associated with us. By "closely associated" is meant primarily

[67] Lusky (1972), p. 709.

[68] Lusky (1972), p. 706.

[69] Parent (1983a), p. 273.

[70] Parent (1983b), p. 344.

[71] Miller (1971).

[72] Parker (1973–1974), pp. 275–276.

[73] Parker (1973–1974), p. 279. Emphasis supplied.

[74] Parker (1973–1974), p. 280.

> what is spatially associated. The objects which are "parts of us" are objects we usually keep with us or locked up in a place accessible only to us. In our culture, these objects might be the contents of our purse, pocket, or safe deposit box, or the pages of our diaries. For some other culture these objects might be eating utensils or the inside of a personal shrine. What these objects happen to be in any given culture is not part of my definition of privacy.[75]

The conception of privacy as a control over information is an important approach as it emphasizes that the person concerned must have a say as to the scope of his or her privacy in differentiated relationships to others and it also brings to light the importance of data protection. However, losing control does not always mean the breach of privacy. For example, in most of the data protection regimes, data controllers have the actual control of data rather than the owner of the data concerned. Yet data controllers are under legal obligation to protect that data according to the provisions of data protection regulations. The right to privacy protects privacy interests of a person even if he does not have a control over his information in a strict sense. Moreover, the scope and extent of control are also not clear. The profound focus of the concept is on the individual control and it disregards the role of society in the regulation of information.

Another shortcoming of this concept is its overreliance on the information. It ignores the privacy of person and the privacy of home where no information is sought. Such conceptualization leaves other interests unprotected such as decisional privacy. Privacy protects a variety of interests including private information and thus must be conceptualized in a way that it encompasses manifold facets and dimensions.

The aforementioned considerations show that the concept of privacy is an open concept. It is not possible to present an abstract account which is so comprehensive and exhaustive that it could be categorized as 'privacy theory of everything'. Therefore, we need other tools that enable us to resolve practical privacy problems and to identify the harms of privacy violations. For that purpose, it is useful to consider the value and importance of privacy as well as the functions it fulfills for both individual and societal wellbeing.

3.3.3 Conceptualizing Privacy on the Basis of Its Value and Importance

The rich theoretical discourse of privacy does not only explain the meaning of privacy and tells us what is privacy; it also dilates upon the question that why protection of privacy is important. We have already explored some of the prominent conceptualizations about the meaning of privacy, namely right to be let alone, concealment of secrecy, limited access to the self and control over information to

[75] Parker (1973–1974), p. 281..

oneself. This section will explain as why people want to be left alone, or why they want to have control over information related to them.

3.3.3.1 Promotion of Intimate and Personal Relations

According to this concept, the main aim of people who are seeking privacy is to form different categories of human relationships. The nature of such relationships could vary from highly intimate to personal and social relationship. The strength and intensity of these relationships are dependent on the level of intimacy found in these relationships. An environment of privacy is required to evolve and flourish this important dimension of human life.

Charles Fried in his seminal essay in the Yale Law Journal recognizes the important value of privacy, which is establish different categories of relationships.[76] According to him,

> privacy is not just one possible means among others to insure some other value, but that it is necessarily related to ends and relations of the most fundamental sort: respect, love, friendship and trust. Privacy is not merely a good technique for furthering these fundamental relations; rather without privacy they are simply inconceivable. They require a context of privacy or the possibility of privacy for their existence. To make clear the necessity of privacy as a context for respect, love, friendship and trust is to bring out also why a threat to privacy seems to threaten our very integrity as persons.[77]

For Fried, essential part of the principles of morality founding such relation demands a broad-based respect from the state as well as from private citizens.[78] Privacy is not *just a defensive right*; rather it establishes the "necessary context for the intimate relations of love and friendship which give our lives much of whatever affirmative value they have".[79]

Robert Gerstein in his brief but emphatic essay terms the absence of external observation as a pre-requisite for intimacy.[80] He believes that without privacy, no intimate relationship could ever exist.[81] Explaining various levels of intimate experience, he distinguishes two states which are observation (when a person observes oneself or anything else) and immersing in intimate experimentation (where one becomes a participant and a part of the experience). To Gerstein, "the fragile unity of the (intimate) experience is broken" when the participants start observation or they become the object of observation.[82] The behavior under someone's observation is completely different from the behavior which one adopts in an intimate situation.

[76] Fried (1968), p. 475.
[77] Fried (1968), p. 477.
[78] Fried (1968), p. 480.
[79] Fried (1968), p. 490.
[80] Gerstein (1978), p. 76.
[81] Gerstein (1978), p. 76.
[82] Gerstein (1978), p. 77.

Gerstein views that any kind of observation without consent is wrong due to interference in autonomy, while the wrong is immense when "the victim of the invasion was submerged in an intimate relationship and therefore did not intend to be observed at all, even by himself."[83] People do not have the right to observe those involved in an intimate relationship because the essential characteristic of "spontaneity" in an intimate relationship cannot be developed otherwise. Resultantly, no intimate relation, having a value for its own sake, can ever grow under an observation and without the opportunity for privacy.[84]

Explaining the importance of intimate relations in human life, Julia Innis states that intimacy is a "common denominator" which connects all the three distinctive accounts of the content of privacy, namely, (a) information based; (b) access based; and (c) decision based.[85] She thinks that an agent possesses privacy only to the extent that he or she has "control over certain aspects of [his or] her life" such as the regulation of privacy about the information related to oneself, access to oneself, and the focus on the intimate decision making. Being the *core denominator* of privacy and involving all the three accounts of privacy content, without the consideration of intimacy "the content of privacy cannot be captured".[86] Innis concludes by offering her "coherent" definition of privacy as,

> privacy is the state of agent having control over a realm of intimacy, which contains her decisions about intimate access to herself (including informational access and her decisions about her own intimate actions).[87]

About the value and importance of privacy, she asserts, "privacy protects our autonomy with respect to our expressions of love, care and liking" because it stems from the respect we extend to persons as "rational choosers" and "autonomous beings" having the capacity to *love*, *care* and *like*.[88]

These considerations provide valuable insights; however, the scope of intimacy should be delimited because it cannot replace privacy as according to Daniel Solove, "[w]ithout limitation to the scope, the word intimacy is merely a different word for privacy".[89] Privacy has many other functions such as the development of psychological aspect of one's personality, which involves mental relaxation and self-actualization.

In line with this, David Feldman presents a broader approach:

> the virtue of privacy is conditioned by the nature of social life. Privacy rights are distinctive because they give control over the boundaries of the spheres of social existence. They express the fact that, in modern, western societies at any rate, individuals live their lives in a number of social spheres, which interlock, and in each of which they have different

[83]Gerstein (1978), p. 78.

[84]Gerstein (1978), p. 81.

[85]Inness (1996), p. 56.

[86]Inness (1996), p. 56.

[87]Inness (1996), p. 56.

[88]Inness (1996), p. 95.

[89]Solove (2008), p. 36.

> responsibilities, and have to work with people in relationships of varying degrees of intimacy.[. . . .] Privacy is largely a matter of being able to choose where, when, and with whom to co-operate or to withhold co-operation, in pursuit of defined objectives.[90]

The concept of privacy where it is connected to the establishment of different kinds of relationship highlights an important function of privacy. Privacy is not important merely due to its instrumental value. Rather, its value is of fundamental character due to the fact that without privacy, the exercise of basic autonomy to enter into relationships is inconceivable. In other words, there is no alternative means to replace privacy if we want to realize such crucial objectives.

3.3.3.2 Safeguarding Individuality and Dignity

> The man who is compelled to live every minute of his life among others and whose every need, thought, desire, fancy or gratification is subject to public scrutiny, has been deprived of his individuality and human dignity. Such an individual merges with the mass. His opinions, being public, tend never to be different; his aspirations, being known, tend always to be conventionally accepted ones; his feelings, being openly exhibited, tend to lose their quality of unique personal warmth and to become the feelings of every man. Such a being, although sentient, is fungible; he is not an individual. (Edward Bloustein 1964)

The philosophical accounts of privacy which connect it to dignity, personhood, individuality and self-fulfillment ardently support its conceptualization as a single-core, unitary and coherent value. They also justify its normative value and effective legal protection on the basis of this theory of privacy.

Edward Bloustein has provided a detailed exposition in his passionate essay, which he had written in support of the "Warrant and Brandeis" view of privacy as "inviolate personality" and in reply to William Prosser's reductionism of viewing privacy as a combination of four distinct torts.[91] He states that Prosser's attempt to disregard privacy as an independent value and considering it as a combination of many other interests[92]—a view reflected in the judgments of many American courts as well as codified under Restatement—is erroneous and needs to be rectified through a general theory of privacy.

Such a theory appeared to be necessary due to importance of a general principle, confusion in courts in dealing with privacy-related cases and modernly sophisticated privacy infringements brought by technological advancements. In contrast to Prosser's main thesis,[93] Bloustein asserts that the fear of rampant press reporting of private facts and their destructive impact on human dignity, integrity and

---

[90] Feldman (1994), p. 51.

[91] Bloustein (1964).

[92] A detailed exposition of Prosser's theory is given in Sect. 3.5.1.1.

[93] Prosser rejects privacy as a new and independent tort which, according to him, is not based on an independent value of its own but rather a blend of four distinct torts aiming at the protection of three different interests of mental tranquility, reputation, and proprietary interest.

autonomy motivated Warren and Brandeis to write their article.[94] He discusses the four "distinct torts", coined by Prosser, one by one.[95] Analyzing the case law Prosser relied on, Bloustein concluded that the value of human dignity was the main factor in the judgments of courts rather than the independent torts Prosser had emphasized. For instance, the intrusion into private affairs of childbirth or telephonic conversation or the infliction of mental distress would not be a reason for relief. Rather, these wrongs are actually affronts to human dignity and individuality. Similarly, in the popular public disclosure cases of Sidis case and Melvin v. Reid, the main issue was not reputation but dignity. According to Bloustein, it does not cause any harm to parents' reputation, if a newspaper publishes the picture of their deformed child. However, parents in that case "are rather mortified and insulted that the world should be witness to their private tragedy", because neither the hospital nor the newspaper have a "right to intrude in this manner upon a private life."[96] In another example, he opines,

> when an author does a sympathetic but intimately detailed sketch of someone, who up to that time had only been a face in the crowd, the cause for complaint is not loss of reputation but that a reputation was established at all. The wrong is in replacing personal anonymity by notoriety, in turning a private life into a public spectacle. [. . . .]Physical intrusion upon a private life and publicity concerning intimate affairs are simply two different ways of affronting individuality and human dignity. The difference is only in the means used to threaten the protected interest.[97]

About the tort of use of name or likeness, Bloustein elucidates that the protected interests are human dignity, individuality and inviolate personality. The perceived right to publicity is not an exact alternative to the privacy right because of the commercial aspect of the former right. To him, 'commanding' the determination of price and the failure to enforce the right to privacy is demeaning to human dignity.[98]

Regarding the tort of putting someone in the false light, Bloustein explains,

> [It] is actionable for the same reasons as the use of a name for a commercial purpose. The "false light" in which the name is used makes the use wrongful for the same reason that the use of the name for advertising purposes does. And, in fact, many of the cases which Dean Prosser cites as actionable for "falsely attributing to the plaintiff some opinion or utterance" . . . . are cases in which a name has been used for advertising purposes. . . .The "false light" and the advertising use are merely two different means of publishing a person's name or likeness so as to offend his dignity as an individual.[99]

Turning to privacy protection beyond law of torts, Bloustein outlines that the three gravamens (i.e. mental tranquility, reputation, and proprietary interests) cannot

---

[94] Bloustein (1964), p. 971.

[95] Prosser's four torts are: (a) intrusion; (b) public disclosure; (c) use of name or likeness and (d) false light.

[96] Bloustein (1964), p. 979.

[97] Bloustein (1964), p. 982. Footnotes omitted.

[98] Bloustein (1964), p. 989.

[99] Bloustein (1964), p. 992.

reconcile the four privacy torts with the constitutional, statutory and common law principles of such protection. Tort law intrusions can be linked to constitutional protection only if such intrusions are considered as a *blow to human dignity or an injury to personality*.[100] Mentioning various cases relating to the Fourth Amendment of U.S. Constitution, he argues that such constitutional protection aims at safeguarding the same interest which the law of tort secures, namely human dignity.[101] Similar is the case with various civil and criminal law statutes that deal with peeping-toms (intrusion), eavesdropping and the disclosure of confidential information. To Bloustein,

> Intrusion and public disclosure are merely alternative forms of injury to individual freedom and dignity.[102]

Jeffery H. Reiman's theory also considers the right to privacy as a 'precondition' to personhood and a fundamental interest entitling everybody to shape her or his destiny.[103] He describes privacy as "a social ritual by means of which an individual's moral title to his existence is conferred."[104] Reiman explains the essential connection of privacy to personhood, which plays a crucial role in providing necessary conditions to the initial creation and the subsequent development of one's *self*. In support of his claim, Reiman presents the features and consequences of the "total institutions" given in the classic study of Erving Goffman, where total deprivation of privacy was one of the main features. In total institutions, all the aspects of privacy such as physical privacy, informational privacy, medical privacy and privacy of the abode are denied to the inmates, resulting into the mortification and vanishing of their self. Totalitarian states have the features of total institutions whereby the residents are denied the ownership and entitlement to "determine when and by whom (their) body is experienced."[105] Reiman asserts,

> Ownership, in the sense we know it, requires control over cognitive appropriation as well. It requires that the individual have control over whether or not his physical existence becomes part of someone else's experience. That is, that the individual be treated as entitled to determine when and by whom his concrete reality is experienced. Moral ownership in the full sense requires the social ritual of privacy.[106]

Same should be the case with the ownership of one's thoughts and memories in the mind, which requires a "social practice...[and should be] treated according to the ritual of privacy."[107] However, the concept of ownership in his theory is different

---

[100] Bloustein (1964), p. 994.

[101] Bloustein (1964), p. 995.

[102] Bloustein (1964), p. 1000. FN omitted.

[103] Reiman (1976), p. 26.

[104] Reiman (1976), p. 39.

[105] Reiman (1976), pp. 40–41. Footnote omitted.

[106] Reiman (1976), p. 42.

[107] Reiman (1976), p. 43.

from the ownership in the sense of proprietary right. It is rather more fundamental and is a combination of both personal and proprietary rights.[108]

Theorists who conceptualize privacy by connecting it to human dignity, personhood and individuality have been successful in presenting a general theory of personal privacy. Edward Bloustein in particular has emphatically attempted to locate the core value of privacy and has interpreted the distinctive torts as affronts to individuality and human dignity in one way or the other. This way, he has successfully tackled the reductionist view of fragmenting the right to privacy into different torts. Connecting this right to human dignity, personhood, inviolate personality and autonomy has paved the way to recognize the constitutionality of the right to privacy. We can find strong arguments in support of the protection of privacy by constitutions in theories belonging to this school of thought.

3.4 Modern Approaches to the Conceptualization of Privacy

The scholarly discourse on the concept of privacy does not end here. Rather than to frustrate the scholars, the complexity of the concept has further intrigued them to approach the issue with innovative methodologies. Some of these approaches are important to be mentioned here under the title of "modern approaches". However, the term "modern" should not be strictly understood in chronological reference as we can discover that the contemporary notions have their traces in relatively early works of Charles Fried (1968), Jeffrey Reiman (1976), and Ruth Gavison (1980). On the other hand, the privacy approaches of Marion Albers (2013, 2014), Helen Nissenbaum (2009), Daniel Solove (2008) and Koops et al. (2016) are contemporary and thus *modern* in the literal sense of the term. Modern scholars have the chronological advantage as they have knowledge and understanding of previous approaches to privacy concept. Thus, their conceptualizations should be rightly expected to offer innovative solutions to the problems of privacy because *inter alia* their approaches have culminated from classical approaches to modern realities of human life. Therefore, they are capable of explicating the conceptual and practical issues associated with the concept of privacy more convincingly.

The strength of modern approaches is that these embrace the protection-challenge and do not declare the nature and value of privacy as vague, confusing and illusive. Rather, the scholars have attempted to look deep into the conceptual conundrum of privacy. A number of important features make their approaches relevant in the modern times of technological and cultural advancement. Modern approaches take into consideration the internet based technological developments as well as the dynamics of publication and broadcasting of the new media. These developments have posed a special challenge to the traditional concepts of fundamental rights and

[108] Reiman (1976), p. 43.

the bifurcation of public and private settings on a spatial basis. The existence of versatility, dynamism and flexibility is another glaring feature of these approaches. Perhaps, these theorists do not stick to an absolutist point of view and most of them are open to change in order to accommodate the emerging issues. They refrain from strict definitional parameters and do not offer exhaustive definitions of privacy and the interests it protects. These concepts cover most of the dimensional areas of privacy such as from spatial privacy (e.g. home), to physical (e.g. body) to communicational (e.g. correspondence) and informational privacy (e.g. data protection) and so on. For such a diverse and expanded scope, most of them recognize the protective levels of constitutional law and also the tort-based relief mechanism.

Marion Albers highlights that privacy has always been characterized by a heterogeneous understanding because there are diverse philosophical dichotomies in its background: firstly, the differentiation between the individual's private matters and the spheres of decision and influence (also) open to others, secondly the contrasting of privacy and the state, which is constitutive for liberal thought, and thirdly the differentiation between privacy and publicness.[109] These basic ideas have areas where they overlap, but nevertheless with different starting points and implications. As a result, the basic understanding of privacy that emerges - privacy assigns something to a person or a group of persons as their own concern and establishes limits to others' access to it—already takes on various nuanced shadings of meaning depending on the context and the description. Varying across cultures and historical epochs, the broad spectrum of topics that is captured by privacy comprises the body, facets of the personality, religious convictions and conscience, spaces such as place of residence, property, close relationships such as partnership and family, or confidential documents and communications. The mechanisms of allocation as one's own are to be understood as broadly as the concept of access, e. g., including invasions of spaces and the body, determination of decisions by third parties, processes of surveillance, or dissemination through the media. This broad and abstract understanding gains even more flexibility once functional approaches to privacy are introduced. After having analyzed the heterogeneity and the need for further development of privacy concepts in this way, Albers points out the crucial legal problem that the traditional basic patterns are linked to the liberal paradigm of fundamental rights and legal protection. However, they are full of prerequisites that have become partly fragile in modern society. Albers emphasizes that the liberal paradigm of fundamental rights is not sufficient to provide a solid background to the sophisticated mechanisms aiming at the protection of heterogeneous *interests*, associated to individuals in their *sociality*.[110] Conceptualizations of privacy and particularly data protection require not only a complex, context-based, multi-level and multidisciplinary understanding but also call for "new legal approaches".[111] Privacy

---

[109] For the following considerations see: Albers (2013), pp. 15–44.

[110] Albers (2014), p. 214.

[111] See for the reasons of complexity and the need for a sophisticated approach with reference to data protection regulatory mechanisms: Albers (2014).

must be guaranteed - or even to some extent: established - through a multifarious bundle of binding provisions and rights. An appropriate protection also requires approaches going above and beyond a focus on the individual.

It is not possible to articulate all modern approaches in a comprehensive manner. However, some reflections and main ideas of specific scholars shall be looked at in more detail because most of the contemporary debates and new regulatory approaches draw on these writings.

3.4.1 Contextual and Multilayered Approaches

Contextual and multilayered conceptualizations can be illustrated with a view to the "*privacy in context*"-approach of Helen Nissenbaum which may be regarded as a comprehensive and nuanced approach.[112] She claims that her approach is "[t]ethered to fundamental moral and political principles, enriched by key social elements, [. . . . and] sufficiently expressive to model peoples' reactions to troubling technology-based systems and practices as well as to formulate normative guidelines for policy, action, and design."[113]

Nissenbaum points out that the current understanding of privacy disputes with respect to the interests, values and principles is not sufficient if it ignores social structures and norms where all these factors operate.[114] The diverse social, political and structural contexts play an important role in the determination of normative enquiries of privacy protection, where "contextual integrity" is a touchstone, demanding appropriateness of the norms of information collection, processing and dissemination. Every arena of life is governed by the norms of information flow and every human activity, events and transaction happen in the context of *place*, *politics*, *convention* and *cultural expectation*.[115] Context in simple words is the "sphere of life" which is beyond the demarcation of public and private bifurcation because, "[e] ach of these spheres, realms, or contexts involves, indeed may even be defined by, a distinct set of norms, which governs its various aspects such as roles, expectations, actions, and practices."[116] The sources of these norms are numerous. Mainly history, culture, law and convention shape the norms of privacy. There are informational norms related to personal information, which are "norms of appropriateness and norms of flow or distribution."[117] Contextual integrity is thus the *benchmark* of

[112]Nissenbaum (2009).

[113]Nissenbaum (2009), p. 11.

[114]Nissenbaum (2009), p. 11.

[115]Nissenbaum (2004), p. 119.

[116]Nissenbaum (2004), p. 119.

[117]Nissenbaum (2004), p. 119.

privacy protection. It is *protected* only when both of the norms of appropriateness and flow are upheld and it is *violated* when either of them is breached.[118]

An important aspect of the theory of contextual integrity is its presumption in favor of *status quo*. Accordingly, the norms of appropriateness and flow should be observed as a normal course, while any deviation from the observance of these norms is regarded as a breach of privacy.[119] Nissenbaum in her contextual integrity theory posits,

> it is crucial to know the context—who is gathering the information, who is analyzing it, who is disseminating it and to whom, the nature of the information, the relationships among the various parties, and even larger institutional and social circumstances. It matters that the context is, say, a grocery store as opposed to, say, a job interview or a gun shop. When we evaluate sharing information with third party users of data, it is important to know something about those parties, such as their social roles, their capacity to affect the lives of data subjects, and their intentions with regard to subjects. It is important to ask whether the information practice under consideration harms subjects; interferes with their self-determination; or amplifies undesirable inequalities in status, power, and wealth.[120]

Nissenbaum does not focus on specific instances of privacy infringements. Considering technology not as a collection of physical devices but as a combination of social contexts, the threat posed by sociotechnical systems to the general societal value of privacy is her primary focus.[121] The threat to privacy is not due to any single breakthrough of technological advancement but due to a full range of technological regime and a *vast array of technology-based systems and practices*, capable of "tracking and monitoring, aggregation and analysis, and dissemination and publication."[122]

Regarding the inadequacy of public/private spaces and the zonal approach for the determination of an intrusion into privacy, she suggests,

> expectations of privacy are even further out of alignment with a dichotomy of zones, even one allowing for shifts. While hardly anyone would claim a right to not be observed attending the Super Bowl, "none of your business" is a perfectly reasonable answer to a passerby on a sidewalk asking your name, even though the sidewalk is most surely a public space and by any standard one's name is not considered private information. Whereas hardly

---

[118] Nissenbaum (2004), pp. 138, 159: "The framework of contextual integrity requires that practices be evaluated in relation to entrenched context- relative informational norms, which in turn requires characterizing them in terms of actors (subjects, senders, receivers), types of information, and principles of transmission. If a novel practice results in a departure from the patterns of flow prescribed by entrenched norms, the novel practice is flagged as a breach and we have prima facie evidence that contextual integrity has been violated. Because it invokes several parameters simultaneously and incorporates conceptual resources for resolving conflicts not found in many other theories, contextual integrity is a more sensitive instrument for identifying privacy breaches. In particular, it avoids the impossible mire into which the overworked public/private dichotomy frequently leads when applied to the messy and contingent realms of privacy." 159.

[119] Nissenbaum (2004), p. 119.

[120] Nissenbaum (2004), pp. 154–155.

[121] Nissenbaum (2009), p. 06.

[122] Nissenbaum (2009), p. 11.

> anyone would assert a right not to be seen on a crowded street, the prospect of radio frequency identification device tags implanted in our clothing, personal effects, or bodies that connect our whereabouts— even in public places— via transceivers and across networks to remote databases is discomfiting.[123]

Nissenbaum does not claim her theory to be a new conception of privacy; rather, she terms it "an alternative conception of informational privacy" based on the criteria of contextual integrity, which is a "justificatory framework for evaluating in moral and political terms the myriad new technology- based systems and practices radically affecting the flow of personal information."[124] She defines *behavior-guiding norms* as which "prescribe and proscribe acceptable actions and practices. Some of them define the relationships among roles and, in this way, the power structures that characterize many familiar social contexts."[125]

Two important strengths of privacy as contextual integrity are firstly, that this framework does not outrightly reject the classical understandings of privacy that are linked to control and access. It takes into account control and access as important determinants of the context. Secondly, the framework of contextual integrity supports the balancing of conflicting values and proposes that policy decisions should be made on the basis of the specific context at stake in the specific case at hand.[126]

The framework of Nissenbaum may be useful in this study for a number of reasons. Firstly, it provides us the possibility to view every problem on case to case basis, and so can be applied to the conflict of free speech and privacy right. Secondly, it fully accommodates the local, societal and cultural peculiarities as the very existence of contextual settings in an analysis which would take the relevant norms into consideration.

There is no doubt that the scholarship of Helen Nissenbaum is singularly comprehensive and systematically convincing. One can find arguments in favor of similar approaches in a number of other writings published long before her work. Charles Fried's account of privacy, which revolves around privacy as an essential element for protection of the values of respect, love, friendship and trust, also refrains from a one-size-fits-all prescription. To him,

> it would be absurd to argue that these concrete definitions and protections, differing as they do from society to society, are or should be strict derivations from general principles, the only legitimate variables being differing empirical circumstances.[127]

According to Fried, to define and protect the right to privacy is the job of legal and social institutions, where *empirical circumstances* are the *legitimate variables*.[128] He suggests,

---

[123] Nissenbaum (2009), p. 116. See for a full account of this view with reference to ICT communication, Nissenbaum (1998), pp. 559–596.

[124] Nissenbaum (2009), p. 158.

[125] Nissenbaum (2009), p. 133.

[126] Nissenbaum (2009), pp. 187, 239.

[127] Fried (1968), p. 485.

[128] Fried (1968), pp. 486–487.

> The delineation of standards must be left to a political and social process the results of which will accord with justice if two conditions are met: (1) the process itself is just, that is the interests of all are fairly represented; and (2) the outcome of the process protects basic dignity and provides moral capital for personal relations in the form of absolute title to at least some information about oneself.[129]

He gives importance to an existing *convention* which can properly rule in the determination of a particular private area. To him,

> Privacy is not, as we have seen, just a defensive right. It rather forms the necessary context for the intimate relations of love and friendship which give our lives much of whatever affirmative value they have. In the role of citizen or fellow worker, one need reveal himself to no greater extent than is necessary to display the attributes of competence and morality appropriate to those relations.[130]

Thus, he accepts that, nevertheless informal social structures play an important role in mutual respect of privacy; still legal rules influence the establishment of the social context of privacy in terms of guaranteeing personal claims of control, while these rules could be comprehended only in certain cultural and institutional backgrounds. "The concept of privacy requires, [. . . .] a sense of control and a justified, acknowledged power to control aspects of one's environment", Fried concludes.[131]

Jeffery Reiman who presents a critique of the Fried's conception, acknowledges the complexity of defining privacy and the elaboration of its social function being *a very complicated social ritual.*[132] To Reiman,

> "Privacy is a social practice. It involves a complex of behaviors that stretches from refraining from asking questions about what is none of one's business to refraining from looking into open windows one passes on the street, from refraining from entering a closed door without knocking to refraining from knocking down a locked door without a warrant."[133]

Ruth Gavison's influential work on privacy also starts from a *neutral* definition of privacy, which has a distinctive character as against reductionist views, and it works coherently in three different contexts. Firstly, it starts with a neutral concept of privacy to identify a loss of privacy and so to further the claims of privacy; secondly, the value of privacy must be coherent for the claims of legal protection; thirdly, the privacy concept must be useful for legal contexts.[134]

---

[129] Fried (1968), p. 487. Citation omitted.

[130] Fried (1968), p. 490.

[131] Fried (1968), p. 493.

[132] Reiman (1976), p. 26.

[133] Reiman (1976), pp. 38–39: "Privacy is a social ritual by means of which an individual's moral title to his existence is conferred. Privacy is an essential part of the complex social practice by means of which the social group recog- nizes-and communicates to the individual-that his existence is his own. And this is a precondition of personhood. To be a person, an individual must recognize not just his actual capacity to shape his destiny by his choices. He must also recognize that he has an exclusive moral right to shape his destiny. And this in turn presupposes that he believes that the concrete reality which he is, and through which his destiny is realized, belongs to him in a moral sense."

[134] Gavison (1980), p. 423.

Gavison's presents the "limited accessibility" criteria to identify when our privacy is lost in different contexts, whereas the reasons for which we claim privacy in different situations are, "the promotion of liberty, autonomy, selfhood, and human relations, and furthering the existence of a free society."[135] The limited access concept of privacy is a *complex* of three independent and irreducible elements of secrecy, anonymity and solitude.[136] According to her,

> A loss of privacy occurs as others obtain information about an individual, pay attention to him, or gain access to him. These three elements of secrecy, anonymity, and solitude are distinct and independent, but interrelated, and the complex concept of privacy is richer than any definition centered around only one of them. The complex concept better explains our intuitions as to when privacy is lost, and captures more of the suggestive meaning of privacy. At the same time, it remains sufficiently distinctive to exclude situations that are sometimes labeled "privacy," but that are more related to notions of accountability and interference than to accessibility.[137]

Gavison rejects the "being let alone" view of privacy, which presupposes nonintervention by the state as:

> the typical privacy claim is not a claim for noninterference by the state at all. It is a claim for state interference in the form of legal protection against other individuals, and this is obscured when privacy is discussed in terms of noninterference with personal decisions.[138]

The typical privacy claims, which she thinks are protected by her neutral concept of privacy, are

> the collection, storage, and computerization of information; the dissemination of information about individuals; peeping, following, watching, and photographing individuals; intruding or entering "private" places; eavesdropping, wiretapping, reading of letters; drawing attention to individuals; required testing of individuals; and forced disclosure of information.[139]

Gavison argues for contextual considerations in explaining a variety of functions of privacy for the wellbeing of the individual because privacy provides "the necessary context" for many essential activities.[140] She convincingly makes her case for "an explicit legal commitment to privacy", where privacy works as a central value and which should recognize the undesirability of privacy losses. Otherwise many important interests would remain unfulfilled.[141] An explicit and general commitment to privacy will go farther than localized approaches and would "colour our understanding of protection in specific contexts". It would focus on systematic breaches of privacy and "could serve as a principle of interpretation, pointing out the need to

---

[135] Gavison (1980), p. 423. Footnotes omitted.

[136] Gavison (1980), p. 433.

[137] Gavison (1980), pp. 428–429.

[138] Gavison (1980), p. 438.

[139] Gavison (1980), p. 436.

[140] Gavison (1980), p. 445.

[141] Gavison (1980), p. 467.

balance losses of privacy, perhaps with presumption in favor of protecting privacy."[142]

3.4.2 Taxonomies and Typologies

Daniel J. Solove is one of the most influential contemporary scholars of privacy law. His work on privacy offers a paradigm shift in the conceptual debates of the definition of privacy, its value, and approaches to its protection. Though he has authored a number of journal articles on various aspects of conceptualization, his book titled *Understanding Privacy* presents a complete account of his unique approach.[143]

Solove is a believer of the immense importance of privacy for the world at large. However, he casts his doubts over the unified meaning of privacy and regards it as a concept in *disarray* because of the absence of consensus on the meaning of privacy, the value it is aimed to protect and its competing value against other opposing values. The confusion about the privacy concept creates practical difficulties in formulating laws and policies aiming at its protection. Solove, therefore, recounts the major prevalent conceptions of privacy, counter-narratives and his own critique. To him, *all* of the prevalent conceptions are either too broad (inclusive of external concepts), too narrow (incapable of explaining all privacy issues) or too vague (having the capacity to be broad and narrow simultaneously). The chief reason for the failure of prevalent conceptions has been identified as consideration of privacy as a "unitary concept with a uniform value that is unvarying across different situations" by attempting to find a core feature or common denominator. He attempts to prove that the conceptualization of privacy is possible without probing the "essence" or core element.

Solove puts forwards a new theory which has four dimensions: method, generality, variability, and focus. The method he adopts is different from the traditional approach of looking for a common denominator. Instead, he uses the analogy of family resemblances for various privacy strands. The aspects of privacy are connected to each other and to the rubric of privacy just like a family, where there is no single common denominator, yet each family member has certain peculiar characteristics which link him to the family he belongs to.

The dimension of "generality" is considered important for every conceptualizing exercise in order to enable the devised theory applicable to a variety of circumstances. However, Solove's approach is cautious in making a generalization which keeps the importance of context as well. In this regard, he has sought guidance from "pragmatism" which calls for a 'balance' between overgeneralization and contextualization. As the pragmatic objective of the theory is to offer guidance for policy

---

[142] Gavison (1980), pp. 467–471.

[143] Solove (2008).

makers, generalization is essential. On the other hand, to deal with specific privacy issues and countervailing interests, the contextual approach is required. However, any theory based on either over-generalization or over-contextuality is counter-productive in the effort of resolving privacy issues.

The third dimension of Solove's theory is "variability" which requires that, due to the changing nature of privacy-demands of history and cultures, the theory must be capable of accommodating such variations. Nothing is inherently private in a static manner. Even the commonly-regarded most private areas of family, body, sex, home, and communications have been subjected to a variety of approaches depending on history and cultures. It requires some level of variability in conceptualization. "A theory of privacy should leave room for cultural and historical variation, but not err by becoming too variable", Solove maintains.

The final dimension of Solove's theory is its focus, which is exceptional from traditional approaches due to its "stability" as the rest of theorists have focused either on the nature of information or subject matter, or on the individual choices, wishes and their expectations of privacy. These elements *per se* cannot be regarded as *inherently* private. Because of the fluidity of these elements, the theories based on them are unable to provide necessary guidance to policy makers for privacy protection. Solove, therefore, contends to focus on the 'actual' problems of privacy. To him, "a privacy problem exists whenever there is a problem from the related cluster of problems we view under the rubric of privacy."[144]

Therefore, he develops a "taxonomy" which focuses on the activities that either *actually* violate privacy or have the *potential* to create "privacy problems". Solove bases the taxonomy of privacy on the four torts enumerated by William Prosser. He also stresses the need to develop new insights due to immense sophistications of the information age. He has identified sixteen privacy problems grouped into a set of four broad categories. The four groups of problematic activities are, with regard to information: (1) collection; (2) processing; and (3) dissemination; while the fourth one is the intrusion.

Surveillance and interrogation are the sub-categories of information collection. Surveillance has been considered problematic historically and many laws outlawing its different forms could be found in many jurisdictions. The evils of surveillance, whether overt or covert, include anxiety and discomfort, suppressing creativity and self-development. In both public places and private settings, it brings "chilling effects that make people less likely to associate with certain groups, attend rallies, or speak at meetings".[145] Similarly, the harms of information collection through interrogation have similarities to both intrusion and surveillance because of its features of probing and information gathering. It is harmful as it has the element of coercion and the magnitude of the harm is directly proportional to the level of coercion exerted by the interrogator.

[144] Solove (2008), p. 76.

[145] Solove (2008), p. 112.

Aggregation is the next problem under Solove's Taxonomy. It is an activity related to information processing where the already existing bits and pieces of information are assembled to make certain conclusions about the data subject. It has a synergic effect in terms of maximizing disclosure of facts. It creates a power imbalance because it empowers one against the other unduly. The aggregation of information collected in small pieces has the potential to wrongly interpret the actual facts associated with the data subject.

Another problem associated with the information processing is identification. It means the establishment of a linkage between the information and the individual. Roger Clark defines it as "the association of data with a particular human being."[146] Identification has some advantages of enhancing accountability as well as curbing fraud. However, it is problematic due to its potential for revealing unnecessary information, distortions of facts and other intrusive characteristics. It is also regarded as an efficient *means of controlling* the data owner by the identifier.

Insecurity of data results in identity theft which is another problem of privacy in Solove's taxonomy that is faced by data subjects. In many instances, even leakages happen from state departments. Insecurity brings the individual to a disadvantageous position where his personal details such as credit card information could be used for fraudulent purposes or criminal activities.

Secondary use of the data also poses many legal and ethical problems. It is defined as "the uses of data for purposes unrelated to the purpose for which the data was initially collected without the data subject's consent".[147] Secondary use violates the right of the data owner to give consent and through that way, it also harms her expectations. The use of data for secondary purpose resembles the tort of breach of confidence, as the user n betrays the trust of the data subject. The tort of breach of confidence has a rich case law in the common law jurisdictions particularly in the United Kingdom. The harms of secondary use include generation of fear, uncertainty, and powerlessness.

The problem of exclusion presented by Solove means the collection of data without giving the right of getting information about the purpose of its collection and usage to the subject. Exclusion has the potential to lead to other problems of unauthorized secondary use and insecurity of databases. It is a fundamental principle of data collection whereby the subject has the right of access to her own data and suggests amendments if required.

After information collection and information processing, a major problematic area according to Solove's taxonomy is the information dissemination. It has been divided into seven areas of: breach of confidentiality, disclosure, exposure, increased accessibility, blackmail, appropriation, and distortion.

Breach of confidentiality is widely recognized in the UK as a tort and the relevant law is invoked whenever a person divulges confidential information while he was

---

146 Roger Clarke, Smart Card Technical Issues Starter Kit, Ch. 3 (April 8, 1998) as referred by Solove.

147 Solove (2008), p. 131.

under a duty to respect secrecy. There is a rich case law that declares a variety of relation as having a fiduciary duty of mutual confidentiality. The importance of confidentiality and the tort action to uphold the breach of confidence is essential for maintenance of important types of human relations—both intimate and professional.

Disclosure is explained by Solove as, "the tort of public disclosure of private facts,. . . .creates a cause of action for one who publically discloses a private matter that is highly offensive to a reasonable person and is not of legitimate concern to the public."[148]

Unlike the confidentiality tort, disclosure does not pre-require the existence of any relationship of trust. That is to say, even a stranger can be sued for the disclosure of private information. The problem of disclosure harms the interest in free speech, autonomy, self-development and democratic self-governance; while these values can be safeguarded through the protection against disclosure. The protection from disclosure also protects from many other financial, emotional, physical, and reputational harms.

Another problem associated with the dissemination of information is called exposure in Solove's taxonomy, which "involves exposing to others certain physical and emotional attributes about a person".[149] Exposure is typically related to the aspects of body and health while disclosure is related to a broad variety of personal data. It is a normal yearn of all human beings to conceal 'animal-like' features or activities. Exposing them in that area certainly causes humiliation and loss of self-esteem. "The need for privacy, and therefore the prevention of exposure, is created by the fact that we have social relationships and concomitant norms of dignity and decorum", Solove maintains.[150]

Increased accessibility is the problem of dissemination and it rises when the access is made easier to the information already available on a limited scale. To Solove, "with increased accessibility, a difference in quantity becomes a difference in quality- it highlights the risk of the harms of disclosure".[151] Increased accessibility maximizes the chances of exploitation of data.

The problem of blackmail is associated with the data dissemination. "Blackmail involves coercing an individual by threatening to expose her personal secrets if she does not accede to the demands of the blackmailer, which often involve paying hush money".[152] Blackmail is generally considered as a criminal act and is punishable in many jurisdictions. Blackmailing causes variety of harms and damages that are responsible for its criminalization, such as economic inefficiency and unlawful enrichment through fraudulent means. Solove considers the disturbance of power balance as a reason for its criminality. To Solove, "[t]he purpose of restricting

[148] Solove (2008), p. 141.

[149] Solove (2008), p. 147.

[150] Solove (2008), p. 148.

[151] Solove (2008), p. 150.

[152] Solove (2008), p. 152.

blackmail is not to limit disclosure but to prevent the threat of disclosure from being used as a tool for exerting power and dominion over others".[153]

The problem of appropriation arises with "the use of one's identity or personality for the purpose and goals of another."[154] Appropriation curbs the choice for a person who desires to present himself to society in a particular manner. Many jurisdictions have laws restraining people from undue advantages at the cost of others, for example, the United States, France, and Germany. Germany regulates appropriation under the law that provides for personality related rights. The harms of appropriation are viewed differently by different scholars. For example, Prosser considers it as a proprietary one.[155] On the other hand, Solove contends that an important dimension of the "loss" under appropriation is its "interference with the freedom and self-development".[156]

Another problem of information dissemination, Solove explores, is distortion. It is related to misrepresenting somebody in relation to the information associated with her, but it is something different than defamation. It is "manipulation of the way a person is perceived and judged by others. It involves the person as inaccurately characterized".[157]

Intrusion is another group of problems, subdivided into intrusion and decisional interference. It involves interference into the lives of others. The harms include disturbance of daily activities and routine life, destruction of solitude and unduly making somebody uneasy. The range of activities are associated with intrusion, as according to Solove, "intrusion need not involve special incursions: spam, junk mail, junk faxes, and telemarketing are disruptive in a similar way because they sap people times and attention and interrupt their activities".[158] Decisional interference is long recognized in American Supreme Court in Griswold v. Connecticut. Decisional interference has the same negative effects as exposure and also the area of human sensitivity is alike i.e. human body and sexuality related aspects.

Daniel Solove's *unique* and *pragmatic approach* emphasizes the problems of privacy from a bottom-up manner rather than to get lost in a hypothetical conceptualization. In other words, Solove focuses on the real and practical problems of privacy and does not strive to look for a common denominator or a core feature in a variety of privacy problems. "Privacy is an umbrella term that refers to a wide and disparate group of related things", he declares.[159] It does not mean that he, like reductionists, rejects the use of the term "privacy" for these values. Rather, he

[153] Solove (2008), p. 133.
[154] Solove (2008), p. 155.
[155] Prosser (1960), p. 406
[156] Solove (2008), p. 156.
[157] Solove (2008), p. 160.
[158] Solove (2008), p. 163.
[159] Solove (2008), p. 45.

advocates the use of the broad term for these issues due to their overwhelming similarities.[160]

In a more recent attempt to conceptualize privacy, Koops et al. present their typology on the basis on their comparative analysis of constitutional protections available to different kinds of privacy as well as of theoretical literature in a variety of jurisdictions.[161] Their typology is different than Solove's taxonomy as against Solove's assertion, they claim that it is possible to conceptualize privacy in a unitary manner on the basis of a set of related concepts. Secondly, they attempt to articulate *privacy as such* and do not engage in the identifications of the harms of privacy. Their study does not exclude other taxonomies and offers to be considered alongside other classifications for a useful insight of the concept of privacy.[162] Koops et al. have also explained the difference between the concepts of taxonomies and typologies, where, "typologies approach the realm of the abstract and the theoretical, whereas taxonomies deal with constructive, concrete, and often empirical entities."[163]

Koops et al. discuss the "most influential typological classifications of privacy" and present an analysis of the constitutional provisions pertaining to privacy from nine jurisdictions and ECHR. Elucidating major doctrinal and theoretical dimensions of privacy, Koops et al. have integrated their findings in a systematic manner to formulate "an original typology of privacy". They have grouped privacy related provisions into five clusters which they call "typology of the objects that the constitutional rights to privacy protect."[164] They present further results in the form of a typology showing eight basic privacy types where each one is connected to informational privacy which has "an overarching" and overlapping character.

Cluster 1 of the typology is about the general right to privacy provided in the constitutions of many countries. Koops et al. find out that the general right to privacy is provided in most of these constitutions but in different manners. Some constitutions expressly mention *privacy* as a protected right while others provide protection to privacy under other constitutional rights. In Cluster 2, they have explained *privacy*

---

[160] Solove (2008), p. 46: "It is no accident that various things are referred to under the rubric of "privacy". They bear substantial similarities to each other. The analogies between different things can be useful and instructive, for we might seek to create similar laws and policies to regulate them."

[161] Koops et al. (2016), p. 483, 576. Koops et al. have analyzed four prominent theoretical works on privacy in a chronological order and have pointed out their limitations. Among them are Westin (1967); Roger Clarke, *Introduction to Dataveillance and Information Privacy, and Definitions of Terms*, http://www.rogerclarke.com/DV/Intro.html. Accessed 26 August 2023. Allen (2011); Finn et al. (2013). According to Koops et al., a common limitation of these works is, for instance, that, "it is not always clear whether the classification is a typology, a taxonomy, or simply an enumerative list." (p. 505). The second limitation is that these conceptions parallel discuss both privacy as a concept and the right to privacy, which confuses the normative dimension of the discussion with the positivist approach and thus most of the conceptions fail to cope with the socio-legal challenges posed by modern technological advancements.

[162] Koops et al. (2016), p. 489.

[163] Koops et al. (2016), p. 495.

[164] Koops et al. (2016), pp. 490–491.

of places and property, aiming at the protection of *home*, *property* and *computers*. Cluster 3 explains *privacy of relations* which includes the protection of *family life*, *the establishment of social relations*, *communications* and *documents*. Cluster 4 enumerates the privacy of the *person* and it includes the protection of *body*, *thought*, *decision making* and *identity*, while Cluster 5 provides the privacy of personal data.

Koops et al. depict their comprehensive methodology in a three dimensional figure showing a zonal distribution on horizontal axis, the two main emphasis of privacy on *freedom from* (or negative freedom) or "being let alone" and *freedom to* "self-development" on the vertical axis. Diagonally, privacy connection with *control* is depicted on the right bottom while its connection with *access* is depicted on the upper left corner of the diagram. The four zones depicted on the upper horizontal axis of the typology figure broadens from the left side to the right side as personal zone (solitude), intimate zone (intimacy), semi-private zone (secrecy) and public zone (inconspicuousness). Under such a comprehensive frame of reference, Koops et al. have allocated their eight *ideal types* of privacy plus informational privacy as an overarching aspect of every type of privacy. Four of eight types of privacies are associated with the *freedom to* (negative freedom) and are also close to the *access* corner of the diagram. They are placed in a way as to show a correlation with different zones of life drawn on the horizontal axis. These four types, which are related to negative freedom or the right to be let alone, are bodily privacy, spatial privacy, communicational privacy and proprietary privacy. The remaining four types are intellectual privacy, decisional privacy, associational privacy and behavioral privacy. These types of privacy emphasize on "freedom to" sort of interests and their goal is to achieve self-development; thus shown in line with the downward entry on vertical axis. The zonal sequence of these types is the same as the other four types, which is respectively (from left to right on horizontal axis) personal zone protected (typified by solitude or isolation), intimate zone (typified by intimacy and limited personal engagement of intimate nature), semi-private zone (typified by secrecy and confidential social interaction) and public zone (typified inconspicuousness during activities in public places). The later four types are nearer to the "privacy as control"-conception because of their association with *freedom to* kind of rights and aiming at self-development.

Koops et al. definitions of eight types of privacy are as following:

Bodily privacy: typified by individuals' interest in the privacy of their physical body. The emphasis here is on negative freedom: being able to exclude people from touching one's body or restraining or restricting one's freedom of bodily movement.

Spatial privacy: typified by the interest in the privacy of private space, by restricting other people's access to it or controlling its use. [. . . .] The home is the prototypical example of the place where spatial privacy is enacted, closely associated with the intimate relations and family life that take place in the home.

Communicational privacy: typified by a person's interests in restricting access to communications or controlling the use of information communicated to third-parties. Communications may be mediated or unmediated, which involve different ways of limiting access or controlling the communicated messages.

Proprietary privacy: [. . . .] typified by a person's interest in using property as a means to shield activity, facts, things, or information from the view of others. For example, a person can use a purse to conceal items or information they prefer to keep private while moving in public spaces.

Intellectual privacy: typified by a person's interest in privacy of thought and mind, and the development of opinions and beliefs. While this can have important associational aspects, it is suitable as an ideal type of the personal zone, as the mind is where people can be most themselves.

Decisional privacy: typified by intimate decisions, primarily of a sexual or procreative nature, but also including other decision making on sensitive topics within the context of intimate relationships. As with spatial privacy, decisional privacy as an ideal type within the intimate zone is closely related to family life.

Associational privacy: typified by individuals' interests in being free to choose who they want to interact with: friends, associations, groups, and communities. This fits in the semiprivate zone since the relationships often take place outside strictly private places or intimate settings, in semi-public spaces such as offices, meeting spaces, or cafes.

Behavioral privacy: typified by the privacy interests a person has while conducting publicly visible activities. These relate to Westin's states of anonymity and reserve and to Cohen's concerns with exposure and transparency.[165]

Informational privacy is the *overarching* aspect of all these types of privacy. It is "typified by the interest in preventing information about one-self to be collected and in controlling information about one-self that others have legitimate access to."[166]

The typology, Koops et al. have elaborated, does not attempt to define privacy or rely on any specific definitional approach to the right to privacy. They have refrained from a normative or prescriptive approach and simply describe *privacy as such.* They arrive at their results mainly through mapping existing theoretical literature and surveying the national jurisdictions in nine countries. Their goal is to identify how the selected jurisdictions have articulated different kinds of privacy within their constitutional frameworks of privacy protection.

3.5 Critical Perspectives on Privacy

The theory of privacy is so rich that one can find an immense variety of perspectives. The foregoing meta-theoretical analysis has already highlighted the prominent perspectives about the concept of privacy. One can see that the majority of scholars not only ardently endorse the moral value of privacy and its psycho-social importance but also advocate its legal protection as a unitary human right. On the other hand, there are also scholarly writings that present a skeptical view of privacy. These critical perspectives range from questioning the conceptual coherence of privacy to blaming its role as detrimental to the welfare of community. The following sections will give an account of these perspectives.

[165] Koops et al. (2016), pp. 567–568.
[166] Koops et al. (2016), pp. 567–568.

3.5.1 *Skeptic Reductionist Critique*

3.5.1.1 Privacy: Not One But Four Torts

William L. Prosser articulated his reductionist view of the right to privacy and categorized privacy violations into four *different* torts. In his seminal article, Prosser presented his reductionist view that the right to privacy is not a single coherent concept. Rather, the infringements of privacy framed under the American case law could be categorized into four distinct torts. This conclusion was a result of his analysis of three hundred cases decided by different American courts. His theory contributed to the development of privacy protection under tort law.

Dilating upon the history and circumstances in which Warren and Brandeis wrote their article, Prosser analyses in detail the American jurisprudence of the right to privacy. He reveals that that the judiciary did not extend an immediate warm reception to Warren's and Brandeis' ideas. For instance, the Court of Appeals of New York rejected the existence of a right to privacy in a case involving unauthorized use of the complainant's name for commercial purposes.[167] To Prosser, initial cases could not provide insights into the scope of the right to privacy, but in the later stage, he was able to draw "definite conclusions" in the process of analysis of hundreds of cases:

> What has emerged from the decisions is no simple matter. It is not one tort, but a complex of four. The law of privacy comprises of four distinct kinds of invasion of four different interests of the plaintiff, which are tied together by the common name, but otherwise have almost nothing in common except that each represents an interference with the right of the plaintiff, in the phrase coined by Judge Cooley, "to be let alone."[168]

He described the four torts as, 1. intrusion upon the plaintiff's seclusion or solitude, or into his private affairs; 2. public disclosure of embarrassing private facts about the plaintiff; 3. publicity which places the plaintiff in a false light in the public eye; 4. appropriation, for the defendant's advantage, of the plaintiff's name or likeness.[169]

Regarding the first tort, Prosser claims that Warren and Brandeis had nothing in mind with these cases, because they were mainly concerned with the publication of private facts. He mentions a number of intrusion related cases adjudicated prior to the publication of their article but still not referred to by them. However, intrusion was afterwards recognized as a full-fledged tort by the US courts and many violations such as wiretapping and eavesdropping were interpreted under its rubric.

Prosser enumerates the pre-requisites of the second tort, which was the primary focus of Warren and Brandeis due to their annoyance on the press of the time. Firstly, the disclosure must be public or at the level of publicity; secondly, the facts upon which the tort action lies must be private ones; and thirdly, the disclosed

[167] Roberson v. Rochester Folding Box Co171 N.Y. 538, 64 N.E. 442 (1902) as cited in Prosser's, William L. "Privacy" Cal. L. Rev. 48 (1960): 383. At page: 384.

[168] Prosser (1960), p. 389.

[169] Prosser (1960), p. 389.

private facts must be considered as offensive by any reasonable person.[170] He considers the disclosure tort as an extension of the defamation tort with the exception of truth as a valid defense. In the disclosure tort too, the protected interest is reputation, which is similar to that of the defamation tort.[171]

The third tort is false light which means either to attribute a verbal utterance to somebody or associate his name or picture to something he has nothing to do with. According to Prosser's analysis, the false light tort is not necessarily connected to defamation and in occasions where it does, defamation action is also valid. Similarly, it is distinct from the disclosure tort as it is not based on true facts but on the invented ones. This tort is considered as a substitute when the defamation suit is deemed inadequate to get relief.

As for the final tort of appropriation, Prosser opines that such protection was available to it in New York and many other places. The courts in many jurisdictions provided recovery to plaintiffs whose names were used for commercial benefits by defendants. This tort is distinct from the other three torts and the interests protected here are neither mental nor reputational, but proprietary.

Although William Prosser has challenged the general privacy theory of Warren and Brandeis, he has refrained to offer his own definition or conceptualization of privacy. He has simply described what American courts were thinking of privacy and how they approached the protection of privacy interests. His descriptive essay does not offer any normative theory of privacy and his 'privacy as four torts' conclusion is based on the analysis of already decided cases. His conclusions do not lead him to categorically opine against the value of privacy. However, his opinion of the incoherence of privacy and the fragmentation of the unity of its concept has made controversial the right-based approach to privacy protection.

No doubt, the theory of *privacy is not a single tort but it is a combination of four torts that have nothing in common* has been so much intriguing that Edward Bloustein has written a detailed and elaborated rebuttal.[172] Looking at the privacy wrongs merely in terms of civil law torts that have no connection to any fundamental value deprives privacy from its constitutional foundation. It becomes very difficult for a privacy tort to sustain against a constitutional value (e.g. free speech) during balancing exercise. Beyond that, the four torts worked out by Prosser are insufficient to cover the diverse range of privacy issues.

3.5.1.2 Privacy: Not Four But Many Torts

Frederick Davis articulated skeptical reductionism with regard to the right to privacy earlier than William Prosser and in a more radical way. He supports the application of torts such as mental distress and proprietary loss as the gravamen for seeking relief

[170] Prosser (1960), pp. 393–396.

[171] Prosser (1960), p. 398.

[172] Please see Sect. 3.3.3.2.

instead of claiming it under the violation of a broad ‘right to privacy’.[173] To highlight the so-called confusion of courts and legislature, he mentions instances of identical interest in the right to privacy with varied nature of relief.[174] Such ambiguity is traced back to the Warren and Brandeis article, which did not find their proposed principles on the case law pertaining to the *right* to privacy and thereby delayed significantly the recognition of privacy as a constitutional right by American courts and other jurisdictions. Highlighting the ‘inconsistency’ of judicial treatment, Davis states that “some courts have based recognition on fundamental principles of common law, others on constitutional mandate, and still a third group, on something called “natural law”.[175] He attempts to draw the relationship of traditional torts of defamation and proprietary torts and opines that defamation is linked to the right to privacy for two main reasons. Firstly, the defense of truth is not absolute in defamation cases and criminal libel. Secondly, a mental feeling is, in fact, the real interest which is ultimately sought to protect by defamation action and that both privacy and defamation are peculiar interests where the injury to each one cannot be precisely demarcated. Relying on these arguments, Davis suggests that the recognition of mental suffering could avoid some confusion.[176] He further argues that considering human personality as ‘property’ has become a very broad concept. On the other hand, the theories of privacy invasion are unable to cover all situations where the injury is inflicted without mental distress e.g. in the event of commercial appropriation. Such event could be better expressed as “expropriation of property rights in personality”.[177] Considering the relationship of causes of legal actions in intrusion cases, Davis says that the changing nature of such wrongs requires the protection under trespass or infliction of mental distress or both because such wrongs have a very remote relation with the right to privacy.[178]

These arguments lead Davis to conclude that the right to privacy is not an independent right but a derivative interest comprised of other important rights. He asserts, “If truly fundamental interests are accorded the protection they deserve, no need to champion a right to privacy arises”. He rejects privacy as a legal concept and claims that it is useful as a sociological notion in the sense of *the pursuit of happiness*, while the property interest attached to one’s personality is much more fundamental.[179]

---

[173] Davis (1959).

[174] Davis (1959), pp. 1–3.

[175] Davis (1959), p. 5. Footnotes omitted.

[176] Davis (1959), pp. 7–9.

[177] Davis (1959), p. 11.

[178] Davis (1959), p. 13.

[179] Davis (1959), pp. 18, 20: “The usefulness of the “right to privacy” as a jural concept can be more easily calculated if “privacy” is recognized as a condition or state achieved when other more elementary interests are safeguarded. Thus, if it is agreed that a person should not be subjected to acts causing mental suffering or emotional distress, and if it is agreed that the inherent utility of personality and circumstances ought to be above piracy or unwarranted expropriation, there arises

This radical rejection of privacy right by Davis has questionable conceptual foundations. On one hand, he is against privacy right as a new concept; on the other hand, he himself suggests introducing a new tort of mental suffering.

His detachment of the tort of intrusion from the right to privacy is also not convincing. Protection of proprietary interests in intrusion cases might be a very rare case as most of the time it is interests related to the dignity and personality right that are aimed to be protected. Furthermore, Davis confuses defamation with privacy. There might be a slight overlap in the facts of a particular case, and it is also possible that a wrong could result simultaneously into both reputational as well as dignitarian damage. Conceptually, however, both defamation and privacy areas have been well explored by scholars where most of them see no confusion between these concepts in a general manner.

The right to privacy cannot be comfortably reduced to some minor torts as it has been legally and theoretically undergone an irreversible maturation. Davis himself accepts the fact that the complete removal of the expression of the right to privacy is not possible due to its strong academic support and its legal evolution.[180]

3.5.1.3 Privacy: Neither a Distinct Right Nor a Tort At All

Starting from the so-called conceptual ambiguity of the right to privacy, Judith J. Thomson[181] questions the popular expression of *the right to be let alone*. She presents many imaginary circumstances in support of her point of view. She downgrades privacy right to a negligible status. Thomson tries to associate the wrong doing with the violation of some other apparent right and concludes that a privacy right's violation is a kind of by-product when another right is violated.

Thomson considers that conceptualizing privacy as a right to be let alone is a narrow approach because it is incapable of covering many intrusions that may not disturb solitude.[182] On the other hand, she also considers this concept as a broad and over inclusive expression because hitting somebody is not letting him alone but still it is not a privacy violation.[183] By giving many hypothetical instances, Thomson views that there are various levels of bad behaviors. Bad behaviors at the lower level are not considered as a violation of rights unless a bad behavior crosses some limits. According to her, a familiar account of rights presupposes that "something" should not be done to the right-holder. For example, "a cluster of rights" is attached to the

no need to protect "privacy". In other words, "privacy" is an interest or condition which derives from and is automatically secured by the protection of more cognizable rights."

[180] Davis (1959), p. 24: "[T]o gather together a number of diverse and explicit tort causes of action under general social concepts without further articulation is to undermine the administration of justice by blurring the lines between deserving and undeserving cases."

[181] Thomson (1975), p. 295.

[182] For example an X-ray device which is developed for sensing the activities of a person who is unaware of it.

[183] Thomson (1975), p. 296.

ownership of a picture. Now whoever owns that picture has the positive and negative rights such as to sell it or to prevent others from viewing it. The viewing of that picture without the permission of its owner would be a violation of the associated negative proprietary right.

Thomson suggests that we have more *stringent* rights on our *persons* as compared to our material goods. We and only we have the right to decide about our body parts as whether to donate them or to sell them. She thinks that preventing outsiders from viewing us is actually an exercise of our proprietary right on our bodies rather than the right to dignity or privacy.[184]

From many instances and suppositions, Thomson concludes that

> the right to privacy is itself a cluster of rights, and that it is not a distinct cluster of rights but itself intersects with the cluster of rights which the right over the person consists in and also with the cluster of rights which owning property consists in. [185]

Elaborating the 'parasitic' status of the right to privacy with the help of instances and their interpretation, she claims that always other rights are being violated *per se* and, as a result, privacy violation also happens. Preempting the question of voluntary dissemination of information, Thomson says that in such cases the "right to confidentiality in respect of personal information" is violated. To Thomson, it is a difficult question to ask whether every right in the privacy cluster is overlapped by other rights due to the disagreement over the definition of the right to privacy. She, however, makes her point with the mentioning of many other rights that are primarily violated in privacy cases e.g. the right to liberty, the right against annoyance, the right not to be distressed etc.

> We are confronted with a cluster of rights-- a cluster with disputed boundaries-- such that most people think that to violate at least any of the rights in the core of the cluster is to violate the right to privacy; but what have they in common other than their being rights such that to violate them is to violate the right to privacy.[186]

Thomson reductionist view is considered as a strong conceptual critique on the unitary concept of the right to privacy. However, her viewpoint has also been severely criticized by other scholars. She does not deny the importance of privacy rights protection but insists on its incoherence and thus she suggests discarding the

[184]Thomson (1975), p. 296, 303: "For if we have fairly stringent rights over our property, we have very much more stringent rights over our own persons. None of you came to possess your knee in exactly the way in which you came to possess your shoes or your pornographic pictures: I take it you neither bought nor inherited your left knee. And I suppose you could not very well sell your left knee. But that isn't because it isn't yours to sell some women used to sell their hair, and some people nowadays sell their blood but only because who'd buy a used left knee? For if anyone wanted to, you are the only one with a right to sell yours. Again, it's a nasty business to damage a knee; but you've a right to damage yours, and certainly nobody else has its being your left knee includes your having the right that nobody else but you shall damage it."

[185]Thomson (1975), p. 306.

[186]Thomson (1975), p. 313.

term. On the other hand, she is happy with the usage of either broader terms such as right to liberty or narrower terms such as the right against annoyance and the right to confidentiality. One fails to understand that what is wrong with the usage of the term of the right to privacy, when it offers a variety of strands and dimensions which are conceptually much clearer than what she suggests. Thomson accepts the usefulness of privacy as a "heuristic device in the case of any purported violation of the right to privacy to ask whether or not the act is a violation of any other right". It shows that the right to privacy cannot be ignored as a rich and mature concept as it provides a valuable explanation to diverse nature of dignitarian and personality related harms. Its conceptual foundations have been further crystalized as a long time has been passed after Thomson wrote her scathing critique of the right to privacy. The right to privacy is currently capable of covering many sophisticated problems associated with technological developments such as online surveillance and data protection.

3.5.2 Is Privacy Detrimental to Society?

As earlier stated, the reductionist critiques on privacy merely focus either on the elaboration of how the courts have interpreted privacy interests (e.g. William Prosser) or on the question of how such interests should be described during legal proceedings (e.g. Davis and Thomson). None of these scholars have denied the importance of the protection of the involved interests. On the other hand, there are critical voices with regard to ascribing a positive value to privacy. Some jurists and scholars consider privacy as counterproductive and argue that it tends to hinder the achievement of one or the other objective. They allege privacy as economically inefficient, detrimental to the public good of the community and against the interests of women as we will elaborate and analyze in the following sections.

3.5.2.1 The Economic Efficiency Critique

In his lecture on the right to privacy, Richard Posner exposes the privacy value to the economic variables of profit and loss and to the principles of demand and supply.[187] In order to set his theoretical framework, he presents an economic analysis of the right to privacy which weighs this right against the economic goals of efficiency and maximization of profits. He starts from the assumption of disregarding private choice as valuable *per se* and privacy as an "instrumental rather than ultimate" value.

Posner considers both prying and privacy as intermediate goods and that concealment and disclosure are economically beneficial. To him, information is concealed for misrepresentation while prying has a benefit of obtaining the actual information. Criticizing the Brandeis' assertion of press catering the idle curiosity,

[187] Posner (1978), p. 393.

Posner says that due to the specialization of the press in prying, it has the ability to obtain economically valuable information with inexpensive means. Posner argues against assigning proprietary rights to personal secrets of people because of the absence of a transaction cost or investment in secrets; while information holders commit fraud during some kind of nondisclosures.[188] He gives the examples where information is available only to those who subscribe to that and where it is obtained through conducting census. In the later case, the subjects have no proprietary rights as they incur no or negligible costs. The absence of costs or any disadvantage is a sufficient reason for snatching proprietary rights from information which is benign and not even discreditable. Apart from proprietary rights, disclosure rectifies misunderstanding in certain situations.[189] Hence, everyone should have the right to ferret out secrets regarding others to protect themselves from disadvantageous transactions and the right to be let alone is not considered as a valid limitation to this right of making economic decisions for oneself.

Posner gives importance to the means by which information is obtained on the basis of economic impacts. He argues in favor of a general tendency and encouragement for making communication generally public rather than to use surreptitious methods and technologies such as wiretapping, which involve significant costs. He suggests: "Society can avoid the additional costs by the simple and relatively inexpensive expedient of providing legal sanctions against infringement of conversational privacy".[190]

The economic analysis of law in general is a controversial area in itself. Regarding the framework of Posner's economic efficiency critique of privacy, it seems to be quite arbitrary as it is not based on any dominant conception of privacy. Rather he assumes a skewed view of privacy for making possible the application of economic principles. He overstretches a limited view of privacy and unjustly extends it to an overall privacy concept. It thus leaves a major theoretical work untouched. The majority of scholars do not consider privacy merely an instrumental value or a secondary right. The strands of privacy are much more diverse. Additionally, the economic approach to privacy does not provide any guidance to the normative balancing of conflicting values and rights.

In particular, Posner's theory of the economic worth of privacy violation is not applicable in developing and traditional societies such as Pakistan. The people in Pakistan consider the non-economic interests of honor, ego, self-respect and tribal image more important than maximization of wealth at the individual level. People are more judgmental than the open societies of United States and Europe. The so-called cost involved in the *frank* disclosure would be disproportionally higher for the information-holder, which is an unbalanced transaction even if we apply Posner's standards. Similarly, there is no power parity in *ferreting-out economically*

[188] Posner (1978), pp. 397–398.

[189] Posner (1978), p. 399: "[A]s when a worker conceals a serious health problem from his employer or a prospective husband conceals his sterility from his fiancée."

[190] Posner (1978), p. 401.

valuable information between, for example, an employee and employer. Due to the power imbalance, this model is not useful to be applied on the media and subjects relationships. Getting exposed once would leave the person deprived forever and the victim will have to face unpredictable consequences. Moreover, we do not have the power to prevent others from blackmailing us on the basis of secret information that they hold due to it disclosure in the media. Thus, the disclosure can lead to non-economic use (or misuse) of information about us such as an instrument of undue social empowerment and subservience. The unforeseen consequences of the disclosure of true information can result into more than merely a *justified harm* to reputation, about which Posner thinks that it is "what others think of us" and so "we have no right to control other people's thoughts".[191]

The assertions that gossip columns are "genuinely informational" because they introduce people to opportunities and dangers make "offensiveness and newsworthiness" as merely a question of cost/benefit analysis in contrast to a value-driven examination. His view that newspapers have no property rights in the photographs published along with the news items confuses public interest publication and unjustifiable disclosure.[192] His approach equalizes both kinds of publications i.e. newsworthy facts and trivial matters, which is against the balancing exercise of privacy interests against other important values.

3.5.2.2 Communitarian Critique

Amitai Etzioni has tried to build a comprehensive case against privacy when it clashes with another value characterized by him as "common good", which is a foundational interest for communitarianism. In his treatise, *The limits of privacy,* Etzioni presents a detailed communitarian perspective of the right to privacy.[193] In the introduction of the book, he raises some pressing and sensitive questions to build his case against personal privacy. He asks whether we would like to employ a person convicted for child molestation or who is an elders' abuser in caring homes. He acknowledges the quandary of balancing privacy with public health and safety and suggests that "good society" does not extend preferential status to one value in comparison to other values.

Etzioni focuses on the two common goods of public safety and public health and analyses their public policy treatment. These common goods have five threads, namely HIV tests, sex offenders' privacy, decryption, ID cards and medical data. Etzioni considers privacy as an individual right which must be, according to the communitarian philosophy, balanced against social responsibilities.

In his analysis of the first area of public policy, Etzioni countervails the public good of saving the life of many children through timely medication against the

---

[191] Posner (1978), p. 408.

[192] Posner (1978), p. 396.

[193] Etzioni (2005).

invasion of mothers' privacy through HIV tests. He argues in favor of the former interest and insists on the enforcement of compulsory HIV tests of pregnant mothers even without their consent in order to diagnose AIDS in fetuses for a prompt treatment.[194]

Afterwards, Etzioni gives a communitarian analysis of American federal law which requires the convicted sex offenders to register with the local authorities after their release from jail at the completion of their punishment (popularly known as Megan's Law).[195] He views that sex offenders have a great propensity of repetitive criminality; therefore they must be kept under a constant supervision. He rejects the existing law as ineffective and offers somewhat out-of-the-box but bizarre suggestion that specially guarded villages should be established for people having a past history of pedophilia where they can live freely, having all the facilities of life such as jobs and shopping malls. Instead of the conventional guards, the inhabitants of the surrounding community should be empowered to keep an eye on their activities.

In the next public policy discussion, Etzioni highlights the threat posed by strong encryption system to public security and other common goods. Hyper encryption is helpful to enhance privacy in the cyber world but this method is used by terrorists, drug dealers and pedophiles for hiding their identities and challenging the law enforcement departments. Five major problems have been identified which are triggered by encrypted internet communication. These are (a) difficulty in acquiring evidence in cybercrimes cases; (b) obstructions in the process of effective criminal investigation; (c) frustrate anti-terrorism efforts; (d) hindrance in intelligence-based operations; and (e) resultantly, it leads to 'greater privacy violations'. The privacy violations become greater when security agencies resort to conventional methods of extracting information through phone hacking and secret video recordings. Above all these contemporary problems, Etzioni expresses his fear regarding some unforeseen "macroscopic danger" such as chemical terrorism, which can be pre-emptively thwarted only if security agencies have the capability to decipher digital communication of perpetrators.

In order to tackle these problems, Etzioni advocates a governmental sponsored *voluntary public key recovery system*. Under these measures, the government provides encryption software to the public whereby the decryption access can be acquired after the legal requirement of search and seizure warrant. He argues that such a voluntary system for backup of a recovery key will provide privacy to public information as well as ensure national security and public safety.[196]

---

[194] Etzioni (2005), p. 18, 42: "The communitarian perspective also enters this analysis by reminding us that a given individual right cannot be used to trump all other considerations, including the common good. Obviously, limiting privacy in the case at hand benefits, not merely the child but also the community."

[195] Etzioni (2005), pp. 43–74.

[196] See Ch 3 p. 81 in particular in: Etzioni (2005).

The utility of universal identifier cards having biometric details is the fourth public policy area explored by Etzioni. Again, he argues in favor of the public good of safety and security against the individual right to privacy. Advocating ID cards and biometric identification mechanism, he counts many of their benefits in the form of tracing fugitive criminals and sexual abusers, tackling income tax evasions, cheating in credit cards, frauds in social welfare benefits, identity-theft, combating illegal arms dealing and unlawful immigration. Likewise, the information contained in these ID cards would be more reliable with an easier retrieval feature. Etzioni claims that ID cards have more public acceptability in America.[197] He attempts to respond to some of the common objections raised by opponents of ID cards and Biometric identifiers; rejecting its connection with totalitarianism as a misconception.

Etzioni analyses the last public policy area of medical records in a different manner than the other areas. Here, he criticizes not the protection of privacy but, in fact, the insufficiency of privacy protection measures. He sees no communitarian interest or public good in the disclosure of medical data; rather considers it worthy of utmost confidentiality. He criticizes the existing practices where personal data regarding medical information is accessible to insurance companies and other private institutions. He supports a strong infrastructure which is protected with passwords and keys to ensure the secrecy of medical information. Furthermore, he suggests strengthening the protection regime with the 'highest rigor of the legal sanctions'.

Etzioni's identification and explanation of the dangers of privacy protection is, no doubt, a thought provoking analysis. However, the solutions of the problems he offers are either impractical or they have the potential to infringe the fundamental values of dignity and liberty. For instance, to arrogate the surveillance of sexual offenders to residents of the community may not be justified in a liberal society. Similarly, the voluntary provision of an encryption key to the government is not practical. The absence of sanctions makes this option as arbitrary, while the governmental sanction in the sense of law enforcement makes it obligatory as against voluntary. Regarding the biometric identity cards, Etzioni is himself skeptical due to the possibility of its abuse and suggests the overseeing of an ombudsman. Still, most of the measures proposed by Etzioni have the potential of new-totalitarianism.

The critique of privacy as harmful to the public good of the community presupposes an ideal community where there exists an absolute parity in social and economic power of members as well as homogeneous goals and priorities of all the members. However, the Pakistani society is very stratified on different grounds. One cannot imagine the establishment of such a perfectly organized order for the protection of collective good. Additionally, the persons associated with media—both journalists and owners—are well-organized and bonded together by their common vested interests in the form of protection of their economic interests from paying fines and compensations to privacy complainants. Therefore, only the state

[197] Etzioni (2005), pp. 117–120.

can protect people's privacy from media intrusions in a positive manner through its institutional mechanisms.

3.5.2.3 Feminist Critique

Catharine A. MacKinnon in the most ardent manner challenges the prevalent debates on decisional privacy especially female choice of abortion. She considers privacy as an instrument of oppressing women because it not only segregates them from each other but also restricts her options to seek public recourse against such opression. To her, "[t]his right to privacy is a right of men "to be let alone" to oppress women one at a time."[198] She doubts the fundamental assumption that women control sex.[199] According to the feminist perspective, the reality is that male exercises greater control over the most affairs while women "feel compelled to preserve the appearance".[200] The misconception regarding female sexual autonomy makes the whole policy debate of abortion regulation a futile exercise. Mackinnon rejects the prevalent approach and highlights problems of gender inequality and forced sex. Secondly, she forcefully introduces another dimension to the political and legal perspective of *pro-life* and asserts that abortion choice is a women prerogative who must decide whether or not to give life to the fetus in her belly.

Mackinnon criticizes the abortion judgments of US courts, which prohibit state intervention in abortion matters on the basis of respecting the decisional privacy of citizens. According to her, these decisions are based on unfounded assumptions regarding gender equality and female sexual freedom, because, "The world without state intervention, the world of states inaction, the private world of Joshua'a abuse and poor women's unfunded abortion, is "the free world.""'[201]

Criticizing the state's approach of abdicating itself from the responsibility of regulating 'private sphere', she terms it as a means of women subordination to male supremacy. In her strong feminist view, it is the man only who controls sexuality and is capable of molding public laws and policies in his favor.[202]

Mackinnon raises a number of objections against the liberal view of the individual right of privacy. She questions the underlying assumption of *gender equality* and *free consent* behind no-state intervention into intimacy and private sphere and declares, "for women, the measure of the intimacy has been the measure of the

[198] MacKinnon (1989), p. 194.

[199] MacKinnon (1989), chapter 10.

[200] MacKinnon (1989), pp. 184–185.

[201] MacKinnon (1989), p. 187.

[202] MacKinnon (1989), p. 188. "*The abortion right frames the way men arrange among themselves to control the reproductive consequences of intercourse. The availability of abortion enhances the availability of intercourse.*"

oppression."[203] These assumptions are based on the feminist perspective that the personal is political and so, the private is public.

Condemning privacy, she asserts that this shield has always been used as a cover for atrocities against women such as battery and marital rape. In this sense, it has remained an instrument to preserve the status quo in the social and political system which is predominantly male dominated. In one of her conclusions, she blames privacy as,

> When the law of privacy restricts intrusion into intimacy, it bars changes in control over that intimacy through law. The existing distribution of power and resources within the private sphere are precisely what the law of privacy exists to protect.[204]

Such feminist insights on privacy are very important as they support the state action to curb female exploitation. The necessity to protect women and children from media intrusions has already been illustrated.[205] In line with the feminist view that the protection of women needs state intervention, the traditional liberal view of the fundamental rights where the state has only a negative role must be judged as being too reduced. The paternalistic underpinnings of the societal strata in Pakistan are not conducive to the development of womens' personalities. Pakistan is suffering from extreme gender inequality and women have special problems and needs. Specifically, the disclosure of their private affairs brings about horrible consequences of ostracism, outcast, as well as to the extent of honor killing. Therefore, these problems need a shrewd and systematic approach by protecting their privacy from media exposure with much stronger regulatory measures. Similarly, privacy should not be a shield to conceal the identities of women harassers even if the issue is related to intimate sphere. Nobody should be allowed to abuse the right to privacy for committing criminal acts. However, a level of privacy is a prerequisite to enable women to report abuse as many cases of sexual misconduct go unreported because women in Pakistan are very concerned regarding their reputation. In such situation, privacy would not be a cover for women rights' abuse, but a shield which could protect the women who complain against harassment and privacy intrusions.

3.6 Limitation(s) of Privacy: Freedom of Speech as a Countervailing Right to Privacy

The above discussion on the concept of privacy shows that philosophers and legal scholars have attempted to explore almost every possible aspect of the right to privacy and it is no more *a concept in disarray*. Sufficient philosophical and theoretical arguments affirm that privacy has a broad scope with a multidimensional

[203] MacKinnon (1989), p. 191.

[204] MacKinnon (1989), p. 193.

[205] See for full review: Section 2.

outlook. Similarly, both normative and descriptive accounts of the right to privacy also highlight the importance of privacy as having inherent as well as strong instrumental value. However, although the review of the prevailing literature on privacy gives an impression of its importance, the insights must not be misinterpreted as if privacy is a 'supreme' value. Privacy is an important human right just like many other human rights such as freedom of speech and the right to have access to information.

Tom Gerety convincingly states:

> A legal concept will do us little good if it expands like a gas to fill up the available space. Take the example of justice: One cannot draw the line where it stops, or starts, in law courts, and with good reason, since such comprehensive and philosophical concepts ought to be everywhere felt but nowhere fixed in our imperfect legal institutions. A properly legal concept must be a principle that translates into a rule; and the rule, in turn, must translate into a set of applications. But no such translations are feasible unless we impose some definite conceptual limits.[206]

Therefore, the concept of privacy is cognizant of the equal importance of other rights. Keeping in view such an accommodating status of the right to privacy, the question of conflict of fundamental rights and its resolving mechanism need to be considered too. The right to privacy is not an absolute right and there may be certain situations where limitation(s) are needed to be enforced on the exercise of the right to privacy in order to protect a more dominant fundamental interest.

The problem of conflict between different rights and values is neither a unique phenomenon nor it could be singularly associated with the right to privacy and free speech conflict. On the contrary, the conflict of fundamental rights is a phenomenon well-known to scholars, lawyers and judges alike. However, to resolve such conflicts has never been an easy assignment for them because such resolution demand answers to a number of questions which belong to different socio-legal and philosophical *discourses*.[207]

One of such problems is the conflict between the right to privacy and right to free speech and freedom of the press. The problems of media's privacy violations in Pakistan[208] does not have a straight forward resolution in the form of imposing blanket censorship or strict content-based regulatory measures by the State. Theo-

---

[206] Gerety (1977), p. 234.

[207] Gavison (1991), pp. 456–457: "First, we need to have a clear analysis of the two competing values involved, what they are, why they are desirable, and how they relate to each other. This may require some conceptual analysis and a lot of moral and human understanding of the ways in which ideals and goals work in our lives and affect other goals that we have as individuals and a society. When we proceed to discuss conflicts between rights, values, or interests, it is crucial that we not lose sight of what we have learned in the first stage by analyzing the different values. We should remember this because situations of conflict are painful. Therefore, we have a tendency, once we have resolved the conflict as we must, to undervalue what we have given up in order to be at peace with the decision that we have adopted."

[208] Section 2.1 of this book (Invasive media practices).

retically, this problem is not *insurmountable*.[209] Different legal approaches have been made to resolve this problem including the concepts of proportionality analysis and balancing exercises.

The following brief introduction to the concept of free speech shall serve two purposes. First, the policy makers should be mindful of the importance of free speech in their attempts to protect privacy and secondly, the absolute free speech defense in privacy cases would be busted by analyzing the claimed protected interests attached therein to the questionable expression.

3.6.1 Free Speech Justifications

Free speech has got a prominent position in the traditional concept of fundamental rights, while on the other hand, "privacy is a relative late comer to the system ofindividual rights".[210] An immense amount of political, legal and philosophical reflections exists which deal with the question of why free speech is important for individual and societal wellbeing and explores different aspects of this fundamental value. The next section provides a brief overview of the arguments in favor of the protection of free speech following Eric Barendt who has summarized these *justifications* and *arguments* into four categories.

3.6.1.1 Arguments from Truth

This set of arguments in favor of free speech focuses on the utility of truth for public good and regards unhindered speech as a way towards discovering truth. These arguments are popularly associated with John Stuart Mill's essay, *on liberty*, but Milton made the same arguments two centuries earlier than Mill.[211] Barendt explains a number of such arguments such as valuing truth as an *autonomous and fundamental good* as well as its utility for the attainment of progress in society. Arguments regarding the significance of free speech for discovering truth are based on the assumption that truth is an objective reality and coherent concept and that a free discussion can authenticate divergent opinions in the so-called "marketplace of ideas". For that matter, J.S. Mill regards uninhibited discussion as a prerequisite to find out the veracity of particular expressions. Discussion is important even for true beliefs in order to get "living truth" rather than "dead dogma".[212]

The theory of J. S. Mill gives immense importance to the truth and uninhibited discussion while it ignores many other values. Sometimes it is necessary to

[209] For a detailed analysis with an American Constitutional law perspective: Emerson (1979).

[210] Emerson (1979), p. 329.

[211] Barendt (2005), p. 07.

[212] Barendt (2005), p. 08.

compromise one value for the sake of other more important values. However, relying on Mill's argument, it is not possible to impose some restrictions which are crucial for social harmony and protection of minorities. On the other hand, the question of whether it would be wise to suppress some unpleasant speech or ideas temporarily, due to their harmful effects for another individual or society in general, is more of a controversial nature. There is there is no straightforward approach to answer this controversy. It poses a challenge the concept of inherent value of truth and leaves it to the observer's analysis to assess a specific expression on case to case basis.

Apart from the discussion over the fundamental or utilitarian value of *truth*, it is also a bold assertion to say that free discussion will always lead us to discover the truth.[213] Barendt gives the example of the Nazi regime's coming into power in 1933 despite of the fact that Weimer Republic supported free political expression in the 1920s. He aptly opines that some restrictions on speech are necessary "to ensure that false propositions do not drive out truths."[214]

In political discourses the truth argument is inapplicable as the truth cannot be taken as a synonym for certainty. Many propositions cannot be objectively tested in a scientific manner. Similarly, it is needless to test the true nature of some absurd statements, which are obviously false.[215]

Additionally, the paradigm of the "free market place of ideas" is criticized for a variety of weaknesses. This paradigm is associated with the famous dissenting opinion of Holmes J. in Abrams v. US. It has influenced the free speech jurisprudence of United States, where the State is not trusted to impose any speech regulations even if these regulations are intended to promote free speech.[216] It advocates the 'no government intervention' in the free exchange of ideas in order to ascertain the truth autonomously, just as uninterrupted market is helpful for a healthy economic competition. Under this theory, any kind of regulatory measure is tantamount to manipulation and ultimately prevents the search for truth. But firstly, the notion of truth is a not a coherent concept. Secondly, it is hard to understand why every kind of governmental intervention in a democracy will be doubted even if it is for the promotion of truth just as economic regulations are imposed for encouraging healthy competition.[217] For example, the floating of various ideas by the press does not always aim at the truth discovery; rather, the maximization of profits is the main motive behind that. It is hard to believe that the press will certainly contribute in the making of a great society if it is completely unrestrained by any kind of regulatory regime. For a variety of good reasons, such as the prevention of conflicts between adverse ideas and pluralism and to tackle deceptive commercial speech, some

[213] Barendt (2005), p. 09.

[214] Barendt (2005), p. 10.

[215] See Barendt (2005), p. 10: Here Barendt gives the example of the statement, "the moon is made of green cheese."

[216] Barendt (2005), p. 11.

[217] Barendt (2005), p. 12.

government interventions in the "market place of ideas" is necessary. To Barendt, "the case has to be made that an unregulated marketplace better serves freedom of speech than other alternatives. And.....it is not really an argument about truth."[218]

3.6.1.2 Arguments from Self-Fulfilment

This approach sees free speech as an essential feature of self-development and considers the imposition of restrictions on expression as harming the growth of personality. According to this approach, freedom of speech is an individual's basic right irrespective of its effects on society as in certain cases it might be inimical to society. This assertion is not consequentialist and considers speech as intrinsically good.

This approach has limitations as it is not clear to what extent free speech is essential to self-development just like other basic necessities of life. If freedom of speech is regarded as worthy of constitutional protection based on its connection with self-fulfillment, the boundaries between speech and other values become blur. Other basic values such as human dignity and privacy are equally connected to self-fulfillment. Similarly, "general freedom is closely linked to self-fulfillment, as is freedom of speech, but that does not mean that the two freedoms are identical. The self-fulfillment rationale for speech easily lends support to arguments which are hard to distinguish from general libertarian or moral autonomy claims", Barendt explains.[219]

The determination of the *actual scope* of free speech becomes a challenge for this theory. If exercising the right to free speech is considered as an important aspect of human dignity and self-fulfillment, it is hard to introduce the consideration that the dignity of others can be infringed as a result of exercise of free speech.

3.6.1.3 Argument of Citizens Participation in Democracy

According to this justification, free speech is necessary for making people capable of fully participating in democracy. In the US context, the writings of Alexander Meiklejohn are considered as upholding these arguments and the German Federal Constitutional Court has also highlighted the role of free speech in public opinion formation.[220] The utility of speech for democratic dispensation highlights political speech. This approach suggests that only *that* speech would get protection which strengthens democracy while any kind of material advocating the overthrowing democratic regime cannot get toleration.

---

[218] Barendt (2005), p. 14.

[219] Barendt (2005), p. 14.

[220] Barendt (2005), p. 18.

The argument from democracy draws on all other arguments for free speech. For example, the encouragement of minorities to express their dissenting views is close to both self-fulfillment and to the argument from truth. Minorities can have better ideas which, if freely allowed, can be helpful to find the truth. According to Barendt, "the argument from democracy has been the most influential theory in the development of contemporary free speech law".[221]

However, if democracy is an objective of free speech, then the regulation of free speech by an elected government for strengthening democratic values should be acceptable. The conclusions of this discourse vary considerably on the ground of what particular view of *democracy* we have in mind. The majoritarian view of democracy might allow speech censures in the interest of society in general. In contrast, the Dworkinian "constitutional democracy" gives basic rights such as freedom of speech a fundamental status that even a majority vote cannot take it away. The majority cannot suppress the right to dissenting speech of minority. Even the discourses questioning the legitimacy of the state would be tolerated under this conception. In any case, these considerations illustrate that free speech is not an absolute right.

3.6.1.4 Suspicion of Government

The fourth argument is based on a general libertarian mistrust of government and its activities to impose curbs on liberties. The other three arguments are positive in nature where free speech is justified on the basis of one or another aspect of its contribution in enhancing human life. In contrast, the justification of speech which is free from governmental regulations is supported with a historical account of speech suppressions by governmental and ecclesiastic authorities.[222] Barendt cites from the popular work of Frederick Schauer who concludes:

> Freedom of speech is based on large part on a distrust of the ability of government to make the necessary distinctions, a distrust of governmental determinations of truth and falsity, an appreciation of the fallibility of political leaders, and a somewhat deeper distrust of government power in a more general sense.[223]

Many positive arguments also support the non-governmental intervention in the free speech, though their reasons revolve around their own premise such as discovery of truth, democracy or self-fulfillment. The negative arguments set aside any role of government to regulate speech in an absolute manner.

However, any free speech theory should provide the possibility for governmental regulation that is necessary to distinguish between constitutionally protected speech and any other expression not covered by constitutional principles. Furthermore, the theory is "parasitic" and mostly justifies its stance on the basis of the other three

221 Barendt (2005), p. 20.

222 Barendt (2005), p. 21.

223 Schauer 86, as cited in: Barendt (2005), p. 21.

positive theories. The over-suspicion of democratically elected government is not justified particularly on the basis of arguments related to what the despotic regimes and authoritative churches did in the past. Furthermore, there are no strong reasons to hold that the constitution focuses *merely* on governmental actions and their negative effects. On the contrary, the regulation of speech in the relationship between private parties and under private law is considered a constitutional duty to protect in European countries such as Germany or France.

3.6.1.5 The Conceptual Necessity of Balancing Privacy with Free Speech

The above discussion shows that both privacy and free speech have their respective limitations. Both are strong contenders in the system of human rights and their curtailment needs strong justification. Privacy and free speech are fundamental rights which have their respective inherent values. None of these rights enjoy an automatic superiority over each other. In such a situation, balancing of these rights by considering their respective instrumentality- e.g. the analysis of specific interests which are being protected- seems to be the only viable choice which can resolve their conflict.[224]

To reconcile both free speech and privacy is not a simple task even if it is acceded that both of these values are important and none of them can assume a superior position at the cost of another. Legislature, judges and legal scholars acknowledge this challenge alike. In the context of online news services and social media too, the balancing of freedom of expression and the right to privacy poses an uphill task. In discussing the possible answer of the question that whether every speech deserves full legal protection, Mark Tunick concludes:

> Speech can have social value even if it does not promote critical thinking; it can have value as a means of individual self-expression even if it does nothing to promote debate about public issues. Even speech that merely entertains has value. But when speech implicates legitimate privacy interests we must weigh the value of free speech against the value of privacy, and in doing so we need to recognize that not all speech deserves the same protection.[225]

These and many other arguments contest the presumption of supremacy of the right to free speech. When it comes to the argument of free press, which is mainly founded on the arguments from free speech, the premise is further weakened due to a number of practical realities. Media and publications are seldom undertaken for the sole platonic reason of promoting free speech. Many other factors are involved which must be taken into consideration when juxtaposing media freedom against the right to privacy.[226] One commentator points out,

---

[224] A detailed explanation of different approaches to 'Balancing of human rights and its justification' is given in Sect. 5.4.1.

[225] Tunick (2015), p. 95.

[226] See Lichtenberg (1987), p. 330: 'Foundations and Limits of Freedom of the Press' (1987) 16 Philosophy & Public Affairs 4, 329 ("(i) More often than not, contemporary news organizations

> A problem with the rhetoric of press freedom is that it often serves more the private interests of media proprietors than it does the public interest, harming both the independence of journalists and the right of the public to know. Concomitantly, although it also has the potential to negatively affect the public's right to privacy, the individualization of that right and its reduction to a material or moral interest rather than anything more fundamental, has meant that privacy rhetoric is also called upon to serve private rather than public interests.[227]

Meiklejohn also rejects bluntly the role of private broadcasting organizations on the ground of their economic interests in communication. According to him,

> The radio as it now operates among us is not free. Nor is it entitled to the protection of the First Amendment. It is not engaged in the task of enlarging and enriching human communication. It is engaged in making money. And First Amendment does not intend to guarantee men freedom to say what some private interest pays them to say for its own advantage. It intends only to make men free to say what, as citizens, they think, what they believe, about the great welfare.[228]

On the other hand, Emerson presents an optimistic view about the conflict of press freedom and privacy. He states:

> [T]he areas of conflict between the right of privacy and freedom of the press are quite limited, and the task of reconciliation is by no means insurmountable. At most points the law of privacy and the law sustaining a free press do not contradict each other. On the contrary, they are mutually supportive, in that both are vital features of the basic system of individual rights. At other points there is only a minor likelihood of conflict. This is true, for instance of the protections afforded privacy through the law of trespass, theft, copyright and the like, where the press has long adjusted to limitations on the gathering of news, and the issues are hardly matters of controversy.[229]

Emerson also provides a recipe of resolving the potential conflict as following:

> In broad outline the resolution of the conflict between the two seems reasonably clear. The purpose of establishing a right of privacy is to protect certain areas of individual autonomy, identity, and intimacy from any intrusion by society at large. This exclusion of collective action would extend to the rules developed by the society for safeguarding freedom of expression. Insofar as the guaranty of freedom of expression serves social interests - in discovering the truth, assuring participation in decision making, and facilitating social change - the individual right of privacy would plainly take precedence over the collective interest. Insofar as freedom of expression serves individual interests – primarily in encouraging self-fulfillment - the two individual rights would seem to be in conflict. In such a situation, however, the guiding principle would be that the exercise of an individual right

---

belong to large corporations whose interests influence what gets covered (and, what is probably more central, what does not) and how.2 (2) News organizations are driven economically to capture the largest possible audience, and thus not to turn it off with whatever does turn it off-coverage that is too controversial, too demanding, too disturbing. (3) The media are easily manipulated by government officials (and others), for whom the press, by simply reporting press re- leases and official statements, can be a virtually unfiltered mouthpiece. (4) Characteristics of the media themselves constrain or influence cover- age; thus, for example, television lends itself to an action-oriented, unanalytic treatment of events that can distort their meaning or importance."

[227] Dawes (2014), p. 18.

[228] Meiklejohn (2000), p. 104.

[229] Emerson (1979), p. 331.

which injures another person would not be favored. Hence, here too the right of privacy would prevail over freedom of expression.[230]

In the nutshell, the theories of privacy, free speech and press freedom highlight the possibility of mutual conflict, whereby one becomes the limitation for another. Conceptual analysis as to their inherent value and to the interests which these values protect call for the need to reconcile. Due to the fact that both privacy and free speech are very broad concepts where both belong to the basic values of human autonomy and dignity, the so-called definitional balancing at the legislative level could not provide perfect solution. However, legal instruments provide a framework for the process of striking fairer and more just balance in any court of law. Ultimately, the problem of reconciliation seems to be resolved by judiciary on the basis of analyzing the actual facts of media intrusions cases in the light of the available and applicable legal rules. This undertaking will require not only the identification of concrete interests supposedly protected by free speech and privacy but also the normative concretization of the broader conceptual underpinnings.

3.7 Conclusions

The study of prominent concepts of privacy, methodologies applied to arrive at a particular conceptual outcome, different perspectives which mostly support and rarely call for discarding privacy, as well as the countervailing status of free speech as a justification for media intrusions has enabled us to work out a framework for balancing these values. Based on the above discussions, following are the major conclusions which would work as a conceptual framework for the comparison of different legal regimes. The framework would offer the parameters and criteria through which the efficacy of a particular legal system in resolving privacy versus free speech conflicts as well as the level of privacy protection shall be judged.

Firstly, the right to privacy is a fundamental right and has its roots in both dignity and autonomy. Dignity and autonomy are the two fundamentals that work as roots for most of human rights including the right to privacy and freedom of speech. Privacy fulfills the deontological criteria in terms of bulging to the same origin of other human rights; it is not an orphan value. 'Privacy as an aspect of human dignity' verifies that it has a strong deontological value and the normative scheme. Its protection should not always require the presence of harmful consequences. Generally speaking, privacy needs protection even if the claimant cannot provide evidence for secondary harms associated with the defendant's action. The accrual of material or nonmaterial damage, however, is relevant at the stage of deciding about the nature and quantum of remedial compensation. But privacy needs protection in certain cases on the basis of *as it is* and may not require further investigation of *what is it good for*. On the other hand, privacy has also a strong instrumental value and many

[230]Emerson (1979), p. 341. Footnote omitted.

scholars consider it as a prerequisite for the nourishment and development of the most fundamental traits of human personality. People need privacy not only for the sake of it but also for establishing human relations of their own choice; they want to exercise their right of controlling outsiders' access to their bodies, premises, information and everything else that could legitimately be perceived as associated to their persona. They also want to be protected from embarrassing situations and are entitled to building their own image in society through legitimate means. These are sufficient entitlements against involuntary media exposures.

Secondly, the formulation of a comprehensive definition for privacy, which could enable courts and policy makers to resolve all the issues in a perfect manner, is not possible. Most of the infringements are context specific. However, the pliability of the concept is not a weakness of the value. Rather, the richness of the concept of privacy is supportive in the resolution of a wide range of practical problems. The ubiquitous infringements of the right to privacy and data protection particularly in the online sphere pose a dire challenge to the conclusiveness of traditional conceptions of morality and normativity. The more a concept would be broad; the more would be the chances of tackling novel problems confronted with that concept. Furthermore, the difficulty of an *exhaustive* definition is not a typical feature of the privacy concept alone. The fundamental values such as the rights of human dignity and autonomy face the same problems, not only of defining them in their own right but also of specifying them in their respective scope and sphere. Therefore, our framework supports a broad definition of privacy and then leaves it to the context of a specific case to find out what particular instance of privacy is invaded and what normative principles should be invoked to remedy the invasion.[231] To reassert, most scholars do not support an inherent delimitation of the right to privacy, but they are open to the adjustment arrangement only where a strong countervailing right or interest (e.g. free speech) needs protection.

Thirdly, privacy is a fundamental human right and its legal protection needs a human rights approach supported by moral and constitutional principles. Any intervention needs to be justified, just as in the case of other fundamental rights. Privacy accepts the right to free speech as a valid justification for its limitation. Whenever there are cases where there is a conflict between these rights and judges have to reconcile these values, this could only be done through balancing exercise. However, both right to privacy and right to freedom of speech have equal values and any kind of presumptive preference in the favor of any of these rights would affect the just and fair balance. This equality is also applicable to media outlets and journalists who cannot claim any special privilege: Their conduct would be judged on the basis of the type of speech that they carry on. For example, political speech

[231] See also for example, Glancy (2000), p. 375: 'At the Intersection of Visible and Invisible Worlds: United States Privacy Law and the Internet' (2000)16 Santa Clara Computer & High Tech LJ 357. "Because privacy law has characteristically evolved by solving a particular type of privacy problem or by reacting to a notorious invasion of privacy, or by protecting a particular type of personal information, it is not surprising that context plays an important role in the diversity of privacy law."

comes on the top of the protection ladder due to its democratic dimension while tittle-tale about private scandals cannot have an equivalent weight in the balancing scale. Similarly, the principle of proportionality must also be taken into consideration in cases where "public interest" is presented as a justification for privacy violation. Any legal approach and protective mechanism which does not consider privacy as a basic right would be unable to protect individual privacy interests whenever these interests are subjected to balancing against other 'established' rights.

Fourthly, the framework acknowledges the importance of free speech, having an inherent value as well as its justifications on the basis of its role in finding out truth, realizing self-fulfillment, ensuring citizens' participation in democracy, and its role as a check on the conduct of government. However, the framework does not support the right to freedom of speech and expression as an absolute value. Fundamental rights and values are not monolithic notions of legal science. Speech is not an absolute reality and it has many forms and manifestations. More than that, the financial dimension of media is an important consideration where there is seldom a platonic journalistic activity and profit maximization is one of the main objectives of many television programs and newspaper publications. This consideration becomes more important in the process of protecting privacy due to the fact that intrusive newsgathering and publications of private information attract more viewers and advertisement revenue.

The framework elaborated until this point is helpful to approach the resolution of the problems of media intrusions into private life in Pakistan as elaborated in Chapter 2. The presentation of a meta-perspective of the theoretical dimensions of privacy along with the strengths and weaknesses of different concepts, modern approaches to conceptualization as well as critical perspectives of privacy highlighted the theoretical richness of the right to privacy. Furthermore, possible limitations on privacy have also been explored. Free speech and press freedom are enshrined values and protected rights. Yet, their interference into the realm of the right to privacy which qualifies for protection must be also justified.

This extensive conceptual study has now enabled us to look deep into the on ground position of the privacy and free speech enforcement in Pakistan and elsewhere by utilizing comparative law methodological principles. These analyses shall provide insights for the prescriptive part of this research work which offers recommendations for privacy law protection in Pakistan.

References

Albers M (2013) Privatheitsschutz als Grundrechtsproblem. In: Halft S, Krah H (eds) Privatheit. Strategien und Transformationen, Stutz Passau, pp 15–44

Albers M (2014) Realizing the complexity of data protection. In: Gutwirth S, Leenes R, Hert PD (eds) Reloading data protection. Springer, Dordrecht, pp 213–235

Allen A (2011) Unpopular privacy: what must we hide? Oxford University Press, New York

Allen AL (1988) Uneasy access: privacy for women in a free society. Rowman & Littlefield

Barendt E (2005) Freedom of speech. Oxford University Press

Beaney WB (1966) The Right to privacy and American law. Law Contemp Probs 31:253
Biehler H, Carolan E, Murphy C (2008) The right to privacy: a doctrinal and comparative analysis. Thomson Round Hall
Birnhack M (2011) A quest for a theory of privacy: Context and control. Jurimetrics 51 https://ssrn.com/abstract=1824533. Accessed 25 Aug 2023
Bloustein EJ (1964) Privacy as an aspect of human dignity: an answer to Dean Prosser. N Y Univ Law Rev 39:962
Bok S (1989) Secrets: on the ethics of concealment and revelation. Vintage, New York
Carolan E (2011) The concept of a right to privacy. https://ssrn.com/abstract=1889243. Accessed 25 Aug 2023
Davis F (1959) What do we mean by right to privacy. SDL Rev 4:1
Dawes S (2014) Press freedom, privacy and the public sphere. J Stud 15:1
DeCew JW (1986) The scope of privacy in law and ethics. Law Philosophy 05:145
Emerson TI (1979) The right of privacy and freedom of the press. Harv CR-CLL Rev 14:329
Etzioni A (2005) The limits of privacy. Basic Books Group, New York
Feldman D (1994) Secrecy, dignity, or autonomy? Views of privacy as a civil liberty. Curr Legal Probl 47:41
Finn RL, Wright D, Friedewald M (2013) Seven types of privacy. In: Gutwirth S, Leenes R, de Hert P, Poullet Y (eds) European data protection: coming of age. Springer, Dordrecht
Fried C (1968) Privacy. Yale Law J 77:475
Gavison R (1991) Too early for a requiem: Warren and Brandeis were right on privacy vs. free speech. SCL Rev 43:437
Gavison RE (1980) Privacy and the limits of law. Yale Law J 89(3):421
Gerety T (1977) Redefining privacy. Harv Civil Rights-Civil Libert Law Rev 12:233
Gerstein RS (1978) Intimacy and privacy. Ethics 89(1):76
Glancy D (2000) At the intersection of visible and invisible worlds: United States privacy law and the internet. Santa Clara Comput High Technol Law J 16:357
Glancy DJ (1979) The invention of the right to privacy. Ariz Law Rev 21:1
Haag EVD (1971) On privacy'. In: Pennock JR, Chapman JV (eds) Privacy. Nomos, XIII
Hallborg RB Jr (1986) Principles of liberty and the right to privacy. Law Philosophy 5:175
Inness JC (1996) Privacy, intimacy, and isolation. Oxford University Press
Koops BJ, Newell BC, Timan T, Skorvanek I, Chokrevski T, Galic M (2016) A typology of privacy. Univ Pa J Int Law 38:483
Kramer IR (1989) The birth of privacy law: a century since warren and Brandeis. Cath Univ Law Rev 39:703
Krotoszynski RJ (2016) Preface: privacy revisited: a global perspective on the right to be left alone. Oxford University Press
Lichtenberg J (1987) Foundations and limits of freedom of the press. Philosophy Public Aff 16(4): 329
Lusky L (1972) Invasion of privacy: a clarification of concepts. Columbia Law Rev 72(4):693
MacKinnon CA (1989) Toward a feminist theory of the state. Harvard University Press
Mark T (2015) Balancing privacy and free speech: Unwanted attention in the age of social media. Routledge
Meiklejohn A (2000) Free speech and it relation to self-government. The Lawbook Exchange Ltd
Miller A (1971) The assault on privacy. University of Michigan Press
Moor JH (1990) The ethics of privacy protection. Library Trends 39:69–82
Moore AD (2003) Privacy: its meaning and value. Am Philosophical Quart 40:215
Nissenbaum H (1998) Protecting privacy in an information age: the problem of privacy in public. Law Philosophy 17:559
Nissenbaum H (2004) Privacy as contextual integrity. Wash Law Rev 79:119
Nissenbaum H (2009) Privacy in context technology, policy, and the integrity of social life. Stanford Law Books
Parent WA (1983a) Privacy, morality and the law. Philosophy Public Aff 12(4):269

Parent WA (1983b) Recent work on the concept of privacy. Am Philosophical Quart 20(4):341
Parker RB (1973-74) A definition of privacy. Rutgers Law Rev 27:275
Posner RA (1978) The right of privacy. Georgia Law Rev 12:393
Prosser WL (1960) Privacy. Calif Law Rev 48:383
Rachels J (1975) Why privacy is important. Philosophy Public Aff 4:323
Reiman H (1976) Privacy, intimacy, and personhood. Philosophy and Public Affairs 6:26
Scanlon T (1975) Thomson on privacy. Philosophy Public Aff 315
Shapiro FR, Pearse M (2012) The most-cited law review articles of all time. Mich Law Rev 110: 1483
Solove DJ (2002) Conceptualizing privacy. Calif Law Rev 90(1087):1092–1126
Solove DJ (2006) A taxonomy of privacy. Univ Pa Law Rev 154:477
Solove DJ (2008) Understanding privacy. Harvard University Press
Thomson JJ (1975) The right to privacy. Philosophy Public Aff 01:295
Warren SD, Brandeis LD (1890) The right to privacy. Harv Law Rev 15:193–220
Westin A (1967) Privacy and freedom. New York Ig Publishing

Chapter 4
Right to Privacy and Freedom of Expression in the Constitution of Pakistan

In order to effectively protect individual's privacy rights from media invasions, judiciary requires legal tools of balancing conflicting rights. A doctrinal analysis of the existing legal regime in Pakistan can help in locating such interpretational tools. Therefore, this chapter will give an overview of the constitutional and legal regime of Pakistan and will herewith identify the gaps before prescribing law reform for an effective privacy right's enforcement.

The Constitution of Pakistan provides protection to both the right to privacy and the right to freedom of speech in its Articles 14 and 19 respectively. However, to answer the question as to why despite such textual references, the people in Pakistan are incapable of invoking compensatory remedies for their privacy violations needs further exploration of fundamental rights principles. For this purpose, the general constitutional framework of the fundamental rights in Pakistan, the protection available to the right to privacy and human dignity, as well as the legal framework available to the right to free speech shall be doctrinally analyzed in the following sections of this chapter.

4.1 Constitutional Framework of Fundamental Rights

4.1.1 Catalogue of Fundamental Rights

The Constitution of Pakistan provides for an extensive list of a variety of fundamental rights in its Chapter I of Part II (from Article 8 to Article 28). Introducing the Constitution and demarcating State's territories, the introductory chapter also recognizes the inalienable right of every person to be dealt with according to law. It grants legal protection to the life, liberty, body, reputation and property in particular, and announces positive and negative liberties where no one shall be obliged to do or

S. Aftab, *Comparative Perspectives on the Right to Privacy*, Ius Gentium: Comparative Perspectives on Law and Justice 109,
https://doi.org/10.1007/978-3-031-45575-9_4

to refrain from anything, which the law does not require.[1] It confers a general guarantee to the people that the legality of every public action must be justified if it hampers any interest related to life, liberty, body, reputation or property. Its broad expression enables people to invoke it in the cases of infringements not covered by the specific provisions of fundamental rights.

Article 9 of the Constitution of Pakistan provides, "No person shall be deprived of life or liberty, save in accordance with law." Article 10 safeguards people from illegal detention and provides the right of defense in a court of law as well as the right to a lawyer. It also obliges the police to produce the person arrested to the nearest magistrate within 24 hours, except in the case of "preventive detention" which has an elaborated procedure in the same Article. Article 10-A entitles everybody to due process of law in all cases of civil and criminal proceedings. Article 11 prohibits slavery, forced labor, and child labor. Articles 12 and 13 protect people against double and retrospective punishments. Similarly, to compel or torture an accused person to be a witness against himself or to obtain evidential material are unconstitutional.[2] According to Article 14 (1), "The dignity of man and, subject to law, the privacy of home, shall be inviolable". Articles 15-18 grant citizens the rights to movement to citizens; right to peaceful assembly; freedom of association and to form political party; and the freedom to do lawful trade, business or adopt any profession. Article 19 grants freedom of speech and expression and guarantees freedom of the press, which are subject to "reasonable restrictions". Article 19A provides the right to have access to information to every citizen, "in all matters of public importance subject to regulation and reasonable restrictions imposed by law."

Articles 20 and 21 grant freedom of religion and protection against religious discrimination. Articles 23 and 24 grant and protect proprietary rights of citizens. Articles 25-28 25A, 26, 27 and 28 declare respectively the right to equal protection of law, the right to free and compulsory education, non-discrimination with respect to access to public places or in joining services, and the right to preserve language and culture.

The Constitution of Pakistan has laid down the "principles of policy" for the public authorities. To act in accordance with these principles is the responsibility of the state functionaries. These guiding principles include the promotion of Islamic way of life, encouragement of local government institutions, discouraging parochial and racial prejudices, ensuring participation of women in the national life, protection of family life and minorities, promotion of social justice and economic wellbeing of the people, enabling people to join Army of Pakistan and the strengthening of bonds with other Muslim countries. These principles are not binding *sensu stricto* and their observance depends on the availability of resources. The contents of these principles

[1] Constitution of Pakistan 1973, Article 4 (2): "(a) no action detrimental to the life, liberty, body, reputation or property of any person shall be taken except in accordance with law; (b) no person shall be prevented from or be hindered in doing that which is not prohibited by law; (c) no person shall be compelled to do that which the law does not require him to do."

[2] Constitution of Pakistan, Article 13 (b) and 14 (2).

are nothing more than moral and ethical guidelines. However, these principles work as an aiding tool of interpretation of the constitutional provisions, especially during judicial review of executive actions.

4.1.2 The Status of Fundamental Rights

Article 8 provides an exalted position to the fundamental rights and declares that any law, custom or usage inconsistent with the constitutional fundamental rights shall be void. It bars the State from making any law in contravention to the constitutional rights. This way, fundamental rights have a superior position in the legal system and the citizens can invoke Article 8 in combination with the relevant fundamental right in the designated courts. The Supreme Court of Pakistan has asserted that these rights are not mentioned in the constitution to enumerate merely the ethical or social ideals of Pakistani society. Rather, these rights could be legally enforced in the highest judicial forums. A right to be called *fundamental* must have two conditions. Firstly, it should not be capable of molding just like the normal legislative instruments but there must be a thorough procedure in the shape of a constitutional amendment if it is necessary to modify or take back a fundamental right.[3] Secondly, there should be an enforcement mechanism whereby the judiciary can declare any executive or legislative violation of these rights as void.[4]

The wording of fundamental rights provisions mostly imposes a negative duty upon the state to refrain from violating these rights and does not clearly express whether or not the state has a duty to protect these rights from encroachments of a third party. However, the jurisprudence of high courts and Supreme Court of Pakistan establishes the protection of fundamental rights as a positive obligation of the State. In Watan Party v. Federation of Pakistan etc., the Supreme Court of Pakistan held that the "State is duty bound to protect the life and property of its citizens in accordance with law against *all* the atrocities".[5] The State is under constitutional obligation to provide *suitable environment and circumstances* where the fundamental rights of citizens can be effectively protected because,

> It is the duty and obligation of the state on account of the various provisions of the Constitution *to provide the atmosphere* based on honesty by providing equal protection of law. Every citizen must be treated equally, dignity of human being life should be maintained,

---

[3] Jabindera Kishore v Province of East Pakistan, PLD 1957 SC 9.

[4] Abul ala Maududi v Govt of West Pakistan, PLD 1964 SC 673.

[5] Watan Party v. Federation of Pakistan etc. Sou Moto case No. 16 of 2011 (PLD 2011 SC 997). Para 122: "it is the duty of the State to protect and safeguard all these Fundamental Rights including the right to life and liberty as envisaged by Article 9 of the Constitution. . .Para 2; "The Provincial Government and the Federal Government owe a duty to the citizens of Karachi to ensure their Fundamental Rights. . ." Para 127: "It is the duty of the Provincial Government as well as the Federal Government to protect and preserve the Constitution, which confers such rights upon individuals." Emphasis supplied.

and liberty of life and honour must be guaranteed as envisaged in the Articles 9, 14 and 25 of the Constitution.[6]

The Supreme Court has elucidated an indirect horizontal effect of fundamental rights as,

> We are therefore clearly of the view that the High Court has plenary power to positively enforce fundamental rights not merely against public authorities but even private parties. Accordingly direction for positive enforcement of fundamental rights against private parties could only be given by the high court in respect of rights guaranteed,[. . .], which might in most cases require enforcement against such parties.[7]

The right to privacy demands a similar proactive approach of the state. It requires refrainment from encroachment by the state as well as proactive protection of the state against private party infringement. By virtue of jurisprudential principles, it becomes easy to establish a case for comprehensive privacy legislation. It is the constitutional responsibility of the state to provide legal instruments to the people so that they invoke relevant concrete rule of law for the protection of their fundamental rights.

4.1.3 The Scope and Enforcement of Fundamental Rights

4.1.3.1 Institutional Arrangements and Judicial Review

The Government of Pakistan has mandated the Ministry of Human Rights to review the human rights situation of the country in order to make the executive functions in-line with the fundamental rights.[8] This legal mandate is of a supervisory and weak executive nature. Most of the functions of this ministry are related to the facilitation of other government departments in terms of coordination, harmonization and information collection regarding human rights issues. Its "Action Plan for Human Rights" does not have any reference to the enforcement of constitutional rights by itself. It merely focuses on the long term goals for introducing legal reforms and strengthening the existing institutional framework for upholding human rights.

On the other hand, the judiciary has a vital role under the Constitution in the enforcement of fundamental rights and it is generally regarded as 'the guardian of fundamental rights'. There is a Supreme Court of Pakistan and five high courts

[6] Commissioner of Income Tax v Messrs. Eli Lilly Pakistan (PVT) LTD. (SCMR 2009 1279). Emphasis supplied.

[7] Human Rights Commission of Pakistan etc. v. Government of Pakistan etc. (PLD 2009 SC 507), para 33.

[8] Government of Pakistan, Rules of Business 1973, Rule 3(3).

i.e. one in each province[9] and in the Islamabad Capital Territory (ICT).[10] The Supreme Court of Pakistan is the highest court of the country in judicial hierarchy, having both appellate and original jurisdiction in human rights cases. Judgments of the Supreme Court have a binding effect in the lower courts' decision-making.[11] Similarly, the decisions of the provincial high courts have a binding effect for all the subordinate courts in the concerned province.[12] Article 184 (3) of the Constitution of Pakistan empowers the Supreme Court to issue an order regarding the question of public importance with reference to the enforcement of fundamental rights. Similarly, high courts can exercise their *writ jurisdiction* under Article 199. According to Article 199, high courts can restrain unauthorized acts of *any person* functioning in connection with the affairs of the government. It can declare unauthorized acts as of no legal effect. High courts can issue directions to produce the person and present him before the court (writ of *Habeas Corpus*); to an office-holder to show his legal authority for holding a public office (writ of *quo warranto*); and to any person or authority for the enforcement of any of the fundamental rights. Remarkably, there is no requirement of public interest involvement for invoking the jurisdiction of high courts. Both Articles thus give the power to the Supreme Court as well as provincial high courts to review the constitutionality of any legislative instrument and executive action. The power of judicial review makes courts the custodian of fundamental rights against the State.

4.1.3.2 Judicial Activism and Public Interest Litigation

The activist role of judiciary to safeguard public interest has become a chief feature of the legal system of Pakistan. The Supreme Court of Pakistan, in a landmark judgment in the case of Benazir Bhutto v. Federation of Pakistan, has relaxed the requirement of *locus standi* and has thus opened the doors for what is commonly known as public interest litigation. It held:

> After all, the law is not a closed shop and even in the adversary procedure, it is permissible for the next friend to move the Court on behalf of a minor or a person under disability, or a person under detention or in restraint. Why not then a person, if he were to act bona fide activise a Court for the enforcement of the Fundamental Rights of a group or a class of persons who are unable to seek relief from the Court for several reasons. This is what the

[9]There are four provinces in Pakistan having High Courts in their respective capitals namely, 1. Punjab (Lahore High Court); 2. Sindh (Karachi High Court), Baluchistan (Quita High Court); 4. Khyber Pakhtunkhwa-former North West Frontier Province (Peshawar High Court).

[10]Constitution of Pakistan, Article 175: Establishment and Jurisdiction of courts.

[11]Constitution of Pakistan, Article 189: "Any decision of the Supreme Court shall, to the extent that it decides a question of law or is based upon or enunciates a principle of law, be binding on all other courts in Pakistan".

[12]Constitution of Pakistan, Article 201: "Subject to Article 189, any decision of a High Court shall, to the extent that it decides a question of law or is based upon or enunciates a principle of law, be binding on all courts subordinate to it".

> public interest litigation/class action seeks to achieve as it goes further to relax the rule on *locus standi* so as to include a person who bona fide makes an application for the violation of any constitutional right of a determined class of persons whose grievances go unnoticed and unredressed. The initiation of the proceedings in this manner will be in aid of the meaningful protection of the rule of law given to the citizens by Article 4 of the Constitution. . .[13]

Due to relaxation of the requirement for a petitioner to be aggrieved and with the exercise of *suo moto* jurisdiction, the Supreme Court and the provincial high courts have been actively and progressively pursuing the protection and enforcement of human rights. With some criticism,[14] the judicial activism is generally appreciated owing to the socio-economic characteristics of Pakistani society. There is a visible social inequality, ignorance about fundamental rights, expensive and long process of litigation, which calls for a vigilant judicial supervision over constitutional rights. The rich case law and strong precedents set during the interpretation of judicial powers regarding the enforcement of fundamental rights confirm a liberal approach, which emphasizes on remedying the infringements rather than to stick to procedural technicalities. According to the prevailing jurisprudence, any member belonging to a particular target group or even to the general public can access the court for enforcement of a fundamental right, provided he proves the *bona fide* nature of his act. There are many instances where the courts take cognizance on the basis of media reports as well as letters and telegrams to the editors of newspapers or to Chief Justices.[15] Furthermore, broadening of the scope and meaning as well as the enforceability of fundamental rights drew an influence on the formulation of legislative instruments and executive measures such as institutional arrangements for preemptive supervision.[16]

The Supreme Court of Pakistan ruled that there must be scientific approach to various electricity projects for the purpose of taking into consideration the environmental impact and health related hazards of electro-magnetic waves. It ordered the Federal Government to form a commission or authority, comprising the environmental sciences' experts for the purpose of evaluating the sustainability of such projects and electrical installations. The Court also held that the development goals must be balanced with the hazardous effects on human health and environment.[17]

---

[13] Benazir Bhutto v. Federation of Pakistan, PLD 1988 SC 416.

[14] Adeel Hussain, 'Mango Scented Sovereignty: Pakistan's Chief Justice Saqib Nisar and Baba-justice' published 17.09.2018 on (Verfassungsblog 17 September 2018) https://verfassungsblog.de/mango-scented-sovereignty-pakistans-chief-justice-saqib-nisar-and-baba-justice/ II) Mohammad Hanif, 'Pakistan's Judges Are on a Mission. But What Is It?' *New York Times* (New York, 01 March 2018) https://www.nytimes.com/2018/03/01/opinion/pakistan-judges-mission-corruption.html. Accessed 26 August 2023.

[15] For details, Hussain (1993).

[16] In Ms Shehla Zia v WAPDA, PLD 1994 SC 693. The Supreme Court of Pakistan has adopted an expansive interpretation of the right to life, encompassing the environmental rights of citizens within its purview. This landmark judgment led to the enactment of the Pakistan Environmental Protection Act 1997, establishing the Environmental Protection Agency as an executive body to oversee environmental matters.

[17] Ms Shehla Zia v WAPDA, PLD 1994 SC 693.

The Supreme Court of Pakistan has taken a unique step by assuming a proactive role to establish "Human Rights' Cell" in order to tackle the "bad governance by state functionaries and exploitation of masses by different interest groups".[18] Judicial activism and public interest litigation are now the hallmarks of fundamental rights enforcement framework.[19] According to the Supreme Court,

> There is a daily influx of large number of applications in HRC from aggrieved persons from all over the country, suffering at the hands of unbridled public functionaries and privileged classes. The trend reveals that courts are ray of hope for disgruntled masses. It is need of hour that such aggrieved persons should be provided required help and support to ensure their fundamental rights, to be able to claim their rights in a confident manner and exploitation in whatever form it may be, curbed for all and once.[20]

There is a wide variety in the subject matter of these cases and the nature of involved interests and rights. Not all of these rights are strictly available against the state or having a strong constitutional dimension but due to liberating the enforcement of various individual interests from procedural technicalities, matters such as the right to receive pension,[21] encroachment on public parks, land and graveyard by private persons and entities,[22] misuse of power, rash driving by public officials,[23] as well as the uprooting/cutting of trees as a result of extension of roads have assumed the status of constitutionally protected rights and have been enforced through judicial mechanism.[24]

In the nutshell, the fundamental rights in the Pakistani Constitution have a strong normative foundation. In case of abridgement, any legislative as well as executive act is subject to judicial review to satisfy the court regarding its constitutionality. Every law and executive order or action must pass the test of constitutionality. If such a test is failed because its enactment or execution would violate any of the fundamental rights, that act is declared as suspended, null, void or even *void-ab-initio*.

---

[18] Supreme Court of Pakistan Annual Report-2017, p. 66. The Human Rights Cell has disposed of 28781 applications in 2017.

[19] For details: Benazir Bhutto case, PLD 1988 SC 388; Darshan Masih v. The State PLD 1990 SC 513 and Margalla Hills Case SMC 20, 2007.

[20] Supreme Court of Pakistan Annual Report-2017, p. 66.

[21] HRC No. 8018-P/2017, HRC No. 3481-S/2017, Supreme Court of Pakistan Annual Report-2017, p. 70.

[22] HRC No. 6465-G/2017, HRC No. 464-P/2016 Supreme Court of Pakistan Annual Report-2017, pp. 71 and 72.

[23] HRC No. 9572-G/2017, HRC No.17000-/2017, Supreme Court of Pakistan Annual Report-2017, p. 71.

[24] HRC No.10923/2017, Supreme Court of Pakistan Annual Report-2017, p. 72.

4.1.4 Limitations on Fundamental Rights

The constitutional provisions which grant fundamental rights also attach certain limitations and conditions to these rights.[25] The Constitution of Pakistan endorses the suspension of a fundamental right during an emergency situation under Article 233.[26] The State is empowered to suspend the fundamental rights to freedom of movement (Article 15), freedom of assembly (Article 16), freedom of association (Article 17), freedom to conduct trade, business or professional activity (Article 18), freedom of speech (Article 19) and the right to protection of property (Article 24). None of these rights provided by the Constitution can restrict the state from making laws or take executive actions after the proclamation of emergency. The idea behind the constitutional limitations on fundamental rights is that individual rights become secondary when the very existence of the state is in jeopardy or an extraordinary situation demands quick and extra-constitutional measures in the so-called larger public interest. The Supreme Court of Pakistan has supported this assertion in many high profile cases where the "doctrine of state necessity" makes the ground to justify the otherwise unconstitutional measures.[27]

The imposition of emergency is a general restraint on many fundamental rights *en bloc*, while there are very few fundamental liberties to which no strings are attached. Generally, there is no concept of absolute rights and most of these rights are subject either to a greater public interest or to the considerations of a possible countervailing right. This feature of fundamental rights in the Constitution of Pakistan is compatible with the theory of fundamental human rights, which recognizes the conflict of rights and offers different resolution mechanisms.

4.2 The Constitutional Protection Available to the Right to Privacy and Human Dignity

4.2.1 Limited Normative Anchors in the Constitution

Privacy is regarded as a fundamental human right embodied in many constitutions of the world. The Constitution of Pakistan also recognizes privacy as a fundamental

---

[25] For example, Article 10 safeguards the citizens from arrest and detention but also exempts the law of preventive detention. Similarly, the penal provisions relating to the blasphemy law and the law on the contempt of court have limitations attached to the right to freedom of speech under Article 19 of the constitution.

[26] According to Article 8 (5): "The rights conferred by this Chapter shall not be suspended except as expressly provided by the constitution."

[27] The theory of necessity was first recognized by Justice Muhammad Munir in Maulvi Tamiz-ud-din case of 1955. Last time, the same doctrine was resorted to by the Supreme Court in the case of Syed Zafar Ali Shah v. General Pervez Musharraf, PLD 2000 SC 869. Supreme Court validated the military coup of General Pervez Musharraf on the basis of this theory.

right. Moreover, the Supreme Court and high courts of Pakistan have granted an important normative position to most of the fundamental strands of the broad right of privacy by developing binding jurisprudential principles.

According to Article 14 (1) of the Constitution of Islamic Republic of Pakistan, "The dignity of man and, subject to law, the privacy of home, shall be inviolable."

The first part of the provision confers an absolute protection to human dignity and it is not subject to any limitation. Privacy of home is protected, too, but it is subject to restrictions as imposed by law. Article 9 of the Constitution also grants a general right, whereby the deprivation of life and liberty is unconstitutional unless such abridgement is according to law. The protection from illegal detention in Article 10 can also be invoked as these provisions indirectly safeguard privacy.

Even if the privacy of home is subject to law such as the criminal law on search and seizure, the Article for the protection of human dignity and privacy is not mentioned in the list of rights that could be suspended in the wake of emergency situation in the country. Article 14 of the Constitution prohibits in an indirect manner the eavesdropping, surreptitious tapping and photographing something inside the house and declares all these to be unconstitutional and un-Islamic invasions on the right privacy. No evidence is acceptable in a court of law if it is gathered by the police through illegal means such as entering the premises without observing the legal procedures and formalities set by the law on search and seizure.[28]

Furthermore, it is evident from the wording of the constitutional text that the state authorities must justify the legality of their intervention in the right to privacy otherwise the action will amount to an infringement of the fundamental right. As a matter of principle, the fundamental right to privacy is inherently inviolable, while interference in the right is an *exception*.

The textual expression of the inviolability of human dignity and privacy under the Constitution of Pakistan is express, but it is very brief and does not mention the concrete areas worthy of protection under the privacy rubric. However, the case law of higher courts has expanded it to some extent and one can find references to some concrete areas and dimensions of privacy. An express construction covering both privacy and dignity of man under an exclusive provision offers an opportunity to judiciary to interpret it for the protection of a variety of human interests.

[28] Manzoor Ahmad v The State, 1990 MLD 1488. The Lahore High Court held at Para 5: "I find that there is substance in the submission of the learned counsel for the petitioner that in view of Article 14 of the Constitution Eaves-dropping, tapping stealthily, photographing something inside the house are invasions on privacy and as such is not permissible under the Constitution as well as in Islam. A Furthermore, the police has entered the premises without observing the formalities of law, hence the evidence so far collected is open to objection."

4.2.2 The Jurisprudence Developed by Superior Courts

The short mention of the privacy of home in the constitution is obviously not sufficient to be invoked in a number of privacy violations. The Courts have attempted to broaden the scope of Article 14 (1) and Article 9 and have enjoined regarding the protection of such aspects of privacy which are not clearly mentioned by the Constitution of Pakistan. The case law dealing with the privacy related interests will helps us in finding out the existing strengths and the remaining weaknesses of privacy enforcement.

Following is an account of the case law to explain how higher courts have interpreted the concepts of right to life, dignity of man and privacy of home. Particularly, it will find out the extent of protection of different strands of privacy through interpretation of the broad constitutional provisions.

4.2.2.1 Leading Judgment of the Supreme Court in the Case of Benazir Bhutto

In the case of Benazir Bhutto,[29] the Supreme Court of Pakistan has discussed the inviolability of right to life, liberty, human dignity and privacy of home in a very detailed and articulate manner.[30] Discussing the significance of these rights, the Supreme Court observed that the right to life under Article 9 cannot be restricted merely to physical existence. Rather, it entails all the essential elements of a quality life in order to "*enjoy it with dignity*". The Court categorically extended the constitutional right of dignity and privacy to all persons without any discrimination and held that even persons accused of breaking law of the land have these rights. Furthermore, the Court emphasized the need for a broader interpretation of the expression "privacy of home" and extended it to places which are not included in the traditional definition of "home". In the words of the then Chief Justice Sajjad Ali Shah, the restricted interpretation of the term "home" i.e. excluding any other place wherever the person might be, is *"illogical and completely out of context"*.[31] The Court held that, "home" even in the literal sense is any place where a person can "enjoy personal freedom" while having a sense of security from outsiders. The Court further elaborated the controversial dichotomy of public and private spaces in a very lucid manner as,

> The emphasis is not on the boundaries of home but the *person* who enjoys the right *wherever he may be*. The term 'home' connotes meaning of privacy, security and non-interference by outsiders which a person enjoys. According to Ballentine's Law Dictionary, "in ancient law French, the word (home) also signified a man". It also defines as "sometimes including not

[29]Ms Benazir Bhutto remained Prime Minister of Pakistan for two times i.e. 1988–1990 and 1993–1996.

[30]Benazir Bhutto v President of Pakistan, PLD 1998 SC 388.

[31]Benazir Bhutto v President of Pakistan, PLD 1998 SC 388.

> only a place of abode, but also support and maintenance". Wider meaning should be given to the word 'home'. The term 'privacy of home' also symbolises the security and privacy of a nature which a person enjoys in his home. The term "privacy of home" cannot be restricted to the privacy in respect of home, the privacy within the four walls of the home. It refers to the privacy, which is sacred and secure like the privacy a person enjoys in his home. Such privacy of home entitles a person to enjoy wherever he lives or works, inside the premises or in open land. *Even the privacy of a person cannot be intruded in public places.*"[32]

The Supreme Court of Pakistan connects the moral roots of privacy to human dignity and emphasizes that the invasion of privacy at outside of home places has similar repercussions for human dignity and honor just like the invasion of privacy inside the home.

> The inviolability of privacy is directly linked with the dignity of man. If a man is to preserve his dignity, if he is to live with honour and reputation, his privacy, whether in home or outside the home has to be saved from invasion and protected from illegal intrusion. The right conferred under Article 14 is not to any premises, home or office, but to the person, the man/woman wherever he/she may be.[33]

Not only, in the Court's view, the fundamental interests of liberty, dignity and autonomy are at stake when telephone conversation is recorded, but once the speaker knows that some unwanted listener is also part of the conversation in a passive way, he cannot speak his heart to the one he intends to. This chilling effect on the right of freedom of speech drawn by the infringement of the privacy of communication is also highlighted by the Supreme Court as,

> once any person's telephone is subjected to eavesdropping, tapping, intrusion or interference of any kind, it interferes with the right of free speech and expression.[....] Therefore, the tapping and eavesdropping of telephone also infringes Article 19 which guarantees that every citizen shall have the right to freedom of speech and expression.[34]

The vulnerability of people is not limited to accessing their private information, but any kind of intrusion into their communication will also bring similar negative consequences. Elaborating and justifying the wide scope of the right to life, the Supreme Court emphatically affirmed,

> With this definition of the word 'life' one would not deter to state that telephone-tapping and eavesdropping mar the protection afforded and guaranteed to the right to life. It infringes the secrecy and privacy of a man which may ultimately be *a source of danger and insecurity*. In this way the liberty guaranteed to a person is also invaded, restricted and circumvented. Therefore, if this exercise is to be considered from any angle, be it constitutional, legal or moral, no justification can be afforded for such reprehensible acts by the officials or the persons at the helm of governance of the country. History is replete with incidents when on breach of such rights Governments have been toppled. Not too far is the incident of Watergate when the President of America for conducting and interfering with the telephones

[32]Benazir Bhutto v President of Pakistan, PLD 1998 SC 388.

[33]Benazir Bhutto v President of Pakistan, PLD 1998 Supreme Court 388.

[34]Benazir Bhutto v President of Pakistan, PLD 1998 Supreme Court 388.

> and communication system of the Opposition had to resign and he was thrown out of office.[35]

Reasonable expectation of privacy in the telephonic conversation has been the subject of some famous international privacy cases such as Olmstead v United States, where Justice Brandeis had presented his historic dissent. The Supreme Court of Pakistan has approached the issue in-line with Brandeis dissent and has thus settled the question by ruling that the telephonic communication is constitutionally protected. It held,

> Normally a person talking on telephone always presumes that his voice is heard only by the person at the other end of the telephone. The telephonic system itself presumes that except the speaker and the listener no one else can hear the talks from one end to the other. This ensures privacy and freedom of speech and a person in the presence of others may not be able to talk so freely or to express himself without any restriction or hesitation.[36]

The Supreme Court of Pakistan imposed a precondition on the state authorities that they have to convince a court of law regarding the urgency of surveillance of a particular person. It held:

> It is unlawful to intercept, reveal the existence of and disclose or divulge the contents of, wire or oral communications, unless the interceptor has previously obtained an order of a Court permitting a wiretap or other interception of the communication, or one party has consented to the interception.[37]

The Court further states that phone tapping and eavesdropping are

> reprehensible, immoral, illegal and unconstitutional act[s] which the authorities finding that there is no clear provision to stop it. [Even the government] indulged in such illegal activities. Our Constitution in clear terms gives guarantee against such violation."[38] Therefore, the Court directs the government to regulate phone surveillance trough legislation so that unconditional and inappropriate practices could be curbed. The Court was so much infuriated by the act of ruling party to phone tapping that it turned down the appeal against dissolution of National Assembly by the President of Pakistan, and held that failure to protect fundamental rights alone was a sufficient ground to dissolve the National Assembly.[39]

Benazir Bhutto case is categorized as a landmark privacy case in the sense that the Court has interpreted and concretized to some extent the general expression of Article 14 of the constitution. The text of the constitution does not confer protection to individual privacy and mentions only privacy of home and dignity of man under its protective scheme. This judgment, however, extended the meaning of home and even ruled that the connotation of "home" and "person" is somewhat similar. In other words, both person and her home enjoy constitutional protection for their dignity and privacy. This judgment further dispelled the confusion regarding

---

[35] Benazir Bhutto v President of Pakistan, PLD 1998 Supreme Court 388. Emphasis supplied.

[36] Benazir Bhutto v President of Pakistan, PLD 1998 Supreme Court 388.

[37] Benazir Bhutto v President of Pakistan, PLD 1998 Supreme Court 388.

[38] Benazir Bhutto v President of Pakistan, PLD 1998 Supreme Court 388.

[39] Benazir Bhutto v President of Pakistan, PLD 1998 Supreme Court 388.

illegality of technological interference into someone's privacy and established that eavesdropping with the help of technology is affront to privacy of home and human dignity.

4.2.2.2 Establishing Broad Privacy Protection

In the case of Ghayoor Hussain Shah v. Gharib Alam, Lahore High Court held that the Constitution of Pakistan does not only guarantee the fundamental right to dignity of man and privacy of his home but the right to life and liberty is also an "inalienable" right of every citizen.[40] The Court rejected the English Common Law maxim which says that the reputation of man dies with his death. Rather, the Court broadened the meaning of reputation from the living beings to the deceased persons and held that the legal heirs are eligible to receive damages in such situation.

In another judgment, summarizing the extent of protection available to *life* in jurisprudence, the Chief Justice of Pakistan held,

> Right to life has been explained and interpreted by the Superior Courts in a large number of cases. It includes right to livelihood, right to acquire, hold and dispose of property, and right to acquire suitable accommodation, which could not hang on to fancies of individuals in authority, and includes all those aspects of life which go to make a man's life meaningful, complete and worth living. It implies the right to food, water, decent environment, education, medical care and shelter. A fundamental right cannot be snatched away or waived off pursuant to any agreement.[41]

These assertions make it clear that this right does not mean to be construed as a protection from homicide or bodily injury. Rather it entails all the basic features even a modern man can think of as required for an enjoyable life subject to other provisions of the constitution. In Watan Party case, the Court held, that the term 'life' in the Constitution of Pakistan does not mean to be used in a restricted way, rather *a wide meaning should be given to enable a man not only to sustain life but-to enjoy [life].*[42]

The protection of life under Article 9 is not restricted to merely the protection of 'animal life or vegetative life'.[43] Rather, the right to a clean atmosphere, guaranty to the other fundamental rights, rule of law, and *a right to have clean and incorruptible administration* for good governance as well as *the right to have protection from encroachment on privacy and liberty* come under its wide sphere.[44]

---

[40] Syed Ghayyur Hussain Shah v GharibAlam, PLD 1990 Lahore 432, para 24.

[41] Chief justice Iftikhar Muhammad Chaudhry, PLD 2011 SC 619 (Suo Motu case no 13 of 2009: In the matter of(Action on press clipping from the Daily "Patriot", Islamabad dated 4-7-2009 regarding Joint Venture Agreement between CDA and Multi-Professional Cooperative Housing Society (MPCHS) for development of land in Sector E-11 Islamabad.

[42] Watan Party v Federation of Pakistan etc. Sou Moto case no 16 of 2011, PLD 2011 Supreme Court 997.

[43] Benazir Bhutto v President of Pakistan, PLD 1998 SC 388.

[44] Benazir Bhutto v President of Pakistan, PLD 1998 SC 388.

The Supreme Court of Pakistan considers the right to life as *sine qua non* for the existence of other rights. It expressly mentions that interventions into this right through illegal seizure and search are not only against the spirit of the right to life and human dignity but are also discriminatory and against the principles of equal protection of law conferred by other provisions of the Constitution. In Shehla Zia case, the Supreme Court held,

> The word 'life' is very significant as it covers all facts of human existence. The word 'life' has not been defined in the Constitution but it does not mean nor can it be restricted only to vegetative or animal life or mere existence, from conception to death. Life includes all such amenities and facilities which a person born in a free country, is entitled to enjoy with dignity, legally and constitutionally.[45]

Ghayoor Hussain Shah v. Gharib Alam case has significance due to the fact that it has broadened the meaning of the abstract term "life" mentioned under Article 9 of the Constitution of Pakistan. The protection of "life" ordained in Article 9 includes all those aspects of human life which is essential for the development of their personality such as the right to privacy.

4.2.2.3 Acknowledging Informational Privacy

Protection of personal information is an important aspect of the general right to privacy. With the arrival of modern devices of data storage, computing and transmission of information, it has emerged as a comprehensive interest in its own right called the right to data protection. Its objectives are not only guaranteeing seclusion but also to ensure transparency in the collection, processing and dissemination of data. The right to data protection is meanwhile acknowledged as an important value and a full-fledged fundamental right. Scholars are reconsidering the conventional moral and legal philosophies to cater the regulatory demands of modern technological developments. Currently, data protection debates regarding the formulation, modification and execution of rules and regulations occupy international forums.

In Pakistan, one can find some general but strong remarks of a high court in the case of M.D. Tahir Advocate v. Director State Bank of Pakistan in favor of the protection of informational privacy.[46] In this case, the validity of a circular issued by the State Bank of Pakistan was challenged through a constitutional petition.[47] Lahore High Court declared both the issuance and contents of the circular as invalid and unconstitutional on the basis of not fulfilling the requirement of Articles 9 (right to life and liberty) and 14 (1) (dignity and privacy).

The Court observed:

---

[45] Ms Shehla Zia and Otherrs. v Wapda, PLD 1994 SC 693, para 12.

[46] State Bank of Pakistan is the central bank of Pakistan, regulating monitory system of Pakistan, created through State Bank of Pakistan Act in 1956.

[47] M D Tahir Advocate v Director, State Bank of Pakistan, CLD 2004 Lahore 1680.

> It is to be noticed that "home", "person" and "life" itself have been granted Constitutional protection from State interference. In Constitutional terms, this is said to be the protection of rights of "privacy". It can hardly be denied, that taking of private information without any allegation of wrong doing of ordinary people is an extraordinary invasion of this fundamental right of privacy.[48]

The Court relied on Pakistani and Indian case law which gives a wide meaning to the term 'life'.[49] It held that the impugned circular "clearly violates the basic jurisprudence of "privacy" conceptions germane in Article 14 of the Constitution". Depositing money in the banks demands a safe and secure environment from all types of public and private peering. The Court remarked,

> The deposits in Banks by ordinary people and citizens constitute manifestly the creation of safe and secure environment for their savings in which the State, much less a banking corporation can attempt to pry into. This Article [14 (1)] of the Constitution corresponds to Article 21 of the Indian Constitution that has been held to be crucial to the functioning of a democratic and free society.[50]

Lahore High Court's judgment in M.D. Tahir case provide a foundation to a comprehensive protective regime for informational privacy in general as well as to the rights related to collection, storage, processing and dissemination of personal data.

4.2.2.4 Limits for Interventions Provided by Law

The Supreme Court of Pakistan affirms in a landmark judgment that the fundamental rights to life, liberty, human dignity and privacy of home enshrined in Chapter II of the Constitution cannot be usurped by a provincial legislation.[51] This judgment was awarded while deciding a constitutional reference, submitted by the president of Pakistan under Article 186 of the constitution.[52] The purpose of the presidential reference was to invoke the advisory jurisdiction of the Supreme Court on the constitutionality of various provisions of a provincial assembly's proposed bill.[53]

---

[48] M D Tahir Advocate v Director, State Bank of Pakistan, Lahore, CLD 2004 1680. Emphasis supplied.

[49] For example: The court referred to Indian court case of Kharak Sing v State of U.P. AIR 1963 SC 1295.

[50] M D Tahir Advocate v Director, State Bank of Pakistan, Lahore, CLD 2004 1680.

[51] Reference No. 2 of 2005.

[52] Article 186 is regarding the advisory jurisdiction of Supreme Court of Pakistan, which says, "(1) If, at any time, the President considers that it is desirable to obtain the opinion of the Supreme Court on any question of law which he considers of public importance, he may refer the question to the Supreme Court for consideration. (2) The Supreme Court shall consider a question so referred and report its opinion on the question to the President."

[53] Hisbah Bill was enacted by the provincial government of religious parties' alliance known as MMA on 14th July, 2005. The act was about the establishment of *Hisbah* institution headed by *Muhtasib* (can be loosely translated as Ombudsman), the main objective of which was to enforce good deeds and prevent sinful acts of the citizens.

The Court had to find out whether or not the provisions of the subject bill- sections 10 and 23 in particular- would be violative of the fundamental rights including the right to life, liberty, privacy and dignity.[54] The Supreme Court unanimously declared most of the operative clauses of the bill (including sections 10 and 23) as unconstitutional and in contradiction to constitutional provisions safeguarding fundamental rights.

One can also find case law where court has adopted a nuanced approach to question of reasonable expectation of privacy. "Reasonable expectation of privacy" is a test generally used in privacy cases for the determination of justifiability of the claim. The claimant has to establish that at the time of infringement, her circumstances were such as she could reasonably desire and expect privacy. The actual application of this test varies a lot across jurisdictions. It is sometimes dependent on the public/private bifurcation of the milieu in which the alleged infringement occurs, while at other times, a more expanded treatment may be given. The relevant situation and conduct of the claimant plays a crucial role in such determination. The concept, however, revolves around the question as when a person can or cannot reasonably expect privacy. The High Court of Sindh has declared privacy as "the very basis of a decent living" and does not require the observance of traditional Islamic veil for a woman who wants to protect her bodily privacy from staring of an outsider. She is not bound to strictly observe Islamic veil in order to reasonably or validly expect privacy for herself. Based on this principle, the Court restrained the defendant from construction of a high-rise building and rejected their stance that the plaintiffs have no right to privacy because no hijab-observing woman was living in the vicinity of that building. It held that the defendant's assertion is "*patently erroneous*" because "the right of privacy exists in the most modern and even permissive societies of the West and is the very basis of a decent living."[55] In this judgment, the Court broadened the scope of reasonable expectation of privacy which cannot be permanently diluted even if, at times, somebody voluntarily chooses to compromise her privacy. The right to privacy is thus not limited to an in-house sphere and one can reasonably expect privacy if she or he goes outside to the public places for recreation purposes. Therefore, the High Court of Baluchistan held:

> The Fundamental Right to 'dignity' (Article 14) will also be violated when the users of the Park are holed in within the pit of the Park. Whilst 'privacy of the home' is specifically recognized as a Fundamental Right (Article 14) people in public spaces are also entitled to limited personal space and privacy given the exigencies of the situation and to the extent that it can be ensured. Couples, families or for that matter any person would be deterred from venturing into the Park if every movement of theirs can be monitored. They would thus

[54] Section 10 was about powers and functions of *Muhtasib* (ombudsman) while section 23 gave immense powers to *Muhtasib* titled as "special powers of *Muhtasib*". For example, according to section 23 of the bill, *Muhtasib* shall have the powers to, "monitor adherence of moral values of Islam at public places", and to discourage and check extravagance, dowry, beggary, entertainment shows, indecent behavior and to advise those found disobeying parents.

[55] Akhtar Ahmad Ghori v Messrs Saima Estate developers, 1989 CLC Karachi 2172.

> effectively be discriminated against in respect of access to a public place; yet another Fundamental Right.[56]

The courts have successfully devised principles that support the proportionate approach in the balancing exercise of various rights. It does not pre-suppose the superiority of one right over the other. Neither has it declared that privacy is an absolute value, or that every kind of communication should be protected from surveillance in all circumstances. It keeps open the possibility of interference into privacy if circumstances of the particular case demands so. The Supreme Court allows phone tapping for the purpose of security of the people. It held, "[i]f at all phone tapping or eavesdropping is to be allowed with legal justification, it can be done only when a *grave risk to the security of the country* is involved."[57] Therefore, the Court principally agrees to the balancing of the right to privacy with other countervailing rights such as security of state and its people. These findings can guide us in the formulating of rules for the balancing of free speech with the right to privacy.

Baluchistan High Court requires the state to refrain from intruding into people houses, while the state can do so in certain exceptional circumstances and with the strict compliance to law.[58] However, the nature of law and its promulgation must also be in line with the requirements of the constitutional provisions. Merely the presence of a law is not sufficient and if the application of the said law causes trouble to fundamental rights, it can be declared as null and void. Applying this reasoning, the Supreme Court, in the case of Mehram Ali v. Federation of Pakistan, tested the constitutionality of Section 10 of the Anti-Terrorism Act, 1997, which was empowering a police officer or any other person of the law enforcement, to enter and search any premises on suspicion of the presence of illegal written or recoded material.[59] The Court declared Section 10 as directly in conflict with Article 14 of the Constitution. It held,

> No doubt, that the above right of privacy is subject to law but such law is supposed to be reasonable and in conformity with the constitutional mandate.[60]

The Supreme Court has criticized the violation of privacy in the guise of issuing merely a Statutory Regulatory Order (SRO) by the Government of Pakistan. Condemning telephone tapings and eavesdropping as "reprehensible, immoral, illegal and unconstitutional act", the apex Court held that the government must have legal justification for telephone taping and eavesdropping, e.g. in case of grave

---

[56] Chamber Of Commerce and Industry Quetta Balochistan v Director-General Quetta Development Authority, PLD 2012 Quetta 31.

[57] Benazir Bhutto v President of Pakistan, PLD 1998 SC 388. Emphasis supplied.

[58] Ghulam Hussain v Additional Sessions Judge, Dera Allah Yar, PLD 2010 Quetta 21: "It is in only certain exceptional circumstances that the privacy of the home can be violated and to do so strict compliance with the applicable law has to be made."

[59] Mehram Ali and others v Federation of Pakistan and others, PLD 1998 SC 1445.

[60] Mehram Ali and others v Federation of Pakistan and others, PLD 1998 SC 1445.

threat to the security of Pakistan.[61] The issuance of executive orders under some law does not legitimize telephone tapping, if the supervision is not justified with the protection of another vital interest, such as grave threat to national security.

4.2.2.5 Summary

In the nutshell, courts in Pakistan have set effective precedents for the policy makers. Through their judgments, the courts have issued restraining orders for the governmental, institutional, corporate or individual actions that were deemed to be violative of the right to privacy. The jurisprudence in Pakistan has highlighted the sensitivity of the issue of privacy and endorses it as a valuable interest. The higher courts have expressed appreciation of privacy in the strongest possible words. Connecting of privacy with the right to life and dignity of man in the judgments shows that judges recognize the inherent value of privacy. On the other hand, one can also find decisions which explain the importance of privacy for the attainment of certain other important goals such as the violation of privacy brings psychological and personality related negative effects. In the case of M.D. Tahir advocate v Director, State Bank of Pakistan, Lahore High Court affirmed, "when one's most private details are taken, it affects the life of the person making him potentially vulnerable and insecure."[62]

The guidelines set by higher courts and the Supreme Court of Pakistan have not been utilized by the concerned authorities to develop legislative and regulatory structure for privacy rights' enforcement. In the absence of a comprehensive privacy law, the constitutional text and jurisprudence developed by courts are nothing more than fragments that need further elaboration. However, the textual mention of dignity and privacy as well as the pro-privacy judgments has made the general legal scheme as conducive to the promulgation of full-fledged privacy legislation.

---

[61] It may be noted here that telephone taping of judges and other important offices was one of the reasons claimed in defense of the dissolution of National assembly by the then President of Pakistan, Mr. Farooq Ahmad Khan Laghari. Supreme Court rejected the petitions filed against that dissolution order, and strongly condemned Intelligence Bureau's (comes under authority of PM) eavesdropping. The court also talked about Watergate scandal which resulted in the collapse of Nixon government.

[62] M D Tahir Advocate v Director, State Bank of Pakistan, CLD 2004Lahore 1680.

4.3 The Constitutional Framework for the Right to Free Speech in Pakistan

4.3.1 Anchors in the Constitution

The Constitution of Pakistan provides the right to free speech to every citizen under Article 19:

> Every citizen shall have the right to freedom of speech and expression, and there shall be freedom of the press, subject to any reasonable restrictions imposed by law in the interest of the glory of Islam or the integrity, security or defence of Pakistan or any part thereof, friendly relations with foreign States, public order, decency or morality, or in relation to contempt of court, commission of or incitement to an offence.

Just like the right to privacy of home, the constitution expressly mentions freedom of speech, expression and freedom of the press. These freedoms are subject to the constitutional restrictions, which apart from being reasonable must have a legal cover in the form of legislation. The interests mentioned in the provisos are all belong to the category of the so called 'public interest', state's interest or societal interest. However, the individual rights could be safeguarded from abuse of the right to free speech under the broad limitation of decency and morality or when those interests are protected by a speaking law. The right to privacy may only countervail this right if there would be a comprehensive legislation on privacy, which expressly defines and enshrines privacy related interests. Such a privacy law would work as a tool for balancing free speech with the right to privacy.

4.3.2 Importance of Free Speech in the Pakistani Jurisprudence

The constitutional jurisprudence of free speech developed by higher courts of Pakistan highlights the importance of free speech and press freedom at one hand and emphasizes the responsibility this right entails on the other hand. The Supreme Court of Pakistan has termed freedom of the press as "the mother of all liberties in a democratic society", and considers it as an essential part of the democratic system because of its role in maintaining checks on the governmental authorities by bringing to public knowledge the transgressions of their legal mandate.[63] Article 19 encases the right to participate in a dialogue without the fear of state interference and the right to remain silent, too.[64] Most of the fundamental rights, including the right to free speech, enshrined in the constitution of Pakistan are both positive and negative rights.

---

[63] Ms Benazir Bhutto v News Publications (pvt) Ltd 2000 CLC Karachi 904.

[64] Province of Sindh v MQM, PLD 2014 SC 531.

The Supreme Court has stated that the communications business derives its sanctity from the constitutional guaranties to the freedom of speech and the right to access to information of public importance.[65] Being a custodian of the viewers' and broadcasters' rights, it is the duty of Pakistan Electronic Media Regulatory Authority (PEMRA) to enforce the rights of free speech and access to information in letter and spirit. PEMRA is authorized to take strict measures, such as cancelling the licenses of television channels or cable operators if they do not perform their *constitutional and legal obligation* of broadcasting in the public interest or violate laws of the land.[66]

Lahore High Court has expressed its understanding of the difference between "speech" and "action" and has recognized their mutual distinction also. Accordingly, the expression of dislike or reservations against a polity does not amount to a crime unless there is a proof of some action to that effect.[67] The constitutional right to free speech was exalted to the extent that even an advocacy for the abolition of territorial sovereignty of Pakistan was declared as a protected speech if such expression does not amount to violent measures.

Peshawar High Court has discussed the justifications of free speech on the basis of its instrumental value. The Court acknowledges the utilitarian value of free speech with reference to the establishment of a peaceful, orderly and just society, where people have a feeling of living in freedom with a constitutional guaranty and assurance of greater security.[68] The Court in an emphatic manner describes all the essential circumstances for an effective exercise of the free speech right, including respecting the privacy of the speaker to enable him speak his heart.

> The police and the people in authority must change their outlook now and stop the unnecessary harassment of the people by censoring the letters of the citizens of Pakistan, tapping their telephones, and keeping a watch on their activities except in the case of the known traitors and treason-mongers because that amounts to the negation of the fundamental right guaranteed to the people by the Constitution. Freedom of expression of one's views is a gift of the Constitution, and it cannot be abridged by the people in authority so long as it is not intended to create a chaos in the country or disrupt or destroy it. [. . .] A man is entitled to his opinion and is within his right to express it. The citizens of Pakistan are free and they must be allowed to live in freedom and the law of the land should conform to this freedom.[69]

The right to freedom of speech and press includes the right to hold opinion and the right to express the opinion in verbal or written form as well as the right to communicate that opinion through any other means. Freedom of the press enshrined in Article 19 protects the right to publish whatever one pleases with unless it transgresses the constitutional limits. Therefore, publication of newspaper must be

---

[65] Dr Shahid Masood v Federation of Pakistan, 2010 SCMR 1849.

[66] Dr Shahid Masood v Federation of Pakistan, 2010 SCMR 1849. Regarding PEMRA, see also Sect. 2.2.

[67] The State v Abdul Ghafar Khan PLD 1957 (W.P.) Lahore 142.

[68] Hussain Bakhsh Kausar v The State PLD 1958 (W.P.) Peshawar 15.

[69] Hussain Bakhsh Kausar v The State PLD 1958 (W.P.) Peshawar 15.

protected and facilitated, otherwise the freedom of press would become a "mockery and delusory".[70]

The Constitution of Pakistan authorises the State to take regulatory measures as a matter of public policy. However, any kind of statutory regulation of speech and press must pass the constitutional test of "reasonableness". For instance, it is "reasonable" to legally require a newspaper to be published on a regular basis in order to prevent it from yellow journalism and blackmailing, while requiring the publisher to ensure his financial viability in the shape of depositing a huge amount of cash as "security" is not a reasonable restriction because it can prevent an intelligent and qualified person from publishing a newspaper.[71] Any such legal and regulatory restriction, which is imposed in a way as to harm the purpose of constitutional protection of the freedom of the press would be unconstitutional.[72] Similarly, it is the obligation of the state institutions to act in a manner, which is supportive with respect to upholding constitutional guaranties including free press.

Article 19 provides limitations of the right to free expression. However, these restrictions must pass the test of reasonableness and overriding public interest.[73] According to Supreme Court of Pakistan,

> Restriction can be imposed and freedom of expression may be curtailed provided it is justified by the "clear and present danger" test that the substantive evil must be extremely serious and the degree of imminence extremely high. The danger should "imminently threaten immediate interference with the lawful and pressing purposes of the law" requiring immediate step to ensure security of the country. Speech would be unlawful if it is directed to inciting or producing imminent lawless action and is likely to produce such action. Speech and conduct are two different concepts. Speech relates to expression and conduct to action. Speech ends where conduct begins but if both are combined the Court has to draw the dividing line. The freedom of expression of views is curtailed or restricted when they threaten clearly and imminently to ripen into conduct against which the public has a right to protect itself.[74]

Mere fear of serious injury is not a justification for the suppression of freedom of speech and there must be reasonable ground that the speech, if practiced, would bring serious evil, and that the feared danger is imminent. The Supreme Court of Pakistan held,

> In order to support a finding of clear and present danger it must be shown either that immediate -serious violence was to be expected or was advocated, or that the past conduct furnished reason to believe that such advocacy was then contemplated. [.....] The effect, weight and impact of speech is to be judged from an overall appreciation by looking to its background, the truthful statement made in it and object with which it has been made. If such a speech makes allegation or defames anyone without any justification, but does not create

[70] Muzaffar Qadir v The district magistrate, Lahore PLD 1975 Lahore 1198.

[71] Muhammad Rafiq Meer v Government of the Punjab PLD 1989 Lahore 12.

[72] Muzaffar Qadir v The district magistrate, Lahore PLD 1975 Lahore 1198: "The Constitutional guarantee of liberty of the press is one of the strongest bulwarks of liberty and any order which violates the freedom of the press would be unconstitutional and void."

[73] Mian Muhammad Nawaz Sharif v President of Pakistan, PLD 1993 SC 473.

[74] Mian Muhammad Nawaz Sharif v President of Pakistan, PLD 1993 SC 473.

lawlessness, disorder, or threat to security or disruption, it will hardly amount to subversion of the Constitution.[75]

The case law related to freedom of expression confirms the importance of this fundamental right and attempts to explore its different levels of protection. Freedom of expression is a crucial rights and the state cannot abridge it on the basis of anticipatory harm. The courts have mentioned "clear and present danger" as a test to justify interference with this right. Furthermore, regulation of the media for an effective exercise of free speech is duly allowed under the constitutional scheme of free speech.

4.3.3 Limitations on Free Speech

Just like many other fundamental right, the right to free speech, freedom of expression and freedom of the press are not absolute rights. These rights entail both kinds of limitations, i.e. firstly specific limitations which have been mentioned in expressed terms; and secondly, limitations which have been derived by the courts from the general restrictions such as reasonability, decency and morality. As the constitution allows for imposing restrictions on Article 19 right to freedom of expression, there are many legal rules in various panel provisions which criminalize certain expressions. For example, the form of speech that can be criminalized in Pakistan includes condemnation of the creation of the State of Pakistan,[76] inducing students to take part in political activities,[77] sale, publication and distribution of obscene books, objects, songs,[78] and the speech covered by criminal defamation provisions.[79]

4.3.3.1 Limitations Expressly Mentioned in the Constitution

4.3.3.1.1 The Glory of Islam

Pakistan is an Islamic Republic and Islam is state religion with many Islamic law penal and civil flavors in its legal system. Therefore, the right to free speech and freedom of expression is subject to the "glory of Islam". The constitutional limitation has been concretized through criminal law and Pakistan Penal Code criminalizes the act or speech of outraging religious feelings of citizens with up to ten years

[75] Mian Muhammad Nawaz Sharif v President of Pakistan, PLD 1993 SC 473.

[76] Section 123-A Pakistan Penal Code 1860.

[77] Section 153-B Pakistan Penal Code 1860.

[78] Sections 292–294 of Pakistan Penal Code 1860.

[79] See for details: Nyazee (2009).

imprisonment.[80] The law also provides for death punishment, life imprisonment and fine for a person who uses derogatory remarks against the Holy Prophet Muhammad.[81] Uttering of words with an intention of wounding religious feelings is also punishable with one-year imprisonment.[82] The normative discussion on the existence, promulgation or the historical background of the making of these laws is outside the purview of this book. However, it is argued that these laws work as a serious prohibition for freedom of speech. Blasphemy laws are,

> essentially a category of prohibitive laws that are meant to curtail certain kinds of speech and hence raise fundamental questions of freedom of speech, as well as of legitimate arenas of state proscription of certain kinds of speech for certain public interest and policy imperatives.[83]

Apart from the fact that the blasphemy law is widely abused, a variety of expressions—from casual conversation to a sticker on motorcycle—have been impugned as blasphemous in the lower courts but the majority of the accused were released at the trial stage.[84] Most importantly, although speech remained to be the central point of judicial discussions, the constitutional protection available to free speech has never been discussed in blasphemy cases.[85] It seems that the courts are absolutely convinced that religious sentiments are a supreme value which cannot be exposed to a balancing exercise during adjudication. Whenever the question of constitutionality of blasphemy laws has been put to the court, it has been straightaway rejected. The constitutional principles such as freedoms of religion and speech have never been successful to stay firm before blasphemous speech or conduct during the process of judicial balancing.[86]

The courts on some occasions have expressed a kind of anger against social media due to the presence of 'blasphemous material' and even have categorically said that the whole social media could be blocked in Pakistan if the trend continued.[87]

An analysis of case law shows that the courts have refrained from the principle of balancing free speech with religious ideals of 'glory of Islam'. No free speech justification could prevail against the interest of Muslim community in preserving

[80] Pakistan Penal Code, Section 295-A: "Whoever, with deliberate and malicious intention of outraging the 'religious feelings of any class of the citizens of Pakistan, by words, either spoken or written, or by visible representations insults the religion or the religious beliefs of that class, shall be punished with imprisonment of either description for a term which may extend to ten years, or with fine, or with both."

[81] Pakistan Penal Code, Section 295-C.

[82] Pakistan Penal Code, Section 298.

[83] Siddique and Hayat (2008), p. 307.

[84] Siddique and Hayat (2008), pp. 322–327.

[85] Siddique and Hayat (2008), pp. 373–377.

[86] Siddique and Hayat (2008), pp. 376–377: "Section 295-C remains unassailed on fundamental rights grounds, in contexts where allegedly blasphemous speech may be actually valid academic or general discussion and dialogue, potentially garnering protection from Article 19".

[87] Shehzad (2017).

their religious sensitivity. Due to this reason, the test of "clear and present danger" has not been applied in cases where blasphemy is the issue. The importance of freedom of expression is thus reflected primarily in judgments involving political speech, the kind of speech that requires strong protection.

4.3.3.1.2 Contempt of Court

Article 19 of the Constitution of Pakistan does not protect speech if it amounts to contempt of court. Article 204 of the constitution empowers the Supreme Court and high courts to award punishments to any person who, "abuses, interferes with or obstructs the process of the Court in any way or disobeys any order of the Court; scandalizes the Court or otherwise does anything which tends to bring the Court or a Judge of the Court into hatred, ridicule or contempt; c. does anything which tends to prejudice the determination of a matter pending before the Court; or does any other thing which, by law, constitutes contempt of the Court....".

Regarding contempt of court, the Supreme Court sets the limits as,

> Fair comments about the general working of the Court made in good faith in the public interest and in temperate language, and fair comments on the merits of a decision of a Court made after the pendency of the proceedings in a case in good faith and in temperate language without impugning the integrity or impartiality of the Judge, shall not amount to the commission of contempt of Court.[88]

The Court held that the contempt of court under Article 204 must be interpreted in conjunction with the Article 19 of free speech and Article 66 of the free speech privilege for members of parliament. The free speech and press freedom should not cross the limits to commit contempt of court. It is, however, no wrong to criticize the judge's public role in good faith keeping in view the due administration of justice because, "Justice being not a cloistered virtue same must be allowed to suffer the scrutiny and respect even through outspoken comments of ordinary man".[89] The court stressed on the need to obtain a balance between the objectives of free speech at one hand and the respect for judiciary on the other hand. It held:

> No doubt that there exists freedom of speech and press, whereby right of expression and publication of opinion are duly guaranteed by the Constitution. However, such rights are controlled and regulated by other provisions of the Constitution. Besides, it is an established principle of justice and fair play that a person is normally free to exercise the right in the manner and to the extent that same does not directly affect or injure any other person. Therefore, limitations placed by the Constitutional provisions and law to freedom of speech or press must be exercised and cannot be overlooked. The person seeking Constitutional protection must simultaneously display his feeling in temperate language without causing scandalization or mala fides or disrespect to any person or institution.[90]

[88] Syed Masroor Ahsan v Ardeshir Cowasjee PLD 1998 SC 823.

[89] Syed Masroor Ahsan v Ardeshir Cowasjee PLD 1998 SC 823.

[90] Syed Masroor Ahsan v Ardeshir Cowasjee PLD 1998 SC 823.

Thus, the court set all the persons associated to newspapers such as journalists, editors and publishers under an obligation to choose a language which is not 'strikingly pungent', or "which smacks of loud bitterness or aimed at emitting intemperate expression or abnormal understanding suggesting scandalization of the Court or cause obstruction to the impartial administration of justice."[91]

On the other hand, the Court has taken a liberal stance and avoids actionably for a bonafide false expression of opinion if it proves to be in the public interest. The defendants in such false but honest speech were held not liable under the entitlement of 'qualified privilege which the newspapers enjoy under Article 19 of the Constitution."[92]

4.3.3.2 Derived Limitations

The jurisprudential principles of free speech revolve around the concept of right with a corresponding responsibility. The Courts expect the journalists to exercise their right of free speech and freedom of the press with utmost care. The abstract terms of "decency" and "morality" provide the opportunity to the courts to derive further limitations of free speech and explain concrete issues under the ambit of the constitutional order.

Article 19 provides both the right to free speech and freedom of the press, but it does not mean that the press has some special right as compared to ordinary citizens. The Supreme Court of Pakistan categorically held,

> The freedom of press is only a specific instance of general right of freedom of speech; persons engaged in newspaper business, cannot claim any other or greater right than that possessed by the persons not in that business. Furthermore the freedom of press is not absolute, unlimited and unfettered. The protective cover of press freedom must not be thrown open for wrong doings.[93]

The press has an obligation to society to work responsibly and must not transgress the constitutional limitations of public order, decency and morality. No defence of good faith will be invoked by media persons in the case of an irresponsible conduct while exercising their due right of fair comment.

> Function/duty of a free press is to act as a watchdog and to disseminate correct and fair accounts of the various *public* events and of other matters in which public may be vitally interested. In the discharge of the above function/duty there may be some occasional lapses on their part which are to be condoned, provided the same do not fall within the ambit of reckless or irresponsible conduct or prompted by malice or any other ulterior motive. The press besides relying upon Article 19 of the Constitution which provides that every citizen shall have the right of freedom of speech and expression and there shall be freedom of press subject to any reasonable restrictions imposed by law which includes contempt law, may

---

[91] Syed Masroor Ahsan v Ardeshir Cowasjee PLD 1998 SC 823.

[92] Sheikh Muhammad Rashid v Majid Nizami PLD 2002 SC 514.

[93] Syed Masroor Ahsan v Ardeshir Cowasjee PLD 1998 SC 823.

press into service Article 18 of the Constitution which guarantees freedom of trade, business or profession.[94]

The constitutional provision for the right to freedom of speech imposes some broad-based duties on the exercise of this right at the same time. If this article is compared with Article 19 of ICCPR[95] or Article 10 of ECHR,[96] the later provisions also limit free speech with the imposition of duty but in both cases, these limitations must be "necessary". The term "reasonable restrictions" is broad and can be interpreted in an open-ended manner.

The elaboration of scope, limitation, and status of free speech by Pakistani higher courts shows that by no means the protection under Article 19 is boundless. The courts have categorically stated that the press cannot claim some any superior value in upholding its, right and has also eluded that the freedom to do business can be a more appropriate interest in some cases. Freedom of the press is only a 'specific instance' of the broad right to free speech and so every intervention would not amount to free speech violation. Similarly, the expressions such as acting in a responsible way, and speech which is directed to any kind of 'lawless' action, is not protected according to the above case law.

[94] Syed Masroor Ahsan v Ardeshir Cowasjee PLD 1998 SC 823.

[95] ICCPR Article 19: 1. Everyone shall have the right to hold opinions without interference. 2. Everyone shall have the right to freedom of expression; this right shall include freedom to seek, receive and impart information and ideas of all kinds, regard less of frontiers, either orally, in writing or in print, in the form of art, or through any other media of his choice. 3. The exercise of the rights provided for in paragraph 2 of this article carries with it special duties and responsibilities. It may therefore be subject to certain restrictions, but these shall only be such as are provided by law and are necessary: *(a)* For respect of the rights or reputations of others; *(b)* For the protection of national security or of public order *(ordre public),* or of public health or morals.

[96] ECHR Article 10: 1. Everyone has the right to freedom of expression. This right shall include freedom to hold opinions and to receive and impart information and ideas without interference by public authority and regardless of frontiers. This Article shall not prevent States from requiring the licensing of broadcasting, television or cinema enterprises. 2. The exercise of these freedoms, since it carries with it duties and responsibilities, may be subject to such formalities, conditions, restrictions or penalties as are prescribed by law and are necessary in a democratic society, in the interests of national security, territorial integrity or public safety, for the prevention of disorder or crime, for the protection of health or morals, for the protection of the reputation or rights of others, for preventing the disclosure of information received in confidence, or for maintaining the authority and impartiality of the judiciary.

4.4 Conclusion: The Need to Bring Privacy Principles Out of the Closet[97]

The analysis of the constitutional regime for the enforcement of fundamental rights brings us to make certain conclusions which will assist us in fulfilling the prime objective of this research. Regarding the general framework of constitutional rights, the courts have interpreted the enshrined expressions such as protection of person's life, human dignity and privacy of home in a liberal manner. Apparently, the courts have focused on the protection of these values rather than to tangle themselves in linguistic labyrinths. The offering of a very broad meaning to the right to privacy poses no jurisprudential impediment for applying our conceptual framework. Has it not been the case, it would have been a theoretical impossibility to counter the narrow views of the courts because Pakistan is common law country and the doctrine of *stare decises* is strictly followed.[98] The black letter law is always viewed in terms of how the courts have interpreted that, and in the words of US Supreme Court justice Charles Evans Hughes, *the Constitution is what the judges say it is.*[99] Hence, there is no difficulty in deriving a broad meaning from jurisprudence where the rights and values of dignity of man and privacy of home have been sufficiently elaborated in a generous manner.

An important feature of the fundamental rights' enforcement in Pakistan is that these rights have a horizontal effect and are not only enforceable against the state but also against the private individuals and entities. The jurisprudence pertaining to the judicial review of legislative and executive function of the state draws on the primacy of constitutional rights and categorically holds that no fundamental right should be left unenforced just because of the fact that the infringer is a private party. This feature gives us the opportunity to extend our conceptual framework, which considers privacy as a fundamental right, on the breaches of privacy rights either by private individuals (such as journalists) or by private entities (such as media and newspaper outlets).

The Constitution of Pakistan provides the right to free speech and expression as well as freedom of the media in its Article 19, but the right is not absolute and the same Article provides limitations on the speech. Any speech which crosses the boundary of constitutional limitations is not a protected speech. The jurisprudence, in the most unequivocal term, rejects the notion of absolute and unbridled speech. Two aspects of the free speech jurisprudence need to be highlighted here. The restrictions on free speech are to protect community rights or, in other words, the state or public interest (i.e. free speech is subject to glory of Islam, security of the state and societal morality). On the other hand, we did not find any useful guidance

[97] Andrew Jay McClurg used this expression in a well cited article about American law. See McClurg (1994).

[98] See generally: Munir (2014).

[99] http://c250.columbia.edu/c250_celebrates/remarkable_columbians/charles_hughes.html. Accessed 26 August 2023.

that how the free speech defence would be scaled against private interests, such as when the content of speech is based on the private information of a person.

A survey of the constitutional regime for the protection of privacy interests reveals the significant deficit where such cherished concepts have no value in the practical realm. The protection available is illusory and needs serious attention to make it available to the common people who suffer privacy problems on a daily basis. These principles need to see the light of the day, and they would only see such light if privacy violations become actionable claims, beyond condemnable diabolic actions. Apart from the constitutional broad and abstract principles, the analysis of the legal regime shows that no legal dispensation is available to the people for the protection of their right to privacy. There are various laws rules and measures which are completely inadequate; both conceptually and practically, for their application on privacy related infringements.[100]

The legal lacuna calls for an urgent attention of the policy makers to fill it with a general privacy law. Before recommending the adequate protective legal regime for privacy, it will be helpful to see how privacy rights evolved in other jurisdictions and that how they tackled the issues related to reconciling free speech with privacy.

References

Hussain Dr F (1993) Public interest litigation. working Paper series no 5, SDPI Islamabad

McClurg AJ (1994) Bringing privacy law out of the closet: a tort theory of liability for intrusions in public places. NCL Rev 73:989

Munir Dr M (2014) Precedent in Pakistani law. Oxford University Press

Nyazee IHK (2009) Media law in Pakistan. Federal Law House Rawalpindi

Siddique O, Hayat Z (2008) Unholy speech and holy laws: Blasphemy laws in Pakistan-controversial origins, design defects, and free speech implications. Minn J Int Law 17:303

[100] See Chap. 7 for a detailed survey regarding privacy related statutes and their respective short comings in their application against privacy infringements.

Chapter 5
Reconciling the Freedom of Expression with the Right to Privacy: Protecting Private Life from Media Invasions Under the ECHR

The foregoing chapters have sufficiently explored the problems of privacy, its conceptual underpinnings, and the absence of operative legal norms in Pakistan for its comprehensive protection. These considerations highlight the failure of the Pakistani legal system to provide protection to the right to privacy against media intrusions. It has become clear by now from the instances of media intrusions that every aspect of human life is vulnerable to get exposed to the public at large. Sufficient evidence has been produced in the form of describing actual contents of different television programs which ascertains the seriousness of the problem of privacy rights' enforcement in Pakistan. The extensive literature review on the concept of privacy certainly verifies that privacy is a crucial human right. The importance of its value is supported by many moral, philosophical as well as instrumental arguments. These conceptual and scholarly writings provide useful guidance for setting parameters to analyze the existing privacy law regimes and their respective effectiveness in a comparative manner. The lessons learned from our analysis will enable us to set standards for a prescriptive model of privacy protection in the shape of devising proposals for an effective legal reform in Pakistan.

As earlier stated, analysis of Pakistani constitutional framework reveals the immense importance of privacy which has been one of the core values connected to the right to life. However, the widespread prevalence of media intrusions into the privacy of citizens show that there exist a wide gap in the protective legal enforcement of the right to privacy and its associated interests. These findings demand a legal response to the problem. Therefore, further research is required, using comparative law methodology, in order to find out how the right to privacy is protected in other legal regimes. Since the European Convention on Human Rights (ECHR) is an overarching international convention that many contracting states have ratified, its norms and jurisprudential principles, as interpreted and applied by the European Court of Human Rights (ECtHR), may offer a valuable resource in terms of guiding principles for the proposed privacy law reform in Pakistan. In order to explore this hypothesis more closely, this chapter presents illustrative cases decided by ECtHR in

S. Aftab, *Comparative Perspectives on the Right to Privacy*, Ius Gentium: Comparative Perspectives on Law and Justice 109,
https://doi.org/10.1007/978-3-031-45575-9_5

which the nature of privacy infringements is comparable to the problems of privacy in Pakistan discussed in Chap. 2. The correlation of Pakistani problems with European solutions would sufficiently justify the relevance of ECtHR for comparative law research. The chapter introduces the jurisdiction of the ECHR and its catalogue of human rights, the ECtHR as authoritative court and the impact mechanisms the human rights established in the ECHR and the decisions of the ECtHR have. We will examine the substance and obligations of these human rights and then look more closely to Article 8 of ECHR which grants every person the right to respect for his or her private and family life, home and correspondence. The last part explores how this right is balanced against other countervailing rights and what balancing rules and criteria the ECtHR has established in its case law to reconcile the right to privacy with the freedom of expression.

5.1 An Overview of Illustrative Cases of Privacy Protection Under the Convention

A cursory look to some cases where the ECtHR provided relief to the victims of press intrusions attracts every researcher to dig deep into such system of protection. For instance, the European Court of Human Rights has set limits for the reporting of rape incidents and subsequent abortions and has held that the assessed intrusion into the victim's privacy was unjustifiable.[1] The Convention provides protection to vulnerable individuals in an effective way as the ECtHR has relaxed the condition of public hearing under the fair trial rule in order to enable them to keep their privacies protected from media and public curiosity.[2] The jurisprudence of the ECtHR has contributed in the development of a concept of *responsible journalism* in the shape of setting legal norms, which the media is required to follow in their newsgathering activities as well as in the publication of sensitive news stories.[3] In the case of Pedersen v Denmark, the Court instructed the journalists to take due care in reporting their stories, refrain from conjectures and make sufficient inquiry to ascertain the truth before they send something to the press.[4]

Another contribution of the ECtHR towards the protection of the right to privacy is that it has rejected the concept of *zero privacy* when the subject is either in the public space or when she or he is a public figure. In the case of von Hannover v Germany No. 1, the Court considered these concepts in a detailed manner and held that public figures have also a right to their privacy and that the exercise of this right

---

[1] See for instance: ECHR, *P. and S. v. Poland*, judgment of 30 October 2012. Application No. 57375/08.

[2] ECHR, *B. and P. v. UK,* judgment of 24 April 2001. Applications No. 36337/97 and 35974/97.

[3] Arden (2015), pp. 242–254.

[4] Pedersen v. Denmark (2006) 42 EHRR 24 as cited in Arden (2015), p. 244.

would not require them to remain inside their homes.[5] This nuanced approach has not only enabled the actual complainants to get remedy for their harm but has also effectively impacted the member states' privacy protection.

5.2 Relevance of European Convention on Human Rights as a Privacy Protection Regime Model

5.2.1 Background of ECHR

The European Convention on Human Rights (ECHR)[6] is a significant International law document, which regulates human rights in most of the European countries. It is an important human rights treaty between the member states of the regional organization called Council of Europe (CoE). This treaty was originally conceived and initiated by ten of the total fourteen member states of the Council of Europe. The Convention was opened for signature on 4th November, 1950 in Rome and came into force on 3rd September, 1953.[7]

The ECHR has the privilege of being the first instrument to give effect to certain rights provided in the Universal Declaration of Human Rights (UDHR) by accruing a binding character to the codified human rights.[8] The Convention refers to the UDHR expressly in its preamble and considers the aim of the UDHR as *securing the universal and effective recognition and observance of the Rights* declared therein. Functionally, the Convention can be compared with the national constitutional jurisdictions, and due to this reason, some commentators qualify it as a *European Fundamental Rights Constitution*, while the European Court of Human Rights also uses the expression of "constitutional instrument of European Public Order".[9] Another important international human rights law instrument is the International Covenant on Civil and Political Rights (ICCPR) of 1966, which more specifically provides human rights and enforces them through international law instruments. Most of the European states have signed and ratified the ICCPR. In order to bring the Convention up to the standards set by ICCPR, the 7th Protocol of ECHR has inserted many human rights which are in line with those standards.

---

[5] ECHR, *Von Hannover v Germany*, Judgment of 24 September 2004. Application No. 59320/00.

[6] Formally known as the Convention for the Protection of Human Rights and Fundamental Freedoms and abbreviated as ECHR. For details: https://www.echr.coe.int/documents/convention_engpdf. Accessed 26 August 2023.

[7] See for the drafting history and development of human rights protection through the ECHR: Ehlers and Becker (2007), pp. 2–10.

[8] See for relevant details about Convention, additional Protocols, and related information: https://www.echr.coe.int/Pages/home.aspx?p=basictexts&c=#n1373906329495859950365_pointer. Accessed 28 August 2023.

[9] Ehlers and Becker (2007), p. 2. Footnotes omitted.

Therefore, the ECHR has more than a regional character as it takes the international human rights law into consideration and the guarantees provided as such meet the standards of universal human rights.[10]

As of now, the Convention rules over approximately 820 million people of 47 jurisdictions, having diverse national legal systems and cultures.[11] Adjudicating and enforcing human rights in such a diverse legal environment make it particularly valuable for a comparative analysis because it will be easy for Pakistan to borrow the pliable legal principles developed by ECtHR for the consumption of all member states.

5.2.2 Establishment of ECtHR and Enforcement of Human Rights Under the Convention

5.2.2.1 Catalogue of Human Rights Under the Convention

The ECHR provides a comprehensive catalogue of human rights and freedoms along with the associated warranties. In section 1 Article 2, it provides protection to the right to life and bans depriving someone of his life extra-judicially. However, clause 2 of Article 2 provides the possibility of lawfulness of the deprivation of life in the event of an absolute necessity as when it is undertaken in self-defense, in the process of arresting someone and in order to quell riots or insurgency. Articles 3 and 4 prohibit torture, slavery and forced labor. Article 5 provides everyone the liberty and security of his person subject to lawful detention as a result of conviction after a fair trial or when it is necessary to bring somebody before the competent authority on reasonable suspicion of criminality to prevent him from absconding. In the case of minor, the educational objectives of detention are also a valid ground. Similarly, the detention of persons suffering from infectious diseases, unsound mind, and addicts is also lawful. Clause 5 further provides the remedy of compensation to persons who are detained in violation of the procedure of the Convention. Article 6 provides the right to fair trial by impartial forum within reasonable time. This article has an important proviso regarding the publicity of trial proceedings.[12] The subsequent para enshrines the presumption of innocence of a person unless proven guilty and that provides that merely charging someone does not make him a criminal or convict. Accused persons are entitled to some basic rights such as the right to be informed, to

---

[10] See for the discussion of universal and regional human rights regime: Ehlers and Becker (2007), pp. 25–32.

[11] See for more details: https://www.coe.int/en/web/portal/home. Accessed 28 August 2023.

[12] Article 6 ECHR: "Judgment shall be pronounced publicly but the press and public may be excluded from all or part of the trial in the interests of morals, public order or national security in a democratic society, where the interests of juveniles or the protection of the private life of the parties so require, or to the extent strictly necessary in the opinion of the court in special circumstances where publicity would prejudice the interests of justice."

defend oneself, right of legal representation, and other ancillary rights. Article 7 is the recognition of the Latin maxim, *Nulla poena sine lege*, and it forbids the awarding of punishment greater than the penalty applicable at the time when the offence was forbidden. However, it does not mean that any brutality can go unpunished because of the absence of law. Article 7 (2) enshrines the principle that in the case of brutal crimes, the general principles of criminal law as recognized by civilized nations shall be applicable.

Article 8 recognizes the right of everyone "to respect for his private and family life, his home and his correspondence". It also prevents the public authority from interference into this right except under the specific conditions enumerated under Article 8 (2) of the Convention. Article 10 provides the right to freedom of expression and its associated rights such as "the freedom to hold opinions and to receive and impart information and ideas". The right to freedom of expression is not absolute and the Convention attaches not only "duties and responsibilities" but it may also be restricted under some conditions enumerated in Article 10(2). Article 9 enshrines the right to freedom of thought, conscience and religion: "Everyone has the right to freedom of thought, conscience and religion; this right includes freedom to change his religion or belief and freedom, either alone or in community with others and in public or private, to manifest his religion or belief, in worship, teaching, practice and observance." There is no bar on the freedom of thought and conscience or on the professing of one or the other religion. These rights and freedoms have an absolute nature under the Convention, however, the *manifestation* of religion and belief is subject to those legal limitations, which are necessary for the maintenance of democratic society and public safety such as health, morals, as well as *for the protection of rights and freedoms of others*. Article 11 provides the right to freedom of peaceful assembly and association and it is subject to similar lawful restrictions. Article 13 is important for the effectiveness of Convention's rights and provides 'teeth' to other rights in the form of connecting the rights to their respective remedies. It says, "Everyone whose rights and freedoms as set forth in this Convention are violated shall have an effective remedy before a national authority notwithstanding that the violation has been committed by persons acting in an official capacity."[13] Regarding the personal scope of human rights in the Convention, its enjoyment is equally available to everybody without discrimination under Article 14. However, it does not mean that member states cannot prevent alien from political activity and their right to free expression, assembly and equal protection can be restricted by high contracting parties.[14]

The important guarantees through Additional Protocols added to the substantive Articles of the Convention.[15] These additional guarantees include the protection of

[13] Article 13 ECHR.

[14] See: Article 14 and 16 ECHR.

[15] For detail information regarding Additional Protocols to the ECHR see: https://www.coe.int/en/web/conventions/search-on-treaties/-/conventions/treaty/results/subject/3. Accessed 28 August 2023.

property, right to educate children, right to free and fair election (1st Protocol Articles 1–3); protection against double jeopardy (7th Protocol Article 4) or abolition of death penalty (13th Protocol Article 1). With the passage of time, the Convention has broadened not only its substantive scope and further guarantees but it has also strengthened the effectiveness of available remedies.

5.2.2.2 Establishment of the European Court of Human Rights (ECtHR)

For an effective enforcement of the enshrined human rights, the Convention has established a judicial body called European Court of Human Rights (ECtHR), which works under the auspices of the Council of Europe.[16] It has the jurisdiction under Article 19 of the Convention in "all matters concerning the interpretation and application of the Convention and the Protocols".[17] Established in 1959, the Court has issued more than 10,000 judgments as well as advisory opinions spanning diverse issues of human rights. The Court is staffed with 47 eminent judges who are elected by the Parliamentary Assembly of the Council of Europe from a list provided by all the member states.[18] The Convention also deals with the operational procedures of the Court and the respective roles of single judge formations, three judges committees, seven judges chambers as well as the Grand Chamber of all the seventeen judges.

Initially, the jurisdiction of the Court was not as strong as we see it today. The member states readily accepted the traditional public international law scheme of filing complaint by one member state against the other member state; however, they were not ready to grant individuals a direct access to invoke ECtHR jurisdiction.[19] Therefore, they introduced a filter where the complainant had to file their complaints in the European Commission for Human Rights first. The Commission and the Member State against whom the complaint was filed would then decide whether or not the complaint should be forwarded to the ECtHR. There were two different procedures for state complaints and individual complaints. Complaint by a state would be directly accepted once the state would assent to the Convention, while an individual complaint to the commission was subject to the separate *declaration of acceptance* by the member state concerned.[20] Of course, it was an ineffective protection mechanism and a hitch in the way to effective remedy for human rights violation. The reluctance of member states to allow individual complaints against

[16] See: https://echr.coe.int/Pages/home.aspx?p=home. Accessed 28 August 2023.

[17] Article 32 of ECHR: "In the event of dispute as to whether the Court has jurisdiction, the Court shall decide."

[18] See: https://ijrcenter.org/european-court-of-human-rights/. Accessed 27 August 2023.

[19] Ehlers and Becker (2007), p. 3.

[20] Ehlers and Becker (2007), p. 3.

them is evident from the fact that only eight declarations of acceptance were submitted until 1958.

A noteworthy breakthrough in the procedural efficiency of the ECtHR occurred on 1st November 1998 with the coming into force of the 11th Protocol, which brought revolutionary change in the filing of complaints and allowed individuals to directly file their applications in the ECtHR.[21] Since then, private individuals and entities can directly approach the ECtHR, besides the possibility that the jurisdiction of the Court can be invoked by any high contracting party against another high contracting party.[22] To Ehler, this revolutionary change was a "decisive factor in the evolution of the system in the last 50 years".[23] The 11th Protocol was added to rationalize the enforcement machinery of the rights and guarantees provided by the Convention. It abolished the Commission and the two-step procedure for individual complaints. Thus it provided the *individual* his right place in the international law arena. It gave a permanent status to the ECtHR to which all the complaints from individuals and states would now rout. In order to check frivolous complaints, a committee comprising on three judges would decide the fate of *manifestly ill-founded* complaints by declaring them inadmissible. However, as this change attracted an unmanageable flood of individual complaints, therefore, the coming into force of 14th Protocol in May 2004 has now empowered a single judge to decide upon the admissibility of complaints and reject the manifestly ill-founded complaints *ab initio*. Before resorting to the ECtHR, exhaustion of all domestic remedies by the applicant is required for admissibility of application.[24]

5.2.2.3 The Impact Mechanism of ECHR in National Jurisdictions and the Nature of Binding Force of ECtHR Case-Law

The ECHR has not laid down any particular procedure to incorporate the Convention into national legal systems of the member states. Article 1 of the Convention merely obliges the High Contracting Parties *to secure to everyone the rights and freedoms* enshrined therein. States become High Contracting Parties who sign and ratify the Convention under Article 59 of ECHR, after which it becomes binding under International law. It has been left to the discretion of the member states to decide on how to incorporate the Convection into domestic law. Resultantly, the method of incorporating the Convention into domestic law varies from member state to member state. For instance, ECHR is superior to its constitution in Netherlands, equal to its constitution in Austria, superior to its ordinary statutory law in Belgium and

[21] See for the text of the Protocol 11: https://www.coe.int/en/web/conventions/search-on-treaties/-/conventions/treaty/155. Accessed 25 August 2023.

[22] Articles 33, 34 ECHR.

[23] Ehlers and Becker (2007), p. 5.

[24] Article 35 (1) ECHR.

France, and equal to its federal acts of parliament in Germany.[25] Similarly, the additional Protocols supplement the Convention and they come into force when the required number of states signs them. A member state is liable under a Protocol only if it has duly signed that particular Protocol. Meanwhile, Article 57 provides the states with the opportunity to make a specific reservation regarding a provision of the Convention and making statement that some law is not in conformity with the Convention. Permissible reservations exempt the reserving state from application of that provisions about which the reservation has been made. However, an important feature of the safeguard mechanism of ECHR is that it does not prohibit the member states from following higher standards of human rights or recognize such human rights as not embodied in the Convention.[26]

As for the implementation of Convention's rights, a minimum requirement is alluded in the preamble that European states being "like-minded and having a common heritage of political traditions, ideals, freedom and the rule of law, to take the first steps for *the collective enforcement* of certain of the rights stated in the Universal Declaration".[27] After ratification of the Convention, the realization of the *collective enforcement* can be seen in the shape of ECtHR, which is a permanent judicial body, whose judgments are usually declaratory in nature and have binding effect under international law on the states who are parties to the proceedings concerned.[28] The Convention also provides an execution mechanism for the final judgments[29] of the ECtHR, which is supervised by the Committee of Minsters.[30] As the Convention is an International law treaty of the regional level, ECtHR has expressly stated its obligation to the codified rules of Vienna Convention on the Law of Treaties, and has also devised further methods of interpretation where it has to fulfill unique interpretational requirements.[31] In case of the establishment of a

[25] Ehlers and Becker (2007), p. 27.

[26] Article 53 ECHR.

[27] Preamble to the ECHR. Emphasis supplied.

[28] See Article 46 of ECHR for binding force and execution of judgments.

[29] According to Article 44, the judgment of the Grand Chamber is final, while the Chamber's judgment becomes final when the parties give declaration that they shall not refer the case to Grand Chamber, or when 3 months passes without any declaration, or when such declaration is rejected by the Grand Chamber.

[30] According to Article 46 (3): "If the Committee of Ministers considers that the supervision of the execution of a final judgment is hindered by a problem of interpretation of the judgment, it may refer the matter to the Court for a ruling on the question of interpretation. A referral decision shall require a majority vote of two-thirds of the representatives entitled to sit on the committee. 4. If the Committee of Ministers considers that a High Contracting Party refuses to abide by a final judgment in a case to which it is a party, it may, after serving formal notice on that Party and by decision adopted by a majority vote of two-thirds of the representatives entitled to sit on the committee, refer to the Court the question whether that Party has failed to fulfill its obligation under paragraph 1. 5. If the Court finds a violation of paragraph 1, it shall refer the case to the Committee of Ministers for consideration of the measures to be taken. If the Court finds no violation of paragraph 1, it shall refer the case to the Committee of Ministers, which shall close its examination of the case."

[31] See for details, Ľalík (2011).

violation of the Convention's right by a state, the Court imposes obligation of both compensatory and restitutory nature. Just satisfaction or equitable compensation is awarded in the former case, while an order for stopping continuous violation and ending the effect of violation to the possible limit is passed in the latter case.

In order to elaborate the exact nature of member's obligation arising from the Convention, different scholars have classified the normative obligations of the Convention's rights into a slightly different form.[32] Rationally, an obligation can either be negative or positive and then there are different dimensions of these obligations. However, Ehler has elaborated six kinds of obligations under the heading of *functions of the Convention rights.*[33] The remaining four functions or obligations of the ECHR are guaranty of equal treatment and equality before law,[34] guaranty of civil right to free elections, procedural rights obligation and obligation to interpret laws in conformity with the Convention. The operation of all these guarantees either requires negative or positive action, which will be further elaborated in the following sections.

5.2.3 *Unfolding the Substance and Obligations of Human Rights*

5.2.3.1 Negative Obligation

The primary focus of the Convention is on the protection of liberty, which obligates the state to refrain from infringements of the Convention's rights at the first place. This kind of obligation is according to the traditional understanding of human rights as basic liberties available against the state. The provisions of many rights start with a connotation of negative obligation as "no one shall be". For example, prohibition of depriving somebody of his life (Article 2), prohibition of torture (Article 3), prohibition of slavery (Article 4), prohibition of punishment without law (Article 7) and prohibition of discrimination (Article 14) expressly restrain the state from infringing these guarantees. Similarly, other rights also demand negative obligation on the part of the state, so as to respect people's right to liberty, private life, freedom of expression and thought. In the cases related to the state's interference with these rights, the ECtHR first determines whether the area is actually protected by the scope of a specific right in the Convention and that whether or not the alleged infringement can be attributed to the state action. The Court then considers both specific

[32] See and compare the classification: Starmer (2001), pp. 139–159; Ehlers and Becker (2007), pp. 32–38.

[33] Ehlers and Becker (2007), pp. 32–38.

[34] The Convention does not support a claim for a general equality in every sphere and it requires that the alleged discrimination must be with reference to the rights enumerated in the Convention. Article 14 prohibits discrimination on any ground in the enjoyment of rights and freedoms provided by the Convention.

limitations attached to some rights and the general limitations provided under Articles 15–17.[35] However, the legality of such limitations is also subject to strict requirements such as that the interference must be in accordance with the law and necessary in a democratic society.[36]

5.2.3.2 Positive Obligations

The scope of an effective protection of human rights demands both positive and negative measures from the state. At a primary level, the state needs to refrain from impairment of citizens' fundamental rights. This is the primary duty of the state, but it is not sufficient for an effective protection as the state has a duty to protect citizens' rights from infringements by a third party. This positive duty of the state requires proactive measures to minimize the risk of fundamental rights infringements such as the provision of legal frameworks to regulate private conflicts. The ECHR acknowledges this dimension of human rights and it imposes certain positive obligations in a straight forward manner and some in an implied manner.

The construction of Article 1—saying that the member states *shall secure to everyone* the rights—has an objective dimension and it demands the high contracting parties more than mere a passive abstention from interfering with the human rights. In order to secure the rights of the people in an effective way, the Convention obligates the member states to take positive measures for an effective protection. Some rights in the Convention demand positive action in a straight forward manner. For instance, the minimum rights of the convicted persons enumerated in Article 6 (Right to fair trial) are that they have to be informed and to provide them legal assistance in case of unaffordability. However, most of the rights demand positive action in a 'discreet' manner, regarding which it is strongly presumed that without positive obligation of the state, these rights cannot be *effectively* enforced.[37]

Positive obligations as a concept of human rights enforcement are typically associated with the European jurisdiction. As a contrast, the scope of fundamental rights under American constitution is, at least in principle, limited to the imposition of negative duty on the state. According to an earlier observation of Judge Posner in the case of Jackson v. City of Joliet, the American constitution is *a charter of negative rather than positive liberties*, while the authors of the Bill of Rights were not concerned for the lack of actions on the part of government; rather they wanted to check the excess of government actions.[38] He stated: "The Fourteenth Amendment,

---

[35] Article 15 is the emergency provision and provides the possibility of derogation of rights in case of war or public emergency; Article 16 restricts political activity of aliens and Article 17 prohibits abuse of Convention's rights.

[36] These concepts shall be explained in detail under the sections that analyze Article 8 and Article 10 obligations.

[37] Starmer (2001), p. 139.

[38] See for a comparative case law of the United States and Germany as well as their contrasting approaches to the scope of basic rights: Currie (1986), p. 864.

adopted in 1868 at the height of laissez-faire thinking, sought to protect Americans from oppressions by state government, not to secure them basic governmental services."[39]

To elaborate these distinctive approaches to the dimensions of human rights, Keir Starmer has made a comparative analysis of two cases: one of the US Supreme Court which is DeShaney v. Winnebago Social Services Department[40] and another from the European Court of Human Rights, which is A v. UK.[41] Both cases are related to the responsibility of the states to protect children from abuse. In the first case, the father of a 3 year old child, named Joshua, used to beat this child severely for a long time to the extent that his brain was permanently damaged. The father was then finally convicted of child abuse. Joshua's mother sued the Department of Social Services (DSS) for not taking effective measures to stop the inflicted violence. The department was in-touch with the child and was fulfilling their routine responsibility such as examining the child and arranging for counseling of the father. The plea was rejected not only at the lower judiciary but the US Supreme Court also rejected the appeal. The Supreme Court observed that the due process clause does not provide protection to citizens against private parties. The due process of law merely forbids United States from depriving individuals of life and liberty but does not demand any affirmative action for the protection of these interests against impairments by private individuals. It stated that the intention behind inserting the Due Process Clause in the Fourteenth Amendment was to prevent the government from abusing its own power so that not to become an instrument of oppressing its citizens.[42] The purpose of due process of right in the constitution was stated as protecting people from the state and not from each other. Based on this reason, the Supreme Court held that, as DSS had no such obligation to protect citizens from other people, they could not be made liable in the Joshua case for any kind of failure to protect.

In a similar case of child abuse by his stepfather i.e. the case of A v. UK, the European Court of Human Rights took a different approach. Though the stepfather was charged and prosecuted for the bodily harm he inflicted on his child, yet he was acquitted as the prosecution could not prove the illegal assault. He had confessed the use of physical force but justified that on the basis of disciplinary measures. In his complaint to the ECtHR, A alleged that the state had failed to safeguard him from his stepfather's ill-treatment. The UK government argued that no direct responsibility could be attached to it in terms of protecting children from maltreatment of step-parents. However, the ECtHR rejected the argument and stated that obligations under Articles 2 and 3 require states to take positive measures to ensure that nobody in their jurisdiction is subjected to inhuman treatment. This obligation also includes the protection from the abuse of other private individuals. It held that children and

---

[39] Jackson v. City of Joliet, 465 U.S. 1049 (1832) as cited in: Currie (1986), p. 864.

[40] (1989) 489 US 189 as referred to in: Starmer (2001), p. 140.

[41] (1999) 27 EHRR 611 as referred to in: Starmer (2001), p. 140.

[42] DeShaney v. Winnebago Social Services Department (1989) 489 at 195–196, as cited in: Starmer (2001), p. 142.

other vulnerable individuals in particular have an entitlement to state protection "in the form of effective deterrence against such serious breaches of personal integrity".[43] The state was held liable for its failure to effectively protect the claimant.

The comparison of American and European judgments illustrates contrasting approaches. The difference of approaches is usually attributed to historical reasons due to which the European Human Rights regime was designed not only to safeguard freedoms from governments but also to protect dignity *effectively*. "This notion of effectiveness runs like a thread through Convention jurisprudence", Keir Starmer comments.[44]

The positive obligation of the member states to prevent private individuals from interference into other private individuals' rights requires the states to take appropriate measures in this regard. For instance, it is the duty of the state to place effective criminal law as well as an enforcement framework in order to deter the offences detrimental to life at one hand, and on the other hand, the state is also obliged to have such operational machinery to prevent or minimize the risk to life from criminal acts.[45] Similarly, almost every right needs proper mechanism to check its infringement from both government and private actions and in the case of an infringement, the victim must have a forum for remedying the infringement.

Keir Starmer identifies five positive duties of the states under the Convention.[46] These duties are:

1. *To put a legal framework which provides effective protection for convention rights*
2. *To prevent breaches of Convention*
3. *To provide information and advice relevant to a breach of Convention rights*
4. *To respond to breaches of Convention rights*
5. *To provide resources to individuals to prevent breaches of their convention rights*

It is obvious that the Convention imposes positive obligations on the member states. However, that does not yet answer the question whether the national judiciary is affected by such positive obligations or not. The Court has clarified this point in Goodwin v United Kingdom. In this decision, it states that both the authorities of the member states as well as their courts are bound under the Convention's positive obligation to take measures for the recognition of the identity of persons.[47] In another case, the Court notes,

> the Contracting States are under a duty to organize [sic] their judicial systems in such a way that their courts can meet the requirements of the Convention. This principle also applies to the execution of the Court's judgments. Accordingly, it is equally immaterial in this context

[43] A. v. UK (1999) 27 EHRR 611, paragraph 22, as cited in: Starmer (2001), p. 143.

[44] Ehlers and Becker (2007), p. 143.

[45] Ehlers and Becker (2007), p. 35.

[46] Starmer (2001), pp. 146–159.

[47] ECHR, *Christine Goodwin v the United Kingdom*, judgment of 11 July 2002. Application No. 28957/95.

> to argue, as the Government did, that the Federal Court could not in any event have ordered that the commercial be broadcast following the Court's judgment. The same is true of the argument that the applicant association should have instituted civil proceedings.[48]

The Strasbourg Court has observed specifically about Article 8 obligations as, "These obligations may involve the adoption of measures designed to secure respect for private life even in the sphere of the relations of individuals between themselves."[49] Similarly, in Cossey v the United Kingdom, the Court observed:

> As the Court has pointed out on several occasions, notably in the Rees judgment itself (p. 15, para. 37), the notion of "respect" is not clear-cut, especially as far as the positive obligations inherent in that concept are concerned: having regard to the diversity of the practices followed and the situations obtaining in the Contracting States, the notion's requirements will vary considerably from case to case. In determining whether or not a positive obligation exists, regard must be had to the fair balance that has to be struck between the general interest of the community and the interests of the individual, the search for which balance is inherent in the whole of the Convention.[50]

In the subsequent para, the Courts says: "The requirement of striking a fair balance could not give rise to any direct obligation on the respondent State to alter the very basis of its system."[51]

In the nutshell, the analysis of substance and obligation of human rights provided in the Convention and as interpreted by the ECtHR reveals more comprehensive protection. This approach is in-contrast to the typical American approach of satisfying merely with the state's abstention from infringements of fundamental rights. The Convention requires the member states to take positive measures and proactive steps in order to protect human rights. This European approach to the protection of human rights will be further explored in order to learn lessons for privacy protection in Pakistan.

5.2.4 Margin of Appreciation

The principle of margin of appreciation offers member states the authority to consider the local circumstances of the particular case when they impose restrictions on human rights or fulfill positive obligations, keeping in view the provisions of the Convention and the standards set by the ECtHR. The ECtHR has explained its 'supervising' role through giving member states such a margin of appreciation. It has nevertheless the power to ascertain whether the standards are satisfactorily applied

---

[48] Vgt Verein Gegen Tierfabriken v Switzerland Appl no 32772/02 (ECtHR, 30 June 2009), para 97. Preference omitted.

[49] ECHR, *X and Y v Netherlands*, judgment of 26 March 1985. Application no. 8978/80.

[50] ECHR, *Cossey v The United Kingdom*, judgment of 27 September 1990. Application No. 10843/84, para 37.

[51] ECHR, *Cossey v The United Kingdom*, judgment of 27 September 1990. Application No. 10843/84, para 38.

according to the principles developed under the Convention. The ECtHR is not willing to replace the national jurisdictions and takes cognizance only if it thinks that proper balance has not been undertaken.[52]

The principle of margin of appreciation was developed by the ECtHR in Handyside v. the United Kingdom in 1976.[53] The Court held that the Convention machinery for the protection of human rights is subsidiary to the national systems where the national states are required to fulfill the task of implementation in the first place.[54] It declared, "[t]o find uniformity in the conception of morality is impossible, so margin of appreciation is essential, but with limitation."[55] The function of margin of appreciation becomes more important when the state authorities, statutory or regulatory as well as judicial bodies, juxtapose competing interests and values. However, the recognition of a margin of appreciation does not prevent the ECtHR from "assessing whether the domestic courts have recognized important factors, performed the balancing test and applied the relevant criteria in a reasonable way."[56] If any party feels aggrieved due to the outcome of such balancing, he or she can apply for relief to the ECtHR. If the application fulfills other admissibility criteria, the Court then tests the reasonability as well as the proportionality of the interference in question.

The principle of margin of appreciation is criticized on various grounds. For instance, the uncertainty of what exactly is required could potentially restrict member states from conforming to the Convention.[57] Mr. P Mahoney, judge of the ECtHR, has conceded that in the process of balancing conflicting rights, Strasbourg barely provides *concrete answers*. But nevertheless, it provides guidance with respect to the philosophy and values on the basis of which the courts of national jurisdictions could weigh such conflicting rights on the basis of their own domestic law.[58]

Margin of appreciation is a necessary tool which binds diverse legal systems into a singular forum of human rights adjudication. It provides the necessary *margin* to member states to meet the Convention's human rights standards while remaining in the sphere of their own local contexts. Nevertheless, it is a reality that the quest to an extreme certainty of law also brings undue rigidity where it becomes difficult for a multi-lateral legal system to conform to one set of rules without compromising the other.

[52] Hertel v Switzerland (25 August 1998), para 46 iii.

[53] Kilkelly (2003).

[54] ECHR, *Handyside v the United Kingdom,* judgment of 07 December 1976. Application No. 5493/72, para 48.

[55] ECHR, *Handyside v the United Kingdom,* judgment of 07 December 1976. Application No. 5493/72, para 48.

[56] Korpisaari (2017), p. 42.

[57] For criticism on margin of appreciation, please see: Korpisaari (2017), pp. 42–46.

[58] Mahoney (2014), p. 578.

Furthermore, margin of appreciation has a utility for any comparative research as it provides a flexible legal regime where the adoption of broad principles is much easier to follow rather than to transplant a complete legal framework. The principle of margin of appreciation reflects the diversity of national and local contexts where these rights actually operate. It recognizes the context-specificities of many jurisdictions. Thus it also provides the opportunity to non-member countries such as Pakistan to borrow the useful principles, and apply them *mutatis mutandis* to cases in hand according to their own circumstances and societal demands.

5.3 Article 8 of the European Convention of Human Rights (ECHR)

Article 8 is the basic legal norm which protects private life and the related interests under the European Convention on Human Rights. It provides:

1. Everyone has the right to respect for his private and family life, his home and his correspondence.
2. There shall be no interference by a public authority with the exercise of this right except such as is in accordance with the law and is necessary in a democratic society in the interests of national security, public safety or the economic well-being of the country, for the prevention of disorder or crime, for the protection of health or morals, or for the protection of the rights and freedoms of others.

The jurisprudence of ECtHR has explained the width and breadth of the scope of this Article and the values and interests attached to it. It is important to explore the concrete areas and the scope of their respective protection.

5.3.1 Protecting Privacy Under the Convention

5.3.1.1 The Meaning and Scope of Private Life

In the case of X v. Iceland, a person complained against the Government of Iceland that he is not allowed to keep a dog. This was prohibited in the municipal laws of his place of residence.[59] His application was declared as inadmissible. The Court stated that the philosophical and moral value elaborated by scholars connects it to the right to live according to the way one wishes while this right does not end there. The right to respect for private life also comprises of "the right to establish and develop relationships with other human beings, especially in the emotional field for the development and fulfillment of one's own personality".[60] However, in the same

[59]ECHR, *X v Iceland*. Judgment of 18 May 1976. Application No. 6825/74.

[60]ECHR, *X v Iceland*. Judgment of 18 May 1976. Application No. 6825/74, paras 86–87.

breath, the Court held that it does not mean that every sphere of human activity could be protected. It rejected the notion that the protection of private life under Article 8 means the protection afforded to "the relationships of the individual with his entire immediate surroundings" and held, "Article 8 of the Convention cannot be interpreted such as to secure to everybody the right to keep a dog."[61]

Rationalizing the scope and application of Article 8, the ECtHR has refrained from devising an exhaustive definition. According to the Court, it is neither possible nor necessary to frame an exhaustive definition for the notion of "private life".[62] The Court categorically rejected the limitation of private life to the "inner circle" of a person's life which he chooses exclusively for himself as this notion will be "too restrictive".[63] The respect for personal life also includes the right to establish and develop relationships with other human beings.[64] Therefore, the Court extended the protection of private life under Article 8 equally to the professional and non-professional nature of activities.

In Van Kück v Germany, the Court has summarized the areas of life which are protected under Article 8. It states:

> [T]he concept of "private life" is a broad term not susceptible to exhaustive definition. It covers the physical and psychological integrity of a person [. . . .] It can sometimes embrace aspects of an individual's physical and social identity [. . . ..] Elements such as, for example, gender identification, name and sexual orientation and sexual life fall within the personal sphere protected by Article 8 [. . . .] Article 8 also protects a right to personal development, and the right to establish and develop relationships with other human beings and the outside world [. . . ..] Likewise, the Court has held that although no previous case has established as such any right to self-determination as being contained in Article 8, the notion of personal autonomy is an important principle underlying the interpretation of its guarantees. [. . . ..] Moreover, the very essence of the Convention being respect for human dignity and human freedom, protection is given to the right of transsexuals to personal development and to physical and moral security.[65]

In short, the broad scope of Article 8 has enabled plaintiffs to invoke it successfully for protecting variety of interests such as interests linked to one's sexuality, family and children, immigration, prisoners, search and seizures, surveillance and data protection, as well as privacy violations of media.[66]

---

[61] ECHR, *X v Iceland,* Judgment of 18 May 1976. Application No. 6825/74, paras 86–87.

[62] ECHR, *Niemietz v Germany*, judgment of 16 December 1992. Application No. 13710/88, para 29.

[63] ECHR, *Niemietz v Germany*, judgment of 16 December 1992. Application No. 13710/88, para 29.

[64] ECHR, *Niemietz v Germany*, judgment of 16 December 1992. Application No. 13710/88, para 29. Similarly, in Axel Springer AG v Germany, the ECtHR said that the concept of private life is broad which cannot be susceptible to exhaustive definition and it includes reputation.

[65] ECHR, *Van Kück v Germany*, judgment of 12 September 2003. Application No. 35968/97.

[66] Stratford (2002), p. 20.

5.3.1.2 The Meaning and Scope of the Protection of Home

The jurisprudence of Strasbourg Court does not construe the term "home" as a residential abode according to the everyday life usage of the term. The meaning and interpretation of "home" in a narrow sense such as to restrict it to residential place is not helpful to protect Article 8 interests effectively. The Court has included professional or business premises in the definition of "home", and the public authorities are required to justify interference thereto as per the test of legitimate aim and the extent to which it is "necessary in a democratic society."[67] The Court has left the demarcation of home to the factual circumstances of every case and has not devised any proprietary, geographical, or residential criteria for a place to be protected under Article 8.[68] Even actual "living" is not necessary in a place so as to call that a "home" and mere ownership of a residential location is sufficient.[69] On the other hand, a rented place of residence or the working place, such as the office, is also protected under Article 8. Thus the fact that one does not own a premise would not automatically exclude it from protection.[70]

The broad scope of the protection of home is complemented by a broad understanding of impairments. In the case of López Ostra v. Spain, the ECtHR held that severe environmental pollution, even if its hazard does not cause serious health issues, can affect human wellbeing. Therefore, it has the capacity to "prevent them from enjoying their homes in such a way as to affect their private and family life adversely".[71]

In the case of Moreno Gómez v. Spain, the ECtHR explains the meaning and scope of the Article 8 protection available to home in the most extensive way and states:

> Article 8 of the Convention protects the individual's right to respect for his private and family life, his *home* and his correspondence. A home will usually be the place, the physically defined area, where private and family life develops. The individual has a right to respect for his home, meaning not just the right to the actual physical area, but also to the

---

[67] ECHR, *Niemietz v Germany*, judgment of 16 December 1992. Application No. 13710/88, para 30: "The Court observes that in certain Contracting States, notably Germany [....], it has been accepted as extending to business premises. Such an interpretation is, moreover, fully consonant with the French text, since the word "domicile" has a broader connotation than the word "home" and may extend, for example, to a professional person's office."

[68] See: ECHR, *Buckley v The United Kingdom*, judgment of 1995. Application No. 20348/92. Also see: ECHR, *Niemietz v Germany*, judgment of 16 December 1992. Application No. 13710/88, para 30: "It may not always be possible to draw precise distinctions, since activities which are related to a profession or business may well be conducted from a person's private residence and activities which are not so related may well be carried on in an office or commercial premises. A narrow interpretation of the words "home" and "domicile" could therefore give rise to the same risk of inequality of treatment as a narrow interpretation of the notion of "private life"".

[69] ECHR, *Gillow v the United Kingdom*, judgment of 14 September 1987. Application No. 9063/80, para 46.

[70] ECHR, *Niemietz v Germany*, judgment of 16 December 1992. Application No. 13710/88.

[71] ECHR, *López Ostra v Spain*, judgment of 09 December 1994. Application No. 16798/90.

> quiet enjoyment of that area. Breaches of the right to respect of the home are not confined to concrete or physical breaches, such as unauthorised entry into a person's home, but also include those that are not concrete or physical, such as noise, emissions, smells or other forms of interference. A serious breach may result in the breach of a person's right to respect for his home if it prevents him from enjoying the amenities of his home.[72]

This broad treatment of the word "home" reminds one of the similar broad interpretation of this term by the Supreme Court of Pakistan, which, in the same manner, does not restrict the protection to the ordinary usage of the term and includes many areas under its ambit.

5.3.1.3 The Meaning and Scope of Correspondence

The term "correspondence" has also been interpreted broadly. The Court noted that the provision mentions the term correspondence without using any adjective to qualify it. No such qualification as based on the means used for communication is required.[73] The Court has applied the protection to a variety of communication processes such as written and verbal communication, personal or commercial communication or any other kind of communication which is made with the help of modern techniques.[74] In Halford v United Kingdom, the Court expressly included telephonic conversation in the definition of "correspondence" and the interpretation of correspondence was not restricted to letters or papers but comprised modern methods of communication.[75] Consequently, digital communication through email or messenger services are entitled to Article 8 protection.

5.3.2 *The Possibilities of Interference with the Article 8 Right*

Under Article 8 (2) of the ECHR, the right to respect of private and family life is not absolute as it provides for the possibility of interference under certain circumstances. Interference with the rights and interests can be made by the member states. However, parties to the Convention have to justify their interference according to

---

[72] ECHR, *Moreno Gómez v Spain*, judgment of 16 November 2004. Application No. 4143/02.

[73] ECHR, *Niemietz v Germany*, judgment of 16 December 1992. Application No. 13710/88, para 32.

[74] ECHR, *Klass and Others v Germany*, judgment of 06 September, 1978. Application No. 5029/71, para 44: "Although telephone conversations are not expressly mentioned in paragraph 1 of Article 8 (art. 8-1), the Court considers, as did the Commission, that such conversations are covered by the notions of "private life" and "correspondence" referred to by this provision." para 41. Amann v Switzerland, App no 27798/95 (ECtHR, 16 February 2000) "reiterates that telephone calls received on private or business premises are covered by the notions of "private life" and "correspondence" within the meaning of Article 8 § 1."

[75] ECHR, *Halford v the United Kingdom*, judgment of 25 June 1997. Application No. 20605/92.

one of the exemptions given in the proviso. Accordingly, the interference must be in accordance with the law, and secondly, it must be necessary in a democratic society with regard to enumerated legitimate aims. The first condition requires *legality* of the action, which means that there must be some legal basis available to justify the interference. The Court has not resolved the query as what does specifically constitute "law" or how exactly the condition of "*prescribed by law*" can be satisfied.[76] However, the mere presence of a legal basis is just a starting point for the Court and not sufficient as a valid justification in all circumstances. The notion of "prescribed by law" also carries the essential characteristics of a law, and those are accessibility, foreseeability and certainty.[77] The second condition of "necessary in a democratic society" does not strictly mean indispensability. The jurisprudence has developed this concept and it is commonly understood as anchoring the principle of proportionality. The means used for the interference must be proportionate to the legitimate aim.[78]

5.4 Balancing Privacy with Other Countervailing Rights

5.4.1 Balancing of Human Rights in Theory

Robert Alexy explains the balancing exercise as a technique of judicial interpretation, which is used for "[t]he determination of the appropriate degree of satisfaction of one principle [right] relative to the requirements of other principles [rights]".[79] Ardently supporting the effectiveness of balancing and proportionality techniques, Alexy differentiates between *norms* and *principles.* Norms are just like rules of positive law, whose characteristic is that if valid and the required applicability conditions are fulfilled, the action they require must be done to ensure compliance and avoid non-compliance. In contrast, principles are *optimization requirements*, which demand that something be realized "to the greatest possible extent given the legal and factual possibilities."[80] Alexy argues that fundamental rights are a combination of principles and norms, and therefore they must be optimally enforced, because "constitutional rights have been intrinsically tied to the principle of proportionality. The applicability of this principle presupposes that constitutional rights have the structure of principles or optimization requirements".[81] In order to repeal the objections that balancing exercises were subjective and irrational, he has

[76] Ehlers and Becker (2007), p. 52.

[77] See for an extensive elaboration: Mountfeld (2001).

[78] Ehlers and Becker (2007), p. 53.

[79] Alexy (2014), p. 52.

[80] Alexy (2014), p. 52. Reference omitted.

[81] Alexy (2009). For a full consideration of Alexy's conception of balancing and proportionality see: Alexy (2010).

presented his *weight formula* in the form of an equation of the related values in symbol forms which he also calls *the law of balancing*. In simple form, he describes this as "[t]he greater the degree of non-satisfaction of, or detriment to, one principle, the greater the importance of satisfying the other".[82]

Nevertheless, the concept of balancing of fundamental rights is not without controversy. There is some criticism from scholars over the exercise of balancing rights, particularly on letting a basic right to be outweighed by utilitarian considerations in the context of national security and public interest. For instance, Dworkin is of the view that only in emergency situation the public interest limitation should be allowed to trump free speech, while in most of the occasions basic rights such as free speech should prevail.[83] Barendt draws on Habermas' argumentation that fundamental rights when exposed to the balancing exercise lose their "normative strengths" and become ordinary policy issues decided by legislatures and administrators.[84] He also shows his concern that no rational criteria can be laid down for the weighing and balancing of fundamental rights with other values, which then creates arbitrariness and unpredictability. However, the balancing exercise is unavoidable in almost every situation where two or more fundamental rights are in a conflicting position. The courts then have to apply rational judgments about the level and circumstances of infringements in a coherent and consistent manner. Barendt explains:

> [B]alancing may be incoherent in principle, and very difficult to apply in practice. The [balancing] process appears to assume that the values underlying the conflicting rights can be measured (or weighed) against each other and a harmonious result achieved. But these values may be incommensurable: how can the individual's interest in privacy be thought less or more valuable than the public's right to be informed? Perhaps choices have to be made in the light of the values ascribed to the exercise of the competing rights in the *context of the particular case*, or under general principles which give greater weight to one value rather than another in cases of conflict.[85]

Başak Çali, who emphasizes the important function of the human rights in tackling the issue of balance of power in society and states, points out that many scholars reject the *absolutism about rights* for one or the other reason.[86] Such rejection compels scholars and practitioners to seek various ways for the resolution of the difficult cases arising out of the necessity to contextualize human rights. The

---

[82] Alexy (2005), p. 573.

[83] Dworkin (1977), essays 7 and 12, as cited in: Barendt (2009), p. 50.

[84] Barendt (2009), p. 49.

[85] Barendt (2009), p. 52. Emphasis supplied and FN omitted.

[86] Çalı (2007), p. 251. See also: p. 261: "An important aspect of human rights provisions is their capacity to give voice to a single individual's claims before the decision making authorities and courts. Human rights claims empower individuals regardless of their relationship with the authorities or their status in the community. These claims are important, precisely because claims that conflict with the economic, political or social goals of elites, majorities, and authorities can be articulated in the form of human rights claims even when legal or constitutional claims are not available."

balancing agenda, in Çali's view, to reconciling mechanism of competing interest related to human rights at one hand and the communal interests on the other hand emerges as one candidate, which is regarded as "a key interpretive principle" in the reconciliatory approach of the European Court of Human Rights.[87] There are arguments that, to accept a circumstantial weightage of some human right would give "a shifting character to human rights principles," where the balancing exercise in question could possibility "swallow up the rights."[88] Çali suggests that only the strong commitment to the principle of proportionality can avoid such criticism on the balancing exercise.[89] The principle of proportionality in the balancing exercise "requires that the objective of the communal aim or interest has to be sufficiently important to limit the right; the measure of the limitation has to be suitable and no more than necessary to defend the communal interest in question."[90]

It is beyond doubt that the main purpose of human rights is to restrain the "consequentialist form of reasoning", the balancing practices thus "require identification of interests, assigning values to them and ultimately to deciding which interest yields the net benefit."[91] The determination of the specific value of an interest based on specific circumstances of the case is also dependent on some conditions such as the application of the principle of proportionality.

On order to counter criticism on the balancing exercise, Robert Alexy presents a three-stage structure of balancing. He elaborates three stages and their importance as:

> The first stage involves establishing the degree of non-satisfaction of, or detriment to, a first principle. This is followed by a second stage in which the importance of satisfying the competing principle is established. Finally, in the third stage, it is established whether the importance of satisfying the latter principle justifies the detriment to or non-satisfaction of the former. If it were not possible to make rational judgments about, first, intensity of interference, secondly, degrees of importance, and, thirdly, their relationship to each other, then the objections raised by Habermas would be justified. Everything turns, then, on the possibility of making such judgments.[92]

These concerns and ideas are important in relation to the uniqueness of human rights principles and laws, as the routine valuation and decision on the basis of merely shifts and tilts of balancing scale would reduce the constitutional foundation of basic rights to contractual transactions. However, it is not possible to avoid all sorts of measures in the reconciliation process of conflicting claims. Therefore, *ultimate balancing process* is a chief feature of human rights adjudication in the ECtHR. This process helps to preserve the unique character of fundamental rights in order to prevent ambiguity in the concept of rights. The circumstances of the case in hand provide an important context to the enforcement of Convention's rights, while the

---

[87] Çalı (2007), p. 253. Footnotes omitted.

[88] Çalı (2007), p. 253. Footnotes omitted.

[89] Çalı (2007), p. 253. Footnotes omitted.

[90] Çalı (2007), p. 253. Footnotes omitted.

[91] Çalı (2007), p. 259.

[92] Alexy (2005), pp. 572, 574.

known principles of balancing exercise by the ECtHR protect rights from being overly-contextualized.

Balancing of human rights is essential in the realm of conflicting constitutional rights. It is not possible for the legislature or framers of the constitution to set the boundaries of fundamental rights in a way as to perpetually avoid the possibility of conflict. It is the domain of judiciary to exercise their informed wisdom and resolve the conflicts between rights, based on the principles of balancing and proportionality. The next section will explore freedom of expression under Article 10 of the ECHR as well as the principles devised and applied by ECtHR on practical issues of privacy and free speech balancing. This exploration will highlight as how the conflicting interests between the right to freedom of expression on one hand and the right to respect private life on the other hand are being taken into consideration.

5.4.2 Freedom of Expression Under Article 10 of the ECHR as a Countervailing Right

Article 10 of the ECHR provides the right to freedom of expression:

1. Everyone has the right to freedom of expression. This right shall include freedom to hold opinions and to receive and impart information and ideas without interference by public authority and regardless of frontiers. This Article shall not prevent States from requiring the licensing of broadcasting, television or cinema enterprises.
2. The exercise of these freedoms, since it carries with it duties and responsibilities, may be subject to such formalities, conditions, restrictions or penalties as are prescribed by law and are necessary in a democratic society, in the interests of national security, territorial integrity or public safety, for the prevention of disorder or crime, for the protection of health or morals, for the protection of the reputation or rights of others, for preventing the disclosure of information received in confidence, or for maintaining the authority and impartiality of the judiciary.

The first para introduces and explains the freedom of expression, which includes freedom to hold opinions as well as protects the exercise of legitimate informational rights. The second para narrates the conditions and limitations that might be imposed for the achievement of given objectives. Freedom to hold opinions is almost an absolute right and is not subject to the restrictions enumerated under second para.[93]

The jurisprudence of the ECtHR explains the importance of freedom of expression and its case law demarcates the boundaries of its scope. In the case of *Thoma v. Luxembourg*, the Court asserts, "freedom of expression constitutes one of the essential foundations of a democratic society and one of the basic conditions for its progress and for each individual's self-fulfilment".[94] In the case of *Handyside v UK*, the Court has explained the scope and limitations of this right. The right to freedom

[93] Report of the Committee of Ministers in: Van Dijk et al. (1998), p. 413, as referred to in: Macovei (2004).

[94] ECHR, *Thoma v Luxembourg* judgment of 29 March 2002. Application No. 38432/97, para 43.

of expression is viewed as an important value for a democratic society and the state is bound to justify any kind of interference with this right as per the criteria of the second para of Article 10. Member states have a margin of appreciation in complying with the Convention's right because "the machinery of protection established by the Convention is subsidiary to the national systems safeguarding human rights".[95] Freedom of expression is therefore not an absolute right and the State can legitimately interfere or can restrict speech based on reasons given in para 2 of Article 10.

In many judgments, the ECtHR has elaborated the objectives of the protection of freedom of expression. These objectives are, broadly speaking, twofold. Firstly, on the individual level, freedom of expression is essential for self-fulfilment and personality development. Secondly, it has also an important function in society in the shape of promotion of democratic processes. It acknowledges the importance of the preeminent role of the press in a democratic state. However, the press must not forget its duties and responsibilities; particularly it must respect other important values such as the reputation of others.[96]

The case law of the ECtHR reveals that complainants have invoked Article 10 successfully for the protection of a variety of expressions. The interference by a member state with the right to free speech is judged with a stringent test of whether or not the action was necessary in a democratic society. If an interference or limitation of the right is based on conditions or restrictions prescribed by law and necessary in the sense of para 2 of Article 10, then it does not amount to an infringement of the freedom of expression. For example, in the case of Engel and Others, the applicant failed to prove that a disciplinary action of the Dutch Government imposed on soldiers for publishing articles against military disciplines was a violation of freedom of expression. [97] The Court held that the Dutch Government action was not intended to snatch away the right to freedom of expression but to punish an abuse of that right.

The ECtHR gives a great regard to political debate and opines that political figures should have a greater patience for criticism by the popular press. Certainly, the press has bounds which they must not violate, yet it is a medium for the fulfilment of the right of the people to have access to information.[98] In Lingens v Austria, the Court held that the conviction of a journalist for an alleged defamation after he used broad value judgmental expression (e.g. immoral, undignified etc.) was necessary neither in a democratic society nor for the protection of the reputation of

[95] ECHR, *Handyside v the United Kingdom*. Application No. 5493/72, para 48.

[96] ECHR, *Prager and Oberschlick v Austria*, judgment of 26 April 1995. Application No. 15974/90, para 34: "The Court reiterates that the press plays a pre-eminent role in a State governed by the rule of law. Although it must not overstep certain bounds set, inter alia, for the protection of the reputation of others, it is nevertheless incumbent on it to impart—in a way consistent with its duties and responsibilities—information and ideas on political questions and on other matters of public interest."

[97] ECHR, *Engel and Others v The Netherlands*, judgment of 8 June 1976. Applications No. 5100/71, 5101/71, 5102/71; 5354/72, 5370/72.

[98] ECHR, *Lingens v Austria*, judgment of 08 July 1986. Application No. 9815/82.

others.[99] The interference was declared as "disproportionate to the legitimate aim pursued" and accordingly a breach of Article 10 of ECHR.[100]

The Court does not treat all kinds of information identically. It makes distinctions on the basis of the quality of information and its objective. In the case of Standard Verlag v Austria, the Court explained,

> They made a convincing distinction between information concerning the health of a politician which may in certain circumstances be an issue of public concern [.....] and idle gossip about the state of his or her marriage or alleged extra-marital relationships[.....] the latter does not contribute to any public debate in respect of which the press has to fulfil its role of 'public watchdog', but merely serves to satisfy the curiosity of a certain readership.[101]

As a result, the Court held that the Austrian Courts in this case validly justified the interference for the protection of the right to respect for private life and successfully balanced conflicting rights.

5.4.3 Balancing Principles in ECtHR Jurisprudence: Prominent Media Related Cases and Leading Judgments on Celebrities and Paparazzi

The above elaboration of Articles 8 and 10 of the ECHR shows that the Convention provides both the right to privacy and free speech in an express manner. Both of these rights have immense importance, not only for their own sake but also for the sake of upholding other human values such as the development of personalities and the maintenance of a viable democratic order. Interestingly, the Convention also provides a "paradigm" for the conflict between the right to respect for private and family life and the right to freedom of expression.[102] The effective enforcement of the right to privacy can result into the curtailment of the freedom of expression in many cases. The conflict of these two rights is obvious and frequent. Jemima Stratford has rightly observed, "one person's right may be another person's wrong."[103] In such situations, the ECtHR resorts to the balancing technique in order to resolve the conflict between different rights' holders. Not only with other rights, but the qualifications attached to both of these rights call for a consideration that whether any of the exceptions could be invoked to justify the alleged infringement. Therefore, the ECtHR, after confirming that there exists an impairment of a Convention right (i.e. Article 8 in case of privacy right) attributable to the state, analyses if such alleged interference was "in accordance with the law" and

---

[99] ECHR, *Lingens v Austria*, judgment of 08 July 1986. Application No. 9815/82, para 47.

[100] ECHR, *Lingens v Austria*, judgment of 08 July 1986. Application No. 9815/82, para 47.

[101] ECHR, *Standard Verlags GmbH v Austria*, judgment of 05 June 2009. Application No. 21277/05, para 52. References omitted.

[102] See for details: Stratford (2002), pp. 13–44.

[103] Stratford (2002), p. 13.

"necessary in a democratic society". Similarly, in case of free speech, no infringement by a public authority is illegitimate if such interference was "prescribed by law" and necessary for the objectives mentioned in Article 10 (2). Thus, none of the right to privacy and freedom of expression has an absolute character. These rights are balanced against the objectives of interference provided along with their provision as well as with each other. For instance, in the case of Krone Verlag GMBH v. Austria, the Court had to resolve such a conflict for which it resorted to balancing exercise.[104] The Court stated:

> The subject matter at issue in this case relates, on the one hand, to the right of the press under Article 10 of the Convention to inform the public on matters of public concern regarding ongoing court proceedings and on the manner in which decisions by the courts are enforced and, on the other, to the State's positive obligations under Article 8 of the Convention to protect the privacy of persons, in particular minors, to whom such proceedings relate. When verifying whether the authorities struck a fair balance between two protected values guaranteed by the Convention which may come into conflict with each other in this type of case – freedom of expression protected by Article 10 and the right to respect for private life enshrined in Article 8 – the Court must balance the public interest in the publication of the information and the need to protect private life.[105]

The Conventional rights system does not recognize a hierarchy of values. Rather, it requires a balancing of various rights in the case of conflict, both on the abstract-typifying level as well as in the concrete case. Introducing the guiding principles on the privacy protection during media coverage, the Consultative Committee of the Convention asserted,

> the right to privacy and the right to freedom of expression are neither absolute nor in any prevailing order to each other, as they are of equal value. In addition, they not only stress the need to achieve a balance between the exercise of these rights, but also specifically call on media to develop their own guidelines.[106]

More recently the ECtHR was confronted with the tricky issue of resolving the conflict between Article 8 and 10 of the Convention in some high-profile cases. The Court utilized the opportunity well and pronounced remarkable judgments. Several decisions that dealt with celebrities and paparazzi elaborated key criteria and principles for balancing the right to respect for private life against the freedom of expression. Through these judgments, the Court changed the paradigm of zero privacy in public places or for public figures. The principles articulated under this jurisprudence have a strong persuasive force for all the jurisdictions whose legal systems have yet to draw frontiers between conflicting territories of privacy and free

---

[104] ECHR, *Krone Verlag GmbH v Austria*, judgment of 19 September 2012. Application No. 27306/07.

[105] ECHR, *Krone Verlag GmbH v Austria*, judgment of 19 September 2012. Application No. 27306/07, para 49.

[106] Consultative committee of the convention for the protection of individuals with regard to automatic processing of personal data-Guiding principles on the protection of privacy In media coverage. Strasbourg, 18 May 2016.

speech. Beyond that, there are other illustrative decisions on invasive media practices.

5.4.3.1 Von Hannover v Germany-I

The case of Von Hannover v Germany I (2004)[107] is one of the noteworthy cases. This case is believed to have "radically altered the rules governing the unauthorized publication" of celebrity exposures in the media.[108]

5.4.3.1.1 Background of the Case

In Von Hannover v Germany I, a complaint was filed in the ECtHR by Caroline von Hannover, the daughter of Prince Reiner III of the State of Monaco, claiming that the Federal Republic of Germany had failed to protect her Article 8 right to respect for private and family life. In her quest to avoid media attention and repel paparazzi of the European tabloid newspapers, she fought tirelessly in many courts of law since 1990. The present complaint was regarding her pictures in German magazines *Bunte*, *Freizeit Revue* and *Neue Post*. These photos were taken at different locations and were depicting the applicant's different activities under different captions. For example, one of the photos published on the front page of *Freizeit Revue* showed her sitting in the corner of a restaurant with her male friend, Vincent Lindon, who himself has been a famous actor. It was captioned as "The most tender photos of her romance with Vincent" ("*Die zärtlichsten Fotos ihrer Romanze mit Vincent*"). Other photos showed her on horseback, referring as "Caroline and the blues. Her life is a novel with innumerable misfortunes, says the author Roig" ("*Caroline und die Melancholie. Ihr Leben ist ein Roman mit unzähligen Unglücken, sagt Autor Roig*"). A photo also showed her with her children as part of an article, entitled as ""I don't think I could be a man's ideal wife" ("*Ich glaube nicht, dass ich die ideale Frau für einen Mann sein kann*")." Seven photos were published in *Bunte* magazine, which depicted her together with the actor and her son. Some photos also showed her in swimsuit captured while she was in Monte Carlo Beach Club. All these photos were published at different times, with different references and texts from 1993 to 1997. She started a long legal battle in different courts of Germany, challenging the infringement of her personality right and her right to privacy as well as her right to the use of her image recognized under sections 22 and 23 of the Copyright Act.[109]

---

[107] ECHR, *Von Hannover v Germany*, judgment of 24 June 2004. Application No. 59320/00.

[108] Barnes (2005), pp. 599–600: "In Von Hannover, the European Court of Human Rights offers an exceptionally clear statement of judicial recognition of the relationship between privacy and personal development. Considering this decision emanated from one of the world's most respected courts, the international community will reap enormous benefits."

[109] ECHR, *Von Hannover v Germany*, judgment of 24 June 2004. Application No. 59320/00.

Not satisfied with the judgments passed by Hamburg Regional Court and then the Hamburg Court of Appeal, she appealed to the Federal Court of Justice, which rejected her appeal in its landmark judgment of 19 December 1995.[110] The Court of justice accepted merely a partial of her appeal, which was related to pictures showing her in a courtyard corner of the restaurant with Vincent. The Court said that even figures of contemporary history par excellence have an entitlement to privacy, but only when they retire to a secluded place. The Court rejected the remainder of her appeal, stating that the public figures should tolerate the publication of pictures which are captured in public places. The applicant then filed a constitutional appeal in the Federal Constitutional Court, which too accepted her appeal in part in its landmark judgment of 15 December 1999. The Court allowed the appeal to the extent of those photos which were showing her children on the basis of Articles 2 (1) in conjunction with Article 1 (1) as well as Article 6 of the German Basic Law. Regarding other photos, however, it dismissed the appeal. Finally, Caroline von Hannover applied to the ECtHR which assessed the case and set the following principles.

5.4.3.1.2 General Principles Devised by the Court

As related to the scope of Article 8 ECHR, the Court held that personal identity such as one's name or picture, as well as physical and psychological integrity comes under the ambit of the protection under the right to respect for private life.[111] Secondly, the primary intention of the guarantee under Article 8 is to ensure the development of one's personality in the course of her relations with other human beings without outside interference. Thirdly, the scope of private life includes the protected zone a person needs for her interaction with other people, even if that interaction happens in a public context. Regarding the scope of protection of one's picture, the Court stated that the determination of whether or not a particular interference is to be assessed in the light of the protection of Article 8 depends on some basic facts. These facts are for instance, the public or private subject matter of the photos and the extent of their dissemination either for a limited purpose or for the consumption of general public.

As related to the nature of obligation[112] of the state under Article 8, the ECtHR explained that the primary object of Article 8 is to protect the individual *against arbitrary interference by the public authorities*. However, the effective protection of the interests related to Article 8 additionally requires positive obligations of the state

[110] The judgments of Federal Court of Justice and German Constitutional Court in Hannover cases shall be discussed in detail in Chap. 6.

[111] ECHR, *Von Hannover v Germany*, judgment of 24 June 2004. Application No. 59320/00, paras: 50, 52.

[112] ECHR, *Von Hannover v Germany*, judgment of 24 June 2004. Application No. 59320/00, paras 57, 58, 71.

in the form of adopting measures "to secure respect for private life even in the sphere of the relations of individuals between themselves".[113] The Court refrained from drawing a *precise boundary* between these two kinds of obligations, and stated that similar principles would rule in the determination of each obligation, where a fair balance must be struck between the competing interests of an individual and community, while *in both contexts the State enjoys a certain margin of appreciation.*[114] Similarly, private life under Article 8 has to be balanced against the freedom of expression under Article 10 of ECHR.[115] The Court reiterated that Convention's guarantees do not intend theoretical or illusory rights. Rather, they aim at rights that are practical and effective.[116]

As related to the importance of freedom of expression and of the press under Article 10, the Court highlighted that freedom of expression constitutes *one of the essential foundations of a democratic society.*[117] Free speech does not only cover favorable or benign information and ideas. Its protection may also extend to offending, shocking or disturbing speech, which is a pre-requisite of a democratic society based on pluralism, tolerance and broadmindedness. Similarly, journalistic freedom also covers a degree of *exaggeration or even provocation.*[118] The press plays an important role in a democratic society. However, it must not overstep certain bounds particularly in the matters related to people's reputation and individual rights.

As related to publication of photos, the Court held that freedom of expression is not limited to publication of information; it extends to the publication of photos as well. The protection of personality rights becomes more important when the matter is related to photos, because the photos published in the tabloid press are usually captured in an environment of frequent harassment. According to the Court, "it induces in the person concerned a very strong sense of intrusion into their private life or even of persecution."[119]

Referring to its case law, the ECtHR emphasized that in order to balance the protection of private life against freedom of expression, it has always focused on the contribution made by the publication of photos or articles in the newspapers to a

---

[113]ECHR, *Von Hannover v Germany*, judgment of 24 June 2004. Application No. 59320/00, para 57.

[114]ECHR, *Von Hannover v Germany*, judgment of 24 June 2004. Application No. 59320/00, para 57.

[115]ECHR, *Von Hannover v Germany*, judgment of 24 June 2004. Application No. 59320/00, para 58.

[116]ECHR, *Von Hannover v Germany*, judgment of 24 June 2004. Application No. 59320/00, para 71.

[117]ECHR, *Von Hannover v Germany*, judgment of 24 June 2004. Application No. 59320/00, para 58.

[118]ECHR, *Von Hannover v Germany*, judgment of 24 June 2004. Application No. 59320/00, para 58.

[119]ECHR, *Von Hannover v Germany*, judgment of 24 June 2004. Application No. 59320/00, para 59.

debate of general interest.[120] Hence, among the crucial factors in balancing the protection of private life against freedom of expression is the extent to which the published articles and photographs contribute to a "debate of general interest". But even if publications contribute to such a debate, still the balancing act must take into account the reasonable and legitimate expectations of the person protected by Article 8 ECHR that his or her private life is adequately respected.

5.4.3.1.3 Application of the Principles and Decision of the Court

In the von Hannover I case, the ECtHR noted that merely the fact of Caroline von Hannover belonging to the Monaco royal family does not make her a public figure. Hence, the nature of her routine activities related to sports, walking or shopping is *purely private*.[121] The Court emphasized the distinction between reporting of facts which, on the one hand, contribute to a debate of general interests in a democratic society such as reports about politicians when they discharge their official tasks, and which, on the other hand, do not make such a contribution but relate exclusively to details of the individuals' private life. The Court clarified that the press discharges its duties as *public watchdog* only in the former case and not in the latter one.[122] The public has also an essential corresponding right to be informed in a democratic society regarding matters of public interest which may, in certain situations, extend to the private lives of politicians. In the instant case, however, the photos of the applicant had no connection with the debate of general interest. The Court considered,

> the publication of the photos and articles in question, the sole purpose of which was to satisfy the curiosity of a particular readership regarding the details of the applicant's private life, cannot be deemed to contribute to any debate of general interest to society despite the applicant being known to the public.[123]

The Court clarified that the interest of the public does not constitute public interest and where there is a question of infringement of Article 8 right, free speech in such circumstances calls for narrower interpretation.[124] Furthermore, the Court necessitated an increased vigilance in the protection of private life due to the advent of new

---

[120] ECHR, *Von Hannover v Germany*, judgment of 24 June 2004. Application No. 59320/00, para 60.

[121] ECHR, *Von Hannover v Germany*, judgment of 24 June 2004. Application No. 59320/00, paras 61, 62.

[122] ECHR, *Von Hannover v Germany*, judgment of 24 June 2004. Application No. 59320/00, para 63.

[123] ECHR, *Von Hannover v Germany*, judgment of 24 June 2004. Application No. 59320/00, para 65.

[124] ECHR, *Von Hannover v Germany*, judgment of 24 June 2004. Application No. 59320/00, paras 66–68.

communication technologies with greater ability to store and reproduce big amount of personal data.[125]

Based on these observations, the Court declared that the German courts' interpretation of the expression "figure of contemporary society par excellence" under section 23 (1) of the German Copyright Act provided for a limited protection to the use of one's image and its application to private figures such as the applicant was not justified.[126] The Court further declared that in order for the state to discharge its positive obligation under Article 8 ECHR, the provision of the German Copyright Act has to be interpreted narrowly. The distinction between absolute and relative public figures must be obvious so that the people know "exactly when and where they are in a protected sphere or, on the contrary, in a sphere in which they must expect interference from others, especially the tabloid press".[127] Similarly, the spatial isolation standard which the German courts used was also declared as too vague. The Court stated that the contribution of the published photos and corresponding articles to a debate of general interest would be a decisive factor in balancing the protection of private life against freedom of expression. Thus it concluded that neither any such contribution was made by photos in the instant case nor the public had any legitimate interest in knowing about Caroline's private life. The only possible interest could be the commercial interest of the magazines in the photos. This, however, could not outweigh the applicant right to an *effective* protection of private life under Article 8. Due to these reasons, the ECtHR confirmed the violation of Article 8 by Germany as the German courts had not undertaken a fair balance between the right to private life and the freedom of expression.

5.4.3.2 Von Hannover v Germany II and Axel Springer AG v Germany

The von Hannover v Germany II-case and the Axel Springer AG v Germany-case have led to two follow-up decisions the ECtHR issued on the same day. An analysis of these judgments reveals an interesting fact that the Court, though it applied similar principles to the facts, yet arrived at different results. The Court further elaborated the balancing principles based on its case law and presented these in a coherent manner. One can say that the general principle of contribution of publication in the debate of general interest explained and applied in the Von Hannover case I was further clarified with adding more relevant factors.

---

[125] ECHR, *Von Hannover v Germany*, judgment of 24 June 2004. Application No. 59320/00, para 70.

[126] ECHR, *Von Hannover v Germany*, judgment of 24 June 2004. Application No. 59320/00, para 72.

[127] ECHR, *Von Hannover v Germany*, judgment of 24 June 2004. Application No. 59320/00, para 73.

5.4.3.2.1 Background of the Cases

Encouraged by the favorable decision in her first case in the ECtHR, Caroline von Hannover and her husband initiated several legal proceedings to get injunctions from the civil courts against the publication of particular photos presented in German magazines. Once again the photos, published in various magazines such as *Frau im Spiegel* and *Frau Aktuell*, were depicting her and her husband in different places. These photos were accompanied with various articles about some aspects of their life. In one of the objected photos, she was depicted as going for a walk during their skiing holidays in St. Moritz, accompanied by an article entitled, "Prince Rainier – not home alone" ("*Fürst Rainier – Nicht allein zu Haus*"), which mentioned the loneliness of the sick and old Prince Reiner and suggested that being unwell, his children should not have left him home alone.[128] Other pictures were depicting the applicants in various activities and places such as in a chairlift or attending the Rose Ball.[129]

Caroline von Hannover started legal proceedings in German civil courts seeking for injunctions against the publication of her photos. The Regional Court of Hamburg granted the injunction, stating that the illness of Prince Reiner and his relation to Von Hannover are not facts that could contribute to a debate of general interest because she does not have any official position and merely family relations are not of a paramount public interest.[130] On appeal of the publishing company, the Hamburg Court of Appeal set aside the judgment of the first instance stating that Article 8 must be balanced with Article 10 and that section 23 (2) of the Copyright Act should not be used to prohibit publications of photos of popular people captured in the public places. It also held that the protection of private life does not necessarily demand the banning of publication of photos captured in public places.[131] Von Hannover again filed an appeal in the Federal Court of Justice on the points of law. Her appeal was dismissed as not according to the concept of graduated protection (*abgestuftes Schutzkonzept*) developed in the case law under section 22 and 23 of the Copyright Act. The Federal Court of Justice stated that in order to assess whether or not some publication portrayed an aspect of contemporary society within the meaning of section 23(1) (1) of the Copyright Act, balancing has to be struck between the right to dignity under Article 1 (1), personality rights 2 (1) of the Basic Law and Article 8 of ECHR against the right to freedom of expression and of the media as well as the public's interest in being informed under Article 5 (1) of the Basic Law

[128] ECHR, *Von Hannover v Germany (No. 2)*, judgment of 07 February 2012. Application No. 40660/08, para 17.

[129] ECHR, *Von Hannover v Germany (No. 2)*, judgment of 07 February 2012. Application No. 40660/08, paras 18, 19.

[130] ECHR, *Von Hannover v Germany (No. 2)*, judgment of 07 February 2012. Application No. 40660/08, para 23.

[131] ECHR, *Von Hannover v Germany (No. 2)*, judgment of 07 February 2012. Application No. 40660/08, para 17.

and Article 10 of the Convention.[132] The Court concluded that photos had an information value in the context of article published alongside. Therefore, the appellant had no legitimate right to stop the publication. The Court also considered other factors such as the method of obtaining the pictures, which was not surreptitious in the instant case.

On invoking the jurisdiction of the Federal Constitutional Court, only partial acceptance to the appeal was granted, The FCC held that the determination of the information value by the Federal Court of Justice with respect to photos and accompanied articles could not be constitutionally objected. Similarly, Prince Ernst August von Hannover too did not get the desired relief from German courts.

Failing to get injunction from German courts, both the applicants applied to ECtHR. In their view, the refusal of the German courts to grant them injunctions against the publication of the photos violated their Article 8 right to respect for private life.

In the Axel Springer case,[133] a famous television actor and hero of a show where he played the role of a police superintendent had successfully obtained injunctions in German courts against the publication of the details of his arrest and previous conviction in prohibited drugs cases. He was arrested by the Berlin police and a small amount of cocaine was recovered from him. The news and follow up articles were published in different sections of German media, which he successfully challenged in different civil courts. Axel Springer, a publishing company feeling aggrieved from the injunctions and penalties imposed on it in Germany, applied to ECtHR on the basis of Article 10.

In both of these judgments, the ECtHR set similar principles and, interestingly, found in the former judgment that there was no violation of Article 8, while in the latter case, the Court held that Article 10 right of the publishing company had been violated.

5.4.3.2.2 Balancing Principles and Criteria Set for the Balancing Exercise by the ECtHR

As for the general principles concerning private life, freedom of expression, and margin of appreciation, the ECtHR almost repeated their whole description of Von Hannover-I judgment. The Court also reemphasized some general principles in both cases and then articulated six-point criteria for balancing both Article 8 and 10 of the ECHR.

The Court stressed that the press plays an *essential role* because of its contribution as a *public watchdog* in a democratic society. It explained that the press has a corresponding *duty* to disseminate information in order for the public to exercise its

---

[132] ECHR, *Von Hannover v Germany (No. 2)*, judgment of 07 February 2012. Application No. 40660/08, para 29.

[133] ECHR, *Axel Springer AG v Germany*, judgment of 7 February 2012. Application No. 39954/08.

right to receive information.[134] The Court also clarified that for the outcome of the case, the Court will make no distinction whether an application has been filed under Article 8 or under Article 10, as both Articles of the ECHR comm*and equal respect*.[135]

The Court laid down six-point criteria in a coherent form, based on the extensive case law of the Court. According to the Court, in the event of balancing exercise of the freedom of expression with the right to respect for private life, the following factors shall be taken into consideration.[136]

Contribution to a Debate of General Interest

The Court clarified that it is an essential criterion to consider the contribution of the newspaper articles and photos to the debate of general interest. However, the Court did not fix the subject of general interest and held that the circumstances of the case will determine what constitutes the debate of general interest. The general interest of the public is not limited to politics or criminality according to the given criteria. Public interest could be extended even to entertainment news such as sports and performing art. On the other hand, reporting the rumors about marital discords of the President of a country or the financial difficulties of a famous singer are not considered as justifiable contribution in the debate of general interest.

How Well Known Is the Person Concerned and What Is the Subject of the Report?

The status of the person in terms of her role and position in the society plays a role in the balancing exercise. It has to be determined whether the person holds a public role and is being reported on this role or whether details of the private life of a private person are spread. According to the Court,

> fundamental distinction needs to be made between reporting facts capable of contributing to a debate in a democratic society, relating to politicians in the exercise of their official functions for example, and reporting details of the private life of an individual who does not exercise such functions.[137]

The press exercises its role as a 'public watchdog' in a democratic society when they disseminate information to the public regarding issues of public interest and its role has more limitations in the case of dissemination of information with respect to private individuals.

---

[134] ECHR, *Axel Springer AG v Germany*, judgment of 7 February 2012. Application No. 39954/08, paras 79, 80.

[135] ECHR, *Axel Springer AG v Germany*, judgment of 7 February 2012. Application No. 39954/08, para 87.

[136] ECHR, *Von Hannover v Germany (No. 2)*, judgment of 07 February 2012. Application No. 40660/08, paras 108–113. ECHR, *Axel Springer AG v Germany*, judgment of 7 February 2012. Application No. 39954/08, paras 89–95.

[137] ECHR, *Von Hannover v Germany (No. 2)*, judgment of 07 February 2012. Application No. 40660/08, para 110.

Prior Conduct of the Person Concerned

The conduct and the role of the person concerned prior to the publication or obtaining of information is also important. Circumstances where the person himself causes the disclosure or gives consent to taking photos or publication of information or photos or reveals himself the data about his personal life to the public media shall also be considered. However, the cooperation of a person in a limited context or for a limited purpose does not give an absolute license to the media for an all-out media assault.

Content, Form and Consequences of the Publication

The way in which the photos or articles are published and the manner in which the press represents the individual in a particular context as well as the extent of the reach of a particular publication are also factors that must be considered in the balancing exercise.

Circumstances in Which the Photos Were Taken and Method of Obtaining the Information and Its Veracity

Not only the context of publication but also the manner in which the photos or information were obtained by the press are relevant. Hence, "the nature or seriousness of the intrusion and the consequences of publication of the photo for the person concerned"[138] are elements that have to be taken into account in the balancing process. The veracity of the information is also an important factor as the proviso of Article 10 requires journalists to act in good faith which is possible only when they would try their best to verify the accuracy of the subject information. They are obliged to provide "reliable and precise information in accordance with the ethics of journalism."[139]

5.4.3.2.3 Application of the Principles and Decisions of the Court

The Court in von Hannover case (No. 2) concluded that the national courts of Germany have taken into consideration the criteria elaborated earlier and that there was no violation of Article 8 rights of the applicant. The Court also approved the verdict of Federal Constitutional Court which had held that the illness of Prince Reiner had an information value for the public and hence that could be regarded as a contribution to the debate of general interest.[140] Similarly, the photos accompanied with the articles were considered in a holistic manner, i.e., not separated from the article and so a factor in such contribution. Responding to a valid apprehension of the applicants regarding the overstretching of the criteria by the media, where it may

---

[138] ECHR, *Von Hannover v Germany (No. 2)*, judgment of 07 February 2012. Application No. 40660/08, para 113.

[139] ECHR, *Axel Springer AG v Germany*, judgment of 7 February 2012. Application No. 39954/08.

[140] ECHR, *Von Hannover v Germany (No. 2)*, judgment of 07 February 2012. Application No. 40660/08, para 118.

circumvent the photos and articles in future and publish that in a way to give a false impression of their connection to the debate of general interest, the Court stated that it was outside of the scope of the instant case and that the Court cannot consider or guarantee future eventualities. It advised the applicants that they could raise the issue in national courts if they would have any such complaint in the future. The Court also explained a third category of individuals which fall in the middle area and can neither be regarded as full-fledged public figures nor as ordinary people. It held that both of the applicants belong to that category where they do not have political offices but still they are much popular and have respective roles in the public arena.

Interestingly, the application of the same criteria brought the Court to an opposite conclusion in the case of Axel Springer v Germany. As the Court did not agree to the balancing exercise undertaken by German courts, it deemed it apt to state every point of the criteria and apply it on the facts of the case. Before arriving at the decision, the Court considered the first bullet of the criteria—contribution to the debate of general interest—and stated that the public usually has an interest in the news where the subject matter is related to criminal incidents. However, other factors such as the position of the accused person and the presumption of innocence come into operation too.[141] Secondly, the Court disagreed with the Hamburg Regional Court's assertion that the actor was not that famous and stated that he was well-known due to his role of a police superintendent in a famous television show which was broadcasted for a long time. However, the Court resorted here to the controversial presumption about public figures that they are role models for their fans and that fans like to follow them and have a legitimate right to get information about their lives. The Court stated,

> [w]hilst it can be said that the public does generally make a distinction between an actor and the character he or she plays, *there may nonetheless be a close link between the popularity of the actor in question and his or her character* where, as in the instant case, the actor is mainly known for that particular role. In the case of X, that role was, moreover, that of a police superintendent, whose mission was law enforcement and crime prevention. That fact was such as to increase the public's interest in being informed of X's arrest for a criminal offence. Having regard to those factors and to the terms employed by the domestic courts in assessing the degree to which X was known to the public, the Court considers that he was sufficiently well known to qualify as a public figure. *That consideration thus reinforces the public's interest in being informed of X's arrest and of the criminal proceedings against him.*[142]

The Court also assessed the conduct of the actor prior to the publication of the impugned orders and held that he himself caused to reduce the legitimate expectation of the protection of his private life due to his appearance in media, where he himself

[141] ECHR, *Axel Springer AG v Germany*, judgment of 7 February 2012. Application No. 39954/08, para 96.

[142] ECHR, *Axel Springer AG v Germany*, judgment of 7 February 2012. Application No. 39954/08, para 99.

brought the details of his private life to the limelight.[143] Regarding the method of obtaining information it held,

> there is nothing to suggest that such a balancing exercise was not undertaken. The fact is, however, that having regard to the nature of the offence committed by X, the degree to which X is well known to the public, the circumstances of his arrest and the veracity of the information in question, the applicant company – having obtained confirmation of that information from the prosecuting authorities themselves – did not have sufficiently strong grounds for believing that it should preserve X's anonymity.[144]

Regarding the impact of the information published in the press and their consequences for the person, the Court stated that the articles did not contain any such expression to vilify and raise false allegations. The Court concluded that the sanctions imposed by German courts are not justified on the basis of the above stated factors and that the sanctions could result into chilling effects on the publisher company. Therefore, the restrictions were held disproportionate to the alleged objective, which resulted into the violation of Article 10 right of the publisher company.

The judgments in both cases were welcomed by the media and free speech advocates as in both instances, free speech prevailed against the right to private life as a result of the balancing exercise of the ECtHR. Some commentators took it as a 'rebalancing' in order to allay the fears of media bodies.[145] In the Axel Springer case, the decision was not unanimous as five judges wrote dissenting views, primarily criticizing the majority decision on the basis of its method of analyzing the balancing exercise undertaken by national courts. They were of the view that the ECtHR should not assume the status of a court of 'fourth instance' by going into details of how the balancing was made. Rather, the Court should restrain itself to the determination whether or not the balancing criteria have been followed. The dissenting judges opined that the Court should not question the balancing exercise conducted by national courts unless it finds a *manifest error or omission*.

The consideration of the nature of a dramatic role of a law enforcer and its relation to his real life arrest as a relevant factor in its contribution to the debate of general interest has also been questioned on the basis that this reasoning cannot be extended to other roles such as doctors.[146] Similarly, in the Von Hannover case, the skiing photo was termed by the Court as capable of contributing to the debate of general interest *at least to some degree* is not entirely convincing. These decisions were also considered as "containing appeasement elements" where member states primarily

---

[143] ECHR, *Von Hannover v Germany (No. 2)*, judgment of 07 February 2012. Application No. 40660/08, para 101.

[144] ECHR, *Von Hannover v Germany (No. 2)*, judgment of 07 February 2012. Application No. 40660/08, para 107.

[145] See for example: Reid (2012).

[146] Reid (2012).

United Kingdom were said to be not happy with some judgments which it considered as ignoring the principle of subsidiarity.[147]

5.4.3.3 Illustrative Judgments of the ECtHR on Invasive Media Practices

Following are some of the illustrative cases, based on such facts that can be correlated to Pakistani media intrusions, which were taken to the ECtHR and where the Court provided either adequate relief to privacy victims or set guiding principles to prevent future infringements.

5.4.3.3.1 Protection of the Victims of Sexual Violence from Media Exposure

One of the problems discussed in detail in Chap. 2 is media's disclosing the names and medical information of the victims of rape in Pakistan. There is no justification for the publication and disclosure of rapes, neither intruding in their lives for the purpose of interviews has any public interest. However, it is a routine exercise of media to report these crimes with souring personal details. There is no comprehensive legal regime or statutory rules which could be invoked by rape victims or their parents to obtain injunctions or to claim compensation for the damage.[148] In contrast, regarding the case law of the ECtHR, the identity disclosure and the disregard for the confidentiality of medical information related to the case are taken very seriously. In the case of P. and S. v. Poland, the Court conceded the traumatic situation of the rape victim, when she and her mother brought the tragedy and the aftermath of their identity disclosure shared with the Court, and claimed a satisfying sum of 60,000 € and 30,000 € respectively.[149] The precise reproduction of her tragic experience in the judgment speaks volumes of how the identity disclosure of a rape victim can stigmatize both the victim and her family that also leads to harassment and discrimination in many cases.[150] Regarding the importance and sensitivity of health related

[147] Fenwick (2012) An appeasement approach in the European Court of Human Rights? https://ukconstitutionallaw.org/2012/04/05/helen-fenwick-an-appeasement-approach-in-the-european-court-of-human-rights/. Accessed 25 August 2023.

[148] The Code for Conduct for electronic media provides in section 8 (6), "Identity of any victim of rape, sexual abuse, terrorism and kidnaping shall not be revealed without prior permission of the victim or victim's guardian where victim is minor." However, the ineffectiveness of the regulatory regime (which has already been explained) makes such ethical standards ineffective.

[149] ECHR, *P and S v Poland*, judgment of 30 October 2012. Application No. 57375/08.

[150] ECHR, *P and S v Poland*, judgment of 30 October 2012. Application No. 57375/08, para 173: "She submitted that the impact on the events concerned in the case had been extremely severe on her. She had been the object of comments expressed in public, in the media and directly to her. A book on the case by an antichoice activist had been published, describing the events in a malicious and distorted manner. Her true identity and details of her private life had leaked to the media. She had suffered because her mother who had tried to protect and help her, was vilified in public. She

data, the Court held, "[r]especting the confidentiality of health data is a vital principle in the legal systems of all the contracting parties to the Convention. The disclosure of such data may dramatically affect an individual's private and family life, as well as his or her social and employment situation, by exposing that person to opprobrium and the risk of ostracism."[151] The Court awarded 30,000 € to the victim and 15,000 € to her mother as compensation for their non-pecuniary damage.

The jurisprudence about rape victims' identity does not accept the arguments in the favor of disclosures of names of victims on various pretexts (already discussed in Chap. 2). Rather, it emphasizes the hazardous psychological and social implications of such privacy breaches. The names of rape victims as well as medical or other data associated to the incident are sensitive information and need to be protected in an absolute manner. The principles devised by ECtHR related to this problem can be of much help for Pakistan in strictly prohibiting such disclosures to the press and media through legal means.

5.4.3.3.2 Protection of Children from Media Exposure

Children become the focus of attention in various newsworthy events, particularly, in cases of either they are accused in some juvenile delinquency or if they are victims of criminality. In both cases, their right to privacy is highly important due to their specific need of rehabilitation and personality development. They are not psychologically strong enough to deal with so much media attention and could easily end up into severe emotional and psychological issues.

In a number of occasions, the ECtHR has rejected the claim that a non-public hearing constitutes a violation of the freedom of expression or the right to a fair trial. The Court held that the right to a fair and open trial may be subordinated to the right to privacy of children and other people. In the case of B. and P. v. the United Kingdom the Court explained that "[t]he proceedings which the present applicants wished to take place in public concerned the residence of each man's son following the parents' divorce or separation" and that "such proceedings are prime examples of cases where the exclusion of the press and public may be justified in order to protect the privacy of the child and parties and to avoid prejudicing the interests of justice".[152] To enable the deciding judge to gain a full and possibly accurate picture of what is beneficial for a child, i.e. regarding his residential options and communication with relatives, the Court held essential that the parents and other witnesses must feel capable of expressing themselves candidly *without fear of public curiosity*

had also been deprived of liberty. Her suffering during the summer of 2008 when the main events took place was intense, but she also suffered later when, for example, her teachers had made inappropriate comments and disclosed to her classmates what had happened to her."

[151] ECHR, *P and S v Poland*, judgment of 30 October 2012. Application No. 57375/08, para 128.

[152] ECHR, *B and P v UK*, judgment of 24 April 2001. Applications No. 36337/97 and 35974/97, para 38.

or comment. This objective cannot be achieved if the proceedings are open to the public and media.

The Court is also very considerate for the rightful welfare of minor offenders, even if they are involved in the most heinous crimes. For instance, in the case of V. versus The United Kingdom, when two minor boys at the age of ten abducted a 2 years old toddler from a shopping center, took him to two miles away and then battered him to death and throw him on the railway track, the Court observed: "It follows that, in respect of a young child charged with a grave offence attracting high levels of media and public interest, it would be necessary to conduct the hearing in such a way as to reduce as far as possible his or her feelings of intimidation and inhibition."[153] The nature of trial and judgments in such cases must keep into consideration the later life and development of the juveniles. The Court termed it essential to take into consideration the age, maturity level and emotional capacities of children and stated that measures should be taken to enable them participate effectively in the legal proceedings.[154] Regarding the publicity of the cases, the Court ordered for the confidentiality of their identities and held the member states responsible to protect such vulnerable under trial juveniles from undue media attention.

The judgments in the cases of Kurier Zeitungsverlag und Druckerei GmbH v. Austria[155] and Krone Verlag GmbH v. Austria[156] are a powerful illustration of how the ECtHR rejects the free speech defense when it comes to the privacy of a child. In this case, the applicant, a publishing company, filed an application in the ECtHR against the payment of compensation to a child and her mother, imposed by Austrian Courts under the Media Act as a result of establishing the violation of their privacy. The issue was related to the excessive maltreatment of a child by her parents. The Court directed officers to take custody of the child. Resistance of the family and the frightening response of the child attracted media who covered those scenes and later on, the applicants published a number of articles along with pictures. On the complaint of the child and her mother against publication, Austrian Courts imposed a fine of 9000 € on Kurier Zeitung for publishing 3 articles, and 130,000 € on Krone Zeitung for publishing 13 articles. Rejecting the complaint, the Court held, "[p]hotographs appearing in the tabloid press are often taken in a climate of continual harassment which induces in the person concerned a very strong sense of intrusion into their private life or even of persecution".[157]

---

[153] ECHR, *V v UK*, judgment of 16 December 1999. Application No. 24888/94, para 87. See also: *T v UK*, judgment of 06 March 1998. Application No. 24724/94.

[154] ECHR, *V v UK*, judgment of 16 December 1999. Application No. 24888/94, para 86.

[155] ECHR, *Kurier Zeitungsverlag und Druckerei GmbH v Austria*, judgment of 17 January 2012. Application No. 3401/07.

[156] ECHR, *Krone Verlag GMBH v Austria*, judgment of 19 June 2012. Application No. 27306/07.

[157] ECHR, *Kurier Zeitungsverlag und Druckerei GmbH v Austria*, judgment of 17 January 2012. Application No. 3401/07, para 48.

5.4.3.3.3 Protection of Private Life of Public Figures from Media Intrusion

The Convention provides protection to the right to privacy of public figures. Personal privacy in public places and of public figures is a controversial area of privacy law and the balancing of free speech and right to privacy pose a great deal of difficulty to judges and regulators alike. However, to announce *zero privacy* either for public figures or in the public places is not accepted by the ECtHR. The principles elaborated in the previous section sufficiently make it clear that the Strasbourg Court has a sophisticated and nuanced approach to resolve this tricky problem. The guidelines devised in the ECtHR's jurisprudence have a great utilization for comparative law study. In the case of Von Hannover v Germany, the ECtHR rejected the German notion of 'person of contemporary history par excellence' under German Arts and Copy Right Law and held that it cannot agree to the domestic court's interpretation, which delimits the protection of private life of the public figures.[158]

5.4.3.3.4 Maintaining Integrity of Court Trials and Proceedings

In the case of Egeland v. Norway, the ECtHR found that the prohibition of journalists from taking and publication of the picture of the accused outside the court's premises in the police car was not a violation of the right to free speech.[159] Before reaching that conclusion, the Court referred to a Principle in the Recommendations of the Committee of Ministers of the Council of Europe, which provides that suspects, accused and even convicted persons partake the protection of Article 8.[160]

In the case of Sciacca v. Italy, the ECtHR rejected the stance of the Italian government that convicted persons' right to privacy could be conquered by the right of the public to be informed or the objective of preventing further offences in the society.[161] In that case, the police took photographs of a person under

[158] ECHR, *Von Hannover v Germany*, judgment of 24 June 2004. Application No. 59320/00, para 72.

[159] ECHR, *Egeland and Hanseid v Norway*, judgment of 16 April 2009. Application No. 34438/04, para 65.

[160] Principle 8 of Appendix to the Recommendation (2003) of the Committee of Ministers of the Council of Europe: "The provision of information about suspects, accused or convicted persons or other parties to criminal proceedings should respect their right to protection of privacy in accordance with Article 8 of the Convention. Particular protection should be given to parties who are minors or other vulnerable persons, as well as to victims, to witnesses and to the families of suspects, accused and convicted. In all cases, particular consideration should be given to the harmful effect which the disclosure of information enabling their identification may have on the persons referred to in this Principle."

[161] ECHR, *Sciacca v Italy*, judgment of 11 January 2005. Application No. 50774/99, paras 30, 31.

investigation and subsequently released them to the media and held a press conference regarding the financial fraud of the person.[162]

5.4.3.3.5 Limitations of General Nature on Journalistic Enterprises Under ECHR

The right to free speech provided in the Convention carries with it "duties and responsibilities" and may be subject to restrictions (para 2 of Article 10). These duties and responsibilities equally apply to journalistic conduct and newsgathering practices. Journalists are required to respect the rights of others in the course of their activities.

With regard to such duties, responsibilities and restrictions over the freedom of expression or media, the ECtHR has explained that it does not intend to direct the journalists how they should make their programs or what they should or should not publish. It believes in the editorial independence and integrity. However, the Court has clarified that editorial autonomy has its limits. In the case of Krone Verlag v. Austria, it stated that editorial independence should not be hampered through micromanagement at the decisional level, but such "editorial discretion is not unbounded."[163] For the Courts, in order to fulfill the vital function by the press as a public watchdog, both the rights of the press to impart information and the right of the public to receive that information must go hand in hand.

The Court has also required the presence of good faith in the dissemination of correct information, even if it happens that information is uncertain at the time of publication and not perfectly precise or accurate. The prevalence of good faith can absolve journalists from liability.[164]

Good faith does not count in creating sensational scenes and intruding into private lives for the purpose of voyeuristic content. Most of the issues and illustrations discussed in the Pakistani media privacy problems (Chap. 2) do not have any kind of lofty objectives as mocking people and reducing them to a state of humiliation show a *prima facie* bad faith. The ECtHR differentiated sensationalist reports from serious reports and has held that the former has no protection if someone is scandalized for no cogent reasons.[165] It also makes a differentiation between objective reporting and

---

[162]ECHR, *Sciacca v Italy*, judgment of 11 January 2005. Application No. 50774/99.

[163]ECHR, *Kurier Zeitungsverlag und Druckerei GmbH v Austria*, judgment of 17 January 2012. Application No. 3401/07, para 47: "Whilst it is true that the methods of objective and balanced reporting may vary considerably and that it is therefore not for this Court, nor for the national courts, to substitute its own views for those of the press as to what technique of reporting should be adopted (*Jersild v. Denmark*, 23 September 1994, § 31, Series A no. 298), editorial discretion is not unbounded."

[164]ECHR, *Fressoz and Roire v France*, judgment of 21 January 1999. Application No. 29183/95, para 54.

[165]See for instance: ECHR, *Stoll v Switzerland*, judgment of 10 December 2007. Application No. 69698/01. Unreported ECtHR Press Release: https://hudoc.echr.coe.int/app/conversion/pdf/?

sensationalistic reporting. In the case of Couderc and Hachette Filipacchi Associés v. France, the ECtHR reiterated "that the public interest cannot be reduced to the public's thirst for information about the private life of others, or to the reader's wish for sensationalism or even voyeurism."[166]

5.5 Conclusion

In the nutshell, the above illustrations sufficiently justify the research premise that the protection of the right to privacy and its balancing with the right to free speech under the European Convention on Human Rights provides a good model for comparative studies. There is a rich human rights jurisprudence available, which can guide us into the resolution of most of the privacy problems related to media practices in Pakistan. After the case law illustrations, we can better understand the actual tools used by ECtHR for privacy right's protection and its reconciliation with the freedom of expression.

It is pertinent to mention here that the discussion of the principles and jurisprudence of the ECtHR is undertaken while keeping in view the main findings provided under the conceptual framework in Chap. 3. To recap those conclusions: (1) privacy as a basic right in its own and due to its consequential value; (2) precision in the definition is neither possible nor required; (3) the interests attached to this broad right need legal protection, interference must be contingent upon specific context; (4) free speech is also neither absolute neither monolithic; and lastly, (5) there is no presumption of superiority between free speech and privacy which means conflicts could only be resolved through balancing techniques while interference must be justified on the basis of legal provisions keeping in view the principle of proportionality.

References

Alexy R (2005) Balancing, constitutional review, and representation. Int J Constitutional Law 3(4): 572–581

Alexy R (2009) On constitutional rights to protection. Legisprudence 3(1):1–7

Alexy R (2010) A theory of constitutional rights. Oxford University Press

Alexy R (2014) Constitutional rights and proportionality. Revus J Constitutional Theory Philos Law/Revija za ustavno teorijo in filozofijo prava 20(22):51–65

Arden M (2015) Human rights and European law: building new legal orders. Oxford University Press

---

library=ECHR&id=003-2208290-2355248&filename=003-2208290-2355248.pdf. Accessed 25 August 2023.

[166] ECHR, *Couderc and Hachette Filipacchi Associés v France*, judgment of 10 November 2015. Application No. 40454/07, para 101.

Barendt E (2009) Balancing freedom of expression and privacy: the jurisprudence of the Strasbourg Court. J Media Law 1(1):49
Barnes RD (2005) The Carolina verdict: protecting individual privacy against media invasion as a matter of human rights. Penn St Law Rev 110:599
Çalı B (2007) Balancing human rights? Methodological problems with weights, scales and proportions. Hum Rights Q 1:251
Currie DP (1986) Positive and negative constitutional rights. Univ Chic Law Rev 53(3):864
Dworkin R (1977) Taking rights seriously. Duckworth
Ehlers D, Becker U (eds) (2007) European fundamental rights and freedoms. Walter de Gruyter
Kilkelly U (2003) The right to respect for private end family life: a guide to the implementation of Article 8 of the European Convention on Human Rights. Directorate General of Human Rights Council of Europe, pp 10–11
Korpisaari PH (2017) Balancing freedom of expression and the right to private life in the European Court of Human Rights-application and interpretation of the key criteria. Commun Law Haywards Heath 22(2):39–50
Ľalík T (2011) Understanding the binding effect of the case-law of the ECtHR in domestic legal order. In: International conference: effectiveness of the European system of protection of human rights, Warszawa Sejm
Macovei M (2004) A guide to the implementation of Article 10 of the European Convention on Human Rights. Human rights handbooks
Mahoney P (2014) The Relationship between the Strasbourg Court and the National Courts. LQR 130:568
Mountfeld H (2001) The concept of a lawful interference with fundamental rights. In: Cooper J and Jeffrey eds Understanding human rights principles. Hart Publishing
Reid E (2012) Rebalancing privacy and freedom of expression. Edinburgh Law Rev 16:253
Starmer K (2001) Positive obligation under the Convention. In: Cooper J, Jowell J (eds) Understanding human rights principles, vol 4. Hart Publishing
Stratford J (2002) Striking the balance: privacy v freedom of expression under the European Convention on Human Rights. In: Colvin M (ed) Developing key privacy rights. Bloomsbury Publishing
Van Dijk P, Hoof GJ, Van Hoof GJ (1998) Theory and practice of the European Convention on Human Rights. Martinus Nijhoff Publishers

Chapter 6
Privacy Protection in ECHR Member States: Germany and the United Kingdom

This chapter will present the privacy law regimes from two signatory states of the ECHR to the extent that these regimes are valuable for the main objective of this work. The chosen model jurisdictions are Germany and the United Kingdom—one civil law country and one common law country. The following sections will analyze the indigenous protection available to privacy interests in the light of the ECHR. The analysis of interaction of Convention's law and principles with the national jurisdictions will help to understand the functionality of the general principles devised under the international law of the ECHR. The principles are not only valuable for the theory of privacy and free speech but they also have a noticeable impact on the national jurisdictions in the shape of refining their approach not only towards the protection of the right to privacy but also towards its balancing against the countervailing right of free speech and public interest. Thus, this comparison will provide us a foundation for developing proposals and prescribing solutions for the main research problem in the subsequent chapter.

6.1 Protection of Privacy in Germany

6.1.1 Overview of Illustrative Cases

Germany is one of the founding members of the Council of Europe and it takes seriously its commitment under international law to the upholding of values protected under the ECHR. The right to respect for private life under Article 8 and the right to freedom of expression under Article 10 of the Convention enjoy an effective enforcement in Germany. In this context, the Federal Constitutional Court has developed illuminating principles and unique doctrinal approaches regarding the optimum protection of these values and their mutual balancing. Following a case by case development of privacy law, its balancing with free speech is elaborated by the

S. Aftab, *Comparative Perspectives on the Right to Privacy*, Ius Gentium: Comparative Perspectives on Law and Justice 109,
https://doi.org/10.1007/978-3-031-45575-9_6

Constitutional Court as well as by civil courts which, in doing so, have to observe the Constitution and the guidelines of the Constitutional Court. An overview of illustrative cases reveals how the German approach to the dilemma of protecting privacy from media intrusion is worthy for comparative law studies not only in its own right but also where the jurisprudence of the ECtHR is duly taken into consideration.

As we have seen in the previous chapter, the refinement of privacy law as well as the balancing principles under the Caroline series of cases by ECtHR has significant importance for a research project in this area of law. Similar cases adjudicated in Germany are not of a lesser value as the German courts have produced many landmark judgments, which clarify different legal and constitutional quandaries arising from the conflict of basic rights. Thus, a highly developed German law regulating the issues around the right to the development of one's personality is capable of protecting the concrete areas of the privacy right of people in cases dealing with the State as well as in conflicts between private parties.[1]

The Lebach case of 1973 is one of such instances where the Federal Constitutional Court has demonstrated that how a right to publish a crime story should be balanced against the subject's right to the re-integration into society.[2] In this case a television channel wanted to broadcast a documentary based on a crime of armed robbery and murder in the village of Lebach that had happened several years ago. The plaintiff, who had been convicted for aid to these acts and was soon to be released after serving several years of imprisonment, was one of the subjects of the documentary. He failed to get injunction from the civil courts against such broadcast and ultimately filed a constitutional appeal on the basis of his personality rights. The Constitutional Court held that the right to the free development of one's personality in combination with the inviolability of dignity protects an autonomous sphere of private life, where the protected individuals can develop and preserve their individual identity. This includes the right to be left alone as well as to be free from external intrusion into private realm. The Court further held that each person may determine for him or herself whether and to what extent certain events from his or her life may be presented to the public. Public reporting of a criminal act by naming, depicting or portraying the delinquent would affect his personal rights, because it negatively qualifies his person in the eyes of the addressees from the outset. Nevertheless, in the process of balancing personality rights with the freedom of the press and broadcasting, reporting on criminal offences, especially serious criminal offences, is possible even with naming and pictures, as long as the reporting and broadcasting are made at the time when the criminal offence or criminal trial have just taken place. But this balancing result must change the more time goes by. Once the delinquent underwent punishment for what he had done in the past he should be given an opportunity to become member of the society just like other people. His interest could have been harmed by the broadcast of the story afresh as the people would have been reminded a forgotten incident. The broadcasting at that later date would hinder

[1] See for instance: Markesinis (1999).

[2] BVerfGE 35, 202.

re-socialization—a right that is also constitutionally protected and that increases the weight of the interests of the delinquent. Under these circumstances, the balancing result turns: If the re-socialization is endangered, a renewed reporting of a crime, on the basis of which the delinquent can be identified, must be refrained from.[3] This judgment of the Constitutional Court thus shows that a balancing process has to take into account all circumstances, involved interests and rights at the relevant point in time. It also has provided a foundation to a relatively new right, popularly known as the "right to be forgotten" or "*Recht auf Vergessen*" in German which postulates that a person has a *right to be let alone* even if he was once a subject of public attention at some point in time in the past and that remaining in the media focus for a while does not mean perpetual abandonment of the right to privacy. This novel right as a facet of privacy and personality rights is to be explained later on in this section.

German law does not protect every kind of speech and the question whether a contribution provides something to the more general dimension of free individual and public opinion forming process, plays an important role in balancing exercises by the courts. The German jurisprudence of both the Constitutional Court (BVerfG) as well as civil law highest court (BGH) is consistent on the denial of 'free speech protection' to utterance which, at the time of the discourse, the speaker knows to be false. In other words, conscious lies are not considered as a protected speech because they would not add anything fruitful to the normatively underlying free individual and public opinion forming process. In the Soraya case, a newspaper had published a fictitious interview of Princess Soraya, the ex-wife of Shah of Iran.[4] The Constitutional Court rejected the free speech defense of the defendant and accepted the civil courts' imposition of heavy damages on the publication. In one of the Caroline von Monaco series of cases, the Federal Court of Justice took a similarly hard stance against a fictitious interview of Princess Caroline von Monaco, which was based on fabricated facts including her intention to remarry.[5] The Court declared that such fabricated publications amount to grave and intense infringement of the right to personality of the subject. In such cases, mere apology of the publisher, his written retraction from the story or printing the correct version of the plaintiff might not be sufficient to correct the loss suffered by the victim. It held that the consistent case law entitles the plaintiffs to monetary compensation in such cases of a grave breach of the personality right.[6]

[3] BVerfGE 35, 202 (226 ff.).

[4] BVerfGE 34, 269.

[5] BGHZ 128,1. Bundesgerichtshof (Sixth Civil Division) judgment of 15 November 1991.

[6] "Infringements of the right of personality like the one before the court are grave intrusions of this kind. In full knowledge of the fact that the plaintiff refused to be interviewed, the defendant created a fictitious interview on problems in the plaintiff's private life and her psychological condition [further details]. In order to increase his circulation numbers and for commercial gain, the defendant exposed the plaintiff's private life to the curiosity and sensationalism of hundreds of thousands of readers. In respect of two of the publications in question this was done deliberately. In the case of the third publication there was at least negligence. [. . . .] Granting monetary compensation has its roots in the consideration that, without such a claim, impairments of a person's dignity and honour

The case law requires both journalists, who are in their quest for serious reporting, as well as paparazzi, who are interested in sensational pictures of celebrities, to be mindful of the personality rights of the subjects particularly in their pictorial stories. The Constitutional Court recognizes personal rights as well as freedom of the press and requires balancing processes. Informational dissemination by the press plays an important role in the formation of public opinion and it makes the press an important ingredient of a democratic society. Behavior of celebrities and politicians worthy of criticism and even minor offences such as traffic violation could be reported if the offender is a public figure whose behavior shows a disregard for traffic laws in the manner of repeatedly rash driving and speed violations. On these considerations, the Court held that a constitutional complaint had no chances of being successful in a case in which a publisher had published a news story and a picture about the traffic violations and suspension of driving license of a famous person.[7] However, the Court also made it clear that the presumption of innocence is a fundamental right which must be considered in the balancing process.

According to the Federal Court of Justice, the imposition of compensation is justified, if paparazzi repeatedly violate the image and personality rights of a son of a celebrity by taking pictures of his daily life activities.[8] If it is clearly communicated by the subject that she or he does not want to be pictured or remain in the limelight and in spite of knowing this, media disregards the wishes, such conduct would be normatively sanctioned because it is either guided by grave negligence or profit motives. Therefore, the violation of personality right entitles the plaintiff to compensation in addition to retraction or preventive injunctions.[9] This case also clarifies

---

would often remain unpunished with the result that legal protection of one's personality starts to wither and decay. In contrast to compensation for pain and suffering, in cases of monetary compensation claimed for an infringement of the general right of personality, the aspect of the victim's satisfaction comes to the fore (reference). Despite doubts raised in legal literature (references), the court upholds this point of view. Moreover, this form of redress is meant also to serve a preventive purpose." BGHZ 128, 1 (Bundesgerichtshof (Sixth Civil Division)) decided on 15.11.1991. Translated by: Snook, available at: https://law.utexas.edu/transnational/foreign-law-translations/german/case.php?id=731. Accessed 02 September 2023.

[7] BVerfG, judgment of the 1st Chamber of the First Senate of June 13, 2006, 1 BvR 565/06.

[8] BGH NJW 1996, 985, VI. Civil Senate (VI ZR 223/94).

[9] "[T]he violation of the right which the defendant has committed against the claimant goes beyond the mere publication of the photos. It acquires its special gravity from the fact that the defendant, by the repeated publication of the photos of the claimant without his consent, has violated his right to his own image with particular obstinacy and, at least by the last publication, has disregarded the claimant's contrary wishes which were expressly stated to it. Besides the repeated breach of the law by the defendant which consisted in the publication of the photos without consent, there was also therefore a conscious and manifest disregard of the stated wishes of the claimant. Besides this, the defendant was acting for its own commercial advantage. This means that the violation of the right which the defendant has committed against the claimant is, through its intensity, the defendant's motive and the degree of its fault, to be assessed as so grave that it requires the granting of a claim to monetary compensation. The special nature of the violation of the right to one's own image consists in the fact that the victim - in contrast to other cases in which he can perhaps demand the retraction or the correction of a statement infringing his personality right - has at his disposal against such a

that a mere relation to someone from the ruling family does not automatically provide paparazzi the right to take pictures of his private life.

More recent case law demonstrates that the Federal Constitutional Court is interpreting the privacy protection norms through a nuanced approach which takes into consideration the realities of modern life in the shape of cutthroat competition in the media for sensationalistic content as well as the technological developments which has the capacity to grant virtual permanency to private images and facts. Therefore, the judgments in the cases of Caroline von Hannover[10] and in the recent "right to be forgotten case"[11] formulate differentiated and partly new guidelines for the media and online platforms. Deciding on a number of appeals, the Constitutional Court in the case of Caroline von Hannover clarified the scope of fundamental rights to one's dignity and privacy against the right to entertaining speech.[12] The two decisions of the Constitutional Court in the "right to be forgotten" cases are historic judgments that succinctly underscore the challenges of the Internet and communication technologies.[13] Both of these judgments were awarded on the same date in somewhat similar constitutional complaints against search engine operators, aiming to remove the links to an archived press article (RTBF-I) and an archived television documentary (RTBF-II) which appear as a result of typing the names of the complainants in the search engine bar. After clarifying jurisdictional issues and the compatibility of the fundamental rights provided by the German Basic Law, the Charter of Fundamental Rights of the European Union (CFREU) and the European Convention on Human Rights (ECHR), the Constitutional Court held that all the relevant norms support the development of a right to be forgotten. Regarding German Basic law, this right requires from the state to refrain from its violation at one hand, and through its indirect horizontal effect, to be protected against violations by other private parties. This right and its multidimensionality are of immense importance due to the fact that digital media and online platforms have blurred the boundaries between social and private sphere. Therefore, they pose a greater threat to the right to personality and the associated values and interests must be balanced by the judiciary in deciding upon complaints. Regarding the balancing of different

---

violation of his right no other defensive option than a claim to monetary compensation. It follows from this that in such a case lower requirements are to be placed than in other cases of a violation of the right of personality on the granting of a claim to compensation." BGH NJW 1996, 985 VI. Civil Senate (VI ZR 223/94), Translated by: Youngs, available at: https://law.utexas.edu/transnational/foreign-law-translations/german/case.php?id=729. Accessed 02 September 2023.

[10] BVerfG Order of 26.02.2008, 1 BvR 1602/07, 1 BvR 1606/07 und 1 BvR 1626/07, available at: https://www.bundesverfassungsgericht.de/SharedDocs/Entscheidungen/EN/2008/02/rs20080226_1bvr160207en.html. Accessed 02 September 2023.

[11] Order of 6 November 2019—1 BvR 276/17—Right to be forgotten II.

[12] This judgment, which explained the concepts of privacy in the public space and for the public figures as well as the requirement of public interest debate, will be discussed in detail in the later part of this chapter.

[13] Orders of 6 November 2019—1 BvR 16/13—Right to be forgotten-I and 1 BvR 276/17—Right to be forgotten-II.

rights, the Court held that search engines are not protected under the freedom of speech, but rather under the right to do business whilst the news platforms are protected under freedom of speech. Additionally, the public right to have access to information is covered by the freedom of information. In order to undertake the balancing exercise, all these conflicting rights shall be taken into consideration. Mainly, the rights of the search engine operator and the right to free speech of the media shall be judged against the right to free development of one's personality. While deciding the protection claim, time would be having a specific weight in the balancing process due to the specific features of internet-based communication. The stored information could be retrieved through search engines and the result could be a continuous and constantly renewed stigmatization. Therefore, it is a duty of the legal system to prevent the eternal availability of private stances, statements and actions using online platforms for public consumption. The Court termed the right to be forgotten as a prerequisite for the freedom to rehabilitate and make a new beginning without restraint. Weighing up the different rights, there are no constitutional objections against obligations of search engine operators, such as delisting requirements, and obligations of media outlets to restrict access to archives or retrieval via search engines.

These illustrative cases show that while many jurisdictions are struggling to formulate a preliminary legal framework for the protection of privacy at one hand and to reconcile this 'nascent' right with the much elaborated and esteemed right of free speech on the other hand, German law on privacy offers a useful model for comparative study. German privacy law regime has reached to a mature posture not only due to its deep constitutional roots in the national legal system but also as a product of cohabitation with the instructive jurisprudence of the ECtHR.

6.1.2 Background: The German Legal System

The German legal system is categorized as belonging to the Romano-Germanic family, which has been developed on the basis of Roman *jus civile* or civil law.[14] The civil law system is differentiated from the common law system on the basis of their respective historical developments. Civil law was "conceived as rules of conduct intimately linked to the ideas of justice and morality", which made the doctrinal approach as an essential feature of this law.[15] Unlike common law which is mostly formulated by judges to resolve the instant cases, civil law evolved as a private law and culminated in the shape of comprehensive codes.[16] Today, civil law is distinguished from the common law on the basis of a few reasons. Firstly, there is

---

[14] See for an introduction of legal families and their relationship: David and Brierley (1978), pp. 1–6.

[15] David and Brierley (1978), p. 1.

[16] David and Brierley (1978), pp. 1–2.

no concept of binding precedents or *stare decisis* in civil law; and secondly, the norms are available in the shape of written codes, legislated by parliaments rather than the judge-made law or unwritten discretionary equity-based principles of common law. Therefore, Germany has a written constitution (German Basic Law—*Grundgesetz-GG*) and a number of legislative statutes ranging from a comprehensive Civil Code (*Bürgerliches Gesetzbuch—BGB*) to sophisticated and specialized legal regimes, among others data protection laws.

6.1.2.1 German Basic Law as the Constitutional Basis

Since it came into effect on 23rd May, 1949, the German Basic Law is the most sanctified document and comes at the top of hierarchy of legal norms and instruments. Article 20 declares that Federal Republic of Germany is a democratic and social federal state where, "The legislature shall be bound by the constitutional order, the executive and the judiciary by law and justice."[17] The Basic Law provides a catalogue of fundamental rights in articles placed at the beginning. The following articles regulate the basic structure of German polity such as the structure of federalism, relations of the federation with the units (*Länder*), composition and competences of state organs, legislative procedures, and the establishment of the judicial system.

6.1.2.2 Provision of Fundamental Rights and Their Enforcement

6.1.2.2.1 Catalogue of Fundamental Rights Under German Basic Law

The German Basic Law provides a comprehensive list of basic rights and acknowledges inviolable and inalienable rights as the basis of peace and justice in the world, Article 1 (2). It starts with declaring the inviolability or untouchability ("Unantastbarkeit") of human dignity in Article 1(1). The state authority is duty-bound to respect and protect human dignity. The basic rights enumerated subsequently are neither sacred slogans nor merely non-binding declarations. Rather, they bind all the three tiers of the state as directly applicable law. Article 2 (1) provides the right to free development of one's personality subject to the rights of others, the constitutional order or the moral law. Article 2(2) entitles the citizens to their rights to life, physical integrity and personal freedom, which may only be interfered in pursuant to a law that complies with all constitutional requirements. The catalogue thus goes on to provide human rights such as the right to equality and nondiscrimination (Article 3); freedom to profess and practice religion or philosophical convictions (Article 4); freedom of expression, arts and sciences (Article 5); special protection of marriage, family, and children (Article 6); freedom of assembly,

[17] Article 20 of German basic Law.

association and movement (Articles 8, 9 and 11); privacy of correspondence, posts and telecommunications (Article 10); and inviolability of home (Article 13).

6.1.2.2.2 Establishment of the Federal Constitutional Court and Its Role

The Federal Constitutional Court of Germany is regarded as a "guardian of the constitution" as it plays a crucial role in constitutional interpretation and so "carries the *Grundgesetz* into current era".[18] The Court was established through the Basic Law (Arts. 92 et seq.) and an Act of Parliament called Federal Constitutional Court Act of 1951 (*Bundesverfassungsgerichtsgesetz*). Unlike traditional Supreme Courts of common law countries, it does not have a dual authority of both the last interpreter of constitution and a last resort of the appeals. Rather, the constitutional matters have been exclusively assigned to it as its sole task. Its current position and importance has been described as,

> [t]oday, the Federal Constitutional Court is one of the most renowned constitutional courts in the world. Conversely, the Court also sees itself as part of an international—and in particular European—network of (constitutional) courts, and takes inspiration from the decisions of foreign courts. Within the European Union, the Court contributes to stabilizing the liberal order by means of the integrating power of the European legal community...[19]

The jurisprudence of Federal Constitutional Court influences the abstract constitutional norms in terms of substituting them in a speaking jurisprudence in the process of case-to-case interpretation. It gives the Court a strong role in the governance-related issues despite the fact of a political system based on separation of powers.[20] Only filing a formal application invokes the jurisdiction of the Court and, unlike the Supreme Court of Pakistan, it has no *sue moto* power to take cognizance on its own initiative. However, the BVerfGG establishes procedures for constitutional complaints that enable the Court to accept or not accept constitutional complaints for decision according to criteria defined by law.

6.1.2.3 Substantive Laws and Their Enforcement

Articles 70 et seq. of the Basic Law confer the law making powers on the federation and units in the form of concurrent legislative and exclusive federal legislative nature as well as the manner to administer and execute the respective matters. The making of federal law is the primary domain of *Bundestag* under Articles 77–78, where the legislative procedure for making new law and amending an existing law has been provided. Under Article 83 et seq., the execution of federal law is the duty of units, partly under the oversight of the federation.

---

[18] Bumke and Voßkuhle (2019), p. 9.

[19] Bumke and Voßkuhle (2019), p. 11.

[20] Bröhmer et al. (2012), p. vii.

The German legal system can be roughly differentiated into two main areas of law i.e. public law and civil or private law. The former regulates the relations between state and its citizens as well as the relations between two public entities of the state while the later regulates purely private transactions. Public law includes the Basic Law at the top level of the hierarchy of norms. Administrative law covers many special legislative and regulatory norms dealing with the executive arm of the state and regulates the operation of the state machinery such as matters related to the affairs of police, environmental protection, tax management, and supply of daily life amenities. The criminal justice system is based mainly on the Criminal Code (*Strafgesetzbuch-StGB*) which provides a detailed account of the definitions of offences and their respective punishments. Similarly, German civil law has a comprehensive and extensive written code for its regulation, called Civil Code (*Bürgerliches Gesetzbuch-BGB*). The Civil Code contains general provisions on obligations and contracts, provisions for the law of torts, provisions related to property law, as well as provisions related to matters of family and succession. Other important laws for the purpose of this research are the Copyright Act regarding Works of Art and Photographs (*Kunsturhebergesetz-KUG*), substantiating some aspects of personality rights such as the right to one's own image, or Press Laws.

The rights and duties enumerated in public and civil laws of Germany are adjudicated by an independent judiciary. The Basic Law has set the powers and functions of the judiciary for adjudication of constitutional and legal disputes. Articles 92–104 of the Basic Law provide rules for the organization and composition of the Federal Constitutional Court (Articles 93 and 94), federal courts (Articles 95 and 96), and the principles of judicial independence, abolition of capital punishment and fair trial (Articles 97, 102 and 103 respectively). The Federal Constitutional Court is authorized to check the constitutionality of laws and of decisions of state institutions. The catalogue of fundamental rights in the Basic Law particularly binds all the state functionaries of legislature, executive and judiciary to that effect. These rights are available to the people against the state functionaries. However, in a landmark judgment in the Lüth case (1958), the Federal Constitutional Court held that fundamental rights could also influence private relations under civil law.[21] As a result, the Constitutional Court can review the judgments of civil courts to determine whether or not the judges have taken into consideration the "radiating effect" of the basic rights on civil law.

6.1.2.4 Third-Party Effect of Fundamental Rights Under German Law

The legal developments, which led the German legal system to an effective protection of privacy, demonstrate a tendency of overlapping of private and constitutional law. The trend of the cases discussed earlier is that one private party institutes a civil suit alleging the other private party for infringement of its interests protected under

---

[21] BVerfGE 7, 198 (203 ff.).

civil law, and then the civil suit gets mature at the appeal stages, culminating into a constitutional law dispensation. This trend is typical not only for German law, as the debate around the interaction of private and public law is an important part of legal theory. One can find a variety of views and arguments, both in support of and against the so-called constitutionalization of private law. The discussions around this issue explore various forms and degrees of the cohabitation of both areas of law.

Traditionally, fundamental rights operated both vertically and horizontally, however, the trend of written constitutions has modified the application of human rights. The dominant prevailing view is that these rights are made available to the people against the state through constitutional arrangements. However, the comprehensive legal, judicial and administrative arrangements for the protection of these rights usually encroach into the realm of private law, which is being designed for regulation of private parties' *inter se* disputes. This is widely acknowledged to a certain extent, although the interference of state machinery into the private law domain of contractual nature is not a welcoming trend according to the liberal theories of democracy and human rights.[22] The question of application of human rights to private parties is expressed as the "third party effect of fundamental rights", where the two primary parties are the right-holder (a natural person) and the state (a public authority). The study of various legal systems reveals many approaches to the tackling of this problem.[23] Aharon Barak has enumerated four such model approaches:[24] (a) direct application model;[25] (b) non-application model;[26] (c) indirect application model;[27] and (d) application to judiciary model.[28] All these models have their benefits and shortcomings or limitations, however, in Barak's opinion,

> the proper model is the indirect (or "cascade" application model). Yet this is not the regular indirect application model, but, rather, a strengthened and augmented indirect application model. [. . . .The] recognition of human rights of one person *vis-à-vis* another inevitably involves limitation and narrowing, as a consequence of the regard for the other's rights. This limitation and narrowing must be evaluated within a particular normative framework. This framework concerns relations between private parties. This is private law. Hence, recognition of human rights necessitates restrictions and limitations set forth in private law itself. Indirect application, therefore, is required.[29]

[22] It is controversial due to the fact that an overwhelming focus on resolving private disputes through resorting to public law principles will eclipse the contractual autonomy of individuals, which is a core area aimed to be protected by political and constitutional setups.

[23] See for example: Barak (1996), pp. 13–42.

[24] Barak (1996).

[25] Barak provides the examples of some judgments from Germany and Switzerland to argue that this approach could be found in these jurisdictions.

[26] To Barak, the Supreme Court of Canada adopted this approach in Dolphin Delivery case.

[27] According to Barak, this model could be found in Germany, Italy, Spain and Japan.

[28] In Barak's view, United States has adopted this model.

[29] Barak (1996), p. 258.

The impact of fundamental rights on private relations or the "third party effect or horizontal effect of fundamental rights" is described in the German expression as "*Drittwirkung der Grundrechte*". Against the background of the right to privacy, this doctrinal construction and the discussions are relevant because of the fact that the threats to the privacy right of individuals are not coming from the state alone. Most of the times other private individuals or entities such as journalists, publishing companies and users of online forums pose greater threats to privacy than the state does. The case law development of the different ingredients of the right to privacy in Germany as summarized below also shows that plaintiff and defendants were mostly private parties.

6.1.2.5 The Status of ECHR and the Impact of ECtHR Decisions on German Law

This chapter is primarily interested in how the protection of privacy is shaped at the level of various contracting states in the light of the ECHR and the jurisprudence of the ECtHR. As an example, we have already explained that Caroline von Hannover applied to the ECtHR against the judgment of Federal Constitutional Court and reached a decision that Germany failed to protect her right to respect of private life provided by Article 8 of ECHR.[30] This judgment drew a decisive impact on the subsequent approach of German courts towards privacy. Before addressing and analyzing this, it is important to briefly discuss the status and rank of ECHR in German law.[31]

As mentioned above in Chap. 5, the ECHR does not provide any procedure for placing itself at a specific position in the national legal systems of member states. Thus, one can find a variety of approaches to its normative status. Article 59 (2) of the German Basic Law provides: "Treaties that regulate the political relations of the Federation or relate to subjects of federal legislation shall require the consent or participation, in the form of a federal law, of the bodies responsible in such a case for the enactment of federal law."[32] The federal legislature consented to the ECHR through a statutory law as per the procedure laid down by the Basic Law,[33] bringing the Convention into force on 3rd September, 1953. The Convention binds the Federal Republic of Germany as a contracting party according to Art. 1 ECHR ("The High Contracting Parties shall secure to everyone within their jurisdiction the rights and freedoms defined in Section I of this Convention"). The Contracting

---

[30] See Sect. 5.4.3.2.3.

[31] This section draws on the analysis of Hans-Joachim Cremer in Cremer (2010), pp. 23–41.

[32] Available at: https://www.gesetze-im-internet.de/englisch_gg/englisch_gg.html#p0412. Accessed 02 September 2023.

[33] Articles 76, 77, 78 and 82 of the Basic Law regulate the procedure for legislating federal law involving both houses of the parliament namely the Federal Legislative Assembly (*Bundestag*) and the Federal Council (Bundesrat).

Parties also have to undertake to abide by the final judgment of the ECtHR in any case to which they are parties, Art. 46 ECHR.

However, the influence of the jurisprudence of the ECtHR goes beyond what Article 46 states solely for the parties in a particular case. The principle position of the German jurisdiction with respect to the nature of the implementation of ECtHR decisions and their relationship with relevant German decisions was elaborated in a controversial judgment of the Federal Constitutional Court in a case known as Görgülü case.[34]

According to the facts in the Görgülü case, the biological father of a child got a decree from Wittenberg Local Court for the custody of his child who had been living with foster parents until then. However, the order was turned down after the foster parents appealed to Naumburg Regional Court. Additionally, this court suspended Görgülü's right of access to his child. After rejection of his constitutional complaint by the BVerfG, he applied to the ECtHR under Article 34 ECHR. The ECtHR decided in favor of Görgülü: By denying the custody and access to his child, the Naumburg Regional Court had violated Article 8 right of the applicant.[35] After the judgment of the ECtHR, Görgülü applied to the Local Court for an implementation of the judgment that granted him periodical access to his child. However, the order issued accordingly was again challenged in the Naumburg Regional Court, which, once again, terminated the right of access to his child. In its decision, this court stated that the ECtHR's judgments have binding force for the Federal Republic of Germany under public international law and that Article 97 (1) of the Basic Law grants autonomy to the judiciary from the Federal Government, and therefore, such international law instruments would not have binding effect for the German courts.

Once again, Görgülü filed a constitutional complaint. In the following judgment, the Federal Constitutional Court developed a detailed reasoning about the status and nature of the binding force of ECtHR jurisprudence in the German national jurisdiction. It explained the status of ECHR and of the decisions of the ECtHR in the following words:

> In the German legal system, the European Convention on Human Rights has the status of a federal statute, and it must be taken into account in the interpretation of domestic law, including fundamental rights and constitutional guarantees (1.). The binding effect of a decision of the ECtHR extends to all state bodies and in principle imposes on these an obligation, within their jurisdiction and without violating the binding effect of statute and law (Article 20.3 of the Basic Law), to end a continuing violation of the Convention and to create a situation that complies with the Convention (2.). The nature of the binding effect depends on the sphere of responsibility of the state bodies and on the latitude given by prior-ranking law. Courts are at all events under a duty to take into account a judgment that relates to a case already decided by them if they preside over a retrial of the matter in a procedurally admissible manner and are able to take the judgment into account without a violation of substantive law (3.). A complainant may challenge the disregard of this duty of consideration

[34] Cremer (2010), p. 25.

[35] Görgülü v Germany App no 74969/01 (ECtHR, 26 February 2004) BVerfGE 111, 307.

> as a violation of the fundamental right whose area of protection is affected in conjunction with the principle of the rule of law (4.).[36]

The Court further passed some remarks in relation to the sovereignty requirement and to the national constitution, the German Basic Law:

> the Basic Law aims to integrate Germany into the legal community of peaceful and free states, but does not waive the sovereignty contained in the last instance in the German constitution. There is therefore no contradiction with the aim of commitment to international law if the legislature, exceptionally, does not comply with the law of international agreements, provided this is the only way in which a violation of fundamental principles of the constitution can be averted.[37]

These observations of the Constitutional Court have been regarded as "skeptical assessment" to determine the binding force of the ECHR and the decisions of the ECtHR in the national legal order.[38] But the Court explained its approach: International treaty law applies domestically only if it has been incorporated into the national legal order in accordance with constitutional law. The constitutional principle of friendliness towards international law (*Gebot der Völkerrechtsfreundlichkeit*)[39] takes effect only within the framework of the democratic and constitutional system of the Basic Law.[40] Nevertheless, it has an impact on the understanding of the national constitution, especially on fundamental rights, and on the understanding of national law.

Firstly, the Convention's principles and the respective decisions of the ECtHR influence the interpretation of the Basic Law. They serve as interpretative guidelines for determining the content and scope of fundamental rights and rule-of-law principles of the Basic Law, provided this does not lead to a reduced protection of these rights.[41]

Secondly, the Court clarified that though the judiciary and administrative bodies cannot avoid national laws and Basic Law on the pretext of conforming to the ECHR, yet,

> the binding effect of statute and law also includes a duty to take into account the guarantees of the Convention and the decisions of the ECtHR as part of a methodologically justifiable interpretation of the law. Both a failure to consider a decision of the ECtHR and the "enforcement" of such a decision in a schematic way, in violation of prior-ranking law, may therefore violate fundamental rights in conjunction with the principle of the rule of law. [. . . ..]Since the European Convention on Human Rights – as interpreted by the ECtHR – has

---

[36] BVerfGE 111, 307, para 30.

[37] BVerfGE 111, 307, para 35.

[38] Cremer (2010), in Humboldt Forum Recht (Vol. 11, pp. 138–146): It refers to an interview of the then President of ECtHR published in *Der Spiegel* November 15, 2004, expressing concern in relation to the judgment of the Constitutional Court.

[39] Article 24 of the Basic Law.

[40] BVerfGE 111, 307 (318 f.).

[41] BVerfGE 111, 307 (317).

> the status of a formal federal statute, it shares the primacy of statute law and must therefore be complied with by the judiciary.[42]

The following para is also worthy of reproduction which explains how the ECtHR judgments could be "taken into account".

> "Take into account" means taking notice of the Convention provision as interpreted by the ECtHR and applying it to the case, provided the application does not violate prior-ranking law, in particular constitutional law. In any event, the Convention provision as interpreted by the ECtHR must be taken into account in making a decision; the court must at least duly consider it. Where the facts have changed in the meantime or in the case of a different fact situation, the courts will need to determine what, in the view of the ECtHR, constituted the specific violation of the Convention and why a changed fact situation does not permit it to be applied to the case. Here, it will always be important how taking account of the decision takes in the system of the field of law in question. On the level of federal law too, the Convention does not automatically have priority over other federal law, in particular if in this connection it has not already been the object of a decision of the ECtHR.[43]

In the nutshell, the standards of the ECHR and the decisions of the ECtHR are strengthened in their legal significance. Looking only at Article 59 (2) of the German Basic Law, the norms of the ECHR have the same force just like federal statutes. However, at a broader level and with a view to the constitutional principle of friendliness towards international law (*Gebot der Völkerrechtsfreundlichkeit*), the ECHR has a further-reaching status because their provisions influence both the understanding of the Constitution and of national law. Similarly, the decisions of the ECtHR reach beyond the specific case and its parties because they must be taken into account in other relevant cases as well.

Practically, it is possible to initiate a constitutional complaint based on the argument that a Conventional right's interpretation by the ECtHR was ignored in the contested decision and that judgments of this Court were not taken into account in the manner required by the Constitution and its principle of friendliness towards international law. If this argument proves to be true, the contested decision simultaneously violates the fundamental rights of the German Basic Law in combination with the rule of law principle (*Rechtsstaatprinzip*).[44] The Federal Constitutional Court acknowledged this possibility of filing a constitutional petition for a disregard of the Convention by not taking its provisions or the jurisprudence of the ECtHR into account.

In the Görgülü case, the Court took this stand in its own decision. As a result, it held that the Naumburg Regional Court had infringed the constitutional right of the plaintiff protected under Article 6 of the Basic Law in connection with the rule of law principle.

[42] BVerfGE 111, 307, paras 47, 53.

[43] BVerfGE 111, 307, para 62. www.bundesverfassungsgericht.de/SharedDocs/Entscheidungen/EN/2004/10/rs20041014_2bvr148104en.html. Accessed 03 September 2023. Note: The English text of the judgment uses abbreviation of "ECHR" instead of "ECtHR".

[44] Hoffmeister (2006), p. 731.

After acquiring a fundamental insight into the status of the European Court of Human Rights (ECHR) and the binding nature of its judgments, it is crucial to explore how the concept of the general personality right and the protection of privacy evolved within the German legal system. Additionally, we will examine how these principles further developed under the influence of the provisions of the ECHR and the judgments handed down by the European Court of Human Rights (ECtHR).

6.1.3 The Development of General Personality Right and Protection of Privacy

Although the German legal system is a system of codified law, yet privacy and personality rights have been developed through case law. The starting point has been scholarly consideration, civil law and decisions of the Federal Court of Justice. Different personality rights were worked out step by step in a piecemeal manner as a legal response to specific concrete problems. An overview of these developments illustrates how the personality law evolved to its present state, what difficulties had to be overcome and what kind of conceptual and interpretative problems encountered the courts. It will become clear from these considerations that, in fact, the real culmination point of these developments was the constitutional dimension of the right to privacy and personality rights, acknowledged and strengthened by the Federal Constitutional Court. The impact of the fundamental rights approach of the FCC in its jurisprudence led the protection of privacy to a more unified and consolidated state and the protection mechanism became more consistent from the initially piecemeal protection. This approach is not only effective for pragmatic considerations of protecting privacy interests and providing satisfactory relief to the victims of intrusions. It is also supported by the theories of privacy which consider privacy right as a unified and multifaceted human right.

6.1.3.1 The Roots of Privacy and Personality Protection in Early Civil Law Torts

The development of the general personality right under German law as an effective normative tool for a variety of human interests is noteworthy, especially in the narrower area of the right to privacy. Both rights were first conceived at the theoretical level by scholars and not by lawmakers or judges. The seminal article on the right to privacy written by Warren and Brandeis was a legal and scholarly response to the press intrusions into various aspects of human personality, where the authors proposed the legal recognition of *general right to privacy* in order to protect *inviolate personality*. In Germany, a prominent scholar Otto Friedrich von Gierke made a somewhat similar proposal in 1895, calling for the recognition of a "general right of personality" (*Allgemeines Persönlichkeitsrecht*).[45] This pioneering idea got the support of many contemporary jurists and is considered as a theoretical milestone towards the legal recognition of a general personality right.[46]

The right to privacy was not codified in Germany despite the prevalence of a legal system having a predominant tendency of codified norms. The demarcation of boundaries of the scope of this right so that to make a clear distinction between the "serious and the trivial" matters, could be one of the explanation for the non-codification of privacy law in Germany.[47] Whatever the reasons might be, the right to privacy or the Gierke's proposed generalized personality right was not incorporated in the German Civil Code of 1900. Rather isolated interests related to personality were recognized by the civil courts through interpretation with a *piece-meal approach*.[48]

The tort or delict provisions[49] of the German Civil Code start from Section 823 and continue till Section 853. However, the most important provisions from a privacy protection perspective are sections 823 and 826. Section 823 provides the liability for the damage as:

> (1) A person who, intentionally or negligently, unlawfully injures the life, body, health, freedom, property or another right of another person is liable to make compensation to the other party for the damage arising from this.
>
> (2) The same duty is held by a person who commits a breach of a statute that is intended to protect another person. If, according to the contents of the statute, it may also be breached without fault, then liability to compensation only exists in the case of fault.

Section 826 provides compensation for "intentional damage contrary to public policy" as:

> A person who, in a manner contrary to public policy, intentionally inflicts damage on another person is liable to the other person to make compensation for the damage.

It is important to note that neither section 823 (1) nor 823 (2) mentions the right to privacy or the general personality right as a protected interest along with life, body, health, freedom or property.[50] Prior to the recognition of the general personality right, the restricted meaning and narrow interpretation have delimited the legal effects of these provisions in providing remedy to the some tortious harms. For

[45] Von Gierke, 1 Deutsches Privatrecht 702 (1895) as cited in Krause (1965), p. 485.

[46] Krause (1965), p. 485.

[47] Krause (1965), p. 485.

[48] Lehman (1968), p. 109.

[49] See for an explanation of both terms: Buckland and McNair (1952), pp. 338–351. Tort or civil wrong—a common law term—is usually construed as the infringement of a legally protected interest or right attached to property or *Ius in Rem* while delict is a civil law term, which is used, for infringement of personality related rights or *Ius in Personum*. The official English Translation of BGB titles Chapter 27 as "Torts", while Markesinis and Unberath discuss these provisions under the title of "The Delict Provisions of BGB" in their treatise.

[50] It will be explained afterwards that how the expression "another right" worked as an important normative tool under German privacy law.

example, in order to qualify for remedy, the impugned action was required to meet the test of "adequate causation" as against the liberal principle of proximate causation.[51] Similarly, the affecting of "enumerated assets (or *Güter*)" could only result in a duty to compensation. Not only some key personality rights such as *honor* was excluded from the protection under the narrow interpretation of the BGB, but *freedom* was also considered narrowly as *freedom from restraint*, while the expression of "any other right" was restrictedly construed as the protection of proprietary rights under the doctrine of *ejusdem generis*.[52]

The second clause of Article 823 BGB entitles a person to claim compensation in the case of violation of particular statutory rights. According to Jon Lehman, "objective rights established by protective laws (*Schutzgesetze*), particularly the Penal Code (*Strafgesetzbuch-StGB*), and by other provisions of the BGB can become subjective rights enabling the injured person to bring an action for damages under the BGB."[53] This provides means to claim for compensation also under civil law if someone proves the infringement of criminal law provisions of 185–187 and 189 of the German Penal Code.

There are further legal provisions applied by German courts for sporadic protection of different aspects of personality. Among these were, for example, the protection of the use of the name under section 12 of German Civil Code and the entitlement of a person to control the nature of dissemination of his or her picture or likeness.

The failure of such a piecemeal approach is exemplified through the *Reichsgericht*'s judgment of 1908, when the sister of renowned writer Friedrich Nietzsche tried to prevent the posthumous publication of a letter written by her brother to his friend. She claimed that the publication of such letters would violate the right to personality of her late brother. In its judgment, the Court announced that the general right to personality was "a stranger to existing civil law".[54] The Court also stated in categorical terms that the BGB did not recognize any general right of personality, and that it protects only specific rights which are protected by statutory provisions either of the BGB or of other law such as the right to one's name, trademarks and copy right related interests as well as the rights related to the publication of one's picture.[55] It then stretched the copyright law by assigning significant literary importance in Nietzsche's letters and granted relief on that basis.

[51] Lehman (1968), p. 110.

[52] Lehman (1968), p. 110.

[53] Lehman (1968), p. 110.

[54] 69 Entscheidungen des Reichsgerichts in Zivilsachen, 401, 403 (1908) as cited in Krause (1965), p. 485.

[55] See the analysis of the same case in: Lehman (1968), p. 112.

6.1.3.1.1 Dr. Schacht Case: General Personality Right as a Constitutionally Guaranteed Universal Right

In a landmark judgment, the so-called Dr. Schacht case, the Federal Court of Justice recognized the constitutional foundation of the general personality right and its influence on the protection the BGB provision of 823(1) provides.[56] According to the facts of the case, Dr. H H G Schacht was a distinguished economist, who used his financial expertise for stabilizing the German currency value in 1923 and so pulled out the country from a devastating inflation.[57] He also served as the president of Reichsbank for 7 years (1923–1930) and politically affiliated with the Nazi party while lobbying for Hitler to become Reich's Chancellor, which eventually happened in 1933. Initially, he supported the rearmament program of the Reich. However, his differences with Hitler on budgetary imbalances which he thought could only be stabilized if the arms' expenses were being cut, led him to his confinement to concentration camp in 1944. Later on in Nuremburg trials, he successfully defended his role and position during the Nazi regime, and afterwards also successfully appealed against the conviction of German people's Court at Stuttgart and thus resumed a successful career.[58]

The instant case started when a weekly journal published an article criticizing his past connection with the Nazi party. He instructed his attorney to send a legal notice to the publishing company of the magazine invoking his "right to reply" under the press law. However, rather than to answer to the notice, the magazine published the attorney's letter in its "Letters from readers" section, with omissions as to the explanation of some facts. The attorney sued the company demanding the company to retract the earlier publication, which gave the impression that he had written to the magazine as one of its readers and not as an attorney for Dr. Schacht. The defendant company constantly refused to publish such a reply insisting that they were not bound under the law to do so. The *Landgericht* (trial court) granted the relief which was overturned by the Court of Appeal (*Oberlandesgericht*) against the decision of whom the jurisdiction of Federal Court of Justice (*Bundesgerichtshof-BGH*) was invoked. This Court reinstated the earlier judgment in a landmark decision that was breaking new ground for privacy and personality rights.

Furnishing reasons for its decision, the Court of Justice referred to earlier judgments where the courts have protected many personality related interests in a sporadic manner, as well as to the academic literature of Gierke and Kohler who *pleaded for the recognition of a comprehensive personality right*. The Court held:

> now that the Basic Law [Constitution of 1949] has recognized the right of a human being to have his dignity respected (Article 1), and also the right to free development of his personality as a private right, to be universally respected in so far as it does not infringe another person's right or is not in conflict with the constitutional order or morality (Article

[56] BGHZ 13, 334.

[57] See the notes to cases in: Markesinis and Unberath (2002), pp. 472–473.

[58] Markesinis and Unberath (2002), pp. 472–473.

> 2), the general personality right must be regarded as a constitutionally guaranteed fundamental right. No further discussion is needed here of whether and how far the protection of this general personality right, the limitation of which requires a balancing of interests, is restricted in particular cases by justified private or public needs, which outweigh the interest in the inviolability of the exclusive sphere of personality; for in this present case it is not evident that the defendant company has any interests worth protecting, which it could use to justify the conduct objected to by the plaintiff. On the contrary, by the defendant company's choice of a way of publishing the request for correction, omitting essential parts of the letter, interests of the plaintiff in the nature of personality rights have been infringed.
>
> While an unauthorised publication of private notes constitutes—as a rule—an inadmissible attack on every human being's protected sphere of secrecy, a modified reproduction infringes the personality rights of the author because such unauthorised alterations can spread a false picture of his personality. In general, not only unauthorised omissions of essential parts of the author's notes are inadmissible, but also additions through which his notes presented for publication only for certain purposes acquire a different colour or tendency from what he expressed in the form chosen by him and the kind of publication he had allowed.[59]

The Court also clarified that any kind of copyright interest would remain unhurt. Applying the principles on the case, the Court held that the defendant company was not entitled to publish the legal notice under "Letters from readers" section of the newspaper and, beyond that, with the omission of key passages. It gave the false impression that the plaintiff was expressing his personal views as a reader of the magazine rather than putting forward the standpoint of his client Dr. Schacht. The Court held the publishing company responsible for the violation of the acknowledged general personality right. Firstly, because the plaintiff had demanded the correction of the facts only and did not authorize the company to publish the letter, which made the contents known to an unintended wide circle of people. Secondly, because the magazine gave a different meaning to the letter, *as the letter acquired a meaning not in conformity with its original composition.* Thus, it was a disparagement of the general personality right and justified to demand for revocation.

The judgment in the Dr. Schacht case, where the BGH introduced the infringement of personality right as the new basis of liability, has been termed as "outright judicial *coup de main*" that also worked as a "birth certificate" for the a direct horizontal effect or *unmittelbare Drittwirkung* of fundamental rights over the private law domain.[60] In its judgment, BGH sweepingly remarked that after the promulgation of Basic Law, which has enshrined Article 1—inviolability of human dignity—and Article 2—the right to development of personality *as a private right to be universally respected* unless it conflicts with the constitutional order or morality. However, the Court did not articulate any constitutional-law basis of going against the textual requirement of the Basic Law. It is clear that the right to inviolability of dignity is available against the state due to historical reasons of state fascism, while Article 1 (3) expressly declares the three branches of the state (legislative, judiciary and executive) as corresponding party of direct application of fundamental rights as

[59]Translated in: Markesinis and Unberath (2002), pp. 412–415.

[60]Brggemeier (2006), pp. 59–82.

effective law.[61] Nevertheless, how sophisticated the conceptions of the horizontal effect or the *Drittwirkung* are and must be, has already been explained.[62] The fundamentals remain unclear in the decision of the BGH.

6.1.3.1.2 Krankenpapier Case: General Personality Right as Another Right

Major case law in the following years further developed and modified the personality right theory founded in the Dr. Schacht case. It is pertinent to mention here that, in the early decisions of the relevant case law, the BGH tended to interpret the basic rights as if they had an immediate binding effect for private parties or, in German expression, *unmittelbare Drittwirkung*.[63] From there, conclusions are drawn to the civil law. In the case of disclosure of medical documents (*Krankenpapiere*), the BGH stated that the Court of Appeal had a correct assumption in terms of acceptance of section 823 (2) BGB claim for the violation of a general right to personality.[64] Relying on the theory of Neumann-Nipperdey-Scheuner, it held that the fundamental rights of the inviolability of dignity and the right of everyone to free development of their personality in Articles 1 and 2 of the Basic Law *are not only directed against the state and its organs, but also applies to everyone in private law transactions.* It further held:

> While it cannot be understood otherwise that it has been declared in Art. 1 Para. 1 Sentence 2 as an obligation of all state power to respect and protect human dignity, and that in Art. 1 Para 3 has laid down basic rights the following provisions, including primarily the right to free development of personality, as a directly applicable law, binding the legislature, the executive, and the judiciary. It is therefore, inevitable to conclude that the general right of personality is to be regarded as an "another right" within the meaning of Section 823 (1) BGB [. . . .] it is out of question that the general right of personality also applies within the Civil law order and that it enjoys legal protection against injuries, which civil law grants in particular in the provisions on tortious acts. It is not only protected in accordance with Section 826 of the German Civil Code, but also the protection of Section 823 (1) of the German Civil Code.[65]

The Court declared that the general personality right has a broad scope just like general clauses of law and also bears similar ambiguity. It cannot be fixed in limits and its boundaries cannot be conclusively determined. The right of man to respect for his dignity and free development of his personality is a "*Muttergrundrecht*" or

---

[61] Brggemeier (2006), p. 64.

[62] See Sect. 6.1.2.4.

[63] Cremer (2010), pp. 50–52.

[64] BGHZ 24, 72 translated from: http://www.servat.unibe.ch/dfr/bz024072.html. Accessed 25 August 2023.

[65] BGHZ 24, 72 translated from: http://www.servat.unibe.ch/dfr/bz024072.html. Accessed 25 August 2023.

"*Quellrecht*" (mother of fundamental rights or a source right).[66] After mentioning the importance of the personality right and the areas it protects, the court stated:

> The general right of personality does not open up the possibility of unlimited enforcement of one's own interests. There can be no question of compensation or injunctive relief existing everywhere, where someone sees is concerned by hindrance from another person. Because the general right to personality is based on the fact that human dignity is to be respected and protected with the possibility of the development of the individual personality, its essential requirements are linked to the fact that in the particular area of life for which it is considered, the personality values the Basic Law wants to protect are important and are affected in the given case. The main limitation is that neither the constitutional order, the moral law nor the rights of others be violated due to the conflicting situations that arise from this [.....] Depending on how things are organized, the scope of the right to privacy may vary to a great extent. Whether in individual cases the right to personality has been violated can only be judged on the basis of careful assessment and consideration of all the circumstances that are important for its demarcation.[67]

6.1.3.1.3 Herrenreiter Case: Admissibility of Damages for Non-material Loss

In the course of development of the German law of liability and damages, the introduction of damages for non-physical wrongs in the "Gentleman Rider" (*Herrenreiter*) case provided the teeth to Civil law, which could be extended to limitless infringements of personality rights.[68] The claimant was a rich man, owner of a brewery, and a participant of a dressed horse riding show. A pharmaceutical company published his picture on an advertisement poster for a drug, which they claimed to be a supplement for sexual potency. He objected to the publication of his picture promoting a controversial drug without his permission. The BGH confirmed the injury to the personality right of the claimant protected under section 823 of Civil Code and 22 of Art and Copyright Act and granted the injunction, prohibiting further publication and circulation. However, a challenge for the Court was how to ascertain whether or not damages for immaterial loss could be claimed under 823 (2) of BGB. Section 253 of BGB applicable at that time generally excluded immaterial damage and was allowing that only if some special law expressly provides to that effect. This difficulty was successfully overcome by the Court while resorting to Section 847, which allows compensation as a result of a broad notion of "deprivation of liberty". The Court considered the new constitutionalized form of private law, overruling the "no-private law protection of a general personality right by the guarantee of human dignity and the right to the free development of the personality".[69]

---

[66] BGHZ 24, 72, para 15 translated from: http://www.servat.unibe.ch/dfr/bz024072.html. Accessed 25 August 2023.

[67] BGHZ 24, 72, para 17–19, http://www.servat.unibe.ch/dfr/bz024072.html. Accessed 25 August 2023.

[68] BGHZ 26, 349.

[69] See Cremer (2010), p. 51. Parenthesis omitted.

In the articulation of its reasons for arriving at the conclusion, the BGH did not agree with the presumptive license fee logic of the Court of Appeal. It stated:

> In truth he claims not compensation for a non-existent pecuniary loss but an appreciable satisfaction for an unlawful attack on his personality protected by § 22 of the Act on Artistic Creations and Articles 1 and 2 of the Constitution. He demands satisfaction for the fact that a widely disseminated poster, by making him, one might almost say, "ride" for the purpose of advertising the defendant's tonic—and a sexual one at that—humiliated him and made him an object of ridicule. In such a situation it is absurd to award damages on the basis of a fictitious license agreement.[70]

Furthermore, the following paragraphs are noteworthy:

> This Senate has already said in its decision in BGHZ 13, 334, 338 that the sacredness of human dignity and the right to free development of the personality protected by Article 2 of the Constitution are also to be recognised as a civil right to be respected by everyone in daily life, in so far as that right does not impinge upon the rights of others and is not repugnant to constitutional order or the moral law. This so-called general right to one's personality also possesses legal validity within the framework of the civil law and enjoys the protection of § 823 I BGB under the designation of "other right" [.....].
>
> Articles 1 and 2 of the Constitution protect—and indeed must be applied by the courts in the administration of justice—what is called the concept of human personality; they recognise in it one of the supra-legal basic values of the law. Thereby they are directly concerned with the protection of the inner realm of the personality which, in principle, only affords a basis for the free and responsible self-determination of the individual and an infringement of which produces primarily so-called immaterial damage, damage expressed in a degradation of the personality. To respect this inner realm and to refrain from invading it without authorisation is a legal command issuing from the Basic Law itself. And it follows from the Constitution that in cases of invasion of this sphere, protection must be given against damage characteristic of such an invasion.[71]

The Court concluded that once such infringement is proved, the equitable compensation could be claimed in monetary terms even for non-pecuniary loss based on the norm of "deprivation of liberty". Otherwise, the protection of inner freedom without a just compensation under civil law will make such protection an illusory idea. It held,

> There is no obvious reason why § 847 BGB should not be extended by analogy to such attacks as injure the right to free exercise of the will, especially where that deprivation of intellectual liberty, just like deprivation of bodily freedom, renders natural restitution impossible. Where such blameworthy depreciations of the personality right are in question, the effective legal protection offered by the Constitution can, in the absence of any special legal provision, be attained only through its inclusion in the injuries mentioned in § 847 BGB, since their injurious consequences are of necessity primarily immaterial.[72]

In the two cases—*Krankenpapier* and *Herrenreiter*—BGH followed slightly different approaches. In the former case, the BGH tended to acknowledge the direct

---

[70] Translated in: Markesinis and Unberath (2002), pp. 415–420.

[71] Translated in: Markesinis and Unberath (2002), pp. 415–420.

[72] Translated by Markesinis, available at: https://law.utexas.edu/transnational/foreign-law-translations/german/case.php?id=739. Accessed 03 September 2023.

horizontal effect of fundamental rights (*Unmittelbare Drittwirkung*) while in the latter case, it tried to dilute that impression.[73] As already explained, discussing the inviolability of human dignity and the right to the development of personality, the Court concluded in the *Krankenpapier* case that these rights are directed not only against the state and its organs, rather these rights could be validly applied in 'private law relations', which means their availability against *anyone*.[74] From this conception, the Court drew its "inevitable conclusion" that "the general personality right is to be regarded as 'another right' within the meaning of sec. 823 (1) BGB. . . ."[75] In the *Herrenreiter* case, the BGH did not repeat this position. Rather, it placed itself more clearly somewhere between direct and indirect third party effect. According to the Court, Article 1 and Article 2 of the Constitution *accord validity* to the general personality right also in the *private law system*, that's why it is protected as 'another right'. To respect the constitutional sphere in the sense of not infringing it in an unauthorized manner is a *legal requirement* (Gebot) flowing from the Basic Law itself and whereby damages work as a constitutional consequence to ensure protection.

6.1.3.1.4 Ginsengwurzel Case: Deriving Personality Right from Constitutional Value System

In a subsequent case, the so-called *Ginsengwurzel* case,[76] the BGH restrained itself from endorsing the direct effect of fundamental rights on the relationship of private parties *inter se*.[77] In 1961, BGH awarded compensation for the infringement of personality right for the non-pecuniary loss in the so-called *Ginsengwurzel* case. According to facts of the case, a professor of international and ecclesiastical law brought a ginseng root from Korea and gave it to his pharmacologist friend for research purposes, who afterwards published an article mentioning the law professor in a thankful manner for assisting him in providing the root. In 1957, a company dealing with a tonic containing ginseng root referred to the law professor in an advertorial piece in widely distributed journals. The defendant company mentioned the name of the plaintiff professor in the advertisement as being an important scientist, who expressed his views on the value of ginseng regarding its aphrodisiac quality.[78] The professor sued the company, claiming that he had suffered an unauthorized attack on his personality right as the advertisement gave the impression that he gave his opinion about a doubtful product for monitory considerations regarding which he had no professional knowledge. While relying on BGHZ

[73] See for analysis Cremer (2010), pp. 48–53.

[74] BGHZ 24, 72, See for analysis, Cremer (2010), p. 50.

[75] BGHZ 24, 72, See for analysis, Cremer (2010), p. 50.

[76] BGHZ 35, 363.

[77] See Cremer (2010), pp. 52–53.

[78] BGHZ 35, 363 as translated in: Markesinis and Unberath (2002), pp. 420–423.

26, 149 (*Herrenreiter* case), he claimed 10,000 DM as satisfaction amount for the damage done to his right to personality.

In its decision, the BGH emphasized that the BGB's focus had been more on proprietary interests of the claimants. It stated,

> When the BGB established that enumeration principle, the high value of the protection of human personality and its special sphere had not received the recognition that it enjoys according to Articles 1 and 2 I of the Constitution. From the standpoint of the BGB, the protection of property interests always stood in the foreground, whereas the personal worth of a human being received only insufficient and fragmentary protection. In recognising a general personality right of mankind and granting it the protection of § 823 (1) BGB, the courts drew for civil law purposes the consequences resulting from the rank the Constitution assigned to the worth of human personality and the protection of its free development. That protection, however, would be incomplete and full of loopholes if an infringement of the personality right did not give rise to a sanction adequate to the violation. Just as the restriction of protection by the law of delict to specific legal interests of a human being has proved too narrow to afford the protection of personality required by the Constitution, so a narrowing of immaterial damages, for immaterial loss to cover only injury to specifically mentioned legal interests, no longer conforms to the value-system of the Constitution. For Article 1 declares it to be an urgent obligation on the public power to protect the sacred dignity of the human being. Article 2 (1) puts the right of a human being to free development of his personality at the head of the fundamental rights.[79]

The BGH affirmed that the abolition of damages for non-pecuniary loss occurred to an infringement of personality right would mean that the injury to the dignity and honor of a human being shall remain without any sanction of the civil law, while the purpose of civil law is to deal with the "disturbance of essential values and makes the doer of injury owe satisfaction to the victim for the wrong done to him."[80]

Another key aspect of the Ginseng judgment is that the Court elaborated the difference between damage to the constitutionally protected concrete area of body, health and freedom, and the violation of personality right in general. Accordingly,

> the factual aspect of an injury to a general personality right is much less specific than where body, health, or freedom is injured. That means that there are many marginal cases where the question is whether the case is one included in the generalised description of violation of the personality and whether, if it does, the unlawfulness is not excluded by the competing rights of the "offender", among which the right to free expression of opinion deserves particular attention. It is precisely where a so-called balancing of interest must take place that the limits of what is allowed are not always easy to fix.[81]

The Court stressed that the condition for just satisfaction arises where the personality right is infringed for *wanton reason* and that no apparent countervailing interest is shown for such violation. Thus, it applied these principles on the instant case and held that the award of money as just compensation by way of satisfaction is duly justified because of the seriousness of the assault on the personality right of the law professor.

---

[79] BGHZ 35, 363 as translated in: Markesinis and Unberath (2002), p. 421.

[80] BGHZ 35, 363 as translated in: Markesinis and Unberath (2002), p. 422.

[81] BGHZ 35, 363 as translated in: Markesinis and Unberath (2002), p. 422.

6.1.3.1.5 Conclusions

The described cases, though adjudicated in the Federal Court of Justice under Civil law, drew a positive impact on the protection of the right to privacy due to an approach of being guided by the provisions of the constitution. The conceptualization of the privacy right as a constitutional value is reinforced by the radiating effect of fundamental rights. The basic requirement of the fundamental rights to get effective protection leads to a clearer picture of privacy law in Germany.

The analyzed judgments are typically cited as examples of the earlier tendency of German higher courts to award more or less direct horizontal effect to fundamental rights. However, the later development in the approach of the BGH clarified the misconception that the fundamental rights enshrined in German Basic Law are also available against private parties or enforceable at the level of private law. In the Ginseng case, the Court did not held in support of the so-called third party application of fundamental rights; rather, it used terminology conveying a broader meaning such as the 'judiciary has drawn such conclusions for implementation through private law'. In the words of the Court, the courts drew for civil law purposes, i. e. for the protection of a general personality right by sec. 823 I BGB, the consequences resulting from the rank the Constitution assigned to the worth of human personality and the protection of its free development.[82]

Against this background, Federal Constitutional Court played a decisive role and supported the constitutionalization of the right to privacy and refined the remaining conceptual and legal ambiguities.

6.1.3.2 The Constitutionalization of Civil Law of Privacy and Personality Rights

In April, 1961, a newspaper published a completely fabricated interview of Princess Soraya Esfandiary-Bakhtiary. Popularly known as Princes Soraya, she was the ex-wife of the Shah of Iran and living in Germany after her divorce. The same paper published another news-story with a brief clarification that the April interview was not given by Princess Soraya. Princess Soraya successfully complained against the newspaper on the ground of her personality right violation. The trial court awarded her DM 15,000. Later on, both the *Oberlandesgericht* (court of appeal) and the *BGH* (Federal Court of Justice) confirmed the judgments of the trial court. Against these judgments, the defendant newspaper filed a constitutional petition in the *Bundesverfassungsgericht* (Federal Constitutional Court).[83]

[82]BGHZ 35, 363 as translated by: Lawson and Markesinis for University of Texas available at: https://law.utexas.edu/transnational/foreign-law-translations/german/case.php?id=738. Accessed 25 August 2023.

[83]BVerfGE 34, 269, Translated by: Rudolf Schlesinger's Comparative Law 6th ed (1998) by Baade, Herzog and Wise; available at the University of Texas's foreign law translation web page:

The FCC then reached a landmark judgment, the Soraya case judgment, in 1973.[84] The Constitutional Court availed the opportunity to give a recap of how there used to be no protection of the right to privacy in the German Basic Law and that how the BGH attempted a breakthrough to provide relief under the "other right" expression of sec. 823 I BGB. By this way, the FCC addressed the normative confusion created by the apparently conflicting texts of sections 253 and 847 of BGB. The Court highlighted that the restriction of damages in the cases of non-material loss under section 253 is a general rule to which section 847 worked as an exception. Resultantly, the plaintiff had to prove some kind of special losses such as loosing job or economic interests according to that textual interpretation. However, the Constitutional Court endorsed the earlier innovative interpretation of the BGH in *Herrenreiter* case, which had removed the impediment in remedying the personality harm and thus provided a foundation for an enhanced protection to the right to personality. The Constitutional Court made these important remarks about the BGH approach to the modification of Civil Law in awarding damages for non-material loss:

> In the decisions dealing with this question, the BGH also pointed to the drastic technological and social changes that have taken place since the enactment of the Civil Code. The development of mass media, hardly predictable in 1900, makes the protection of an individual's personality right more important and more difficult in our day. Therefore, the BGH held, a court which takes the value system of the Constitution seriously can no longer feel bound by § 253 of the Civil Code insofar as that provision denies recovery for non-pecuniary damages even in cases of grave injuries to an individual's personality right.[85]

The defendant raised objections mainly on the competency of judges to interpret the law contrary to a legal rule (section 253 of BGB). The objections emphasized that judges should not announce monetary award for non-monitory damage where the legal rule had expressly precluded that. Rejecting the appeal against the previous judgments and holding that the reinterpretation of section 253 by judges in the Ginseng case was legitimate, the FCC included an important passage to its judgment, which clarifies the positivist versus interpretationist dilemma:

> occasionally, the law can be found outside the positive legal rules erected by the state; this is law which emanates from the entire constitutional order and which has as its purpose the 'correction' of written law. It is for the judge to 'discover' this law and through his opinions give it concrete effect. The Constitution does not restrict judges to apply statutes in their literary sense when deciding cases put before them. Such an approach assumes a basic completeness of statutory rules which is not attainable in practice . . . The insight of the judge may bring to light certain values of society . . . which are implicitly accepted by the constitutional order but which have received an insufficient expression in statutory texts. The judge's decision can help realize such ideas and give effect to such values.[86]

---

https://law.utexas.edu/transnational/foreign-law-translations/german/case.php?id=721. Accessed 25 August 2023.

[84] BVerfGE 34, 269.

[85] BVerfGE 34, 269.

[86] BVerfGE 34, 269.

The Constitutional Court articulated the findings in earlier judgments of the BGH in a more precise manner, stating that the respect for dignity and personality right is (1) *also a private law right*; (2) to be *respected* by everyone; (3) it is protected by *sec. 823 (1) BGB*. Civil courts have acknowledged the existence of this right under the 'radiating effect' of Basic Law. The FCC explained:

> The judicial process in which the contested decisions were made was a civil litigation that had to be decided under the private law system. The Federal Constitutional Court does not have to review the interpretation and application of civil law as such. However, the objective order of values contained in the constitution's fundamental rights also affects private law; it is a fundamental constitutional decision for all areas of law. The Federal Constitutional Court is responsible for ensuring that this "radiating effect" of the constitution is observed. It therefore checks whether the decisions of the civil courts are based on a fundamentally incorrect view of the scope and effectiveness of a fundamental right or whether the result of the decision itself violates the fundamental rights of a party. [.......]The Federal Constitutional Court (BVG) has no reason to contest this case law of the Federal Court of Justice (BGH) on a constitutional law basis. The value system of fundamental rights finds its center in the human personality and its dignity, which can develop freely within the social community [....] Such protection can above all claim the private sphere of man, the area in which he wished to be alone, make his own decisions and does not wish to be interfered with by interventions of any kind [....] In the field of private law, this legal purpose is also served by the legal construction of general personal right; it fills in gaps in personal protection that remained here despite the recognition of individual personal rights and had become more and more palpable over the course of time for various reasons. The Federal Constitutional Court therefore has never reproved the recognition of a general personality right in the jurisprudence of the civil courts.[87]

However, this announcement must be taken together with the Court's extensive clarification of the qualification of civil suits, which the Court ordered to be the exclusive purview of civil courts. It held:

> It is up to the ordinary courts to interpret the relevant provisions, which, when making their decision, must take into account the influence of fundamental rights on civil law. The Federal Constitutional Court is solely responsible for ensuring that the ordinary courts observe the fundamental rights norms and standards; As part of this task, it has to examine whether the contested decision reveals design errors that are based on a fundamentally incorrect view of the importance of a fundamental right, in particular the scope of its scope of protection, and are also of some importance for the substantive legal case [....] There is no room here for a further examination [....], A rejection decision may not depend on whether the complaint was only for injunctive relief or revocation or payment of compensation for pain and suffering; however, the factual weight of the fundamental rights violation alleged by the complainant cannot give reason to go beyond the basic scope of the examination set out. In particular, the Federal Constitutional Court is not authorized to review the factual findings of the Appeal Court and their assessment, or even to replace them with its own.[88]

The Court also highlighted the special character of the general personality right and the difficulty to fix the boundary of its scope:

---

[87] Translated into English at: http://www.servat.unibe.ch/dfr/bv034269.html. Accessed 25 August 2023. These excerpts are also translated into English in: Cremer (2010), pp. 54–55.

[88] BverfGE 54, 148 (References omitted).

> Because of the peculiarity of the general right of personality, the case law of the Federal Constitutional Court, like that of the Federal Court of Justice, did not conclusively describe the content of protected law, but rather worked out its characteristics based on the case to be decided. For example, privacy, secrecy and privacy are recognized as protective goods of general personality rights.[89]

Later on, e.g. in the Caroline Von Monaco I judgment of 1998,[90] the Federal Constitutional Court has arrived at clearly separating the general personality right of the constitutional sphere from the general personality right developed in civil law even though the latter is always influenced to a certain extent by the former.

Hans Stoll has summarized the interaction of private and constitutional rights in these terms:

> Every Citizen whose fundamental rights have been violated by an act of State may appeal to the *Bundesverfassungsgericht* for relief. In that regard, an act of state may also be a judgment rendered by a civil court. Admittedly, the *Bundesverfassungsgericht* does not control the application of ordinary rules of private law, but it is competent to set aside a judgment whenever it represents a basically wrong view of the scope and importance of a fundamental right. Thus in many of its decisions the *Bundesverfassungsgericht* has established 'signpost', showing the way to the correct interpretation and progressive development of private law in conformity with the fundamental rights under the Basic Law.[91]

The above narration of the evolutionary development of the general personality right shows that privacy has a strong normative foundation in German law today. The first bold and innovative step of the BGH in its Dr. Schacht judgment turned into a rich case law. Additionally, the rulings of the FCC enter the picture which have elaborated a protection of the very diversified nature of privacy interests that is hardly covered by any other legal system.

Schwartz and Peifer analyze the German concept of personality right as

> Germany's unitary concept of a right of personality has proven similarly successful. It supplies a highly abstract framework, one with deep philosophical elements, around which a complete German cosmology of tort privacy has been constructed. Its great merit for the German legal system is to furnish a theoretical vantage point from which judges and scholars can engage in the necessary confrontation with potentially messy facts and inconsistent categories.[92]

6.1.4 Unfolding the Substance and Obligations of Personality Rights

As explained earlier, the Federal Constitutional Court has successfully differentiated the general personality right protected under private law and the constitutionally

---

[89] BverfGE 54, 148.

[90] BVerfGE 97, 125.

[91] Stoll (1999), pp. 33–34.

[92] Schwartz and Peifer (2010), p. 1929.

protected general personality right under Article 2 (1) in combination with Article 1 (1). The latter "serves to strengthen protection for the development and presentation of the individual personality and simultaneously secures the fundamental condition for human existence."[93] Thus, the overall legal and constitutional regime of privacy protection works well to safeguard both outward broader freedom of action at one hand and also a personal sphere with a narrow scope on the other hand, which definitely goes far beyond the protection of solely 'right to be let alone'.

Markesinis summarizes the great variety of violations for which German law has awarded damages or injunctions under the right to personality development regime. These areas are, appropriation of likeness; unlawful release of an insured person's medical record; neighbor snooping; unnecessary publicity about an impending divorce of a member of the aristocracy; the publication of a telephone conversation; the unauthorized opening of sealed mail; the unauthorized imitation of the voice for advertisement purpose; and photographing a public figure in a public place.[94]

If an intrusion is connected to a specifically guaranteed freedom, the relevant special guarantee will be invoked. Therefore, the rights and interests attached to privacy such as personal privacy, confidentiality, informational self-determination, right to identity, right to the rightful representation in the media and so on could be successfully protected provided they meet the required legal criteria. Otherwise, the general right to personality takes effect. However, the so-called "catch-all"[95] quality of the combination of specified personality rights and the general right to personality does not provide an absolute protection. There is always the possibility of a limitation of these rights by another specific guarantee which is in conflict with them.[96]

6.1.4.1 General Right to Personality and Concrete Personality Rights as Catch-All Right

6.1.4.1.1 The Right to Privacy

The general right to personality includes as a more specific right, among others, the right to privacy in a narrow sense, i. e. the right to protect personal and private information from public disclosure under Article 2 (1) in combination with Article 1(1) of the German Basic law. This right has a dual function. On one hand it protects interests of the nature of the 'right to be let alone', while on the other hand, it protects interests, which are a prerequisite for the general freedom of action. The following case law of the Federal Constitutional Court as well as of the Federal Court of Justice

---

[93] Bumke and Voßkuhle (2019), p. 108.

[94] Markesinis (1999), pp. 56–57.

[95] See for details: Bumke and Voßkuhle (2019), p. 106.

[96] In Sect. 6.1.4.3, we will analyze this more closely with regard to freedom of expression and the media.

demonstrates how this normative setup protects a variety of privacy related interests. These interests can outweigh the countervailing interests during the balancing exercise.

The Federal Constitutional Court confirmed a violation of the right to privacy protected under Article 2 (1) in conjunction with Article 1 (1) in a case where a government agency as employer used the divorce related documents of an employee only to initiate disciplinary proceedings.[97] According to the Court, divorce records are subject to confidentiality in accordance with Article 2 (1) in conjunction with Article 1 (1) Basic Law and this aspect of personality can be interfered only if it is legitimated by, among other requirements, the principle of proportionality in relation to protecting an overweighing public interest. However, in the instant case, the investigators requested for access to files, for which it had not been sufficiently clarified whether they could contain relevant information for the disciplinary proceedings at all; furthermore, other sources for obtaining the necessary information had not been sufficiently examined. The Court emphasized that divorce matters are not absolutely protected from examination in the process of disciplinary investigations, because such matters are also discussed in courts in order to pass judgments delimiting the strict confidentiality of such matters. However, in the case to be decided, an access to the contents of the divorce documents violated the principle of proportionality.

In the *Postöffnung* case (mail opening case), the Federal Court of Justice (BGH) held that the unauthorized opening of the sealed letter constituted a violation of the addressee's right to the general right to personality.[98] In this case, a spouse of the divorced couple had her office in the same building as her former husband where they used to live and had her mailbox over there. The plaintiff (former wife) accused the defendant (former husband) of opening three letters addressed to her, one after the other, with different lame pretexts as there was no reason for confusion. Accepting her appeal, the BGH reasoned that the infringement triggers injunctive relief under tort law. The value contained in Article 10 of the Basic Law protecting the inviolability of the secrecy of correspondence against the state impacts private relations because, "the area of communication, which is a significant part of people's way of life and self-fulfillment, needs to be shielded from the curiosity of third parties." The Court further held that communication is a vulnerable area, where the confidentiality plays an important role. The disturbance of confidentiality affects the personalized nature of such communication. Its protection from outsiders is a matter of law when such protection has been expressed clearly such as sealed envelopes and clearly addressed letters.[99]

In the so-called Gretna Green case, the Federal Court of Justice held that the press must not make the private sphere of a person a subject of discussion in public at

[97] BVerfGE 27, 344.

[98] Bundesgerichtshof Urt. v. 20.02.1990, Az.: VI ZR 241/89 (Postal opening case).

[99] Bundesgerichtshof Urt. v. 20.02.1990, Az.: VI ZR 241/89 (Postal opening case).

large; unless there is a sound reason for that.[100] The claimant is entitled for compensation for non-material damage in case the press reports in an embarrassing manner about the private sphere, which also includes sore family relationships. In the Greta-Green-case, a minor girl of a rich German craftsman, the plaintiff, fell in love with a British boy living in Berlin and she wanted to get married to him against her father's wishes.[101] The couple left Germany secretly and fled to Britain in order to commemorate their wedding in the historic Gretna Green town of Scotland. A reporter of the Scottish Daily Mail offered his services to find her whereabouts with a condition that he would publish an article about the couple's romance with pictorial depiction. The plaintiff agreed. This arrangement successfully brought the plaintiff's daughter back to Berlin. According to the arrangement, the journalist published an article with pictures in Daily Mail Scotland. However, the claim arose when the German *Bild-Zeitung* also published the same article and picture with extra spicy headings such as "Father has his daughter pursued" and "the son-in-law's left jacket was not baggy enough".[102] Rejecting the defendant's plea that the information was already disclosed in Scotland, the Court considered the publication of full personal details of private affairs unlawful and imposed DM 7500 on the editor liable for such publication and private disclosures to the public at large.

The general right to personality also protects telephonic conversation and any use of such conversation is subject to prior permission of the participants. The Federal Court of Justice held in the case of a CDU Chairman's appeal against the publication of his leaked telephonic conversation with the Secretary of the party:

> Everyone, even a politician appearing in the public arena and seeking publicity, has in principle a claim protected by Arts 1 and 2 of the Basic Law to the safeguarding of his private sphere, to which others only have access insofar as he allows them to see it. In this private sphere he must be safe from control and censorship by the public, otherwise the basis on which his personality can be realised and develop would be endangered. All the events and expressions of life of this personal sphere are in principle protected by the right of the personality to self-determination in this way.[103]

6.1.4.1.2 Right to One's Identity

The German legal regime provides substantive legal tools for the protection of one's identity and the choice of presenting oneself to the general public. A person is normally identified with her name or her photo. These two symbols may not be exactly used to identify a person and some description of the personal characteristics or the use of graphic narrations could be used to reveal the identification of a person

---

[100] BGH (26.02.1965) IV ZR 204/63.

[101] Stoll (1999), pp. 39–40.

[102] Stoll (1999), p. 39.

[103] BGHZ 73, 120 Bundesgerichtshof Federal Supreme Court, Sixth Civil Senate. Translated by Raymond Youngs for University of Texas foreign law webpage, available at: https://law.utexas.edu/transnational/foreign-law-translations/german/case.php?id=737. Accessed 25 August 2023.

in one or another context. Therefore, German law does not only protect the exact names and pictures but also the *likeness* of a person. This is a more comprehensively approach of protecting the identity. The protection of the combination of name, picture or likeness secures the right to correct the description of one's life in case it is presented to the general public by somebody else and to present oneself before the general public. The right to personality offers the protection of name and picture as its "special manifestations". It protects these areas not only from a non-material injury but also prohibits the unauthorized commercial use of these features.[104]

The right to one's name is covered by sec. 12 BGB which entitles a person against unauthorized use of her name:

> If the right of a person to use a name is disputed by another person, or if the interest of the person entitled to the name is injured by the unauthorised use of the same name by another person, the person entitled may require the other to remove the infringement. If further infringements are to be feared, the person entitled may seek a prohibitory injunction[105]

As for pictures of a person, taking photographs and publishing them is part of the media activities. Photographs provide a sense of reality and liveliness to the news stories. The purposes of images published in newspapers depend on the nature of the publication as well as on the context of a specific publication. Some pictures are related to the articles enclosed, while other pictures tell the story themselves—rather make a news story instead of supporting the written story.

The protection of one's own picture has its constitutional basis in the right to personality under Article 2 (1) in combination with Article 1 (1) of the German Basic Law and by this way one can exercise this right on many ways to control one's likeness. This constitutional right has been substantiated by sections 22 and 23 of the Law on Copyright to Works of Fine Art and Photography 1907. According to section 22:

> Images may only be distributed or publicly displayed with the consent of the person depicted. In cases of doubt, consent is deemed to have been given if the person pictured has received remuneration for being shown. After the death of the person depicted, the consent of the relatives of the person depicted is required for a period of 10 years. Relatives within the meaning of this law are the surviving spouse or life partner and the children of the depicted person and, if there is neither a spouse or life partner nor children, the parents of the depicted person.

Section 23 provides some exceptions to the requirement of consent under section 22. For example, a picture/portrait of someone from contemporary history can be published without consent if such distribution does not abridge any other legitimate right. The understanding of both "contemporary history" and "legitimate interests" have been elaborated in the jurisprudence. The latter include the depiction of the

[104] See: Marlene Dietrich Case BGH 1 ZR 49/97. Translate by Raymond Youngs, available at: https://law.utexas.edu/transnational/foreign-law-translations/german/case.php?id=726. Accessed 25 August 2023.

[105] Chapter 12 German Civil Code (BGB), English translation available at: https://www.gesetze-im-internet.de/englisch_bgb/englisch_bgb.html#p0048. Accessed 25 August 2023.

intimate sphere, the distribution of images which create a dangerous situation for the subject or particular violations of commercial interests of the person from contemporary history. An analogous application of sec. 1004 of the German Civil Code (BGB) provides the remedy for such an interference with the right to image, in the shape of eliminating the interference through legal injunction.[106]

The application of sections 22 and 23 of the Law on Copyright to Works of Fine Art and Photography follows a systematic doctrinal approach. Firstly, it is ascertained that whether or not the alleged right's violation comes under the ambit of section 22; secondly, whether or not the distribution is justified with a view to section 23 (1) of KUG; thirdly, whether any other legitimate interests of the right-holder has been infringed or not.

Regarding the scope of protection of this law, it is mostly restricted to the 'person' of an individual, and can be invoked where the *Bildness* (portrait of person) is in question, or where any kind of material conveys sufficient information with respect to the actual recognition of a person. The protection is not restricted to static photos and it covers motion pictures such as video footages or films showing the person.[107] However, an artistic representation in the form of caricature, even if the person is recognizable, may not come under the ambit of this Act. An image of the person which is technologically manipulated (montage) is something which is different from a caricature as in a caricature the viewer knows the artistic dimension. In one of its decisions, the Federal Constitutional Court declared a manipulated picture of the plaintiff as a violation of his self-determination of presentation of himself before the general public.[108] All in all, the substantiation of an aspect of the personality right

[106] Section 1004 BGB: "Claim for removal and injunction: (1) If the ownership is interfered with by means other than removal or retention of possession, the owner may require the disturber to remove the interference. If further interferences are to be feared, the owner may seek a prohibitory injunction. (2) The claim is excluded if the owner is obliged to tolerate the interference."

[107] For detail scope, see: Vahrenwald (1994), p. 209.

[108] BVerfG 1 BvR 240/04 (14 February 2005) Translated by Raymond Youngs, available at: https://law.utexas.edu/transnational/foreign-law-translations/german/case.php?id=1499. Accessed 10 July 2021. Paras 24 and 25 explain the distinction between a caricature and other manipulated pictures: "The photographic image of the head contains an incorrect message because of the technical manipulation, even if the complainant is still identifiable in spite of the manipulation. How far such an invasion needs to be accepted in the context of a satirical image also depends on whether the observer of the picture can recognise the manipulative alteration, and therefore definitely cannot come to the mistaken conclusion that the person depicted looked like that in reality. Recognisability of the distortion is for instance for the most part a characteristic of a caricature. But that is not the position here. The picture of the head used for the montage claims to be a photograph, and gives the reader no clue that the facial features have been manipulated. Nor does any such clue follow from the fact that the remainder of the image can clearly be recognised as having the character of fiction. This does not apply to the picture of the head. A photograph conveys information about the person photographed without the use of words. Photos suggest authenticity and observers of them assume that the person depicted looks like that in reality. But this assumption is not justified with a graphic manipulation which alters a person's appearance and which can be effected today with relative simplicity by technical means. The holder of the right of personality admittedly has no right to be perceived by third parties only as he would like to see himself

complements the general personality right; it does not exclude it. In other words, sections 22 and 23 of the Law on Copyright to Works of Fine Art and Photography do not preclude the affected person from resorting to the legal remedy under Civil Code in the case of failure to be protected under this law, such as in the case of merely taking picture without distribution.[109]

The broader right to one's image has been elaborated by the Federal Constitutional Court in a number of cases. A study of the Caroline von Monaco (Hannover) series of cases provides useful jurisprudential principles and guidelines regarding various aspects of this right and its value vis-à-vis other interests such as public interest.[110] This right includes the right to have control over one's image in a restricted form as the Constitutional Court does not recognize a right of a person to be portrayed to others only as one wishes to be.

The right to one's fair identity and the protection against unfair portrayal (e.g. in the form of imagery) or description (e.g. in the form of textual representation) is more comprehensive and covers typical common law torts of unauthorized commercial appropriation and also the tort of false light. In the former case, the German courts have devised the principle in cases of using someone name or likeness for commercial purposes.

False light cases usually fall somewhere in-between defamation and privacy violation. The plaintiffs have a right to correct any misperception created by the publication and a right to reply against false allegations or misrepresentation. In the *Schmid-Spiegel* Case, the Constitutional Court upheld the right to reply in a series of allegations and counter allegations between the weekly magazine Der Spiegel and Mr. Schmid, a high-ranking state judge.[111] In this case, Der Spiegel magazine, infuriated with the earlier speech of Mr. Schmid in favor of strikes against employers, dubbed him as a communist sympathizer. Mr. Schmid hit back in a strongly worded verbal reply in which he equated the political reporting of Der Spiegel to pornography. He was successfully sued for criminal libel action, which was confirmed by Gottingen regional Court. However, the Federal Constitutional Court cancelled the decrees at the appeal stage on the basis of the right to free speech. The Constitutional Court analyzed the content of the Spiegel article as well as the

(references omitted), but he does have a right that a photographically constructed image of him should not be distorted by manipulation if it is made available to third parties without his consent. The message of the picture in any case becomes incorrect if the photo is altered beyond changes purely caused by the reproduction process and insignificant for the content of the message. Such manipulations affect the right of personality regardless of whether they are undertaken with a good intention or with an intent to harm and whether readers assess the alteration as advantageous or disadvantageous for the person represented. The assertion of facts which as a rule is conjured up by the pictorial image always becomes inappropriate if it goes beyond reality in relation to the person depicted."

[109] For a detailed discussion regarding taking photo without consent even if distribution is not the aim, see: Vahrenwald (1994).

[110] E.g. 101 BVerfGE 361 (Princess Caroline of Monaco II—1999) as translated in Kommers and Miller (2012), pp. 486–491.

[111] BVerfGE 12, 113 (Schmid-Spiegel Case 1961).

communication made and evidence provided by Mr. Schmid that he had openly criticized Bolshevism. Disregarding these facts, the magazine published a false and misleading news story. The Court held in an unwavering manner,

> If Der Spiegel had through its reporting about the complainant laid open to the justified suspicion of not reporting reliably, then an appropriate contribution to public debate might also consist in correspondingly criticizing Der Spiegel generally as a vehicle for such a mode of portrayal. *Der Spiegel*, thus, had given occasion for a denunciatory judgment. . .and had therefore in principle to put with such a judgment, even if it reduced its reputation.[112]

In the landmark judgment of the Eppler Case, the Constitutional Court decided that the general right to personality protects a person from the attribution of a statement not issued by him. i. e. from putting words into someone's mouth.[113] Referring to earlier judgments, the Court emphasized the broad nature of the right to personality leading to the result that it can be dealt only on case-to-case basis. In the case in hand, the Court set the principle that it would be sufficient for an infringement of the general right to personality to put words into someone's mouth in case that this negatively affects one's own image as seen by others. The decision is a landmark judgment because the private or intimate sphere of life were not involved in this case. Thus, the Constitutional Court differentiated from then on quite sharply between the right to privacy in a narrower sense, the protection of which comprises merely a part of the right of personality, and the general right to personality which encompasses a variety of interests, can then be, as we have seen, specified in various facets, and can be continuously developed to address new threats.

6.1.4.1.3 Informational Self-determination

In another landmark judgment, the Census Act Case,[114] the Federal Constitutional Court recognized the existence of the right to data privacy and informational self-determination based on the Article 2 (1) in combination with Article 1 (1) of the German Basic Law. The judgment came as a result of filing a constitutional petition by more than a hundred citizens challenging the constitutionality of the Federal Census Act 1983. All German citizens were required to fill a detailed questionnaire about their life such as occupation, income, education, as well the means of transport they used.[115] As the German constitutional jurisprudence understands the right of personality as being open to new threats and dynamically evolving and determines the scope of content of the right on a case to case basis, the right to informational self-determination came under its ambit this time. The threats that come along with the possibilities of automated data processing had reached public awareness. The

[112] BVerfGE 12, 113 (Schmid-Spiegel Case 1961) as translated in: Kommers and Miller (2012), p. 453.

[113] BVerfGE 54, 148 (Eppler Case 1980).

[114] BVerfGE 65, 1 (Census Act Case 1983).

[115] BVerfGE 65, 1 (Census Act Case 1983).

Court elaborated the possible dangers to the personality development of a person in an environment of uncertainty about the level of information the State or private institutions have access to. "If someone is uncertain whether information about unusual behavior is being stored and recorded permanently in computer banks, or does not know whether it will be used or passed on, he will try not to attract attention by engaging in such behavior", the Court warned.[116] Similarly, if public authorities note and register details of participants of a public assembly, people would start avoiding participating in such assemblies although they have a right to exercise their right of assembly in an effective and unimpaired manner. Against the background of these considerations and with a view to the threats of modern data processing technologies, the Court held that under Article 2 (1) in tandem with Article 1 (1) of the Basic Law, the state must protect individuals from "unlimited collection, storage, use, and transmission of personal data as a condition for free personality development".[117] Individuals have a right "to, in principle, decide themselves on the disclosure and use of their personal data."[118] This seems to be more convincing approach to the determination of scope of protection as it is according to the principle of autonomy and informational self-determination.

The judgment then describes the limitations on the right to personality and its offshoot of informational self-determination; it is not an absolute right but can be limited and regulated by constitutional statutes on the basis of Article 2 (1) of the Basic Law. Limitations require a statutory basis, specifying the conditions and scope of the limitations in accordance with the principle of legal clarity. The state is required to clearly convey to the citizens the purpose for which and the conditions under which data is acquired. In principle, personal data may only be collected and used for statutorily defined purposes. Furthermore, the principle of proportionality must be observed. The Court held, among other considerations, that it would be unconstitutional if personal data were processed such as to result in reconstruction or release of comprehensive personality profiles of individuals.[119] Additionally, the state is duty bound to adopt organisational and procedural safeguards to protect the right to informational self-determination against threats resulting from the use of automatic data processing.[120]

The Court, though sustaining most of the provisions of the Census Act, required the State not to continue with the same statute unless legislature amends certain

---

[116] BVerfGE 65, 1 (Census Act Case 1983) as translated in: Kommers and Miller (2012), p. 410.

[117] BVerfGE 65, 1 (Census Act Case 1983) as translated in: Kommers and Miller (2012), p. 410.

[118] BVerfGE 65, 1, Headnote 1., https://www.bundesverfassungsgericht.de/SharedDocs/Entscheidungen/EN/1983/12/rs19831215_1bvr020983en.html. Accessed. Cf. also Phillipson and Fenwick (2000), pp. 660, 662–663: "'Informational autonomy' [. . . ..] refers to the individual's interest in controlling the flow of personal information about herself [. . . ..]". See also the extensive analysis of the decision in: Albers (2005), pp. 151 ff. Accessed 25 August 2023.

[119] BVerfGE 65, 1 (Census Act Case 1983) as translated in: Kommers and Miller (2012), p. 411.

[120] Cf. BVerfGE 65, 1, Abstract available at: https://www.bundesverfassungsgericht.de/SharedDocs/Entscheidungen/EN/1983/12/rs19831215_1bvr020983en.html. Accessed 25 August 2023.

sections of the Act. This requirement delayed the census for at least 4 years. Among the key impacts of the Census Act judgment is its far-reaching significance in having provided a constitutional basis for data protection laws.

6.1.4.1.4 Right to Resocialization and Right to be Forgotten

Reporting a crime with all the relevant details of name and likeness of a suspect is a serious invasion into the personality right. Therefore, it must be justified with view to the freedom of expression or of the media or to the public right to access to information. In this regard, to obtain knowledge about current crimes may be regarded as a sufficient public interest justification, keeping in view the principles of proportionality. In the Lebach case, which has already been presented in the overview of illustrative cases,[121] the Federal Constitutional Court held

> [i]f someone breaches the peace by attacking or injuring fellow citizens or the legally protected interests of the community, he or she must not only suffer the criminal punishment provided by the law but also must accept, as a matter of principle, that in a community committed to freedom of communication the public has an interest in receiving information through normal channels about an act the criminal committed.[122]

However, it does not mean that this right of society to access information is absolute. Rather, it will always be subject to proportionality test whenever the question of personality rights of a person is involved. In the Lebach case, the Court further explained the proportional dissemination of news, stating that it is not always permissible to disclose the identity of a convicted person such as name or picture; the intrusion has to be justified that whether or not the public interest could be served without such disclosures.[123] Beyond that, a person who has already been convicted for his crime and undergone the punishment, in principle, cannot be brought back to the public light for his old conduct. "Not only must prisoners be prepared to reenter human society, society must in turn be prepared also to accept them", the Court asserted.[124] Under Article 2 (1) in tandem with Article 1 (1) of the Basic Law, the criminals are entitled to have the opportunity of rehabilitation and so to become a normal member of society once again after undergoing the sentence for their crime. Keeping these considerations at the forefront, the Court ordered,

> In any case, a televised report concerning a serious crime that is no longer justified by the public's interest in receiving information about current events may not be rebroadcast if it

[121] See Sect. 6.1.1.

[122] BVerfGE 35, 202 (Lebach Case 1973), as translated in: Kommers and Miller (2012), p. 481.

[123] BVerfGE 35, 202 (Lebach Case 1973), as translated in: Kommers and Miller (2012), p. 482. In the Courtroom television case (2001), the First Senate of FCC held that it was not unconstitutional if a law enforces ban on the live coverage of court trials, BVerfGE 44, 103 (2001). In this judgment, the Court viewed that regularly the rights of defendants are more important than the media industry's right to broadcast court proceedings.

[124] BVerfGE 35, 202 (Lebach Case 1973), as translated in: Kommers and Miller (2012), p. 483.

> endangers the social rehabilitation of the criminal. The criminal's vital interest in being reintegrated into society and the interest of the community in restoring his or her social position must generally have precedence over the public's interest in a further discussion of the crime...[125]

The "right to be forgotten", which also has already been mentioned in the overview,[126] is a relatively recent facet of the protection of personality rights under Article 2 (1) in combination with Article 1 (1) of the Basic Law. It draws on case law since the Lebach-decision, but is broader in scope. Its background are the challenges of the change of communication on the Internet. The Court held:

> Given the realities of Internet communication, time is a specific factor to be considered when deciding on a person's claim for protection. The legal order must protect the individual against the risk of being indefinitely confronted in public with their past opinions, statements or actions. Only when it is possible for matters to stay in the past do individuals have a chance at a new beginning in freedom. The possibility for matters to be forgotten is part of the temporal dimension of freedom.[127]

This novel right has, however, certain limits. For example, it does not include the right to request that all information relating to one's person be deleted from the Internet or the right to filter and restrict the publicly accessible personal information according to one's own preferences.[128] Moreover, it can be restricted, provided that the restricting legal acts are constitutional, and requires a balancing with other freedoms and rights, especially the freedom of expression and the media.

6.1.4.1.5 General Personality Right as Subsidiary Right

The right of personality under Article 2(1) of the Basic Law in conjunction with Article 1(1) over time has been, as we have seen, concretized in various facets.[129] They protect more specific human interests related to personal privacy and confidentiality, right to one's identity, right to one's own name, picture or image, right to informational self-determination or right to be forgotten. In cases where none of these facets can be referred to, the general right to personality may offer protection because it has the role of a subsidiary right. In result, the combination of specified personality rights and the general right to personality fulfils catch-all functions. Thus, the constitutional protection of personality rights in German Basic Law has

---

[125] BVerfGE 35, 202 (Lebach Case 1973), as translated in Kommers and Miller (2012), p. 483.

[126] See Sect. 6.1.1.

[127] Order of 6 November 2019—1 BvR 16/13—Right to be forgotten-I, Headnote 2b, www.bundesverfassungsgericht.de/SharedDocs/Entscheidungen/EN/2019/11/rs20191106_1bvr001613en.html. Accessed 28 August 2023.

[128] Order of 6 November 2019—1 BvR 16/13—Right to be forgotten-I, Headnote 2c, https://www.bundesverfassungsgericht.de/SharedDocs/Entscheidungen/EN/2019/11/rs20191106_1bvr001613en.html.

[129] See also as an overview of the development in the jurisdiction of the FCC: Nettesheim (2011), pp. 17ff.

the ability to cover unforeseen future infringements and can constantly be refined and advanced.

6.1.4.2 Constitutionality of Interference: "Gesetzesvorbehalt"

German constitution, just like many written constitutions of the world, provides for the possibility to impose occasional legitimate restrictions on fundamental rights. This legally admissible restraint of fundamental rights is known as *Gesetzesvorbehalt.* It can be loosely translated as 'legal reservation' of fundamental rights. This principle provides that interferences with the fundamental right are allowed if they are justified under the constitutional law and meet all constitutional requirements.[130] The possibility of interference through limitation of fundamental rights can either be expressly mentioned in the constitution itself, such as authorizing the legislature to restrict the right through legislation, or the constitution can include this possibility in an implied manner. for example, in comprising other equally protected constitutional rights, so that conflicts must be solved through balancing procedures. Many provisions of fundamental rights in the Basic Law contain specific limitation clauses in the form of the possibility of statutory restrictions or enumerating the conditions for the regulation of basic rights. The express limitation in sentence 3 of Article 2 (2) of the Basic law which provides, "[t]hese rights may be interfered with only pursuant to a law", and Article 8 (2) restricting the freedom of assembly are the examples of restraining clauses given in the Basic Law. The provisions whereby no such provisos are attached could be restricted in the event of their conflict with countervailing basic rights.

It is of utmost importance that the law aimed at delimiting fundamental right must be according to substantive and formal constitutional requirements. In other words, the delimiting law has its own limitation too, which is described with the expression of *Schranken-Schranken* or limit on limits.[131] A major *limit on this limitation* is that the restraining law must not negatively affect *the very core of the fundamental right.*[132] The *principle of proportionality* is the most relevant example of limits on limits. It requires that the interference must not only be in the pursuit of a legitimate aim but moreover the use of suitable means to achieve the aim, which are also least possible intrusive as well as proportionate to the legitimate objective of interference.

---

[130] Bumke and Voßkuhle (2019), pp. 52–72.

[131] See more closely for the requirements for such a limiting legislation: Bumke and Voßkuhle (2019), p. 53.

[132] Article 19 (2) of German Basic Law.

6.1.4.3 The Right to Freedom of Expression and of the Media as a Countervailing Right

Article 5 of the German Basic Law protects the freedom of expression, the press and broadcasting, arts and sciences as:

> (1) Every person shall have the right freely to express and disseminate his opinions in speech, writing and pictures, and to inform himself without hindrance from generally accessible sources. Freedom of the press and freedom of reporting by means of broadcasts and films shall be guaranteed. There shall be no censorship.
>
> (2) These rights shall find their limits in the provisions of general laws, in provisions for the protection of young persons, and in the right to personal honor.
>
> (3) Arts and sciences, research and teaching shall be free. The freedom of teaching shall not release any person from allegiance to the constitution.

6.1.4.3.1 The Protected Areas Under Article 5 of the Basic Law

The text of Article 5 Basic Law shows that the German Constitution does not only protect free speech or expression, but goes beyond that and provides many communication-related rights. The expression of opinion and its dissemination extends to almost any form. The right of the people to acquire information from generally accessible sources is included. As the freedom of the press and of broadcasting are expressly mentioned, these are no more secondary values derived from the general freedom of speech or from the right of the people to have access to information in the shape of media broadcast and publication. Article 5 Basic Law also prohibits censorship. Clause 2 provides that these rights shall not be absolute but could be limited by statutory laws which have to comply with the constitutional requirements, in particular serve a legitimate objective, among others, the protection of other persons' rights, e. g. the right to personal honor, that are overweighing in the balancing of interests.

Article 5 (1) 1 Basic Law primarily focuses on the protection of "opinion" in its various facets. In the famous "soldiers are murderers" case,[133] the Federal Constitutional Court precisely mentions the respective interests protected under the right to express and dissemination of opinion:

> In contrast to assertions of fact, opinions are characterised by the subjective attitude of the person expressing himself to the object of the statement [reference omitted]. They contain his judgment about facts, ideas or persons. The protection of the basic right relates to this personal attitude. It therefore exists independently of whether the statement is rational or emotional, well founded or groundless, or regarded by others as useful or harmful, valuable or valueless [references omitted]. The protection does not only relate to the content of the statement, but also to its form. The fact that a statement is formulated in a polemical or hurtful way does not remove it from the area of protection of the basic right [references

[133] BVerfGE 93, 266–312, Translated by: Youngs and Markesinis, available at: https://law.utexas.edu/transnational/foreign-law-translations/german/case.php?id=620. Accessed 28 August 2023.

> omitted]. Further, the choice of the place and time of a statement is protected. The person making the statement does not only have the right in general to make his opinion known. He may also choose for it those circumstances from which he expects the widest dissemination or the strongest effect of making it known.[134]

The focus on opinion in the free speech jurisprudence raises the question of whether and to what extent statements of facts come under the protective shield. The Constitutional Court has differentiated the effects and level of protection of both opinion and fact utterance. In the Holocaust denial case, it explains the relationship between facts and opinions in these words:

> Assertions of fact are on the other hand in the strict sense not statements of opinion. In contrast to such statements, the objective relationship between the statement and reality predominates. In this respect they are also open to an examination of their truth content. But assertions of fact do not, for this reason, automatically fall outside the area of protection of Art 5 (1) sentence 1 GG. Since opinions are, as a rule, based on factual assumptions, or take a position in relation to factual circumstances, they are in any case protected by the basic right insofar as they are the prerequisite for the formation of opinions which Art 5 (1) GG in its totality guarantees [reference omitted].
>
> Consequently, the protection of assertions of fact ends at the point where they cease to contribute anything to the formation of opinion that is presupposed in constitutional law. From this point of view, incorrect information is not an interest worthy of protection. The Federal Constitutional Court has thus consistently held that an assertion of fact known or proved to be untrue is not covered by the protection of freedom of opinion [references omitted]. The requirements for a duty to be truthful may nevertheless not be laid down in such a way as to harm the functioning of freedom of opinion so that even permissible statements are not made because of the fear of sanctions [references omitted].[135]

This differentiated approach to the scope of protection of Article 5 (1) Basic Law highlights the relevance of the question whether a contribution provides something to the more general dimension of free individual and public opinion forming process that can be classified, as we have already seen in the overview of illustrative cases,[136] as an underlying principle of the entire article. Article 5 (1) covers the expression of personal opinion as protected speech even if it is exaggerated, wrong or far from the actual reality. For an opinion, it is not required to be truthful or reasonable. The scope of protection is extended to the statements of facts because they provide a foundation over which opinions are being built and thus are an element of the free individual and public opinion forming process. It is, however, outside of the boundary of constitutional protection when knowingly false statements of fact, in other words, conscious lies are supplied because they could not be said to contribute positively to the public discourse. As a result, the general law can easily restrict such false statements and may also impose requirements, such as an obligation to verify the accuracy of factual statements before making them, to the extent possible.

---

[134] BVerfGE 93, 266–312.

[135] BVerfGE 90, 241–255 (Auschwitz lie), Translated by: Youngs, available at: https://law.utexas.edu/transnational/foreign-law-translations/german/case.php?id=621. Accessed 28 August 2023.

[136] See Sect. 6.1.1.

Whether something is a statement of fact or opinion must be determined by carefully interpreting the expression in context. Beyond that, it is not merely the utterance, which is protected, as separating utterance from the effects it exerts on the minds of the audience would be nonsensical.[137]

In the CSU-NPD-case taken as an example, the Constitutional Court applied these principles and held that the statement, "The CSU is the NPD of Europe" is a sweeping expression of opinion in the background of a heated election campaign. The FCC rejected the lower court's ruling, which had taken this statement as "an incorrect statement of fact".[138] The Court also considered the respective public standings of the parties as of "vital importance", and viewed that while balancing, the private or public life of the parties would also have an impact on the conclusions. "A person who voluntarily exposes himself or herself to public criticism forgoes part of his or her protected private sphere", the Court held.[139] For political parties, the test is more stringent and they must accept even caustic remarks.

Article 5 (1) 2 of the Basic Law guarantees the freedom of the press and freedom of reporting by means of broadcasts and films. The press includes all printed products suitable and intended for distribution to the general public. It also covers, to an extent that is disputed in detail, content available on the Internet. All activities related to press work are protected, from the acquisition of information to the dissemination of news and opinions.[140] Protected are, for example, the access to the press profession, the media-specific information gathering, the secrecy of the information sources, the editorial work, as well as time, place and modalities of the distribution of the press product or the decision of media outlets to make past press articles permanently available to the public in archives.[141] However, the content of a press report—statements of facts or expressions of opinions—is not covered by the freedom of the press, but by the freedom of expression.[142] The protection of broadcasting also extends to communications on the Internet. The central function of broadcasting is the dissemination of freely accessible, diverse and comprehensive programs that are independent from the state, the market and individual societal groups, and this is seen as a prerequisite for the free individual and public opinion forming process protected by Article 5 Basic Law. The State must secure by

[137] More closely to the interpretation of Article 5 Basic Law Grimm (1995), pp. 1697 ff.

[138] 61 BVerfGE 1 (CSU-NPD Case 1982) as translated in: Kommers and Miller (2012), p. 464.

[139] 61 BVerfGE 1 (CSU-NPD Case 1982) as translated in: Kommers and Miller (2012), p. 464.

[140] BVerfGE 103, 44 (59)—Courtroom television case (2001).

[141] See Order of the FCC of 6 November 2019—1 BvR 16/13, https://www.bundesverfassungsgericht.de/SharedDocs/Entscheidungen/EN/2019/11/rs20191106_1bvr001613en.html, Right to be forgotten I, Rn. 94.

[142] Cf. Order of the FCC of 6 November 2019—1 BvR 16/13, https://www.bundesverfassungsgericht.de/SharedDocs/Entscheidungen/EN/2019/11/rs20191106_1bvr001613en.html, Right to be forgotten I, Rn. 94.

regulatory measures that this function can be fulfilled appropriately.[143] Once again, the content as such, i. e. statements of facts or expressions of opinions—is not covered by the freedom of broadcasting or the media, but by the freedom of expression.

Article 5 (3) of the Basic Law protects arts and science, which includes the making and publishing of caricatures. The Constitutional Court extends the constitutional protection to every kind of arts and restrains judiciary to go into the determination of good or bad arts.[144] However, there must be some criteria, in the Court's opinion, to separate art from non-art. The caricatures under scrutiny were also acknowledged as work of arts, which needed creativity. However, anybody making a work of art must consider the right to dignity of another person and his personality rights. Therefore, the Court upheld a Regional Court's judgment in which portraying a politician, Franz-Josef Strauss, in a caricature in an undignified way—pig involved in sexual activity—was termed as violation of personality right. The Court held in the "Political Satire case",

> [t]he fact that Strauss is a public figure who is in the midst of public fight of opinions does not deprive him of his human dignity and does not justify defamatory statements injurious to the personality right, not even in the name of artistic freedom.[145]

6.1.4.4 Reconciling Free Speech with Privacy Right in German Case Law: The Legal Framework for Balancing

Freedom of opinion and of the media are, just like personality rights, not absolute rights. Article 5 (2) of the Basic Law includes a 'legal reservation' (*Gesetzesvorbehalt*)[146] and enumerates limits as containing in general laws and in the laws providing protection to personal honor or to young persons. If rights are qualified by provisos attached to them, the legislator can restrict or regulate them; however, the scope and limits of the laws and administrative action also need to be checked for extra-constitutionality due to the "limits on limits" the Basic Law provides for. Although freedom of arts and sciences does not contain any constitutional limitation, they are not absolutely guaranteed; they can be limited with a view to other equally protected constitutional rights.[147] Any restricting or regulating law must be according to substantive and formal constitutional requirements, especially to the principle of proportionality.

---

[143] See Order of the FCC of 20 July 2021—1 BvR 2756/20 et al., https://www.bundesverfassungsgericht.de/SharedDocs/Entscheidungen/EN/2021/07/rs20210720_1bvr275620en.html. Accessed 28 August 2023.

[144] BVerfGE 75, 369 (Political Satire Case 1987) as translated in: Kommers and Miller (2012), pp. 465–467.

[145] BVerfGE 75, 369 (Political Satire Case 1987) as translated in: Kommers and Miller (2012), p. 468.

[146] See Sect. 6.1.4.2.

[147] See Sect. 6.1.4.2; cf. also: Jouanjan (2009), p. 874.

Balancing the competing rights and values having constitutional protection or public interests, as well as the determination of any *proportionate* interference of legislative instruments in the exercise of a fundamental right are special features of German constitutional jurisprudence. Kommers considers balancing as the optimization of various competing constitutional values.[148] The concept of objective value of rights is active in the background here which demands the proper enforcement of rights rather than tangling into the confusion of conflicting interest that cancel each other's values.

The proportionality test involves three steps to judge any act of parliament purportedly impinging on a fundamental right. These steps can be explained in terms of three questions: Firstly, whether the legal means used are appropriate to achieve a legitimate aim (*Eignung*); secondly, whether the means used have, in comparison to equally suitable means, the least invasive character for the concerned fundamental right (*Erforderlichkeit*); and thirdly, whether these means prove to be proportionate in the process of balancing the negative consequences for the data subject and his or her right against the positive consequences for the intended objective (*Angemessenheit*).[149]

The German approach regarding the application of proportionality principle during the judicial review and balancing of various fundamental rights or public interests is in place since the 1950s and perhaps singular worldwide. It is meanwhile followed by many European and non-European countries having a judicial review system. Similarly, it is also used by international judicial forums, in particular the ECtHR and ECJ.[150] This legal framework is regarded as "one of the most sophisticated and rational systems that has ever been devised" for the balancing of conflicting constitutional values of human rights.[151]

Whenever the expression of opinion encroaches upon the right of other private persons, it cannot straightaway trump other private rights. Instead, a conflicting situation arises which must be resolved through the exercise of balancing.[152] The result of such a balancing exercise depends on the circumstances of each case and no value is given an inherent superiority over the other values(s). For instance, the Constitutional Court decided in the Lüth case in favor of upholding free speech right after it was established that the call for boycott was not due to any personal grudge or for personal economic benefit. It held,

> The protection of speech is entitled to less protection when exercised to defend a private interest - particularly when the individual pursues a selfish goal within the economic sector - than speech that contributes to the intellectual struggle of opinions...[153]

[148] Kommers and Miller (2012), p. 66.

[149] Cf. already Sect. 6.1.4.2.

[150] Grimm (2007), p. 384.

[151] Markesinis (1999), p. 47.

[152] BVerfGE 7, 198 (Lüth Case 1958) as translated in: Kommers and Miller (2012), p. 446.

[153] BVerfGE 7, 198 (Lüth Case 1958) as translated in: Kommers and Miller (2012), p. 447.

The Constitutional Court also considers the potential impact of the speech and its content in the balancing exercise. In the same judgment, it held "Where the formation of public opinion on a matter important to the common good is concerned, private and especially individual economic interests must, in principle, recede."[154]

The Constitutional Court often highlights that it is not inclined to give preference to any of the values of freedom of speech, press and broadcasting against personality right because both constitutional rights are "essential aspects of the free democratic order of the Basic Law"; and the courts shall try its best to reconcile both values.[155] Only insofar as such a reconciliation is not possible, then the court would decide in favor of one or the other right on the basis of the situation in the given case scenario. In the Lebach case, the Constitutional Court held,

> In so doing, the court must consider both constitutional values in their relation to human dignity as the nucleus of the constitutional value system. Accordingly, the freedom to broadcast may have the effect of restricting claims based on the right to personality; however, any damage to "personality" resulting from a public broadcast may not be disproportionate to the significance of the publication to free communication.[156]

The Constitutional Court has provided some principles for the balancing exercise in the Lebach case. Firstly, the right to personality or to honor always trumps a knowingly false utterance. Secondly, in the case of true statements that are related to the innermost intimate sphere, the right to privacy trumps the right to free speech. Thirdly, in every case of a serious affront to dignity, the court gives preference to dignity due to its absolutely inviolable status in the Basic Law. If the damage is not closely connected to human dignity, the exercise of balancing will take place.[157] In the following, we take a look at the series of Caroline von Monaco-cases to show how sophisticated the balancing exercise can become.

The facts related to Caroline von Monaco (later on von Hannover) series of cases have already been discussed in Chap. 5. These cases show a long series of her legal battle against different newspapers and magazines. The publishing companies were accused of the violation of her personality rights protected by the German Civil Code or the Copyright Act regarding Works of Art and Photographs,[158] due to their publication of articles and photos which were bringing her private life into public focus. One of such cases ended in a landmark judgment of the Federal Constitutional Court of Germany, where the Court laid down principles of privacy protection and its balancing with the right to free speech in a lucid manner.[159] On invoking the

---

[154] BVerfGE 7, 198 (Lüth Case 1958) as translated in: Kommers and Miller (2012), p. 448.

[155] BVerfGE 35, 202 (Lebach Case 1973), as translated in: Kommers and Miller (2012), pp. 479–483.

[156] BVerfGE 35, 202 (Lebach Case 1973), as translated in: Kommers and Miller (2012), p. 481.

[157] BVerfGE 35, 202 (Lebach Case 1973), as translated in Kommers and Miller (2012), p. 485.

[158] Cf. Sect. 6.1.3.1.

[159] BVerfGE 101, 361. English Translation is available online at the website of Federal Constitutional Court: https://www.bundesverfassungsgericht.de/SharedDocs/Entscheidungen/EN/1999/12/rs19991215_1bvr065396en.html. Accessed 28 August 2023.

jurisdiction of ECtHR in a successful attempt to reverse the judgment, the Court further refined this controversial area, ruling that the right to privacy protected under the general personality right provided by Article 2 (1) in conjunction with Article 1 (1) of the Basic Law is not strictly restricted to domestic sphere. As a result, it is possible for an individual to exercise the right to privacy even outside home, depending on typical circumstances of each case. The protection of privacy becomes secondary when a person consensually makes available his private matters to the public for commercial reasons. Article 5.1 (2) of the Basic Law covers images and texts which may be related to private context or public life. However, a person cannot impose her wish on others such as to be portrayed according to her desires.

The right to privacy stringently protects typical intimate matters, such as protecting the content of one's diaries from disclosure, confidential communication between husband and wife, the intimate sphere of sexuality, social deviancy and diseases.[160] After intimate sphere there comes private sphere, where the provision of some physical space for relaxation is necessary in order to develop one's personality; otherwise, the development will be "seriously impaired". Public figures are entitled to have the existence of this sphere. Private sphere is not restricted to domestic sphere as "the area of withdrawal [. . .] do not end at the walls of one's house or at the boundaries of one's property"[161] However, where there comes wellbeing of the children, the Court gives special attention to their privacy.[162]

Regarding balancing of conflicting issues related to fundamental rights, "the civil courts must observe the meaning and the scope of the fundamental rights that are affected by their decisions to assure that their normative content be preserved at the level of judicial application of the law as well."[163]

In the case of publication of photo of a "person from contemporary history", no permission as a principle required as per section 23 of KUG. However, there is difference between the status of "absolute person of contemporary history" and "relative person of contemporary history". Absolute person of contemporary history has been defined as, "who have not attracted public attention at a certain point through their involvement with a specific event of contemporary history but instead encounter general public attention, independently of single events, on account of their status and their importance."[164] While, a person who does not fulfill this requirement, and comes to public light with reference to some event would become automatically a relative person of contemporary history. The public has a legitimate interest in knowing about persons of contemporary history due to their role model

---

[160] BVerfGE 101, 361. References omitted.

[161] Compare this to the liberal interpretation of Article 9 right to life by the Supreme Court of Pakistan discussed in Sect. 4.2.2.1 of this book.

[162] BVerfGE 101, 361, para 83: "The sphere in which children can feel free from observation by the public and develop free from such observation must therefore be protected in a more comprehensive way than in the case of adults."

[163] BVerfGE 101, 361, para 93.

[164] BVerfGE 101, 361, para 106.

character in order to ascertain that whether or not their actual behavior is in consonance with their public portrayal.[165]

Applying the above principles, the Constitutional Court endorsed most of the principles and standards developed by the Federal Court of Justice, particularly with reference to section 23 of KUG, under which it had interpreted the term "legitimate public interest". The only constitutional requirement under Article 6, where the protection of parents personality gets an enhanced position with reference to taking care of their children, was upheld by the Court.

Regarding other parts of the complaint, the Court held that the publication of photos of the appellant was constitutionally permissible due to interest of the general public in being informed. However, the public cannot be given unlimited access to every photo in which they are interested in. The Court held that the facts regarding the use of method to take the photos and that whether or not the taking of the pictures resulted into a gross intrusion of the appellant's privacy remained in doubt and thus do not affect the result of the judgment.

6.1.5 German Privacy Protection Under the Influence of the ECHR and the ECtHR

The German courts got an opportunity to re-evaluate balancing results and to refine their balancing approaches under the guidance of the Von Hannover I judgment of the ECtHR. It is pertinent to mention that Constitutional Court had announced the Görgülü judgment after just 4 months of the Von Hannover I judgment.[166] The decision the Federal Court of Justice (BGH) arrived at on 06.03.2007 already benefited from the fact that the Görgülü judgment imposed a duty on the jurisdiction "to take into account the guarantees of the Convention and the decisions of the ECtHR as part of a methodologically justifiable interpretation of the law".[167] The Court referred in its decision to the jurisprudential principles of the ECtHR in a favorable manner.[168] Furthermore, the Federal Constitutional Court's also approved the constitutionality of the BGH's approach after it decided on constitutional petitions against that judgment.[169]

---

[165] BVerfGE 101, 361, para 110: "[T]he privacy that is worthy of protection, to which the so-called absolute persons of contemporary history are also entitled, requires (1) a local seclusion to which someone has withdrawn to be alone; (2) that this wish to be alone is recognisable by an objective person; and (3) that the person, confiding in the seclusion, behaves in a manner in which he or she would not behave in the broad public."

[166] Cf. Sect. 6.1.5.

[167] BVerfGE 111, 307, para 47.

[168] BGH, Urteil vom 06.03.2007—VI ZR 51/06. https://openjur.de/u/79043.html. Accessed 28 August 2023.

[169] BVerfGE 120, 180.

In the new series of cases, Princess Caroline successfully obtained injunctions from a district court, which restrained the publisher of the magazine "*Frau im Spiegel*" from a republication of pictures showing her with her husband on skiing vacation in St. Moritz. These pictures were published as pictorial illustrations to three articles, one about the skiing vacation itself, another one about the upcoming "Rosenball" in Monaco and the last one about Prince Reiner's deteriorating health conditions. On the appeal of the publisher, Hamburg Regional Court overturned the restraining order. Princess Caroline challenged this decision in the Federal Court of Justice, appealing to restore the injunctions of the district court. After the balancing exercise of weighing the fundamental rights of both the parties which are protected by Article 2 (1) in conjunction with Article 1(1) of the Basic Law on the one hand and Article 5 (1) of the Basic Law on the other, the BGH arrived at the result that the publication of the pictures was not justified in the first two cases and only lawful in the last one.

What is novel about the BGH's decision is the explicit reference to the ECHR and the jurisprudence of the ECtHR: The BGH emphasized that Article 8 (1) of ECHR must also be taken into account when considering the limits of general right to personality. Relying on the case law of the ECtHR as well as German higher courts, it modified the test of absolute/relative person of contemporary history, and rather resorted to a new mechanism of "variable protection". That means that the Court gives importance to a variety of factors rather than to follow the narrow view of the status of the person in society (absolute or relative person of contemporary history). All the possibly associated rights and interests of privacy and freedom of the speech or the press and people's right to have access to information must be considered. The Court confirmed that during balancing process, entertainment is to be considered as a protected area. However, in line with the ECtHR jurisprudence, entertainment would have less value vis-à-vis personality rights of media subjects. Public interest in the publication of pictures is an important element but the right of being informed is not unlimited. Rather the principle of proportionality should determine the tilt of balance to one or the other right in a particular situation. The fact that a person belongs to contemporary society par excellence is not an absolute license to take their picture everywhere.

Applying the principles on the impugned publication of pictures, the BGH prohibited the republication of the pictures accompanying the article in the magazine "*Frau im Spiegel*" about the skiing vacation of von Hannover and her husband because the article itself and the accompanying pictures lacked the required newsworthiness. They provided no information about a historical event and were no contribution to a debate of general interest, while on the other hand, the couple was on vacation, which belongs to the core area of privacy protectable even for celebrities. The Court explained:

> When making the necessary balance between the freedom of the press and the applicant's general right to personality, it must be borne in mind, in accordance with the principles of case law set out above, that it plays a decisive role whether the press releases new and true information of general interest for public opinion formation or whether the Informational value for the public - as here - essentially consists of entertainment without social relevance.

> [. . . .] In the latter case, there is no public interest in information that should be taken into account that would allow an image to be published against the will of the person depicted (Section 23 Paragraph 1 No. 1 KUG); the person depicted does not have to accept the impairment of their privacy and thus their general right of personality, which is regularly included in the image publication, without consent (§ 22 KUG). In this respect, the defendant's appeal against the ruling of the first instance must therefore be rejected without the violation of a legitimate interest of the person depicted (section 23 (2) KUG) being important.[170]

Regarding the picture in the context of the Rosenball-event, the Court stated that although the Rosenball is an event of public interest having social relevance, the picture of skiing of the couple had no information value which could add anything to the information, which is related to mere entertainment, and so of a low value vis-à-vis the applicant's right to privacy and general personality rights. Thus the later rights outweigh the public interest in disseminating the picture, and further publication was announced as prohibited. However, regarding the republication of the picture in the context of the article reporting about Prince Reiner's illness, the Court found that the illness of the potential ruler and the behavior of his family members during that period was an issue of contemporary history. The article dealt with the behavior of family members during the prince's illness—being on vacation in St. Moritz—and to substantiate and illustrate this reporting by the publication of the picture was justified. Its publication was regarded as no violation of the privacy or the general personality rights of Von Hannover.

The novel approach of the BGH thus incorporated most of the principles of the ECtHR's decision Von Hannover v Germany I as we have already elaborated in Chap. 5. According to Hans-Joachim Cremer, "the court meant to emphasize the new *abgestuftes Schutzkonzept*, the new scheme of variable protection, and to send a signal to Strasbourg that it had definitely adjusted its interpretation of sec. 23(1) KUG to the Convention requirements."[171]

After the decision of the BGH, both the publisher and Princess Caroline von Hannover filed constitutional petitions in the Federal Constitutional Court, challenging the respective parts of the judgment where they did not find a relief. The Court rejected all appeals and approved the new scheme of variable protection developed by the BGH.[172] It held that this novel approach to be in accordance with the relevant provisions of the Basic law for personality rights protection and freedom of the press.

In its judgment, the Court frequently referred not only to its own case law but also attempted to relate its own jurisprudence with the jurisprudence of ECtHR. It emphasized that the interpretation of German constitutional jurisprudence needs to be responsive of Convention's demands as the rights guaranteed under the

[170] BGH, Urteil vom 06.03.2007—VI ZR 51/06, para 34. https://openjur.de/u/79043.html. Accessed 28 August 2023.

[171] Cremer (2010), p. 87.

[172] BVerfGE 120, 180.

Convention should work as interpretative tools in order to determine the scope of protection of fundamental rights of the German Basic Law.

> The guarantees of the Convention and the case-law of the European Court of Human Rights further serve as aids in interpreting the content and scope of fundamental rights at the level of constitutional law, insofar as this does not result in a limitation of or derogation from the protection offered by any human rights or fundamental freedoms under the Basic Law – which is not desired by the Convention itself.[173]

Unfolding the scope of protection of the right to personality, the Court held that the protection granted by the right to respect of the private life in Article 8 ECHR covers, in conformity with the constitutionally guaranteed protection of personality rights, the sum of all personal, social and financial relationships which make up the private life of each individual. The extent to which, in the given situation, the individual's expectations of privacy are justified, must be considered Article 8 ECHR can also include a right to be protected against the publication of pictures by the media. Regarding Article 2 in conjunction with Article 1 of the German Basic Law, the Court pointed to both the right to one's own image and the guarantee of privacy.[174] It further explained their scope of protection:

> The right to one's own image does [...] grant the individual a means of exerting influence and taking decisions as far as the creation and use of pictorial recordings of his person by others is concerned. The need for protection arises above all as a result of the possibility that the image of a person in a particular context may be removed from that context and reproduced by third parties at any time under circumstances which the person concerned cannot control. [...] In addition to the right to one's image, the fundamental right to protection of personality rights also comprises protection of private life. There are several aspects to this protection. Thematically it affects in particular those matters, which the holder of the fundamental right would tend to withhold from public mention or display. Spatially, private life includes an individual's area of retreat, which ensures that he may centre himself and relax, in particular in the domestic sphere but also outside the home and which helps to realise the need "to be left alone" The boundaries of the protected private sphere cannot be generally or abstractly determined.[175]

Regarding the guarantee of freedom of the press, this guarantee includes the right to freely determine the manner and focus as well as the contents of the publication and also the decision as to whether and how a media product is to be illustrated. Thereby, the protection of freedom of the press covers the publication of pictures of persons with the report they are to illustrate. Even entertaining contributions concerning prominent persons, for instance, are covered by the protection of freedom of the press. Entertaining reports about celebrities are also protected by freedom of the press as they also can contribute to the opinion-forming.[176] The Constitutional Court highlights that the activity of the press also falls within the freedom of expression and the freedom of transmission and receipt of information and opinions guaranteed

---

[173] BVerfGE 120, 180, para 52. References omitted.

[174] For these facets see Sects. 6.1.4.1.1 and 6.1.4.1.2.

[175] BVerfGE 120, 180, paras 46 and 47.

[176] BVerfGE 120, 180, para 42. References omitted.

by Article 10 ECHR. These freedoms cover, in principle, the publication of photographs to illustrate a media report and have particular importance in cases of a contribution to matters of public interest.[177]

Both the right to personality and the freedom of the press are under legal reservation and regulated by statutory laws. Within their framework, civil courts have to carry out the balancing exercise by considering all relevant factors and weighing the conflicting interests such as the situation in which the person concerned is photographed or the circumstances under which the photograph was taken on the one hand and the freedom of the press to decide about the nature and style of its own content or its aim to create public interest in a particular story on the other hand. The Court stated:

> It is primarily the task of the civil courts to have regard to the fundamental provisions of the Basic Law taking into account the prescriptions of the European Convention on Human Rights in interpreting and applying the civil-law provisions on the weighing of different interests that are protected by law. In order to do so, the courts shall ascertain the diverging interests concerned and the extent to which they have suffered detriment. The opposing positions are to be placed in relation to one another in view of the concrete circumstances of the individual event, so that they are each duly taken into account.[178]

The Constitutional Court found a way to justify its rejection of both appeals. According to Cremer, "[a]ll of this proves the *Bundesverfassungsgericht*'s efforts to harmonise the standards of the constitution and the Convention. The *Bundesverfassungsgericht* is taking the ECHR's and ECtHR's influence on German constitutional law seriously and trying to reconcile its case law with that of the Strasbourg Court. The *Grundgesetz* is flexible enough to allow such an adaptation."[179]

The new approach of German courts towards the enhanced protection of personality rights due to incorporating the balancing principles of Von Hannover v Germany I was acknowledged by the ECtHR in the subsequent case of Von Hannover v Germany II. The ECtHR held, that "the new case-law of the Federal Court of Justice, endorsed by the Federal Constitutional Court, afforded greater weight to the protection of personality rights, as evidenced by the fact that an injunction was imposed on publication of two of the initial three photos."[180] It approved the application of the new approach by the Federal Court of Justice (BGH) and found that various photos of the applicants neither contained information related to an event of contemporary society nor there used to be any contribution of these photos in the debate of general interest. On the other hand, it also endorsed the opposite outcome of the application of the same criteria, which qualified the article in relation to the illness of Prince Reiner as an event of contemporary history. Thus the

---

[177] BVerfGE 120, 180, paras 57 and 58.

[178] BVerfGE 120, 180, para 74. References omitted.

[179] Cremer (2010), p. 92.

[180] ECHR, *Von Hannover v Germany (No. 2)*, judgment of 07 February 2012. Application No. 40660/08, para 78.

publication was ordered to be justified along with the illustrative picture of his children during holidays. The ECtHR accepted the reasons of the German courts stating,

> the photos in question, considered in the light of the accompanying articles, did contribute, at least to some degree, to a debate of general interest. It would reiterate, on this point, that not only does the press have the task of imparting information and ideas on all matters of public interest, the public also has a right to receive them.[181]

The ECtHR then summarized:

> The Court observes that, in accordance with their case-law, the national courts carefully balanced the right of the publishing companies to freedom of expression against the right of the applicants to respect for their private life. In doing so, they attached fundamental importance to the question whether the photos, considered in the light of the accompanying articles, had contributed to a debate of general interest. They also examined the circumstances in which the photos had been taken. The Court also observes that the national courts explicitly took account of the Court's relevant case-law. Whilst the Federal Court of Justice had changed its approach following the Von Hannover judgment, the Federal Constitutional Court, for its part, had not only confirmed that approach, but also undertaken a detailed analysis of the Court's case-law in response to the applicants' complaints that the Federal Court of Justice had disregarded the Convention and the Court's case-law.[182]

All in all, we can conclude that the judgments of the ECtHR not only contribute to the theoretical underpinnings of privacy law, but also impact the member states approaches to privacy protection in the subsequent cases. Personality rights on the one hand and the freedom of expression and of the media on the other hand are balanced with each other in sophisticated balancing processes.

6.2 Protection of Privacy in the United Kingdom

6.2.1 The Nature of British Tabloid Press

The powerful British tabloid media, well known internationally for its sensationalistic and salacious coverage of the politicians, royals, and media and sports celebrities results in ethical controversies on daily basis.[183] The recent coverage of the former Duke and Duchess of Sussex (Prince Harry and his wife Megan Markle) is one of such examples of the obsession of British tabloid media with public figures, which apparently resulted into the eschewing of the Royal position by the couple and they decided to leave Britain. The non-native origin of the Duchess is generally

[181] ECHR, *Von Hannover v Germany (No. 2)*, judgment of 07 February 2012. Application No. 40660/08. para 118.

[182] ECHR, *Von Hannover v Germany (No. 2)*, judgment of 07 February 2012. Application No. 40660/08, paras 124 and 125.

[183] See for example: Deacon (2004), p. 09.

considered as a catalyst of the celeb-news hunger of the British media, the pungency of which proved to be unbearable for them and, therefore, they moved to Canada.[184]

The intrusive British media practices do not only result into a casual heart burn to the person who values media ethics, but many a times, these end in serious breaches of fundamental rights. A recent example would be the publication of an extensive extract of a leaked private letter of Meghan Markle to her father. She has started and won a legal battle on the basis of misuse of private information, data protection and copy rights violations against the popular tabloid *Mail on Sunday*.[185] This is not a singular example of transgression. In the past, British media have caused a much greater furor. The popular "phone-hacking scandal" associated with the 158-year old tabloid, *News of the World*, caused its closure in 2011. The controversy hatched when British investigators found that in the years 2005–2007, *News of the world*, owned by American media tycoon Rupert Murdoch, along with a number of other British newspapers were involved in phone hacking of politicians, members of Royal families and a number of other public figures. In 2011, the *News of the World* outraged all and sundry when *The Guardian* revealed that the phone of a missing teenage girl, who was later on confirmed by Surrey police to be murdered, was also hacked by *News of the World*. This tabloid had not only listened to voicemails but also deleted some of the voice messages in order to make space for the new messages.[186] The deletion of the messages misguided the investigators and gave a false hope to her family who thought that she was alive and she deleted the messages herself. This media-related scandal has been in the global headlines and it drew far and wide effects in almost all media-related sectors of political, financial, legal, regulatory, as well as academic sectors.[187]

6.2.2 Overview of Illustrative Privacy Cases

In such an intrusive media environment, the case law related to privacy claims provide valuable illustrations for learning lessons through a comparative analysis. These court cases show a gradual development from a complete denial of the right to

[184] See: Hirsh (2020).

[185] BBC report: Meghan sues Mail on Sunday over private letter. https://www.bbc.com/news/uk-49901047. See also news report regarding decisions of the court: https://www.theguardian.com/uk-news/2022/jan/05/meghan-one-pound-mail-on-sunday-privacy-invasion. Accessed 28 August 2023.

[186] See: Nick Davies and Amelia Hill: Missing Milly Dowler's voicemail was hacked by News of the World. *The Guardian* (online 4 July 2011), https://www.theguardian.com/uk/2011/jul/04/milly-dowler-voicemail-hacked-news-of-world. Accessed 28 August 2023.

[187] See for instance Jane Martinson's analysis: "The phone-hacking scandal is over. So what's changed?", The Guardian 11 December 2015, available at: https://www.theguardian.com/media/2015/dec/11/the-phone-hacking-scandal-is-over-so-whats-changed. Accessed 28 August 2023.

privacy to the modification of existing tort law norms in the United Kingdom in order to fulfill its international law obligation under the ECHR.

In a 1991 case,[188] the Lord Justices had highlighted that there was no right to privacy in English law. This case was related to a very grave violation of the right to privacy of a television celebrity: A reporter of *The Sunday Sport* intruded into his hospital room at a time when he was undergoing treatment for his severe injuries sustained as a result of a road accident. Lord Justices Glidewell, Bingham and Leggatt were in agreement to acknowledge that the fact of the case in hand was *a graphic illustration* for the parliamentary consideration of statutory protection of privacy, because both common law and statute lacked an effective protection for such a long time that it needed to be expressly recognized by the parliament.

The judgment of the House of Lords in the case of Wainwright v Home office is an illustration of a non-media case. A public authority—home office—unlawfully strip-searched the claimants, a mother and her mentally impaired child, on their visit to prison. The proceedings arrived at the House of Lords and it had to decide whether a cause for invasion of privacy was recognized by English common law or not. The House of Lords refused to recognize the tort of invasion of privacy through judicial way. It held that Article 8 of ECHR did not oblige them to recognize the right to privacy as a principle of law *per se*, and therefore, only the legislature could create such a right. Thus, the judges categorically refused to go ahead with the development of a right to privacy through the common law.

It was only in the landmark cases of Campbell v Mirror Group Newspapers Ltd. (2004)[189] and Mosley v News Group Newspapers Ltd. (2008),[190] that the English judiciary started using the traditional breach of confidence tort to provide relief to privacy infringements as a result of misuse or disclosure of private information. In the Campbell case, Naomi Campbell, who had earlier publicly stated that she did not take drugs, sought damages for breach of confidentiality against the Mirror Group Newspapers Ltd. for publishing articles about her drug addiction and photographs as she was leaving a Narcotics Anonymous meeting. The House of Lords stroke a detailed balancing exercise between the plaintiff's right to respect for her medical treatment information under Article 8 of ECHR against the newspaper's freedom of speech under Article 10 of ECHR and its associated right to publish photos of a celebrity. It held that the plaintiff right under Article 8 outweighed the newspaper company's right to publish the details of her treatment (i.e. name and pictures of the clinic Narcotics Anonymous), and so the defendant was held liable for damages. Similarly, in the Max Mosley case, the News Group Newspapers Ltd. was held liable by the Queen's Bench for the publication of an article about the claimant, titled "F1 boss has sick Nazi orgy with 5 hookers", in *News of the World* as well as an edited

[188] Kaye v Robertson [1991] FSR 62.

[189] Campbell v Mirror Group Newspapers Ltd [2004] UKHL 22.

[190] Mosley v News Group Newspapers [2008] EWHC 1777 (QB).

video footage secretly filmed by one of the ladies on its website.[191] The Court imposed huge damages of £60,000 on the company.[192]

The legal system of the United Kingdom and illustrative cases such as these as well as the UK's influential press and media industry offer an interesting comparative model to explore how the conflicting interests are being reconciled. The following sections shall also analyze the extent to which UK courts have been successful in their compliance to the standards of ECHR, in particular Article 8 and 10 ECHR, and where the loopholes in their approach are that make the effective protection of privacy problematic for this jurisdiction.

Before going into the details, it is important to provide a brief introduction to the British legal system, its judiciary and important legal norms.

6.2.3 Background: The Legal System of the United Kingdom

A unique feature of the British legal system is the absence of a written constitution or a codified single document having the force of a *Grundnorm*. Nevertheless, there are some historical documents which worked as seed for modern constitutional conventions, but today they are relevant for historical references only. Historically, the British legal system has its root in the *Magna Carta* of 1215, a monarchic decree under the seal of King John, which diminished absolute kingship by subjecting orders of the king to the approval of the Council of Barons and due process of law beneath the kingship. The Bill of Rights of 1689 is another significant document which laid the foundation of English parliamentary sovereignty. Article 9 of the Bill of Rights conferred certain privileges to parliament such as free election of its members and the protection of free speech inside the parliament and the exemption from arrest was granted to Member of Parliament. In 1911 and 1949 further restrictions were imposed on the House of Lords which practically made the House of Commons as the sovereign body. In 1928, every adult man and woman was finally entitled to vote to elect members of parliament under the Representation of the People (Equal Franchise) Act.

Generally, there is no hierarchy between various acts passed by the parliament. However, very few legal instruments have been expressly recognized as having constitutional status. Among them are the Human Rights Act of 1998 and the Constitutional Reform Act of 2005.[193] The Human Rights Act incorporated the

[191] Mosley v News Group Newspapers [2008] EWHC 1777 (QB), para 01.

[192] Both cases are presented more closely in Sect. 6.2.5.2.

[193] R (HS2 Action Alliance Ltd) v Secretary of State for Transport [2014] UKSC 3, para 207: "The United Kingdom has no written constitution, but we have a number of constitutional instruments. They include Magna Carta, the Petition of Right 1628, the Bill of Rights and (in Scotland) the Claim of Rights Act 1689, the Act of Settlement 1701 and the Act of Union 1707. The European Communities Act 1972, the Human Rights Act 1998 and the Constitutional Reform Act 2005 may now be added to this list. The common law itself also recognises certain principles as

ECHR into the English legal system and the Constitutional Reform Act established the UK Supreme Court, which started its functions on 1st October 2009. Prior to these reforms, the upper chamber of the UK Parliament (House of Lords) was performing judicial functions for more than two centuries. It used to be the court of initial trials for Lords (known as peers) and for certain impeachments, while it remained a final court of appeal in the UK functioning under the Appellate Jurisdiction Act 1876 which composed an Appellate Committee of the so-called Law Lords. Gradually, either different Acts of Parliament formally resulted in the destitution of its powers or in *de facto* manner, its functionality faded away unless it ceased to exist in October 2009.

Replacing the judicial function of the House of Lords, the Supreme Court is now the highest court of appeal in all civil and criminal matters. However, due to the doctrine of parliamentary sovereignty, it has no power of judicial review of the legislative instruments and it cannot challenge an Act of Parliament on the basis of its *ultra vires* to the constitution or any of the fundamental rights. Though, the Supreme Court can review executive action under delegated legislation to ensure the legality of their discretion and compatibility of a subordinate bye-law to the parent statute. On the judicial front, the UK Supreme Court heads the hierarchy of a variety of judicial bodies, starting from magistrate courts for criminal cases and county courts for civil litigation to different benches and divisions of the High Court (e.g. Queen's Bench, Chancery Division) and then the Court of Appeal which is comprised of two divisions (Criminal Division and Civil Davion).

The legal system of the United Kingdom is based on parliamentary sovereignty rather than on the principle of separation of power or constitutionalism. According to the well-known constitutional theorist, Dicey

> The principle of Parliamentary sovereignty means neither more nor less than this, namely, that Parliament thus defined has, under the English constitution, the right to make or unmake any law whatever; and, further, that no person or body is recognised by the law of England as having a right to override or set aside the legislation of Parliament.[194]

There is no special mechanism to formulate constitutional principles and no statute can be challenged in any court of law. The supreme legislative authority British parliament is proverbially expressed, "Parliament can do everything but make a woman a man, and a man a woman."[195]

There are two main primary sources of legal norms in the legal system of the United Kingdom. Firstly, Acts of parliament as legislations passed by the British Parliament are important.[196] Secondly, common law is another primary source of

---

fundamental to the rule of law.[. . . .T]here may be fundamental principles, whether contained in other constitutional instruments or recognised at common law, of which Parliament when it enacted the European Communities Act 1972 did not either contemplate or authorise the abrogation."

[194] Dicey (1982), pp. 3–4.

[195] Dicey (1982), p. 5.

[196] For instance Police and Criminal Evidence Act 1984, Public Order Act 1986, Human Rights Act 1998, Constitutional Reform Act 2005 and different devolutions Acts etc.

law in the UK. Known as judge-made law, common law is comprised of the case law or *ratio decidendi*, and binding rules set by high ranking courts to be followed by lower level courts dealing with similar subject matter. These rules have the same force of law just like parliamentary statutes and in many cases the interpretation of different aspects of a criminal and civil law statute is highly dependent on judge-made law. A common law principle can only be repealed by an express statute of parliament on the same subject, through appeal to a higher ranking court (e.g. Supreme Court can overrule a decree of High Court), or when the new rule is the latest in chronological order. In common law jurisdictions, lack of certainty on a legal point due to either absence of a relevant case law or multiplicity of precedents usually result into the frustration of the due process of law.

Regarding codified statutes, no single criminal law or civil law code exists in the UK. Instead, a number of statutory instruments and common law rules are available for invocation. For instance, the civil law (private law) of obligation is mainly comprised of contractual, tort law and unjust enrichment principles.

Tort law is quite developed and it has many different categories which the claimants may invoke according to the nature of their claim. Many types of tort based causes of actions are available to claimants in the absence of or besides a criminal liability or contractual remedy. However, this variety has a negative effect on the scope of tort law, which is regarded as closed-ended, and has no open-ended causes of action. In other words, the claimants are required to link their claim to a specific category of tort, for instance negligence and public safety related torts, or special torts such as defamation, trespass and breach of confidence. Damages and injunctions are the traditional remedies available to claimants against tort-feasers. The claimants resort to *inter alia* the tort of breach of confidence in privacy violation cases in the absence of any statutory remedy. Historically, an equitable doctrine of the breach of confidence has been used in a piecemeal manner to fill the gap existing due to the absence of a common law tort of privacy breach.[197] This doctrine has now been further developed under common law to fulfill the obligation under Article 8 of the ECHR incorporated by the Human Rights Act of 1998.

---

[197] The body of laws called equity was a separate legal arrangement administered in the Court of Chancery in cases where there would no common law rule be available with the main royal courts. The Judicature Reforms Acts of 1873–75 merged the Chancery Court with other establishment and resultantly, common law and equity is now understood as fused, with some controversy. See for example: Burrows (2002), pp. 1–16.

6.2.4 Protection of Privacy Interests Before the Human Rights Act

6.2.4.1 A Brief Account of the Failed Attempts to Formulate Privacy Tort Law in UK

Historically, the United Kingdom does not follow the strict standards of privacy protection as, in contrast to Germany, for example, court cases titles contain the full names of litigants even in the criminal litigations.[198] Legal commentators have long realized the fact that English law neither recognizes "the right to be let alone" as judge Cooley had coined nor personal privacy is protected as a matter of right with a corresponding duty imposed on other persons in order to prevent infringements of the same right.[199] An article published in The Modern Law Review of 1962 issue succinctly analyzed the legal problem and lamented the slow-or-no-response of the English law to the protection of privacy.[200] According to the author Brian Neil, "[i]t seems remarkable that English law, which in many other fields has kept pace with changes in the public *mores,* should have so far failed to evolve any general concept of privacy."[201] Seemingly the article had been written as a reaction to the failed legislative attempt in the British Parliament to enact a general right to privacy.

In 1961, Lord Mancroft initiated a Bill called "The Right to Privacy Bill" in the House of Lords. Lord Mancroft was successful to push the Bill to Second Reading and then to the Committee stage. However, at the end of the session, the Bill died a natural death.[202] Passing of that Bill would have definitely placed the United Kingdom among the pioneering jurisdictions formally recognizing and protecting the general right to privacy. As a key feature of the Bill, the right to privacy was recognized as an essential value to maintain human dignity. The explanatory memorandum explained the purpose as "to give every individual such further protection against invasion of his privacy as may be desirable for the maintenance of human dignity while protecting the right of the public to be kept informed in all matters in which the public may be reasonably concerned."[203] It was a very comprehensive bill and contained most of the necessary principles such as giving the definition of wrongs as well as the articulation of defenses, e. g. reasonable public interest.

The need for legal protection and the deficiency of English law in providing effective protection to people from intruders into their private sphere was also highlighted by academicians. For instance, Professor Winfield wrote about privacy as early as in 1931. These historical facts reveal that not only inside of the British Parliament but outside of the Parliament too, concerns were expressed against long

---

[198] Arden (2012), p. 11.

[199] Neill (1962), p. 393.

[200] Neill (1962), p. 393.

[201] Neill (1962), p. 400.

[202] Neill (1962), p. 393.

[203] As cited in: Neill (1962), p. 393.

range cameras and tape recorders. Therefore, since very long, legal commentators have tried their best to persuade legislators to establish laws protecting privacy. "It is submitted that although it is now extremely unlikely that a court would be persuaded to recognise any general right of privacy the law may not be altogether powerless to guard the individual against the more offensive intrusions," emphatically suggests Sir Brian Neil in his 1962 law journal essay.[204]

In yet another failed attempt for law reform, Brian Walden MP's Privacy Bill was withdrawn in its Second Reading in 1969.[205] The Government though undertook to probe the matter in a comprehensive way which resulted in the publication of "Privacy and the Law Report", recommending legislation for the protection and creation of a general right of privacy.[206] Raymond Wacks gives a long account of different reviews and reports with conflicting conclusions regarding what should be the effective way of privacy protection (judicial interpretation of available torts or legislation), which he terms as *déjà vu*.[207] However, the realization of the importance of the right to privacy and the gravity of the threat to it from various actors, primarily from the press, can be observed as a common element in all these exercises. A more recent example is the Report of Calcutt Committee, published in 1990. The Committee was chaired by David Calcutt QC. This report concluded that though there is a problem of privacy, there is no strong case to support the "statutory tort of infringement of privacy".[208] He however changed his stance in another report of 1992, titled "Review of Press Self-Regulation" and recommended that due to failure of the press self-regulation, the Government should consider the introduction of a tort of privacy infringement through legislation. Similarly, the national Heritage Committee of the House of Commons also expressed dissatisfaction with the working of the Press Complaint Commission, and forwarded a recommendation for the introduction of civil and criminal liabilities through Protection of Privacy Bill. The British Government's reluctance to introduce such a Bill can be judged by the fact that it compiled a comprehensive paper titled *Privacy and Media Intrusions* that has rejected statutory intervention to control media intrusions of people's privacy. It contains the consultation paper on privacy infringements issued by Lord Chancellor's Department as well as the National Heritage Committee Report.

There are many excuses not to enact a privacy protection statute; however, "the real reason is the blocking power of the English press".[209] Another common excuse is presented which is about the difficulty of defining the right to privacy. However, it does not hold water as in many countries, this right has not only been defined but its violation is also successfully and effectively remedied through a variety of legal

[204] Neill (1962), p. 401.
[205] Wacks (2013), p. 26.
[206] Wacks (2013), p. 27.
[207] Wacks (2013), p. 29.
[208] Wacks (2013), p. 27.
[209] Markesinis (1990), p. 806.

instruments.[210] Other arguments put forward that laws protecting privacy would discourage investigative journalism or that the judges are not the suitable agents for regulation of speech and this should be left to self-regulation or to Government regulatory bodies such as Press Complaint Commission. These pretexts do not hold water as media's important role for the democratic order does not mean that all the wrongs committed by tabloids should also be granted a status of absolute legal protection. Tabloids in the United Kingdom are well-known for their yellow journalism. On the other hand, the inability of the regulator to check journalistic wrongdoings has also been highlighted in many fact-finding reports.[211] The argument that a statutory protection of privacy will give judges the power to balance free speech with the right to privacy and that they are not capable of reconciling free speech with other interests, is not convincing either. Markesinis answers this apprehension in a counter argument, saying that if judges cannot be trusted for such an assignment, how far trade unions of newspaper could be trusted for such a lofty exercise. Therefore, he suggests that the patchy measures can only be reformed through statute where the legislature should work out the principles for the relevant privacy area and the judges should then put those principles into action, which will generate meaningful case law over the period of time.[212]

6.2.4.2 The Problem of Privacy Wrongs Without Remedy

Before the Human Rights Act of 1998, no direct remedy was available in the English law for invasion of personal privacy. This fact has been admitted by the English judiciary in many occasions where, in spite of the apparent violation of personal privacy, the judges felt powerless to announce a remedy in order to compensate the wrong.

The English judges on many occasions emphatically stressed the importance of privacy for individual autonomy and maintenance of dignity. In Marcel v Commissioner of Police for Metropolis, Browne-Wilkinson VC observed that the collection of information by various Government agencies such as revenue department and offices of social and health services were jeopardizing individual freedom and declared that "[t]he dossier of private information is the badge of the totalitarian state."[213]

---

[210] Markesinis (1990), pp. 802–808. See also p. 806: "[I]t has been done in a variety of ways [such as] by statute; in Germany, mainly by imaginative courts following a very common law and casuistic method (though, on occasion, also helped by specific statutes such as the *Kunstrurhebergesetz* of 1907, article 22 of which in combination with para 823 I BGB, would have given Mr Kaye a civil remedy)".

[211] Markesinis (1990), p. 806.

[212] Markesinis (1990), p. 808.

[213] Marcel v Commissioner of Police for Metropolis, [1992] 1 All ER 72.

The judgment of the House of Lords in Kaye v Robertson[214] is a perfect example, where the problem of the lack of laws protecting privacy in England was intensively highlighted. According to the facts of the case, the plaintiff, Mr. Gorden Kaye, was a well-known comedian and a star of a popular comedy series on television. In January 1990, Mr. Kaye suffered serious injuries on his head and brain in a dangerous road accident, was resultantly hospitalized and even remained on the life support machine for several days in the intensive care. Owing to his large fan following, public and media admission was restricted after he was shifted to a private room of the hospital. Such measures were important in the interest of his recovery and to prevent secondary infections. Notices were pinned at the doors of the ward and private hospital room conveying these visiting restrictions, and these notices contained instructions for visitors to see the staff before visiting who had a list of the desired family and friends only. On 13th of February, 1990, a photographer and a journalist, who were working for subeditor of Sunday Sport, Mr. Robertson, succeeded to prowl into Mr. Kaye's private room, ignoring and disregarding the instructions displayed on the notices. The photographer took many photos of Mr. Kaye and of his surroundings. According to the tape produced before the court as evidence for defense, Mr. Kaye did not object to these activities. However, after some time, the nursing staff ejected the journalist and photographer through security staff.

A friend of Mr. Kaye applied for injunction *inter alia* to stop the publication of the interview and photos taken in the hospital room. His solicitor based the claim for injunction on libel, malicious falsehood, and trespass to the person and passing off. Although the medical condition of Mr. Kaye was sufficient evidence to prove that he was not fit to provide an informed consent, yet, in the trial court the defendants claimed to have secured Mr. Kaye's consent. The judge granted injunctions with very comprehensive terms and restrained the defendants and their servants or agents from publishing or distributing the photographs, statements, or any other record obtained as such during the so-called scoop. The defendants were ordered to handover "any tape-recording, notes of interview or photographs obtained or taken by any servant or agent of the Second Defendants in Charing Cross Hospital on 13th February 1990 and any copies of negatives thereof."[215]

They appealed against the injunction, which was allowed. Lord Justice Glidewell gave his famous reason for arriving at this decision: "It is well-known that in English law there is no right to privacy, and accordingly there is no right of action for breach of a person's privacy. The facts of the present case are a graphic illustration of the desirability of Parliament considering whether and in what circumstances statutory provision can be made to protect the privacy of individuals."[216] He then analyzed all the available traditional common law torts one by one and ruled out most of the torts to have been committed except for "malicious falsehood." For the tort of malicious falsehood too, the calculation of damages would be a difficult task in his opinion.

---

[214] Kaye v Robertson and another (1991) FSR 62.

[215] As reproduced in: Kaye v Robertson and another (1991) FSR 62.

[216] Kaye v Robertson and another (1991) FSR 62.

Lord Justice Bingham showed similar concerns regarding the failure of common law. To him, "[t]his case nonetheless highlights, yet again, the failure of both the common law of England and statute to protect in an effective way the personal privacy of individual citizens." He accepted the fact that despite the fact that "[t]he defendants' conduct towards the plaintiff here was "a monstrous invasion of his privacy", yet English law could not rectify the harm accrued as such. According to Lord Justice Bingham,

> [i]f ever a person has a right to be let alone by strangers with no public interest to pursue, it must surely be when he lies in hospital recovering from brain surgery and in no more than partial command of his faculties. It is this invasion of his privacy which underlies the plaintiff's complaint. Yet it alone, however gross, does not entitle him to relief in English law.[217]

In his concluding remarks, he further stated, "[w]e cannot give the plaintiff the breadth of protection which I would, for my part, wish. The problems of defining and limiting a tort of privacy are formidable, but the present case strengthens my hope that the review now in progress may prove fruitful."[218]

In a similar passion, Lord Justice Leggatt, agreed to both judgments and expressed their inability to grant proper and deserving relief under English law. The Lord concluded,

> We do not need a First Amendment to preserve the freedom of the press, but the abuse of that freedom can be ensured only by the enforcement of a right to privacy. This right has so long been disregarded here that it can be recognised now only by the legislature. Especially since there is available in the United States a wealth of experience of the enforcement of this right both at common law and also under statute, it is to be hoped that the making good of this signal shortcoming in our law will not be long delayed[219]

The privacy right's advocates have criticized in strong words the English judiciary's approach in this case and its impact on the subsequent cases. According to Markesinis,

> [t]his unfortunate decision has subsequently been treated as authority for the proposition that English common law does not encompass a privacy tort, and its influence has acted as a dead hand on any potential for developing remedies against privacy intrusions" [....] Kaye remains a compelling demonstration of the limits of both existing English law and of the limitations of an approach that relies upon inadequate existing remedies to protect privacy.[220]

One can find a similar declaration also in relatively earlier decisions. It was made by Sir Robert Megarry in 1979, with respect to telephone tapping by the police.[221] The attorney for the plaintiff acknowledged the fact that there was no general right of privacy in English law, yet he based his claim on the special right of communicating

---

[217] Kaye v Robertson and another (1991) FSR 62.

[218] Kaye v Robertson and another (1991) FSR 62.

[219] Kaye v Robertson and another (1991) FSR 62.

[220] Markesinis et al. (2004), p. 158.

[221] Malone v Commissioner of Police of the Metropolis [1979] 2 All ER 620.

on the telephone without 'molestation'. This was declined by the Court. Sir Robert Megarry stated,

> this case seems to me to make it plain that telephone tapping is a subject which cries out for legislation. Privacy and confidentiality are, of course, subjects of considerable complexity. Yet however desirable it may by that they should at least to some extent be defined and regulated by statute, rather than being left for slow and expensive evolution in individual cases brought at the expense of litigants and the legal aid fund, the difficulty of the subject matter is liable to discourage legislative zeal. Telephone tapping lies in a much narrower compass; the difficulties in legislating on the subject ought not to prove insuperable; and the requirements of the convention should provide a spur to action, even if belated. This, however, is not for me to decide. I can do no more than express a hope, and offer a proleptic welcome to any statute on the subject.[222]

In R v Khan, a case for excluding some evidence from the criminal trial which was obtained by police through bugging devices installed clandestinely in the private property of the accused, Lord Nolan expressed his views as,

> [t]his brings one back to the fact that, under English law, there is in general nothing unlawful about a breach of privacy. The appellant's case rests wholly upon the lack of statutory authorisation for the particular breach of privacy which occurred in the present case and the consequent infringement, as the appellant submits, of article 8.[223]

6.2.4.3 The Causes of Action in English Law Before HRA

The legal actions under the law of tort such as trespass, nuisance, harassment and breach of confidence have been traditionally resorted to by claimants who sought protection or compensation for privacy related infringements.[224] All these instruments have one or more shortcomings. Thus, one can say that those were not an alternative to a coherent legal regime for privacy protection. Most of these torts have not been traditionally designed to protect privacy interests, which are deeply attached to the very "person" of individuals. Rather, these torts mostly focus on the proprietary interests attached to property rights. For example, a plaintiff failed to get remedy for aerial photographs of his estate when he applied under the tort of trespass, because the plaintiff could not establish that the alleged act contained all the ingredients to be liable for censuring as such.[225] Obviously the ingredients of the tort of trespass, being a concept of property law, could not be established in aerial overflights, as Griffith J observed, "I can find no support in authority for the view that a landowner's rights in the air space above his property extend to an unlimited

[222] Sir Rober Megarry in Malone v Commissioner of Police of the Metropolis [1979] 2 All ER 620.

[223] R v Khan [1997] AC 558, 581 as cited in Neill (1999), pp. 17–18.

[224] For a detail analysis of pre-HRA privacy claimants instruments and the proposed impact of HRA (or ECHR for that matter) see: Neill (1999), pp. 1–28.

[225] Bernstein of Leigh v Skyviews & General Ltd [1978] QB 479.

height."[226] However, it was a clear case of aerial surveillance, an area that would be protected under the right to privacy.

Similarly, an action under the tort of nuisance can be initiated if the lawful enjoyment of one's property is hindered. This action is attached to the property for its proprietary fringe benefits and it is not a personality right. Therefore it comes into action when the right to land is somehow intervened. A person, who is not an owner but a licensee and has limited proprietary rights, cannot take benefit out of this cause of action.[227]

The tort of harassment has criminal law roots and no one will encourage its use against journalists because the UK's Protection from Harassment Act of 1997 does not contain any definition of the term 'harassment', while its defences from the application of the Act include such broad expressions as 'detection' of crime.

Among the common law traditional torts, the tort of breach of confidence has usually been used for the privacy rights infringements. This tort needs a detailed discussion.

6.2.4.4 The Tort of Breach of Confidence

The absence of the general right to privacy in the United Kingdom, however, does not mean that all of the privacy related interests of the claimants were always left without a remedy. The tort of breach of confidence was the main legal instrument which was used to provide relief to some of the claimants, though in a piecemeal manner. It is invoked mainly on the basis of disclosure of confidential information to parties neither privy to such a relationship of confidence nor entitled to receive the subject information. In order for the claim under the breach of confidence tort to succeed, a three-element test was first introduced by Sir Robert Megarry in Coco v A N Clark[228] and afterwards affirmed by a series of case law of the House of Lords, notably in A-G v Guardian Newspaper[229] as well as in Campbell v MGN.[230] Accordingly, an action for the breach of confidence could be successful if firstly, the information is of confidential nature or has *the necessary quality* of confidence; secondly, the circumstances in which such confidential information is divulged import *an obligation of confidence*; thirdly, there is an *unauthorized use of that information to the detriment of the party communicating it*.[231]

The importance and suitability of breach of confidence as an alternative action for the violation of privacy rights was formally acceded by the Younger Committee in its report on privacy, which declared breach of confidence as "the most effective

[226] Bernstein of Leigh v Skyviews & General Ltd [1978] QB 479, para 487.

[227] Neill (1999), p. 6.

[228] Coco v A N Clark (Engineers) Limited [1969] RPC 41, 47–48.

[229] A-G v Guardian Newspaper (No. 2) (1990) 1 AC 109.

[230] Campbell v Mirror Group Newspapers Ltd [2004] UKHL 22.

[231] Coco v A N Clark (Engineers) Limited [1969] RPC 41, 47–48.

protection of privacy in the whole of our existing law, civil and criminal."[232] However, many scholars such as Raymond Wacks do not agree with such an optimistic view regarding the breach of confidence tort. Wacks opines, "though 'privacy' and 'confidence' often overlap, the action for breach of confidence provided an unsuitable means by which to safeguard privacy."[233] The action under the tort of breach of confidence "is inappropriate because it is, quite simply, based on a different theory. Its main purpose is to protect the business interests of the plaintiff rather than his interests in preserving privacy".[234] One can find other arguments which focus on the importance of various human relationships that necessitate an obligation of confidence for their sustenance, and any misuse of the legal tool of breach of confidence—even for the protection against privacy invasions—will jeopardize this crucial aspect of mutual human involvement.[235]

Owing to the three essential ingredients for a successful action, breach of confidence has many limitations impeding it to become an effective remedy for the protection of private information. Firstly, the requirement of confidentiality in a relationship may not always be fulfilled for a successful action against a newspaper which has published personal information without taking permission from the claimant.[236] Secondly, the claimant may not show any detriment other than mental distress in a privacy case, and so his case may qualify for injunctive relief but cannot get damages in the absence of tangible loss. Thirdly, it is complicated to fulfill the requirement for personal information not to be 'in the access of public' in the internet related cases. Fourthly, the action under breach of confidence, according to Wacks, "is available only to the person to whom the obligation of confidence is owed, and it is only the person who has actual, imputed, or constructive knowledge that he or she is acting in breach of confidence who may be sued."[237] If interpreted in a strict manner, this would also work as a limitation in cases where the claimant sues a newspaper for unwanted publicity. Wacks concludes that breach of confidence action has been inadequate for many privacy related claims, because the action is mainly concerned with "(a) disclosure or use rather than publicity; (b) the source

[232] Para 87 of the Report of the Committee on Privacy chaired by Kenneth Younger.

[233] Wacks (2013), p. 68.

[234] Wacks (2013), p. 16.

[235] "The confidences we bestow upon our close companions are gifts of friendship. We signal our friendship by rendering ourselves vulnerable. We place ourselves at another's mercy - to be discreet, or blow the gaffe. The strength (or weakness) of a personal relationship is often exhibited in the way we respond to this challenge, both as confiders and confidants. To subject these natural incidents of friendship and other personal relationships to legal scrutiny and judgment may weaken the ties that bind us. To protect the individual from invasions of privacy is one thing - it can be achieved by direct limitations upon press freedom. To achieve this by casting him adrift from his fellows, by imposing obligations of confidentiality upon them is another, and, for this writer at least, should lie beyond the competence of judges to prescribe." Wilson (1990), p. 56.

[236] See: Wacks (2013), pp. 76–81.

[237] Wacks (2013), p. 77.

rather than the nature of the information; and (c) the preservation of confidence rather than the possible harm to the claimant caused by its breach."[238]

On the other hand, scholars such as Gavin Phillipson and Helen Fenwick, in their pre-human rights case law analysis, have argued that the application of the tort of breach of confidence was so limited that it had always left privacy claims unremedied, particularly in the cases where reporters photograph either through telephoto lenses or when they secretly record conversation for their newspapers.[239] They have referred to English case law related to all the three essential elements for a successful breach of confidence claims. In their view, the judges have adopted a quite liberal interpretation in order to cover situations of privacy wrongs which are not covered by the strict application of the three-elements-formula. "[T]he developments described above significantly widen the circumstances in which the duty of confidence will be imposed with the result, it is suggested, that many of the activities of reporters engaged in uncovering private facts may now be caught by the law of confidence", they have remarked. However, in order to comprehensively resolve the privacy problems, they concede the opinion of Raymond Wacks that the breach of confidence tort does not sufficiently provide remedies in *all* privacy invasion cases; such as the cases of physical intrusion without obtaining useful information or where the claimant himself has caused a limited or conditional disclosure.[240] These cases would be left without a remedy due to the limited scope of the breach of confidence tort. Furthermore, the breach of confidence tort cannot withstand against the public interest defense such as freedom of information or free speech because of the fact that it is difficult to establish a countervailing public interest in the maintenance of confidentiality of information. Thus, Fenwick and Phillipson conclude:

> [T]he doctrine [of breach of confidence] has become more clearly focused on the private interest of the plaintiff in maintaining confidentiality, rather than on the accompanying public interest in so doing, with the result that the public interest in the free flow of information may more readily prevail since it may have no clear countervailing *public* interest with which to compete.[241]

6.2.5 *The Enactment of Human Rights Act (1998) and the Impact of ECHR*

The enactment of the Human Rights Act of 1998 (hereinafter HRA), which came into force in October, 2002, incorporated the European Convention on Human Rights into English law. Section 2 of the HRA states:

---

[238] Wacks (2013), p. 78.

[239] Fenwick and Phillipson (1996), p. 453.

[240] Fenwick and Phillipson (1996), p. 453.

[241] Fenwick and Phillipson (1996), pp. 454–455.

A court or tribunal determining a question which has arisen in connection with a Convention right must take into account any—

(a) judgment, decision, declaration or advisory opinion of the European Court of Human Rights,
(b) opinion of the Commission given in a report adopted under Article 31 of the Convention,
(c) decision of the Commission in connection with Article 26 or 27(2) of the Convention, or
(d) decision of the Committee of Ministers taken under Article 46 of the Convention,

whenever made or given, so far as, in the opinion of the court or tribunal, it is relevant to the proceedings in which that question has arisen.

Section 6 of the Act declares that it is unlawful for any public authority to act in a way which is incompatible with the Convention right while section 6 (3) includes courts, tribunals, and actions of any persons who performs functions of public nature. According to section 7 of the Act, if person claims that a public authority acted in a way which is incompatible with a Convention right, may bring proceedings against the authority under this law in the appropriate court or tribunal, or rely on the Convention right or rights concerned in any legal proceedings, but only if he is (or would be) a victim of the unlawful act.[242] Similarly, the Human Rights Act has made the Convention rights as part of the law by placing them under Schedule I.

Judges and legal scholars were equally excited for the protection of privacy in a comprehensive manner. They were hoping that the lacunae pointed out in the breach of confidence tort would now be removed and that slowly and gradually a new tort of the breach of privacy would emerge. It was expected that the HRA would provide a better opportunity to English judiciary to "develop and re-balance" the common law in order to protect dignitarian aspects of human life and personal autonomy.[243]

The obligation under Article 8 ECHR to ensure respect for private and family life does not only restrain public authorities from violating it but the same obligation may also require the public authorities to take measures to protect individuals from other private parties—the so-called horizontal application.[244] Moreover, the ECtHR is keen to optimally protect both the interests of individuals as well as of community and calls for a balance between these values.[245] These features of the ECHR were thought to be capable of forging the 'inchoate nature' of the breach of confidence where Articles 8 and 10 of ECHR read with section 12 of HRA "will provide an organizing principle around which the uncertainties inherent in the action, particularly the conflict between the demands of privacy and press freedom, may be

[242] Section 7 of Human Rights Act 1998 reads *inter alia*: "Proceedings: (1)A person who claims that a public authority has acted (or proposes to act) in a way which is made unlawful by section 6(1) may (a) bring proceedings against the authority under this Act in the appropriate court or tribunal, or (b)rely on the Convention right or rights concerned in any legal proceedings, but only if he is (or would be) a victim of the unlawful act."

[243] Fenwick and Phillipson (1996), p. 662.

[244] See Sect. 5.2.3.2 for a detailed analysis of positive obligations of the member states under ECHR.

[245] See observation of ECtHR in Cossey v. The United Kingdom as cited in Sect. 5.2.3.2.

resolved" and this way it will also provide a "normative impetus" in resolving typical privacy cases.[246]

Phillipson and Fenwick conclude, "the action for breach of confidence is now ripe for development into a privacy law in all but name, and may provide a more effective and subtle means of protecting privacy than commonly thought."[247]

6.2.5.1 Initial Confusion of Incorporation: The Cases of A v B plc and Wainwright v Home Office

As earlier stated, almost everybody who was interested in the protection of privacy in UK had attached their hopes to the passing of Human Rights Act. Most scholars and privacy advocates were expecting judicial activism in the interpretation of the HRA provisions in line with the law of the ECHR. However, in the case of A v B plc, the Court of Appeal disappointed to some extent those who had hoped that appropriate privacy protection would be developed. In this case, the claimant Mr. A, a premiership football player, applied for injunctions against the defendants B and C. The injunction referred to restraining B—a national newspaper—from publishing stories which a woman 'C' had sold to B on the basis of English law of confidentiality. These stories concerned extramarital affairs of the claimant with women including C. The court granted the interim injection which was subsequently challenged by defendant B in the Court of Appeal. The Court of Appeal, while allowing the defendant's appeal, ruled that any judicial interference with the freedom of the press must be justified, where merely the protection of confidentiality could not be a valid ground for such interference through injunction. The Court laid down some general 'guidelines' for determination of the cases seeking injunctions against disclosure of confidential information.

Lord Woolf CJ of the Court of Appeal acknowledged the incorporation of the ECHR into domestic law of the UK through the Human Rights Act 1998, which demands the consideration of applications for injunctions for restraining disclosure and publication of "confidential information" in the context of Articles 8 and 10. Lord Woolf explained:

> These articles have provided new parameters within which the court will decide, in an action for breach of confidence, whether a person is entitled to have his privacy protected by the court or whether the restriction of freedom of expression which such protection involves cannot be justified. The court is able to achieve this by absorbing the rights which articles 8 and 10 protect into the long-established action for breach of confidence. This involves giving a new strength and breadth to the action so that it accommodates the requirements of those articles.[248]

[246] Fenwick and Phillipson (1996), pp. 660–693.

[247] Fenwick and Phillipson (1996), p. 693.

[248] A v B plc [2003] QB 195, para 4.

The *tension* between these articles requires a judicial balancing through attaching proper weight to both rights. Lord Woolf accepted the relevance and coherence of Strasbourg jurisprudence in Articles 8 and 10 as

> These decisions are valuable sources of the principles which the articles embrace. The decisions do however tend to repeat the same principles in successive cases in order to apply them to different situations. The citation of a single case may therefore be all that is required.[249]

By providing guidelines to the judiciary for proper balancing and in order to save their time spent in reading bulky authorities, he explained that how freedom of expression should be placed in the balancing scale; because section 12 of HRA calls for proper care to the satisfaction of the judge in restricting a publication in the exercise of the statute. Therefore,

> Any interference with the press has to be justified because it inevitably has some effect on the ability of the press to perform its role in society. This is the position irrespective of whether a particular publication is desirable in the public interest. The existence of a free press is in itself desirable and so any interference with it has to be justified.[250]

Lord Woolf opined that the content of speech, i.e. political speech or mere gossiping, is of little relevance. To him, the court should not interfere with the publication in the first place. Otherwise, it has to justify any such interference "regardless of the quality of the material."[251] Similarly, he considered that neither the content nor the form of reporting is a matter for the courts to deal with. Rather the press regulator (PCP in that case), as well as *the customers of the newspaper concerned* could adequately decide in respect of the press content and its dissemination pattern.[252]

In another 'guideline', Lord Woolf persuaded other judges that seeking a new tort for the protection of privacy may not serve any purpose, and, "an action for breach of confidence now will, where this is appropriate, provide the necessary protection."[253]

The requirement for the proof of confidential relationship has been relaxed as according to A v B plc, "[a] duty of confidence will arise whenever the party subject to the duty is in a situation where he either knows or ought to know that the other person can reasonably expect his privacy to be protected."[254] So the required relationship can be both expressly created as well as inferred from the circumstances. Similarly, the breach of confidence tort can be invoked in the case of intrusion in situations where a reasonable expectation of privacy could be found. However, procuring information through illegal means should not get, according to the

[249] A v B plc (2003) QB 195, para 9.

[250] A v B plc (2003) QB 195, para 11 (iv).

[251] A v B plc (2003) QB 195, para 11 (v). Para xiii too emphasize this point: "Whether the publication will be attractive or unattractive should not affect the result of an application if the information is otherwise not the proper subject of restraint."

[252] A v B plc (2003) QB 195, para 48.

[253] A v B plc (2003) QB 195, para 11 (vi).

[254] A v B plc (2003) QB 195, para 11 (ix).

Court, an automatic restraining injunction on the basis of breach of confidence as there might be other remedies for such unlawful activities.[255]

Lord Woolf dedicated much space to the privacy of public figures and media and people's interest in their lives. He, however, passed controversial judgments about these concepts. In his words,

> Where an individual is a public figure he is entitled to have his privacy respected in the appropriate circumstances. A public figure is entitled to a private life. The individual, however, should recognise that because of his public position he must expect and accept that his actions will be more closely scrutinised by the media. Even trivial facts relating to a public figure can be of great interest to readers and other observers of the media. Conduct which in the case of a private individual would not be the appropriate subject of comment can be the proper subject of comment in the case of a public figure. The public figure may hold a position where higher standards of conduct can be rightly expected by the public. The public figure may be a role model whose conduct could well be emulated by others. He may set the fashion. The higher the profile of the individual concerned the more likely that this will be the position. Whether you have courted publicity or not you may be a legitimate subject of public attention. If you have courted public attention then you have less ground to object to the intrusion which follows. In many of these situations it would be overstating the position to say that there is a public interest in the information being published. It would be more accurate to say that the public have an understandable and so a legitimate interest in being told the information. If this is the situation then it can be appropriately taken into account by a court when deciding on which side of the line a case falls. The courts must not ignore the fact that if newspapers do not publish information which the public are interested in, there will be fewer newspapers published, which will not be in the public interest. The same is true in relation to other parts of the media.[256]

He also made wrong inferences from Council of Europe Resolution No. 116 5 of 1998, which said nothing of the sort.[257]

---

[255] A v B plc (2003) QB 195, para 11 (ix).

[256] A v B plc (2003) QB 195, para 11 (xii).

[257] Lord Woolf CJ reproduced these paras: "6. The Assembly is aware that personal privacy is often invaded, even in countries with specific legislation to protect it, as people's private lives have become a highly lucrative commodity for certain sectors of the media. The victims are essentially public figures, since details of their private lives serve as a stimulus to sales. At the same time, public figures must recognise that the special position they occupy in society – in many cases by choice – automatically entails increased pressure on their privacy. 7. Public figures are persons holding public office and/or using public resources and, more broadly speaking, all those who play a role in public life, whether in politics, the economy, the arts, the social sphere, sport or in any other domain. 8. It is often in the name of a one-sided interpretation of the right to freedom of expression, which is guaranteed in Article 10 of the European Convention on Human Rights, that the media invade people's privacy, claiming that their readers are entitled to know about public figures. 9. Certain facts relating to the private lives of public figures, particularly politicians, may indeed be of interest to citizens, and it may therefore be legitimate for readers, who are also voters, to be informed of those facts. 10. It is therefore necessary to find a way of balancing the exercise of two fundamental rights, both of which are guaranteed by the European Convention on Human Rights: the right to respect for one's private life and the right to freedom of expression. 11. The Assembly reaffirms the importance of every person's right to privacy, and of the right to freedom of expression, as fundamental to a democratic society. These rights are neither absolute nor in any hierarchical order, since they are of equal value. 12. However, the Assembly points out that the right

Applying the guidelines to the facts of the case, Lord Woolf underlined the Court of Appeal's criticism on the judgments under appeal. Firstly, any interference of the courts in the publication of information has to be justified and merely an assumption of public interest would not be a sufficient reason for allowing injunction against a newspaper.[258] Second criticism focuses the lower court's acknowledgement of extra-marital relationship as capable of maintaining the legally protected confidentiality. Lord Wolf declares "objectionable" the approach of lower court to equate both extra-marital relations and the relationship of marriage. He declares that no protection could be extended to the former social arrangement.[259]

Yet another controversial statement was given which, if adopted, would give only a meager and rarest chance to the protection of the right to privacy for public figures. He asserted,

> Footballers are role models for young people and undesirable behavior on their part can set an unfortunate example. While Jack J was right to say on the evidence which was before him that A had not courted publicity, the fact is that someone holding his position was inevitably a figure in whom a section of the public and the media would be interested.[260]

Based on these approaches, the Court set aside the injunction and allowed the appeal of the publisher. This judgment can be considered as a blow to the development of the right to privacy even if it would be through the path of breach of confidence law. It has put onus on the plaintiff to establish that a publication would disclose information related to a relationship of confidence. It has also diluted to a great extent the right to privacy of public figures; and could be cited as one of the exemplary case law which provides justification for zero privacy to the sportsmen and other celebrities.

Wainwright v Home Office is perhaps the first case where the House of Lords rejected the possibility of the existence of a remedy for a general tort of invasion of privacy. It communicated in a strong voice that no "freestanding" or general right to privacy existed ever in the United Kingdom.[261] Lord Hoffmann rejected the idea of 'creating a new right'. He saw that as something very different from the extension of contemporary legal principles and compared any such exercise to the distortion of law.

According to the facts of the case, Ms Wainwright and her mentally incapacitated son were strip-searched by the prison staff before they could meet another son in the prison who was charged of murder and the possible use of drugs. This incident

---

to privacy afforded by Article 8 of the European Convention on Human Rights should not only protect an individual against interference by public authorities, but also against interference by private persons or institutions, including the mass media."

[258] A v B plc. QB 195, para 43 (i).

[259] A v B plc. QB 195, para 43 (ii).

[260] A v B plc QB 195, para 43 (vi).

[261] See Clare Dyer, 'Law lords rule there is no right to privacy - Decision disappoints mother and son strip-searched in jail' *The Guardian* (Online 17 October 2003) https://www.theguardian.com/uk/2003/oct/17/lords.prisonsandprobation. Accessed 28 August 2023.

happened in January 1997. The strip search badly affected the family to the extent that the boy suffered from psychiatric issues.[262] They filed a successful suit for damages on the basis of suffering of mental stress and the invasion of privacy The judge of the County Court awarded them 3500 and 4500 GBP respectively in compensation and aggravated damages. He came to this result on the grounds of a cause of action he derived from the action for trespass and by reasoning that the law of tort should give a remedy for any kind of distress caused by an infringement of the right of privacy protected by article 8 ECHR to which the common law could be adapted although the HRA had not yet come into force. The Court of Appeal, however, accepted the appeal, dropped the damages with respect to Ms Wainwright and reduced the damages in the case of her son. Thereupon, they appealed to the House of Lords. Among their arguments was that a general tort of invasion of privacy could be derived under which the searches of both Ms Wainwright and her son were actionable.

In the subsequent decision, Lord Hoffmann gave his famous opinion against the recognition of any general cause of action for invasion of privacy in UK.[263] He stated that the English courts have so far refused to formulate 'a general principle' of privacy invasion.[264] He mentioned the three key judgments which are, in his opinion, not only "flat against a judicial power to declare the existence of a high-level right to privacy", but also do not suggest that the judiciary should do so. According to his views, only the legislature could establish it.[265] He distinguished between "identifying privacy as a value which underlies the existence of a rule of law [. . .] and privacy as a principle of law in itself". In his eyes, only the former approach is compatible with the way the common law works.[266]

Furthermore, he stated that there is nothing "in the jurisprudence of the ECtHR under Article 8 ECHR which suggests that the adoption of some high level principles of privacy is necessary to comply with article 8 of the convention."[267] He also interpreted the judgment of the ECtHR in Peck v United Kingdom in a way, that it does not call for a general tort for the invasion of privacy, but in fact highlights the need for legal rules in the regulation of CCTV operations. According to him, the enforcement of the HRA had further weakened the argument of legal lacuna as "Sections 6 and 7 of the Act are in themselves substantial gap fillers; if it is indeed the case that a person's rights under article 8 have been infringed by a public authority, he will have a statutory remedy."[268] He adds that it is doubtful whether article 8 ECHR, although it guarantees a right of privacy, treats it as an impairment

[262] According to psychiatric report, he suffered from severe Post Traumatic Stress Disorder (PTSD); he had already learning issues and his mental age was 12 year old.

[263] Wainwright v Home Office [2003] UKHL 53, [2004] 2 AC 406.

[264] Wainwright v Home Office [2003] UKHL 53, [2004] 2 AC 406, para 19.

[265] Wainwright v Home Office [2003] UKHL 53, [2004] 2 AC 406, para 26.

[266] Wainwright v Home Office [2003] UKHL 53, [2004] 2 AC 406, para 31.

[267] Wainwright v Home Office [2003] UKHL 53, [2004] 2 AC 406, para 32.

[268] Wainwright v Home Office [2003] UKHL 53, [2004] 2 AC 406, para 34.

and requires a remedy in damages, irrespective of whether the defendant acted intentionally, negligently or accidentally.[269] Furthermore, the creation of a general tort would pre-empt the controversial question of the extent, if any, to which the Convention requires the state to provide remedies for invasions of privacy by persons who are not public authorities.[270]

Lord Hoffmann dismissed the appellants' claim, the other four Lords agreed with his opinion in this respect, and the appeal finally was dismissed.[271] The decision demonstrated that not only the question of the existence of a general tort of invasion of privacy triggered some controversy but also the consequences of the incorporation of the ECHR, in particular, Article 8 ECHR were in need to be further elaborated.

6.2.5.2 Using and Modifying Indigenous Legal Tools for Compliance with ECHR in Campbell v MGN and Max Mosley v News Group Newspapers Ltd.

Naomi Campbell has been a well-known fashion model, acknowledged in the decision of the House of Lords Campbell v. Mirror Group Newspapers Limited in these words: "Hers is a household name, nationally and internationally. Her face is instantly recognisable. Whatever she does and wherever she goes is news."[272] She filed a suit against the owner company of the "Mirror" newspaper as a response to publishing a pictorial account about her attendance at a rehabilitation clinic—Narcotics Anonymous—in order to recover from alcoholism and drug addiction. The overall language of the article was disingenuously sympathetic as it headed, "Naomi: I am a drug addict", with a praiseworthy start as "Supermodel Naomi Campbell is attending Narcotics Anonymous meetings in a courageous bid to beat her addiction to drink and drugs."[273] The newspaper also presented an exaggerated frequency of her attendance at meetings in the clinic. A paid freelance photographer while concealing himself in a parked car took her photographs, showing her in the whereabouts of the clinic.

Naomi Campbell started legal proceeding on 1st of February, 2001, the same day the Mirror published the story. That further infuriated the newspaper company which Jack J then published a very critical article on 5th of February. The article heading was: "After years of self-publicity and illegal drug abuse, Naomi Campbell whinges about privacy." In another op-ed, the newspaper wrote: "If Naomi Campbell wants to live like a nun, let her join a nunnery. If she wants the excitement of a

[269] Wainwright v Home Office [2003] UKHL 53, [2004] 2 AC 406, para 51.

[270] Wainwright v Home Office [2003] UKHL 53, [2004] 2 AC 406, para 34.

[271] Wainwright v Home Office [2003] UKHL 53, [2004] 2 AC 406, paras 52–53.

[272] Campbell v Mirror Group Newspapers Ltd [2004] UKHL 22, para 1.

[273] Campbell v Mirror Group Newspapers Ltd [2004] UKHL 22, para 2.

show business life, she must accept what comes with it."[274] On 7th of February, the "Mirror" published another offensive article.[275]

Miss Campbell claimed damages for breach of confidence and also compensation under the Data Protection Act 1998. The court upheld Miss Campbell's claim with a modest award of £2500 plus £1000 for aggravated damages. On appeal of the newspaper company, however, the judge's order was discharged on the ground, first of all, that the media is entitled to 'put the record straight', if public figures assume a false image or issue false statements about their lives.[276] Miss Campbell challenged the verdict in the House of Lords.

The House of Lords held the Mirror Group Newspapers company liable to a certain extent by majority vote. In his opinion, Lord Nicholls of Birkenhead held that though there is no "over-arching, all-embracing cause of action for 'invasion of privacy'", yet the law for the protection of various aspects of privacy is developing on a fast pace.[277] Unlike in the case A v B plc, it was emphasized that there is no precedence between the freedom of speech and the right to privacy whenever courts have to decide on competing claims such as in this case:

> Both are vitally important rights. Neither has precedence over the other. The importance of freedom of expression has been stressed often and eloquently, the importance of privacy less so. But it, too, lies at the heart of liberty in a modern state. A proper degree of privacy is essential for the well-being and development of an individual.[278]

The nomenclature of the breach of confidence-tort at one hand and its requirements on the other hand was modified as this cause of action had "firmly shaken off the limiting constraint of the need for an initial confidential relationship".[279] Lord Nicholls stated:

> Now the law imposes a 'duty of confidence' whenever a person receives information he knows or ought to know is fairly and reasonably to be regarded as confidential. Even this formulation is awkward. The continuing use of the phrase 'duty of confidence' and the description of the information as 'confidential' is not altogether comfortable. Information about an individual's private life would not, in ordinary usage, be called 'confidential'. The more natural description today is that such information is private. The essence of the tort is better encapsulated now as misuse of private information.[280]

Furthermore, he recognized that the values enshrined in articles 8 and 10 could be made *part of the cause of action for breach of confidence*. In the same vein, he acknowledged and clarified the so-called horizontal application of human rights with respect to articles 8 and 10 ECHR. The values embodied in these articles "are as much applicable in disputes between individuals or between an individual and a

---

[274] Campbell v Mirror Group Newspapers Ltd [2004] UKHL 22, para 8.

[275] Campbell v Mirror Group Newspapers Ltd [2004] UKHL 22, para 9.

[276] [2003] QB 633, 658.

[277] Campbell v Mirror Group Newspapers Ltd [2004] UKHL 22, para 11.

[278] Campbell v Mirror Group Newspapers Ltd [2004] UKHL 22, para 12.

[279] Campbell v Mirror Group Newspapers Ltd [2004] UKHL 22, para 14.

[280] Campbell v Mirror Group Newspapers Ltd [2004] UKHL 22, para 14.

non-governmental body such as a newspaper as they are in disputes between individuals and a public authority."[281] And "Articles 8 and 10 call for a more explicit analysis of competing considerations than the three traditional requirements of the cause of action for breach of confidence".[282]

Lord Hoffmann joined in his opinion, explaining the impact of ECHR on the English law of torts as,

> In recent years, however, there have been two developments of the law of confidence, typical of the capacity of the common law to adapt itself to the needs of contemporary life. One has been an acknowledgement of the artificiality of distinguishing between confidential information obtained through the violation of a confidential relationship and similar information obtained in some other way. The second has been the acceptance, under the influence of human rights instruments such as article 8 of the European Convention, of the privacy of personal information as something worthy of protection in its own right.[283]

Regarding the horizontal application of ECHR, Lord Hoffmann stressed that, although the HRA is now an equivalent of Article 8 ECHR and enacted as part of English law, it is not directly concerned with privacy invasions by private persons and section 6 of the Act imposes an obligation only against public authorities.[284] Nevertheless, what human rights law had done was, in his view, "to identify private information as something worth protecting as an aspect of human autonomy and dignity. And this recognition has raised inescapably the question of why it should be worth protecting against the state but not against a private person".[285] The legal developments of the causes of action after the incorporation of ECHR show that the center of gravity in such cases has been shifted towards a human rights' approach. The law does not merely protect confidential information but in fact,

> it focuses upon the protection of human autonomy and dignity - the right to control the dissemination of information about one's private life and the right to the esteem and respect of other people.[286]

In the outcome of the case, all those involved in the decision agreed that there must be a balancing of rights and that neither free speech nor privacy has an intrinsic preference or automatic priority.[287] In contrast, they did not fully agree on how to weight and relate the protected interests to each other.

Lord Nicholls of Birkenhead divided the questions into five categories: (1) the fact of Miss Campbell's drug addiction; (2) the fact that she was receiving treatment;

[281] Campbell v Mirror Group Newspapers Ltd [2004] UKHL 22, para 17.

[282] Campbell v Mirror Group Newspapers Ltd [2004] UKHL 22, para 19.

[283] Campbell v Mirror Group Newspapers Ltd [2004] UKHL 22, para: 46. According to Lord Hoffmann, the new principle which omits the requirement of a pre-existing confidential relationship was accepted as representing current English law by ECtHR in Earl Spencer v United Kingdom (1998) 25 EHRR CD 105.

[284] Campbell v Mirror Group Newspapers Ltd [2004] UKHL 22, para 49.

[285] Campbell v Mirror Group Newspapers Ltd [2004] UKHL 22, para 50.

[286] Campbell v Mirror Group Newspapers Ltd [2004] UKHL 22, para 51.

[287] Cf. Campbell v Mirror Group Newspapers Ltd [2004] UKHL 22, paras 55 and 138.

(3) the fact that she was receiving treatment at Narcotics Anonymous; (4) the details of the treatment—how long she had been attending meetings, how often she went, how she was treated within the sessions themselves, the extent of her commitment, and the nature of her entrance on the specific occasion; and (5) the visual portrayal of her leaving a specific meeting with other addicts.[288]

Regarding the first and the second category, the publication by the newspaper was considered justified. Naomi Campbell had repeatedly stated in public, she did not take drugs. Lord Nicholls stressed that "where a public figure chooses to present a false image and make untrue pronouncements about his or her life, the press will normally be entitled to put the record straight".[289] This opinion was shared across the members of the Appellate Committee.

Regarding the other questions of the case, all agreed on the fact that somebody is a public figure or media celebrity does not justify in itself the publication as it is possible that a person attract or seek publicity about a particular aspect of her life, "without creating any public interest in the publication of personal information about other matters."[290] However, the results of the balancing exercise were varying. Lord Nicholls dismissed the appeal on the grounds that the disclosure of the treatment by attendance at Narcotics Anonymous meetings was only an additional information of an unremarkable nature, that the non-publication of this information would have robbed a legitimate newspaper story of attendant detail and that the photograph, which was not challenged for the clandestinely of its taking, but for its content, added nothing of an essentially private nature.[291]

Lord Hoffmann based his dismissal mainly on the consideration that journalism must have some margin of choice in the way it chooses to present their story. Regarding the difference between photographs and information in the written form, he opined that there is no fundamental difference except that photos are more vivid and attractive. Particularly, the "famous and even the not so famous who go out in public must accept that they may be photographed without their consent, just as they may be observed by others without their consent."[292] However, that does not mean that such photographs could be published to the world at large, because, "the widespread publication of a photograph of someone which reveals him to be in a situation of humiliation or severe embarrassment, even if taken in a public place, may be an infringement of the privacy of his personal information."[293] Lord Hoffmann though mentioned many relevant factors and substantial issues required to be weighed against each other. Yet, the conclusions he drew were not favorable in terms of privacy protection. In fact, he preferred a very pragmatic approach favoring

[288] Campbell v Mirror Group Newspapers Ltd [2004] UKHL 22, para 23.

[289] Campbell v Mirror Group Newspapers Ltd [2004] UKHL 22, para 24.

[290] Campbell v Mirror Group Newspapers Ltd [2004] UKHL 22, para 57.

[291] Campbell v Mirror Group Newspapers Ltd [2004] UKHL 22, paras 25 et seq.

[292] Campbell v Mirror Group Newspapers Ltd [2004] UKHL 22, para 73.

[293] Campbell v Mirror Group Newspapers Ltd [2004] UKHL 22, para 75.

the press as a "commercial enterprise". Before rejecting the appeal, he concluded his dicta as:

> No doubt it would have been possible for the Mirror to have published the article without pictures. But that would in my opinion again be to ignore the realities of this kind of journalism as much as to expect precision of judgment about the amount of circumstantial detail to be included in the text. We value the freedom of the press but the press is a commercial enterprise and can flourish only by selling newspapers. From a journalistic point of view, photographs are an essential part of the story. The picture carried the message, more strongly than anything in the text alone, that the Mirror's story was true. So the decision to publish the pictures was in my opinion within the margin of editorial judgment and something for which appropriate latitude should be allowed.[294]

Lord Hope of Craighead accepted that the press has a margin of appreciation in their decisions of editorial nature, of the language to be used for conveying their stories to the public and as to whether or not to accompany the printed word by the use of photographs. However, the margin of appreciation is not absolute and when somebody contests such decisions on the basis of a private right's infringement, the public interest in the publication of news will need to be balanced with the private interest of the claimant. The touchstone for such balancing, according to him, will be to analyze against the background of the jurisprudence of the ECtHR, "whether publication of the material pursues a legitimate aim and whether the benefits that will be achieved by its publication are proportionate to the harm that may be done by the interference with the right to privacy."[295]

Recognizing the Article 8 right to respect for private life of Miss Campbell, the Lord judge stated,

> it is not enough to deprive Miss Campbell of her right to privacy that she is a celebrity and that her private life is newsworthy. A margin of appreciation must, of course, be given to the journalist. Weight must be given to this. But to treat these details merely as background was to undervalue the importance that was to be attached to the need, if Miss Campbell was to be protected, to keep these details private. And it is hard to see that there was any compelling need for the public to know the name of the organisation that she was attending for the therapy, or for the other details of it to be set out. The presentation of the article indicates that this was not fully appreciated when the decision was taken to publish these details. The decision to publish the photographs suggests that greater weight was being given to the wish to publish a story that would attract interest rather than to the wish to maintain its credibility.[296]

Due to these reasons, he allowed the appeal with a conclusion,

> Despite the weight that must be given to the right to freedom of expression that the press needs if it is to play its role effectively, I would hold that there was here an infringement of Miss Campbell's right to privacy that cannot be justified. In my opinion publication of the third, fourth and fifth elements in the article [...] was an invasion of that right for which she

---

[294] Campbell v Mirror Group Newspapers Ltd [2004] UKHL 22, para 77.

[295] Campbell v Mirror Group Newspapers Ltd [2004] UKHL 22, para 113.

[296] Campbell v Mirror Group Newspapers Ltd [2004] UKHL 22, para 120.

is entitled to damages. I would allow the appeal and restore the orders that were made by the trial judge.[297]

Baroness Hale of Richmond, mentioning the Wainwright v Home Office case, explained the powerlessness of common law to protect the right to privacy. She also analyzed all the relevant concepts with an exceptional nuanced manner and dissected the broad rights and their various categories. She emphasized that all of the information published related to the physical and mental health of the claimant as well as to the treatment she was receiving and therefore was both private and confidential at the starting point. Analyzing the free speech defense of MGN against the claim of privacy invasion, she stated that in the categories of speech deserving of protection in a democratic society, political speech is on the top of the list. No democracy is possible without free political speech, while intellectual, educational and artistic speeches have their own place in a democratic dynamic society. The news piece under consideration could be categorized as educational, detailing Miss Campbell 'faults and follies' and revealing 'lies and hypocrisy'. Baroness Hale then arrived at the result that, on the one hand, the newspaper had a right to keep the record straight in the public interest, as far as the issue in question was the use of illegal drugs and Miss Campbell's rehabilitation treatment. On the other hand, the textual and photographic disclosures of information regarding treatment at the Narcotics Anonymous, its location, her arrival and leaving timings, showing her with other attendants of the clinic were unnecessary and the story could be published and conveyed without many details. Based on these arguments, the Lady judge concluded to allow the appeal and restore the order of the judge.

Max Mosley v Newsgroup Newspapers Ltd. is another important case. Max Mosley, the founder and president of Fédération Internationale de'Automobile (FIA), sued the publishers for an invasive article in its "News of the World"—issue of 30 March, 2008. The article headed as "F1 BOSS HAS SICK NAZI ORGY WITH 5 HOOKERS" with the subheading "Son of Hitler-loving fascist in sex shame".[298] The newspaper and its website contained lurid details of an orgy of the claimant with five prostitutes involved in sadomasochist acts. The article was accompanied by a number of photographs extracted from a videotape recorded by one of the prostitutes who concealed a camera in her clothes. An interview of one of the prostitutes was also published on the website—headed as *EXCLUSIVE: MOSLEY HOOKER TELLS ALL: MY NAZI ORGY WITH F1 BOSS*.[299] This attracted another suit. After the original publication, the information about the event spread through other newspapers and on the Internet.

Mosley based his claim, *inter alia*, which is relevant for issues of privacy protection, on the breach of confidence and unauthorised disclosure of personal

[297] Campbell v Mirror Group Newspapers Ltd [2004] UKHL 22, para 125. References omitted.

[298] Mosley v News Group Newspapers [2008] EWHC 1777 (QB), para 01. Note: Max Mosley's father, Oswald Mosley was leader of the British Union of Fascists in the 1930s.

[299] Mosley v News Group Newspapers [2008] EWHC 1777 (QB), para 02.

information. As a result, he regarded his right to respect for privacy as protected under Article 8 of ECHR being infringed.

Justice Eady of the High Court of Justice framed the issues and, with references to post-HRA case law such as *McKennitt v Ash* [2008] and Campbell v MGN, further contributed to the development of the English law on the protection of private information in the shadow of Articles 8 and 10 jurisprudence of the ECtHR. It led him to mention the new methodology for approaching the resolution of such cases in the form of relaxing the requirement for a pre-existing relationship of confidence. According to Justice Eady, "The law now affords protection to information in respect of which there is a reasonable expectation of privacy, even in circumstances where there is no pre-existing relationship giving rise of itself to an enforceable duty of confidence."[300] The judgment asserted that if a reasonable expectation of privacy can be confirmed, the court must carry out the next step of weighing the relevant competing Convention rights in the light of an "intense focus" upon the individual facts of the case. The approach changed the focus to an intensive consideration of all the relevant factors and is definitely against the previous generalised media version, which said that public figures must have less privacy due to their role model position.[301]

Justice Eady followed the Strasbourg steps of finding out the interference to the convention right and then balancing the protected and impaired privacy interests with the countervailing interest, keeping in view the principle of proportionality. Regarding recording and photographing of the intimate acts done at a private property, it is easy to decide that it attracted Article 8 of the Convention.[302] This conclusion led to another step—*the ultimate balancing test*—to find out whether or not the countervailing public interest justified the intrusive behavior of the newspaper concerned. Answering the question of public interest justification of the invasion, Justice Eady considered the possible objectives of public interest. Among them could have been the detection and exposing criminal activities in the instant case. He opined that, even if any significant breach of the criminal law could be discovered, this is not a limitless defence for invasion of privacies of people, as even police cannot install CCTV camera to detect use of illegal drugs in a house. He rejected the plea that Mr. Mosley was inciting or aiding an offence of assault in terms of bodily harm, punishable under the Offences against the Person Act of 1861.[303] Hence, no such sexual offence was committed the exposing and communication of which could serve public interest. The allegation of offences such as the keeping of brothel or Nazi themed acting[304] were not proved. Regarding sexual conduct, the law protects

[300] Mosley v News Group Newspapers [2008] EWHC 1777 (QB), para 07.

[301] Mosley v News Group Newspapers [2008] EWHC 1777 (QB), para 12.

[302] Mosley v News Group Newspapers [2008] EWHC 1777 (QB), para 104.

[303] Lord Justice Eady termed it as the most artificial argument. Mosley v News Group Newspapers [2008] EWHC 1777 (QB) para 113.

[304] Mosley v News Group Newspapers [2008] EWHC 1777 (QB), para 122: "I have come to the conclusion (although others might disagree) that if it really were the case, as the newspaper alleged,

even weird preferences.[305] The Judge held that according to the *new rights-based jurisprudence*, remedies should not be refused for infringements of human rights because some actions of the claimant were distasteful; rather *the private conduct of adults is essentially no-one else's business*.

The Lord Justice goes on to emphasize referring to Strasbourg jurisprudence as:

> When the courts identify an infringement of a person's Article 8 rights, and in particular in the context of his freedom to conduct his sex life and personal relationships as he wishes, it is right to afford a remedy and to vindicate that right. The only permitted exception is where there is a countervailing public interest which in the particular circumstances is strong enough to outweigh it; that is to say, because one at least of the established "limiting principles" comes into play. Was it necessary and proportionate for the intrusion to take place, for example, in order to expose illegal activity or to prevent the public from being significantly misled by public claims hitherto made by the individual concerned (as with Naomi Campbell's public denials of drug-taking)? Or was it necessary because the information, in the words of the Strasbourg court in Von Hannover at [60] and [76], would make a contribution to "a debate of general interest"? That is, of course, a very high test. It is yet to be determined how far that doctrine will be taken in the courts of this jurisdiction in relation to photography in public places. If taken literally, it would mean a very significant change in what is permitted. It would have a profound effect on the tabloid and celebrity culture to which we have become accustomed in recent years.[306]

To answer the question as *who* has to decide what can possibly be sufficient public interest so that to justify a privacy invasion, Lord Justice Eady made an extensive referral to case law on the matter and concluded that it has to be determined solely by the court *ex post facto*.[307]

Lord Justice Eady also tackled the question of the calculation of damages as,

> [i]t is well established that an award of exemplary damages may only be made in circumstances where an element of punishment is thought appropriate by the court *and* the amount

---

that the Claimant had for entertainment and sexual gratification been "mocking the humiliating way the Jews were treated", or "parodying Holocaust horrors", there could be a public interest in that being revealed at least to those in the FIA to whom he is accountable. He has to deal with many people of all races and religions, and has spoken out against racism in the sport. If he really were behaving in the way I have just described, that would, for many people, call seriously into question his suitability for his FIA role. It would be information which people arguably should have the opportunity to know and evaluate. It is probably right to acknowledge that private fantasies should not in themselves be subjected to legal scrutiny by the courts, but when they are acted out that is not necessarily so."

305 Mosley v News Group Newspapers [2008] EWHC 1777 (QB), para 127: "it is not for the state or for the media to expose sexual conduct which does not involve any significant breach of the criminal law. That is so whether the motive for such intrusion is merely prurience or a moral crusade. It is not for journalists to undermine human rights, or for judges to refuse to enforce them, merely on grounds of taste or moral disapproval. Everyone is naturally entitled to espouse moral or religious beliefs to the effect that certain types of sexual behavior are wrong or demeaning to those participating. That does not mean that they are entitled to hound those who practise them or to detract from their right to live life as they choose."

306 Mosley v News Group Newspapers [2008] EWHC 1777 (QB), para 131.

307 Mosley v News Group Newspapers [2008] EWHC 1777 (QB), para 171.

> to be awarded by way of compensation (including aggravated damages) is not sufficient to serve a punitive as well as a compensatory function.[308]

He arrived at £60,000 as award for damages for the invasion of Mosley's his right to privacy.

The judgments in the landmark cases in the post-HRA privacy law have shown that the judiciary is trying its best to make their approach compatible with the law of the ECtHR in order to fulfil the statutory requirement under the HRA. There is no doubt that the reference to the EctHR-jurisprudence had influenced UK's privacy law in the form of an enhanced protection to privacy on the one hand and also in the shape of a nuanced balancing technique on the other hand. However, the lack of a strong constitutional foundation of their tort-based actions is a major reason for uncertainty in this area of law. Scholars are of the view that the tort of breach of confidence cannot be stretched to the extent to provide comprehensive protection to most of the privacy-related interests as opposed to the recognition of a general right to privacy.

6.2.6 *Analysis: Can the Extension of Breach of Confidence Be an Alternative to a Full-Fledged Privacy Tort?*

Even before the coming into force of the HRA, Sir Brian Neil, appreciates the optimism of the judiciary regarding better protection of privacy under the tort of breach of confidence. He, however, expresses his dissatisfaction over the future practice of giving confidential information a *prima-facie* right to protection.[309] He proposed that any such approach should work as a simpler route towards the development of the right to privacy, particularly, the focus should be on the nature of information and not on the duty of confidence. "Such a development will also emphasise that one is trying to safeguard the dignity and privacy of the individual rather than the confidentiality of his private communication."[310] He expresses his apprehension that the extension of the breach of confidence will not protect some privacy interests such as the right to one's publicity. He concludes:

> I hope and anticipate that once the Convention has been incorporated into English law the courts will become increasingly willing to give effect to the principles underlying it. In time therefore the dignity of the individual should assume a fresh importance and, though the freedom of speech and the freedom of the media will remain very powerful counterweights, I hope that in appropriate cases they will not be allowed to act the part of trump cards. There may be lessons to be learned from the jurisprudence of other countries that in this field as in

[308] Mosley v News Group Newspapers [2008] EWHC 1777 (QB), para 176. He ruled that exemplary damages were not admissible in privacy infringements case due to absence of statutory or common law authority/precedents, and also due to fear of failure of the test of necessity and proportionality.

[309] Neill (1999), pp. 27–28.

[310] Neill (1999), pp. 27–28.

> others the courts must seek to balance conflicting rights and try to find the point of equilibrium.[311]

Markesinis *et al* have presented a detailed analysis of the legal developments of English privacy law in the post-HRA jurisprudence. They have expressed their *concerns* as "the incremental, pragmatic approach to protecting privacy via the fig-leaf of confidence is distorting and obscuring the need for a principle-led approach."[312] According to them,

> the reliance on confidentiality to address privacy issues instead of developing a proper tort of privacy has so far prevented the courts from addressing these questions as carefully as they should. This lack of clarity demonstrates the conceptual distortions induced by reliance on confidentiality as opposed to a more explicitly privacy-orientated approach.[313]

In the post-HRA cases of A v. B plc and Campbell, public interest was discussed as an interest connected to freedom of expression. Public interest in the publication of private information was inappropriately juxtaposed with the private interests of the plaintiffs to protect their privacy. To Markesinis et al, "there is also a public interest in protecting personal privacy";[314] while privacy protection also ensures other vital public good such as the societal interest in the rehabilitation of criminal or protecting individuals from undue harassment.[315]

They conclude their article with the following critical remarks:

> Indeed, it could even be seen as a capitulation before lazy assumptions as to the impossibility of defining a tort of privacy, couched in the language of pragmatism and deference to Parliament. If this was acceptable thirty years ago, it does not seem so now given the clear requirement imposed by the Human Rights Act for the courts to give effect in the common law to the principles and values explicitly protected in the ECHR, including the Article 8 privacy guarantee. Thus, instead of a principled approach based upon the recognition of privacy, the Law Lords have opted for the timid, obfuscating approach that has repeatedly been proved flawed, lacks clarity, and produces more not less litigation.[. . .] the reliance upon the law of confidence is likely to prove misguided and incapable of protecting the private life of individuals from illegitimate intrusion.[316]

Gavin Phillipson has also shown his reservations about the 'judicial ambivalence' towards the introduction of the legal right of privacy into English law. He opines such an approach as inadequate "both normatively and structurally."[317] He asserts:

---

[311] Neill (1999), p. 28.

[312] Markesinis et al. (2004), p. 172: "Wishful hankering for a factual approach that does not bother with issues of principle or foreign comparative material is likely to ensure greater confusion, a longer and more tortuous process of developing the law. . ."

[313] Markesinis et al. (2004), p. 153.

[314] Markesinis et al. (2004), p. 157.

[315] Markesinis et al. (2004), p. 158.

[316] Markesinis et al. (2004), p. 206.

[317] Phillipson (2003), p. 726.

> the failure to locate definitively the doctrinal status of Article 8 in the common law has, [.....] resulted in a lingering attachment to principles and values deriving not from privacy, but from orthodox notions of confidentiality that has continued to dog efforts to delineate clearly the new style action in confidence from the old. Perhaps most importantly of all, the courts continue to exhibit this deep ambivalence towards the place and value of privacy in English law in their determination to treat the right to private life merely as a narrowly construed and grudgingly recognised exception to press freedom.[318]

Though English judiciary now uses the terminology of the misuse of private information, its origin is undoubtedly connected to the breach of confidence tort, which cannot be ignored. Breach of confidence tort is an equitable action which is based on good faith. It attempts to protect informational privacy, while the claims for damages in such cases are mostly focusing on pecuniary considerations rather than on rectifying a dignitarian harm. It is argued that this approach would make it difficult for ordinary individuals to precisely balance free speech and privacy and that it has the potential to "undermine structural underpinnings of the law of tort" if human rights principles are applied to private law.[319] So far, this approach has failed to answer many questions, for example, whether this new tort is limited to information misuse or mere intrusion or retrieval of information without publication would also be an actionable infringement. Though the English courts have demonstrated an apparent generosity in relaxing the conditions of a pre-existing confidential relationship in privacy-related claims, yet one sees the limitation of this 'generosity' in some cases.

Coherence is one of the essential characteristics of any legal regime in a given jurisdiction as well as in a given area of law. It needs to be determined whether the "shoehorning" approach of protecting the broad right to privacy from the new misuse of private information brings such coherence in the application of common law or not. Studies have shown that in this area of law, "legislative intervention is not only desirable, but necessary."[320]

References

Albers M (2005) Informationelle Selbstbestimmung. Nomos Verlagsgesellschaft mbH & Co. KG

Arden LJ (2012) Media intrusion and human rights: striking the balance - public lecture. Cardiff Law School, p 11

Barak A (1996) Constitutional human rights and private law. Rev Const Stud 3:218

Brggemeier G (2006) Constitutionalisation of private law-the German perspective. In: Barkhuysen T, Lindenbergh S (eds) Constitutionalisation of private law. Brill Nijhoff

[318] Phillipson (2003), p. 758.

[319] Giliker (2015), p. 783: "this will not resolve the current conceptual confusion as to the interests this tort will seek to protect, its content or future direction."

[320] Giliker (2015), p. 783.

Bröhmer J, Hill C, Spitzkatz M, Wahiduddin S (eds) (2012) 60 years German basic law: the German constitution and its court. The Malaysian Current Law Journal Sdn Bhd

Buckland W, McNair AD (1952) Roman law and common law: a comparison in outline. Cambridge University Press

Bumke C, Voßkuhle A (2019) German constitutional law: introduction, cases, and principles. Oxford University Press

Burrows A (2002) We do this at common law but that in equity. Oxf J Leg Stud 22(1):1–16

Cremer HJ (2010) Human rights and the protection of privacy in tort law: a comparison between English and German law. Routledge-Cavendish

David R, Brierley JE (1978) Major legal systems in the world today: an introduction to the comparative study of law. Simon and Schuster

Deacon D (2004) Politicians, privacy and media intrusion in Britain. Parliam Aff 57(1):9

Dicey AV (1982) Introduction to the study of the law of the constitution. Liberty Classics

Fenwick H, Phillipson G (1996) Confidence and privacy: a re-examination. Camb Law J 55(3):447

Giliker P (2015) A common law tort of privacy? The challenges of developing human rights tort. SAcLJ 27:761

Grimm D (1995) Die Meinungsfreiheit in der Rechtsprechung des Bundesverfassungsgerichts. Neue Juristische Wochenschrift, pp 1697 ff

Grimm D (2007) Proportionality in Canadian and German constitutional jurisprudence. Univ Toronto Law J 57:383

Hirsh A (2020) Black Britons know why Meghan Markle wants out: it's the racism. Daily New York Times https://www.nytimes.com/2020/01/09/opinion/sunday/meghan-markle-prince-harry.html. Accessed 27 Aug 2023

Hoffmeister F (2006) Germany: status of European Convention on Human Rights in domestic law. Int J Constit Law 4:722

Jouanjan O (2009) Freedom of expression in the federal republic of Germany. Ind Law J 84:867

Kommers DP, Miller RA (2012) The constitutional jurisprudence of the Federal Republic of Germany. Duke University Press

Krause HD (1965) Right to privacy in Germany - Pointer's for American legislation. Duke LJ 481

Lehman JA (1968) The right to privacy in Germany. N Y Univ J Int Polit 1:106

Markesinis B (1990) Our patchy law of privacy—time to do something about it. Mod Law Rev 53: 802

Markesinis B (1999) Privacy, freedom of expression, and the horizontal effect of the Human Rights Bill: lessons from Germany. Law Q Rev 47

Markesinis B, Unberath H (2002) The German law of torts: a comparative treatise. Hart Publishing

Markesinis B, O'Cinneide C, Fedtke J, Hunter-Henin M (2004) Concerns and ideas about the developing English law of privacy (and how knowledge of foreign law might be of help). Am J Comp Law 1:133

Neill B (1962) The protection of privacy. Mod Law Rev 25:393

Neill B (1999) Privacy: a challenge for the next century. In: Protecting privacy. Oxford University Press

Nettesheim M (2011) Grundrechtsschutz der Privatheit. Veröffentlichungen der Vereinigung der Deutschen Staatsrechtslehrer 70

Phillipson G (2003) Transforming breach of confidence? Towards a common law right of privacy under the Human Rights Act. Mod Law Rev 66(5):726

Phillipson G, Fenwick H (2000) Breach of confidence as a privacy remedy in the human rights act era. Mod Law Rev 63(5):662–663

Schwartz PM, Peifer KN (2010) Prosser's "Privacy" and the German right of personality: are four privacy torts better than one unitary concept? Calif Law Rev 1:1925

Stoll H (1999) The general right to personality in German law. In: Markesinis B (ed) Protecting privacy. Oxford University Press
Vahrenwald A (1994) Photographs and privacy in Germany. Entertain Law Rev 6(5):205
Wacks R (2013) Privacy and media freedom. Oxford University Press
Wilson W (1990) Privacy, confidence and press freedom: study in judicial activism. Mod Law Rev 53(1):43–56

Chapter 7
Recommendations: A Privacy Law for Pakistan

The width and depth of privacy violations by the media in Pakistan, in particular the gravity of media intrusion into the privacy of vulnerable people, have been pointed out in the second chapter of this research. After having dealt in detail with the theoretical foundations of privacy and having analyzed both the protection of privacy and freedom of expression in the Constitution of Pakistan and the conflict regulation frameworks in the ECHR, Germany, and UK, we are now capable of presenting concrete recommendations, based on the findings of the previous chapters, for the protection of privacy interests as well as for the balancing mechanism to resolve conflicts of privacy with other interests, especially free speech and public interest. This research proposes that the legal protection of the right to privacy through an act of parliament is the only effective way to resolve the problems highlighted in the course of this research.

In order to present concrete recommendations, it is a prerequisite to look deep into the existing legal instruments and to find out the nature of legal gap which must be filled by the proposed privacy law in Pakistan. The proposed law reform endeavor will codify a variety of privacy infringements as actionable wrongs, where it would become possible for the aggrieved persons to compensate the harm afflicted on their legally protected interests. Our extensive account of different theories about the concept of privacy has revealed that privacy has not only strong moral roots but also performs a number of important functions.[1] Due to its inherent and instrumental value, the proposed law reform for the protection of privacy is not amenable to any sort of theoretical repudiation. Furthermore, the comparative analysis of the similar legal problems supports the plausibility of the proposal of legislative intervention. Jurisdictions that can be consulted for comparative analysis offer, as we have seen in previous chapters of this book, a valuable guidance for, among others, the proposed protective mechanism in terms of the demarcation of the scope of the right to

[1] See Chap. 3 of this book.

S. Aftab, *Comparative Perspectives on the Right to Privacy*, Ius Gentium: Comparative Perspectives on Law and Justice 109,
https://doi.org/10.1007/978-3-031-45575-9_7

privacy, the identification of concrete areas of its protection, balancing mechanisms of the countervailing interests as well as the nature of remedies which should be available to the complainants.

The first part of this chapter will look at the possibility of a piecemeal protection of privacy under the existing Pakistani laws and will highlight different provisions which could possibly be invoked for the protection of specific privacy interests. It will also present the obstructive elements of laws where either the wording of a legal instrument or the legal theory of an area of law frustrates the effectiveness of such invocation attempts. Finally, it highlights the fact that statutory protection is the best solution to the privacy problems in Pakistan. The second part explains guiding principles for the proposed statute. These principles are developed after using the findings from our analysis of both the privacy theories as well as the comparative model jurisdictions of ECHR, Germany and the United Kingdom. The part concludes with proposals for remedies for breaches of privacy.

7.1 The Possibility of an Appropriate Privacy Protection Under Existing Norms

7.1.1 Revisiting the Constitutional Foundations for Privacy Protection

Even though there are only limited normative anchors on privacy in the text of the Pakistani Constitution, the jurisprudence, in particular on Article 9 and Article 14 (1) of the Constitution of Pakistan, has used the existing normative anchors for a broader understanding of their scope of protection and recognized the need for privacy protection. The Supreme Court of Pakistan draws on the liberal and dynamic interpretation of the fundamental rights and insists on extending maximum benefits of the constitutional guarantees to the citizens.[2] As a result, the right to privacy is covered to a certain extent by the protection available through the right to life. Article 9 is an open ended guarantee to a variety of vital interests related to human beings as the term 'life' in the Constitution has not been used in a restricted and pedantic manner such as 'to be alive'. Rather, this article protects the basic enjoyment of life as well as maintaining an adequate level of living with the guarantee of freedom and basic rights.[3] Furthermore, the right to life is not only enshrined *per se* but it has been declared as a prerequisite for the protection of other fundamental rights.[4] In the case of Article 14 (1), it also provides an indirect protection against

[2] See Sect. 4.2.2.1 for a detailed elaboration and analysis of Benazir Bhutto case.

[3] See Sect. 4.2.2.1.

[4] See Sect. 4.2.2.2 for elaboration of the word "life" by Supreme Court of Pakistan in Shehla Zia case.

eavesdropping, surreptitious tapping or photographic by state authorities for the purpose of obtaining evidence or for nabbing those involved in immoral activities.[5]

In the nutshell, there is nothing in the Constitution of Pakistan, which disregards the right to privacy or prohibits its statutory protection. The broad understanding that can be drawn from the case law provides a foundation to legislation on the relevant rights and obligations. We have also discussed that the right to free speech is subject to a variety of limitations and legal reservations.[6] Thus, the proposal presented here for the statutory recognition as well as effective protection of the general right to privacy will not generate any constitutional dilemma and it is in accordance with the spirit of constitutional rights if these are construed in a comprehensive manner. In particular, the law of privacy will work as a concretization of the rights to life, human dignity and privacy of home provided in Article 9 and Article 14 (1) of the Constitution of Pakistan.

7.1.2 The Treatment of Privacy-Related Interests in Different Legal Instruments

In the following, a survey of relevant laws is given with a doctrinal outlook. These laws have a potential to be invoked against privacy infringements. It is important to see whether or not, and to what extent the right to privacy which also has, as we have seen, its place in the catalogue of fundamental rights of the Constitution of Pakistan has been translated into the legal protection of its various components.

7.1.2.1 Intrusion into Privacy and Trespass Law

The tort of intrusion is one of the four 'distinct' torts under the rubric of the right to privacy. William Prosser describes it as "Intrusion upon the plaintiff's seclusion or solitude, or into his private affairs" and that the interest protected by the intrusion tort is a mental one, which usefully fills the gap left by trespass, nuisance and intentional infliction of mental distress.[7] According to Edward Bloustein, "intrusion is demeaning to individuality, is an affront to personal dignity".[8] The tort of intrusion upon

[5] See Sect. 4.2.1 for case law reference.

[6] See Sect. 4.3.3 for constitutional restraints on the exercise of the right to free speech.

[7] See Sect. 3.5.1.1 for Prosser's conceptualization of privacy.

[8] Bloustein (1964), p. 973. See Sect. 3.3.3.2 for details about Bloustein's conceptualization of privacy as an aspect of human dignity.

seclusion was inspired[9] by Warren and Brandeis who underscored the importance of privacy, solitude and sensitivity to publicity in their famous article on privacy.[10]

The Pakistan Penal Code mentions the act of intrusion only where it is committed for the purpose of insulting the modesty of a woman.[11] No legal remedy is available for intrusion where its outcome is the invasion of privacy only.

The act of intrusion has some resemblance with the trespass. Both are, however, different concepts. As a successor of the British common law system, the criminal law in Pakistan covers the common law's concept of trespassing into someone else's house, chattels and other immovable property such as land. According to Pakistan Penal Code,

> Whoever enters into or upon *property in the possession of another* with intent to commit an *offence* or to intimidate, insult or *annoy* any person in possession of such property, or, having lawfully entered into or upon such property, unlawfully remains there with intent thereby to intimidate, insult or *annoy* any such person, or with intent to commit an offence, is said to commit "criminal trespass."[12]

The requirement of possession shows that it is an associated right attached to the right to property. Secondly, it pre-requires the prevalence of *mens rea* or criminal intent on the part of the trespasser.

To some scholars, the remedy for a violation of privacy can be found *inter alia* in trespass actions.[13] However, the generally accepted view is that privacy intrusion and trespassing into property are quite different concepts. The latter is a concept of property right which is deemed as an unauthorized interference in the enjoyment of proprietary rights, in the manner of attached to, ancillary, or consequential to the ownership of a house, land and chattels. On the other hand, intrusion into privacy has a constitutional dimension and, as earlier stated, a linkage with the very core of dignity and the general personality right.

Nevertheless, the remedy for both the wrongs could be coincided as it has been typically in vogue in common law cases.[14] According to Lord Mance, trespass is nearer to privacy in many "things that we regard as essentially private, we do or say

---

[9] See Sect. 3.4.2 for details about Solove's taxonomy of privacy.

[10] See Sect. 3.3.1.1 for a detailed exposition of Warren and Brandeis conception of privacy as a "right to be let alone".

[11] According to Section 509 of Pakistan Penal Code: "Whoever, intending to insult the modesty of any woman, utters any word, makes any sound or gesture, or exhibits any object, intending that such word or sound shall be heard, or that such gesture or object shall be seen, by such woman, or intrudes upon the privacy of such woman, shall be punished with simple imprisonment for a term which may extend to one year, or with fine, or with both".

[12] Section 441, Pakistan Penal Code Act XLV of 1860. Emphasis supplied. Lurking house trespass has been define in Section 443 of Pakistan Penal Code as, "*Whoever commits house-trespass having taken precautions to conceal such house-trespass from some person who has a right to exclude or eject the trespasser from the building, tent or vessel which is the subject of the trespass, is said to commit "lurking house-trespass.""*

[13] See for example: Davis (1959).

[14] See for details: Gerety (1977), p. 233.

in our own homes away from the public eye".[15] Still, trespass is capable only of protecting property rights and the legal interests attached to that property. The action under trespass law provides no protection to a person who is not entitled to the proprietary rights of a house or land where the intrusion takes place. For example a visitor to another person's property such as the home or gym owned by the second person would not be entitled to a claim for intrusion into his privacy under trespass law even if the owner has installed a secret camera and films the visitor. Thus trespass law "provides no protection against modern, long-distance means of scrutiny, by acoustic detection or telephoto lens."[16]

A survey of the Pakistani case law during this research could not find a single instance where a media person has been charged under the penal provisions of trespass law. The inbuilt practical difficulties in the trespass law and a huge conceptual variance are the reasons why trespass law cannot be applied against media persons. Practically, the determination of specific intent on the part of the trespasser has been articulated in the penal provisions. Therefore, the intrusive newsgathering activities cannot be incriminated under trespass law because of the fact that the absence of criminal intention is a strong defense.

The peculiar characteristics of the Pakistani society suggest that intrusion must be considered as a strict liability offence where the presence or absence of a particular intent or even negligence is immaterial and the mere intrusive act is punishable *per se*. The nature and gravity of harm due to a privacy violation, its prevalence and frequency in the media landscape in Pakistan as well as an overwhelming urgency for a strict legal regime are some of the important factors that demand such a legal approach. [17] The use of secret cameras, entering without permission with concealed identities and deceiving the dweller by impersonation carry with itself immense harm, more than the one against which the property law concept of trespass protects. The amount of fine and punishment for trespass in the Code shows that it is regarded merely as a kind of inconvenience to the otherwise enjoyment of proprietary rights.[18] On the other hand, intrusion into privacy needs a much more comprehensive approach due to the magnitude of harm it may bring.

It is obvious that trespass law is not meant for application in media excesses cases. It is neither practicable nor intended for that purpose and has never been invoked against intruding paparazzi. The right to privacy is linked to the dignity and personality rights of an individual. The legislative intention behind trespass provisions does not seem to be making it for the protection of the right to privacy. Trespass provisions are aimed to protect proprietary rights rather than the personality related interests. Due to this reason a nominal punishment has been prescribed for a

---

[15] Mance (2009), p. 268.

[16] Mance (2009), p. 268.

[17] See for details: Restatement (Second) of Torts (1977), clause 520. See also: Solove and Schwartz (2012).

[18] As for the punishment of criminal trespass is concerned, it is imprisonment for 3 months or a fine of Rs. 1500/- or both according to Section 447 of Pakistan Penal Code.

trespasser.[19] On the other hand, the punishment for a serious criminal intrusion of privacy is much higher even in the liberal countries such as the United States, which has a more liberal approach towards privacy.[20]

The risk to human life and liberty due to a violation of privacy is all the more in Pakistan.[21] The intrusion into private life can only be minimized if serious intrusion into the privacy of other person is legislated as a criminal offence.

7.1.2.2 Regulation of Surveillance

Surveillance of citizens conducted by the government primarily for security purposes is regarded as a challenge to individual autonomy and civil liberties. Many measures of the government come under the ambit of surveillance such as visual monitoring through CCTV cameras, which observe people's movement and physical activities in the public places, phone tapping, internet data monitoring, online communication analysis and data mining. Surveillance in the shape of CCTV monitoring, phone tapping and profiling has always been a concern to the majority of legal scholars, judges, jurists and human rights activists. It is condemned even in the United States despite the fact that Americans have great sensitivity for their security after 9/11. The sarcastic BIG BROTHER IS WATCHING YOU expression, coined by George Orwell in his masterpiece "1984", has become popular for government surveillance, which links surveillance to digital dictatorship and a hegemonic character of the modern public policies.

There are many evils, both instant and potential, associated with surveillance. Surveillance is a modern system of social control, which has chilling effects at the individual and societal level. It diminishes the originality of human thought processes as well as disrupts his routine activities. Surveillance creates a feeling of discomfort, confusion and unknown fear. Potentially, the monitoring through CCTV and other surveillance methods could be used as a tool to oppress other important rights and liberties such as freedom of speech, freedom of movement and freedom of association. To Professor Nissenbaum, it "constitutes injustice and even tyranny".[22] Quoting Allen Westin, Solove remarks that surveillance is harmful in both public and private settings; and that not only the actual surveillance but also the fear of surveillance forces the people to modify their actual behavior.[23] Similarly, Schwartz

---

[19] Three months imprisonment or Rs. 1500 fine.

[20] See for example New Jersy V. Dharum Ravi where, in an intrusion case, the defendant was convicted with 30 days in jail, 300 h of community service, 3 years' probation and 10,000$ fine by the trial court. Note: The judgment has been recently suspended with an order for fresh trial by the appellate court.

[21] For details see Chap. 2 of this book.

[22] Nissenbaum (2004). See Sect. 3.4.1 for the understanding as how the disregard for the contextual integrity during information processing may amount to surveillance.

[23] Solove (2008), pp. 106–112. Also see Sect. 3.3.2 for surveillance as a major problem of privacy and its practical evils.

has also voiced his concerns regarding potential threats to society at large. He asserts that "[w]hen widespread and secret surveillance becomes the norm, the act of speaking or listening takes on a different social meaning."[24]

The Supreme Court of Pakistan has also declared unconstitutional every state's activity which amounts to surveillance and where no prior court order is obtained.[25]

Due to the poor law and order situation coupled with the lack of awareness among masses regarding their rights, a tacit approval exists to different methods of surveillance in Pakistan. Therefore, the direction of the Court took many years to be complied with through passing an appropriate law. Currently, the Investigation for Fair Trial Act of 2013 provides detailed procedures for surveillance and interception. It regulates the powers of law enforcement and investigative agencies by authorizing them to collect evidence through the use of "modern techniques and devices" only for the scheduled crimes which include terrorism and anti-state activities.[26] The prior warrant of the court is a prerequisite for surveillance activities undertaken by security agencies. Accordingly, the application is made by a high ranking officer to the relevant high court after it is being approved by the minister, along with the necessary record of the suspicious conduct. After consideration of the record, the judge may issue the surveillance warrant and can also modify the conditions related to it.

The enactment of this law is a positive step in the direction of taking the right to privacy seriously as it provides a preventive mechanism for state surveillance. However, the strict confidentiality regarding the warrants of surveillance and the whole procedure is obstructive to an authentic analysis about its efficacy and transparency. No data is available to ascertain how many people under surveillance were actually involved in the "scheduled offences".[27] Secondly, the laws that provide a basis for surveillance contain very broad definitions for 'anti-national activities'. For instance, The Prevention of Anti-National Activities Act 1974 defines "anti-national activity" as "anything done by such individual or association, whether by committing an act or (i) which is intended, or supports any claim, to bring about, on any ground whatsoever, the secession of a part of the territory of Pakistan from the Federation, or which incites any individual or group of individuals to bring about secession. . ."[28] This construction has an immense potential of political abuse.[29] At times, a mere criticism of some governmental policy is interpreted as against the national interest and the person or association is then dubbed as 'anti-national'.

---

[24] Schwartz (1999), p. 1651.

[25] See Sect. 4.2.2.1 for the detailed considerations of the Supreme Court of Pakistan regarding surveillance in Benazir Bhutto case.

[26] See the preamble of The Investigation for Fair Trial Act 2013.

[27] The Schedule I is annexed to the Investigation for Fair Trial Act 2013 which contain several laws prohibiting anti-national and terrorist activities.

[28] Section 2 The Prevention of Anti-National Activities Act, 1974.

[29] See the views of Human Rights Commission of Pakistan's Secretary General views on such laws: Rehman (2015) Laws cut out for abuse. *Daily Dawn* (Online 19 February 2015). https://www.dawn.com/news/1164460. Accessed 28 August 2023.

A major shortcoming of this law is that it does not provide any remedy for the person who is being subjected to surveillance in contravention of the procedure provided by this law. This is an example of the lack of effective protection of the right to be let alone, which is usually available against the state interference.

The existing surveillance law does not provide for any balancing mechanism between the fundamental right of privacy against the state's security interests. It is understandable that if a well-established constitutional right to protection against the state intrusion into the seclusion of people is not effectively remedied, the problem of media intrusion is even more complex. It involves conflicting interests of private parties, which requires a more sophisticated approach to tackle the balancing challenge of these interests. Media in Pakistan also uses interception devices and all the possible surreptitious methods of newsgathering but there is no law to regulate such activities.[30] The procedural requirements in the Investigation for Fair Trial Act are strictly for the purpose of regulating state's security agencies' behavior in their collection of information, but this law cannot be invoked against the media for their so-called investigative journalism.

The privacy threats associated with all forms of stalking and spying must be addressed through comprehensive legislation that allows for a balance between various aspects of the right to privacy and other crucial public interests, such as freedom of speech..

7.1.2.3 Privacy of Home and Search and Seizure Regulation

The right to privacy and dignity of man entail the protection from illegal searches by the police and other state agencies. In some countries, constitutional protection has been granted against unnecessary searches and the forfeiture of private property.[31] The purpose of search and seizure regulation is protecting private personalities and properties from actions of public authorities just like trespass law provides protection from other private parties.

The Constitution of Pakistan provides no express protection from unreasonable search and seizure, except in the manner of a general commitment to the rule law i.e. declaring that everyone shall be treated in accordance with law[32] and her/his entitlement to due process.[33] The Code of Criminal Procedure (Act of 1898) contained the procedure for search. It authorizes the court to issue a search warrant if there is reason to believe that the summoned person would not provide documents or any other evidentiary material he possesses and where the presentation of such

---

[30] See Chap. 2 for details.

[31] See for example 4th Amendment of US Constitution (protection against unreasonable searches and seizures) as well as Article 13 (inviolability of home) and Article 10 (privacy of correspondence, posts and telecommunications) of the German Basic Law.

[32] Article 4 of the Constitution of Pakistan.

[33] Article 10A of the Constitution of Pakistan.

documents has an evidentiary value in the adjudicating process.[34] The magistrate can also authorize the police officer through issuance of warrant to search any place which is used for depositing stolen property, activity of forgery and for "the deposit, sale, manufacture or production of any obscene object".[35] The same provision also authorizes the police to seize the property, documents and seals.[36] Furthermore, the person who is in charge of the subject place is under legal obligation to cooperate with the police in terms of facilitating their entry.[37] The search operation shall be made in the presence of "two or more respectable inhabitants of the locality" and can also be attended by the occupants of the place.[38] The relevant police officer can also conduct search without the pre-required warrant where he has "reasonable grounds to believe" that any material in connection to the investigation could be found only if a timely action is being undertaken.[39] The concerned police officer is required to record the grounds and details of the searching action.

In spite of the availability of legal provisions, the abuse of power on the part of police officials is a common phenomenon.[40] The police usually enter the house without a warrant and intimation to the inhabitants. They take advantage of Section 165 and justify their actions on the basis of 'urgency'. The Police Order 2002, which aims to regulate the police department and to make them service-oriented and accountable to the people through redefining their duties and responsibilities, has become ineffective in curbing police accesses.[41] Though police laws provide penalty against the violation of unlawful search and seizures,[42] yet due to a powerful institution and weak citizenry, these laws are only black letters and nothing more.

Just like the law of fair trial and investigative procedures, the provisions related to search and seizure are irrelevant for the problems of privacy in Pakistan elaborated in Chap. 2. The entry of media people into private premises is not regulated by any law in Pakistan. They enter public places such as hotels, massage parlors, video-rental shops, and restaurants in order to record footages and obtain content for their so-called investigative programs.

---

[34] Section 96 of Code of Criminal Procedure (Act of 1898).

[35] Section 98 of Code of Criminal Procedure (Act of 1898).

[36] Section 98(1)(C) of Code of Criminal Procedure (Act of 1898).

[37] Section 102 of Code of Criminal Procedure (Act of 1898).

[38] Section 102 of Code of Criminal Procedure (Act of 1898).

[39] Section 165 of Code of Criminal Procedure (Act of 1898).

[40] Justice Project Pakistan, *Abuse of Juveniles by the Faisalabad Police,* Allard K. Lowenstein International Human Rights Clinic (Yale Law School, June 2014).

[41] Human Rights Watch Report, *This Crooked system-Police Abuse and Reform in Pakistan* (2016).

[42] See for example, Punjab Police Order 2013, Section 156, (i.e. "Penalty for vexatious entry, search, arrest, seizure of property, torture").

7.1.2.4 Publication of Private Facts and Defamation

The interests related to human reputation are covered by defamation law in Pakistan. However, there is no law or tort based legal action available to victims of privacy violations in order to rectify their damage as a result of publications revealing intimate or private information.

The common law tort of defamation has been codified in a statutory form in Pakistan, which is called Defamation Ordinance of 2002. Like many countries of the world, the criminal law also covers defamatory offenses and makes them punishable with imprisonment and fine. A person feeling defamed has the option to initiate either civil or criminal or both proceedings. Seeking remedy under one statute does not jeopardize the right of the person to apply for another legal dispensation.

Privacy and reputation are both aspects of human dignity and linked to personality rights.[43] Some kind of procedural overlapping might be observed during the balancing exercise with free speech, public interest or journalistic privilege of newsgathering and dissemination of information. However, the nature of both reputational wrong and privacy wrong is different and it cannot be assumed that the laws meant for the protection of reputational interests could be invoked to protect the interests in privacy. In defamation cases, the truth of the matter that causes reputational harm is an absolute defense against a defamation suit. On the other hand, the revelation of true private information may provide a solid ground for legal action. A commentator clarifies this overlap as,

> Because its principles are designed to protect a fundamentally different legal interest, reputation, defamation law does not readily accommodate privacy protection as one of its aims or rationales. Defamation law should prevent people making false and disparaging statements about others in public; privacy law should allow individuals to control what true, but private, information about themselves is disseminated in public and what remains private. Any privacy protection afforded by defamation law has been or should be incidental or indirect at best. [.....] Properly understood, it is not the function of defamation law to protect a plaintiff's privacy.[44]

Another scholar emphasizes,

> In defamation law only statements that are false are actionable; truth is, almost universally, a defense. In privacy law, other than in the false light cases, the facts published are true; indeed it is the very truth of the facts that creates the claimed invasion of privacy. Secondly, in defamation cases the interest sought to be protected is the objective one of reputation, either economic, political, or personal, in the outside world. In privacy cases the interest affected is the subjective one of injury to the inner person. Thirdly, in defamation cases, where the issue is truth or falsity, the marketplace of ideas furnishes a forum in which the battle can be fought. In privacy cases, resort to the marketplace simply accentuates the injury.[45]

---

[43] See Chap. 3 for the concept of privacy in general and Sect. 3.3.2 for the concept of privacy as control over personal information.

[44] Rolph (2007), p. 3.

[45] Emerson (1979), p. 333.

The utterance or publication of content that damages reputation is regulated under the civil and penal laws of defamation. In case of defamation, Pakistan Penal Code (PPC) provides for criminal proceedings under Sections 499–502; while civil remedy could be sought under Defamation Ordinance of 2002. Both Defamation Ordinance and PPC define defamation in their own ways and have no mention for privacy.

Defamation is defined under the civil law as,

> any wrongful act or publication or circulation of a false statement or representation made orally or in written or visual form which injures the reputation of a person, tends to lower him in the estimation of others or tends to reduce him to ridicule, unjust criticism, dislike, contempt or hatred shall be actionable as defamation.[46]

Pakistan Penal Code defines defamation as,

> Whoever by words either spoken or intended to be read, or by signs or by visible representations, makes or publishes any imputation concerning any person intending to harm, or knowing or having reason to believe that such imputation will harm, the reputation of such person, is said except in the cases hereinafter excepted, to defame that person.[47]

These definitions clearly mention the requirement of falsity of the defamatory act or utterance. The truthfulness of any publication and oral statement is a valid defense under both criminal and civil law statutes. It is deviating from privacy torts where truthfulness and tendency of harm in the alleged act cannot be invoked as a material defense.

However, the case law pertaining to defamation can be useful for assessing privacy cases due to the relevancy of jurisprudence on the defenses such as assent, public interest or privileged communication. Similarly, the criteria used in defamation cases for the calculation of damages can also work as a guideline for privacy wrongs.

7.1.2.5 Data Protection Regime

Data protection is an important area which is related to the notion of informational privacy. It has now been granted a status of a full-fledged fundamental right in important legal instruments such as the General Data Protection Regulation of the European Union and the Convention for the Protection of Individuals with regard to Automatic Processing of Personal Data of the Council of Europe.[48] Moreover, legal scholarship also favors the recognition of data protection as a fundamental right

[46] Defamation Ordinance 2002, section 3.

[47] Pakistan Penal Code (Code XLV of 1860), Section 499.

[48] According to Article 1 of the Convention for the Protection of Individuals with regard to Automatic Processing of Personal Data, "The purpose of this Convention is to secure in the territory of each Party for every individual, whatever his nationality or residence, respect for his rights and fundamental freedoms, and in particular his right to privacy, with regard to automatic processing of personal data relating to him ("data protection")."

"next to privacy".[49] In some respects, data protection is more broad-based than privacy particularly in terms of its functions. In contrast to a general privacy right, data protection requires more sophisticated laws and institutional measures for its effective enforcement. The functional objectives of data protection laws are not only to protect informational privacy but also to ensure transparency in the collection, processing and dissemination of data. Regardless of whether data protection is recognized as an independent right or as an aspect of a broader privacy right, its instrumental value is well received in the courts of law around the world.[50]

The advent of the internet and modern communication technologies and devices carry an immense amount of data ranging from non-significant to highly sensitive bits of information. It has significantly attracted the activists, academia and policy makers to formulate some kind of regulatory mechanism in order to minimize the threat to the right to privacy as well as to curb the inappropriate use of personal data.[51] A major aim of these regulatory mechanisms is to enable the person, whose data is subjected to collection and processes, to exercise her data-related fundamental rights in the best possible way. One can find many national, regional and international law instruments dealing with this particular area of online and offline human activities.[52] Legal rules and principles devised as such regulate a range of facets such as the collection, storing, processing, dissemination, amendment and deletion of personal data.

Pakistan is lagging behind in providing data protection rights to its citizens as it does not have any kind of data protection law at the moment. It is in spite of the fact that there are 195 million cellular subscribers, 120 million 3G/4G subscribers, 123 million broadband internet connections.[53] In 2005, a data protection bill was drafted but it has never been presented in the parliament.[54] A bare perusal of the proposed law shows a very bleak picture of the policy makers' understanding of the data protection issues. According to the Draft Bill, the data subjects have no rights available against the state and government functionaries. Section 4 of the bill explicitly provides exemption to the data related activities of the government.[55]

---

[49] Tzanou (2013).

[50] See for example the unanimous judgment of a nine-member bench of the Supreme Court of India in Justice K. S. Puttaswamy (Retd.) and Anr. vs Union of India and others (issued 24th August 2017).

[51] For a detailed analysis of the challenge of Internet regulation see: Kotzur (2022).

[52] See for a detailed analysis of different approaches to the regulation of Internet and data protection rights, Veit (2022).

[53] Pakistan Telecommunication Authority. https://www.pta.gov.pk/en/telecom-indicators. Accessed 28 August 2023.

[54] http://media.mofo.com/docs/mofoprivacy/PAKISTAN%20Draft%20Law%202nd%20Revision%20.pdf.

[55] According to Section 4 of the Bill, "This Act does not apply to the processing of personal or corporate data carried out by federal, provincial or local government. (2) The federal government, in respect of local data only, by notification in the official gazette, may exempt any public or private sector, entity or business from the operation of this Act."

Likewise, the bill does not provide for an effective enforcement mechanism in the form of institutional arrangements. According to its provisions, the data subject can file a complaint to the session judge against the data controller for enforcement of the rights and interest related to the data.[56] The session judge is authorized to direct 'any person' to investigate regarding the complained issue and if the complaint is found to be correct an injunction or a fine of up to Rs. 1,000,000 (around 80,000 Euro) can be imposed upon the data controller.[57] The right of appeal is given against the order of the session judge which will be filed before the relevant High Court.[58] Here again, the law has a very broad construction as the determination of proper territorial jurisdiction is not a simple task due to data processing activities in the digital world.

7.1.3 Why Statutory Protection of Privacy?

The above survey of the relevant laws highlights the textual, theoretical and practical difficulties to extend these laws to privacy infringement cases in a piecemeal manner. This scenario makes it imperative to formulate a comprehensive statute for the concretization of the fundamental right to privacy. The benefits of such a statute are immense for the legal recognition as well as enforce of the right to privacy and its various strands. It will prove to be a legal game changer if a statute is enacted which defines the right to privacy, explains its scope and identifies different interests attached to it, underlines the infringements of privacy as well as codifies the important principles of justified interference and balancing.

An express statutory protection of the right to privacy will bring legal certainty in terms of clarifying people's right and liabilities. To balance freedom of the press with the right to privacy, it requires "to translate the basic right of privacy theory into legal doctrine in the privacy tort area" so that, at one hand, the person has a full knowledge of the extent to which her privacy is protected and, on the other hand, "the press must [also] be able to assess its potential liability for infringement, and the judicial system must have appropriate guidelines for accommodating these often conflicting interests."[59]

The codification of a right to privacy and the declaration of associated wrongs as actionable would work as deterrence for the media industry; journalists would then think twice before any kind of intrusive practices and new gathering for voyeuristic programs. According to Daniel Solove,

> [t]he law works best when it can hover as a threat in the background but allow most problems to be worked out informally. The threat of the lawsuit helps to keep people in check. Without

[56] Section 18(2) of the draft bill of Data Protection Act 2005.

[57] Section 18 (3–5) of the draft bill of Data Protection Act 2005.

[58] Section 18 (8) of the draft bill of Data Protection Act 2005.

[59] Emerson (1979), p. 341.

> the lawsuit threat, people who defame other people or invade their privacy can just thumb their nose at any complaints.[60]

It is a centuries' old general principle of law that 'where there is a right there is a remedy' (*ubi jus ibi remedium*). The Constitution of Pakistan provides a right to dignity of man and privacy of home but this right is of less value due to the absence of an effective remedial mechanism. Similarly, Article 4 of the constitution provides for equal protection of law. The purpose of this Article is that no wrong shall go unremedied and it is used usually to fill the legal lacuna where there is a violation of a right but no respective remedy. In many occasions, the Supreme Court of Pakistan has held that fundamental rights must be liberally interpreted in order to make sure their enforcement rather than to block the remedy due to strict interpretation.[61] The same approach was followed by the Court in the Shehla Zia case, where the Supreme Court of Pakistan held that environmental rights come under the ambit of Article 9 right to life.[62] A similar activist approach can be adopted for the violation of people's privacy where the problem is there but no legal instrument or authority is in place to resolve it in a legal way. The introduction of privacy law is essential to fulfill the constitutional requirement emanating from Articles 4, 9 and 14 because privacy is such a right which is without an effective remedy.

It is not easy for the judiciary, in spite of a case law based legal system, to introduce an actionable right for which no precedent or *stare decisis* could be found in case law. According to Taylor,

> if [the courts] were to introduce a considered right of privacy, it would be a step that appeared to be very legislative in nature. While everyone in the legal system is used to the idea of the courts making law nowadays, there are still some things which it is appropriate for the legislature alone to do.[63]

To Taylor, the so-called bold law-making judgment of the court will suffer from three main difficulties:

> courts are not democratically elected, and major changes in the law by them therefore run into problems of democratic legitimacy; and courts cannot really conduct investigations into the effects of changes they may be considering. Unlike the legislature, they cannot set up committees to hear all interested parties before making a change. In the area of privacy, in which many interests compete for consideration, this is precisely what would be desirable before any change is introduced.[64]

In the United Kingdom, we have seen the difficulties of protecting privacy solely through case law where the judiciary has been consistently resisting such a bold step;

---

[60] Solove (2007), p. 123.

[61] See Sect. 4.1.2 for details about the status of fundamental rights in the constitutional framework of Pakistan.

[62] See Sect. 4.1.3.2 for a description of judicial activism and its impact on the law making process, especially in the case of Ms. Shehla Zia v Wapda.

[63] Taylor (2000), p. 270.

[64] Taylor (2000), p. 269.

it was only after the promulgation of the Human Rights Act 1998 that they recognized the misuse of private information as an actionable wrong.[65]

The case of Pakistan is quite a different one. Although Pakistan has inherited the majority of its substantive and procedural statutes from UK, it has codified most of the common law and has a written constitution. The torts like libel and slander have been codified under the Defamation Act, but there is no statute or case law regarding a breach of confidence. The Trust Act regulates the fiduciary relationship, which is purely a concept of property law and has nothing to do with the disclosure of confidential information. Obviously, the victims of privacy violations do not have an option to invoke some kind of supranational body such as the ECtHR. These circumstances call for a legal reform to formulate a privacy law and recognize privacy violations as an actionable wrong capable of remedy.

The formulation of an effective law for the protection of the right to privacy will also fulfill international law obligations of Pakistan, arising from the Universal Declaration on Human Rights.[66]

7.2 The Guiding Principles for the Proposed Privacy Law of Pakistan

7.2.1 Explicit Recognition of the Right to Privacy and Its Concretization

In the light of the Supreme Court of Pakistan's interpretation of Article 14 (1) and Article 9 (right to life), the right to privacy has to a certain extent a constitutional guaranty along with all the interests attached to this right.[67] It, however, needs a legislative enrichment and refinement. The legislature should not only recognize it in explicit terms but its violation must also be made an actionable wrong capable of legal remedy. The abstract character of the constitutional right could be effectively protected only after its concrete areas and strands are protected through an Act of parliament.

The right to privacy has strong moral roots in the basic human values of liberty and dignity.[68] Violations of the right to privacy may cause a serious affront to human

[65] See Sect. 6.2 in general and Sect. 6.2.5 in particular for protection of the right to privacy in UK after Human Rights Act 1998.

[66] Article 8 UDHR: "Everyone has the right to an effective remedy by the competent national tribunals for acts violating the fundamental rights granted him by the constitution or by law." Article 12 UDHR: "No one shall be subjected to arbitrary interference with his privacy, family, home or correspondence, nor to attacks upon his honour and reputation. Everyone has the right to the protection of the law against such interference or attacks."

[67] See Sect. 4.2 of this book for details.

[68] See Chap. 3 of this book.

dignity and can snatch away the victim's liberty. Acknowledging the importance of these basic values, the meaning and interpretation of "life" by the Supreme Court of Pakistan duly enshrines the right to live life with dignity where all the ingredients required for its enjoyment are available to people.[69] A life without an expectation of privacy cannot be said a worth living life and such a situation would be against the spirit of moral law as well as the spirit of the Constitution of Pakistan.

Therefore, the state of Pakistan is duty-bound under the jurisprudence not only to refrain from violation of citizens' privacy but also to provide an "atmosphere" in the shape of legal instruments under which the victims of privacy could seek remedies against such infringements.[70] It is duty of the legislature to ensure that no wrong should go without the prevalence of an appropriate legal remedy. In the similar vein, privacy law should be enacted which has both substantive provisions and procedural rules for an effective, expeditious, inexpensive and enabling adjudication of privacy related abuses. This law should provide a definition of privacy, an explanation of the attached interests, an elaboration of actions which harm these interests, the nature and kinds of available remedies, the exceptions or possible defenses available to the defendants along with jurisdictional and procedural matters such as specifying the forum of initiation of legal action under this law.

The following sections will offer some recommendations and a framework for articulating different provisions of the proposed privacy law statute. This proposed statute will draw on the theory of privacy and the approaches of legal regimes established in the ECHR, Germany and the United Kingdom that have been analyzed more closely in the previous chapters.

7.2.2 Definition of Privacy Right and Interpretation of Different Terms

It has been sufficiently clarified in Chap. 3 that the formulation of a precise definition of privacy has been a theoretical challenge. The European Court of Human Rights (ECtHR) has expressed similar views that the broad concept of the right to respect for private life under Article 8 of ECHR is incapable of an exhaustive definition.[71] The theoretical underpinnings of privacy also reveal a rich diversity of concept which could not be contained holistically in a single definitional exposition.[72] Therefore, the proposed statute should rely on a broad description of the right to

[69] See Sect. 4.2 for interpretation of Article 9 (right to life) by the Supreme Court of Pakistan.

[70] See Sects. 4.1.2 and 4.1.3 for the status and scope of fundamental rights under the constitutional framework of Pakistan.

[71] See Sect. 5.3.1 for ECtHR's approach towards the protection of the right to private life, specifically considerations of the Court in the cases of Niemietz v. Germany (§ 29) and Peck v. the United Kingdom (§ 57).

[72] See Sect. 3.2 for richness of the concept of privacy.

privacy in the form of elaborating and expanding the brief text of Article 14 (1) and Article 9 of the Constitution as well as concretizing the sporadic and piecemeal directions of the higher courts regarding the right to privacy.[73] However, the statutory definition must mention its violation as an actionable wrong, which entitles the plaintiff to claim legal remedy against the wrongdoer under this law.[74]

The statute may be titled as "Protection of Personal Privacy Act". It should be passed by the *Majlis-e-Shoora* (Parliament)[75] as a federal law.[76] Being a federal law, its territorial jurisdiction would extend to the whole of Pakistan.[77]

The following proposed description shall provide a broad foundation for further substantiation and concretization of associated interests. It would work as an introduction of the right to privacy to the legal system of Pakistan.

(a) *Every person has a general right to privacy. This right includes but is not limited to the right to inviolability of his personal privacy, private life, home, personal information and correspondence.*[78]
(b) *No interference with these rights and interests is legitimate if made without a valid consent of the right-holder except in circumstances where any other constitutional right, or personal interest duly protected by law or an overwhelming public interest outweighs the general right to privacy and the interests protected under this law.*
(c) *Any interference, which could not be sufficiently justified by countervailing rights and interest, shall be regarded as a breach of this Statute.*

---

[73] See Sect. 4.2.2 for the jurisprudence of the right to privacy developed by superior courts.

[74] Eady (1996), pp. 243, 249: "It is all the more important that the protection of such "rights" should not be left to develop in accordance with the subjective impressions of individual judges. It is better that some steps are taken by way of legislation, even if it does not prove possible to embrace every aspect of privacy that one might wish, in an ideal world, to protect.[.....] The starting point is to focus on the kind of behavior which is regarded as most objectionable and, correspondingly, upon the areas of life which it is thought most desirable to protect; and then to devise wording sufficiently precise to cover those matters. One needs also to define, so far as possible, the scope of the exceptions or defences that one wishes to put in place and, in particular, to rein in the unruly steed of "public interest."

[75] Article 50 of the Constitution of Pakistan introduces Parliament as, "There shall be a Majlis-e-Shoora (Parliament) of Pakistan consisting of the President and two Houses to be known respectively as the National Assembly and the Senate."

[76] Article 70 of the Constitution of Pakistan provides legislative process of introduction of the bills and passing them from both houses. These bills become Acts of Parliament (also known as statutes) after the President of Pakistan sign them.

[77] Acts of Parliament or statutes are generally enforced in the whole of Pakistan unless there is any express territorial or subject matter-related exemption. Article 3 of the Constitution provides that the State shall ensure the elimination of all form of exploitation, while Article 7 defines "the State", which includes Federal Government and Parliament. Matters related to broadcasts and other forms of communication and copyrights fall in the Federal Legislative list. Furthermore, most of the criminal and civil laws are passed by Parliament and extended to provinces such as contract law, defamation law, penal laws, prevention of electronic crimes (which penalises illegal access and damage to data and information systems), civil and criminal procedure code and so on.

[78] This definition is a combination of Article 14 (1) and Article 9 of the Constitution of Pakistan.

(d) *The breach of the rights and interests protected under this law may attract civil and criminal liability to the extent of the gravity of interference; and the plaintiff shall be entitled to civil remedy for the violation of his or her right to privacy.*

7.2.3 Explanation of the Key Terms

The above description underlines basic expressions and key terminologies that are used in privacy related legal proceedings. The proposed law must define and explain these terms in order to draw the boundaries of rights and liabilities created under the proposed 'Protection of Personal Privacy Act'. It is not possible to demarcate strictly the substantive scope of the enshrined interests. The circumstances of a particular case would assist judges to determine the nature of damage and fix liability accordingly. However, the legislature can introduce some certainty in the manner of enumerating what is included and what is not included in the scope of a particular term.

Based on the theory of privacy in Chap. 3 and the insights offered by model jurisdictions such as the ECHR, Germany and the United Kingdom, the following meanings and interpretation are recommended to be formulated in the proposed 'Protection of Personal Privacy Act'.

7.2.3.1 Meaning of "Person"

In law, the term "person" is used for both natural and juristic persons as well as entities which are capable of holding rights and liabilities. For example, corporations, trusts, territorial entities and so on come under the definition of "person". However, "person" in the proposed Protection of Personal Privacy Act strictly refers to a natural individual only and it does not include juristic persons. The connection of privacy with human dignity and personhood as well as the functions it performs in the manner of protection and promotion of different levels of human relations make it a humanistic value. Therefore, no corporate entity or the juristic personality formed by the presumption of law, should have such entitlement under this law. However, the protection under this law may be extended to non-personal or juristic entities, tangible and intangible sphere (e.g. places, reputation and sentiments) on occasions where such transgression draws an impact on the life of one or more natural persons.

Another issue is that whether it is required that the complainant must be a *living* person or whether a breach of privacy could also be claimed on behalf of a dead person. In this regard, Pakistani case law has consistently extended the personality-related interests, such as reputation, to dead persons as well. Pakistani law has rejected the common law maxim, which says that the reputation of a person dies with his death. Case law has established that such interests are inheritable to the successors of the person who has been posthumously defamed. A similar approach can also be found in the German jurisprudence, where the dignity of person does not vanish immediately after his death; rather, it continues until a span of 10 years passes.

Thus, the "person" means here a natural individual—living or recently dead. The legislature can set a reasonable limitation period after death for the commencement of a claim under the proposed privacy law.

7.2.3.2 Interpretation of "General Right to Privacy"

"General right to privacy" means a legal right which enables the person to develop one's personhood in a unique manner and is not only available against the state but against the world at large. A general right to privacy goes beyond the protection of the typical *negative liberty* as a result of the fulfillment of positive obligations to which the State is bound, i. e. of the necessity of proper measures for protecting privacy.[79] This dimension is in accordance with the Pakistani constitutional jurisprudence (discussed in Chap. 4) which provides that a meaningful protection to the right to life needs more than the basic amenities of life.[80] Thus, the addressees of the right are comprehensive: On the one hand, the state is prohibited from violating the right to privacy of its citizens; on the other hand, private parties such as individuals and entities are also obliged not to interfere with this right.

7.2.3.3 Interpretation of "Personal Privacy"

The proposed Protection of the Personal Privacy Act is based on human rights provided by the Constitution of Pakistan and international law covenants. Therefore, it strictly deals with the individual's right of privacy and the related values and interests. It excludes other forms of confidentiality such as secret information related to state or trade secrets regarding a commercial activity of a person or corporation. There are laws and measures for secrets and confidential information related to the state which do not have a fundamental rights' dimension. Trade and business secrets must also be protected in their own way.

7.2.3.4 Interpretation of "Private Life"

The protection of "private life" means the protection of all possible areas of one's personhood, which plays a role in the development of his or her personality. These

[79] See Chap. 3 for the concept of privacy.

[80] Article 4 (1) of the Constitution of Pakistan also provides, "To enjoy the protection of law and to be treated in accordance with law is the inalienable right of every citizen, wherever he may be and of every other person for the time being within Pakistan."

areas could not be strictly enumerated or demarcated due to the fact that human personality and its developmental essentials could not be precisely conceived. The open-ended and flexible protection and the assessment of factual circumstances of the specific case are the only legal mechanism to encounter preemptively the legal challenges posed to personality rights by technological advancement.[81] This facet not only protects individual in his or her seclusion but also in the sphere of his or her interaction with other human beings and in the interface of the right-holder with other living species (for example pets) as well as nonliving things (for example electronic gadgets). Private life in the context of this law should be viewed in a broader framework, in contrast to the classic liberal view which focuses on the individualistic self that desires a space of one's own—away from any outside interference at any level. Development of personality is not an ascetic project. The regulation of this realm must take into consideration this bipartisan and symbiotic relation of the individual's self and the society in which it culminates.[82]

Only some of the concrete areas of a broad right to the protection of private life can be mentioned here as examples. The rights which are related to personal identification such as the right to one's name, the right to one's image and personal integrity (including psychological and physiological integrity) are protected in the consistent case law of jurisdictions deliberated in the previous chapters.[83] Thus, the proposed Protection of Personal Privacy Act should cover the protection of these areas.

7.2.3.5 The Meaning of "Home"

The term 'home' used in the proposed Act is not restricted to its traditional meaning, where it is used to denote a place of abode. Article 14 (1) of the Constitution of Pakistan expressly mentions the privacy of home as inviolable. The binding case law of the superior courts related to the interpretation of "home" is in consonance with the jurisprudence of the ECtHR as both emphasize to construe a wider meaning of the term.[84] According to these principles, the protection is focused on the *person* and

---

[81] For details see: Van der Sloot (2015).

[82] Cohen (2013), p. 1905: "Privacy shelters dynamic, emergent subjectivity from the efforts of commercial and government actors to render individuals and communities fixed, transparent, and predictable. It protects the situated practices of boundary management through which the capacity for self-determination develops."

[83] See for example: *ECHR, Von Hannover v Germany (No. 2), judgment of 07 February 2012. Application No. 40660/08, para* 95. *ECHR, Axel Springer AG v Germany, judgment of 7 February 2012. Application No. 39954/08, para* 83.

[84] For Pakistani case law please refer to: Chamber of Commerce and Industry, Quetta Balochistan v. Director-General Quetta Development Authority, PLD 2012 Baluchistan 31, "[P]eople in public spaces are also entitled to limited personal space and privacy given the exigencies of the situation and to the extent that it can be ensured. Couples, families or for that matter any person would be deterred from venturing into the Park if every movement of theirs can be monitored." Benazir Bhutto v. President of Pakistan, PLD 1998 Supreme Court 388, "The emphasis is not on the

not on a place, which has no connection with any identifiable individual. A person's protection may not be denied due the fact that he or she was not inside a residential abode. Protection of home covers work places,[85] public streets,[86] and public parks and so on. Similarly, "his home" does not portray a proprietary connection. It is not required that the person must be a rightful owner of the property to expect privacy in a particular place.[87]

7.2.3.6 The Meaning of "Personal Information"

Personal information means any information, which is related in any manner to an identifiable person. It includes private and sensitive information. The determination of personal information worthy of protection under this law should also depend on the circumstances of a particular case. The limitation of being intimate or sensitive should not be included as a prerequisite in the definition of personal information. It is obvious that the nature of information is a relevant fact in the process of fixing liability for an alleged access to information or its disclosure. However, it is the *context,* in which the information is accessed or used, that plays a crucial role in assessing any actual or foreseeable harm from the intrusion on personal information.[88]

In order to determine the legitimate desirability for the protection of certain information, the tool of "reasonable expectation of privacy" is widely used.[89] According to Raymond Wacks, private information means "those facts, communications, or opinions which relate to an individual and which it would be reasonable

---

boundaries of home but the *person* who enjoys the right *wherever he may be*." ECtHR also considers "home" as an autonomous concept which may not be strictly classified and only factual circumstances would reveal whether or not habitation could be a prerequisite for demarcating "home". See: Chiragov and Others v. Armenia § 206; Winterstein and Others v. France, § 141; and Niemietz v. Germany, § 30.

[85] ECHR, *Niemietz v Germany*, judgment of 16 December 1992. Application No. 13710/88, para 29–31.

[86] See: ECHR, *Peck v United Kingdom*, judgment of 28 January 2003. Application No. 44647/98.

[87] ECHR, *Menteş and Others v. Turkey*, judgment of 24 January 2018. Application No. 23186/94, para 73; ECHR, *Buckley v. the United Kingdom*, judgment of 29 September 1996. Application No. 20348/92, para 54.

[88] Solove (2002), p. 1146: According to Solove, "Privacy is a dimension for a wide variety of practices each having a different value- and what privacy is differs in different contexts."

[89] For example, according to Consultation paper on civil liability for invasion of privacy by the Sub-committee on privacy of the Law Reform Commission of Hong Kong: "The test for determining whether information about an individual is private or not may be based on the location at which the information is revealed or the nature of the personal information in question." (p. 97) "Insofar as individuals have a reasonable expectation of privacy in information about an individual' s private communications, home life, personal and family relationships, private behavior, health and personal financial affairs, the law should protect such information from being made public against their will." (p. 99)

to expect him or her to regard as intimate or sensitive and therefore to want to withhold, or at least to restrict, their collection, use or publication." [90] Requiring the plaintiff to prove that why his or her personal information should not be accessed or used has the potential to result into further disclosure. The term "reasonable" is by itself a loaded term and it may not leave some persons and places at a disadvantageous position because of the absence of expectation of privacy. For example, one may argue that some persons such as public figures and children may not reasonably expect privacy in all circumstances or that the information collected at a public place may not be 'reasonably expected' to be protected from disclosure. However, the determination of the desire or expectation of privacy requires a nuanced approach. The judges should consider many factors in addition to the nature of information, place of information, the informational norms and more importantly, the determination whether or not it violated the 'contextual integrity'.[91] According to Mark Tunick,

> [T]he reasonableness expectations of privacy cannot wholly depend on prevailing practices and existing understandings. While social practices are important sources for determining which methods of observation are legitimate, it is important that we be able to criticize practices that undermine important values, even if those practices have become widely shared. People living in Nazi Germany could expect little privacy in their homes given widespread surveillance practices; but that those practices were widespread does not mean they were legitimate. While the prevalence of a practice or technology of observation is an important indicator of its legitimacy, not all practices or uses of popular technology are acceptable.[92]

7.2.3.7 "Correspondence"

The term "correspondence" here means the letters, emails or other forms of messages written from and addressed to an identifiable individual whereby the communication of a private message or information is aimed. Such letters are sent in sealed envelopes with the addresses clearly marked so that to ensure the correct recipient. It does not include correspondence of public nature such as public notices. Private correspondence is one which is not normally shared by the addressee with all and sundry and is kept secretly. In modern times, "correspondence" also includes emails, mobile text messages, recorded audio messages and all other messages which are sent by the internet applications providing "Inboxes" for private communications.

[90] Wacks (2013), p. 13.

[91] Nissenbaum (2004).

[92] Tunick (2015), p. 69. References omitted.

7.2.4 What Constitutes an "Interference"?

For a successful claim of privacy breach, a person has to establish the occurrence of interference into his or her privacy rights. The establishment of a violation of privacy or the breach of privacy under the proposed 'Protection of Personal Privacy Act' is dependent on a preceding interference. Any interference becomes a breach if not justified by the defences provided in the second part of clause b.

Just as privacy is not capable of an exhaustive definition, the formulation of "interference" into privacy cannot be elaborated comprehensively. For instance, an analysis of a variety of English legislative instruments shows that five different categories of interference into privacy are regulated. These are "unwanted listening and audio recording; unwanted watching, photography and/or filming; unwanted access to personal documents; unwanted access to home and personal belongings; and harassment."[93] However, these areas are regarded as "neither coherent nor comprehensive".[94] It is due to this reason that many legal instruments, aimed at protecting a variety of interests, are involved in the regulation of interference. On the other hand, the *interference* into the rights and interests protected under the proposed privacy law for Pakistan will be more coherent due to its foundational element of privacy and its focus on the general right to privacy.

Normally, media interferes into people's privacy through intrusion and publication of personal information. Intrusion is not limited to physical intrusion. The use of any kind of technological device for the purpose of observing the person, such as through the use of long distance cameras, paparazzi or any other similar method, would also constitute an interference.[95]

In order to determine various forms of interference into privacy, the taxonomy developed by Daniel Solove offers an elaborated guide, which may be resorted to by judges in their analysis of a particular situation so that to decide whether or not an alleged activity or interaction constitutes an interference. On his taxonomic presentation of the problems of privacy, he explains *inter alia* privacy invasion through intrusion and decisional interference; information collection through surveillance and interrogation; information dissemination through activities such as disclosure, exposure, appropriation and distortion.[96]

---

[93] Moreham (2014), p. 143.

[94] Moreham (2014), pp. 143, 155: "Haphazard development has led to duplication in some areas and gaps in other. As a result, potentially serious interference with physical privacy are beyond legislative reach."

[95] For actual and potential threats to privacy due to modern technological developments, see Finn, Wright and Friedewald (2013).

[96] Solove (2006). Note: Solove's order of different problems and their effects has not been followed here as he considers intrusion as a result of collection, processing and dissemination of information, while merely intrusion sans collection of information should also be regarded as an interference. Secondly, information processing has not been mentioned here as it is more related to data protection, while the remaining ingredients of taxonomy sufficiently explicate the concept of

In the nutshell, an articulated definition of “interference” which encircles every possible instance of interference into privacy is as complicated as the concept of privacy itself. Only some of the interpretative tools could be mentioned. These descriptive tools along with the diverse functions performed by privacy could guide judges in their analysis of a specific activity alleged by the plaintiff as ‘interference’ into his or her privacy.

7.2.4.1 Defenses and Exemption from Liability

Both the theories of privacy and the enforcement of privacy rights in the model jurisdictions that have been analyzed in this research reveal that the right to privacy is not an absolute right. Articles 9 and 14 (1) of the Pakistani Constitution ensure that no person shall be deprived of life and liberty “save in accordance with law” and guarantee the privacy of home “subject to law”. Therefore, the defendant has the opportunity to prove that his interference was legitimate and does not constitute a breach of the right to privacy or of this proposed law. Due to these reasons, the proposed privacy law makes a distinction of legitimate and illegitimate (or tortious) interferences.

While applying the provisions of the proposed law, the courts should consider the following factors to determine whether an interference into a privacy right qualifies a breach of privacy under this law.

7.2.4.1.1 Validity of Consent

A legitimate interference would be one which is made after an informed, effective and valid consent of the right-holder.

The first prerequisite of a valid consent in privacy cases is the legal capacity of the person. The person must be capable of exercising his or her free will and must not be in such circumstances where he or she is under duress of any kind. For instance, media persons in Pakistani conduct interviews of the accused persons and detainees in the police custody. As these people are not capable to resist orders of law enforcement persons and are in an exceptional and coercive situation, any given consent cannot be claimed to be lawful and interviews are a grave violation of the right to privacy. Similarly, journalists also entice the victims by saying that the publication or broadcasting of their stories will help in their access to justice and the issue will be highlighted in the media. Such tactics negatively affect the legality of consent which is not given voluntarily and free of inappropriate influence and therefore cannot be validly enforced for a legitimization of the interference.

---

interference. For details see Chap. 4 in general for the concept of privacy, Sect. 3.3.1.1 for the concept of privacy as a right to be let alone and Sect. 3.4.1 for Solove’s taxonomy.

The person must also be of full age. A minor cannot be presumed to be capable of giving informed and valid consent.

Consent is not a permanent license for an absolute disclosure of private facts or publication of private information. A person should be allowed to revoke the consent at a later date if he or she recognizes the seriousness or importance of the issue related to his or her privacy right. For instance, a person may give consent to a journalist for taking his or her photograph in a certain situation, while afterwards he or she comes to know that the context in which it would be published would either be offensive or that the coverage might put him or her in a false light. Thus, the consent should also be generally revocable and particularly if the journalist had acquired the consent through misrepresentation of facts.

7.2.4.1.2 Relevancy of Intention

The breach of privacy should be regarded as actionable *per se*. Neither the existence of intention on the part of the tortfeasor nor the proof of special damages should be required. The disclosure in good faith cannot be an absolute defense and the defendant would have to prove how the public interest could not be better served without the violation of the plaintiff's privacy. In media cases, regard may also be made to the best practices of media associations. As for the proof of damages, the defamation law of Pakistan does not require the occurrence of a special damage.[97]

7.2.4.1.3 Balancing of the Right to Privacy with Countervailing Rights and Public Interest

As earlier stated, the right to privacy is not an absolute value. Not every kind of desire for privacy can be legally protected under all circumstances. The defendant can take the plea that his act of intrusion into the privacy of the other person or the disclosure of private information was a result of the exercise of his legal or constitutional rights and thus falling under the public interest defense. Traditionally, the right to freedom of expression is regarded as a contestant value. In reality, both of these interests have a metaphorical hate-love relation.[98] It is very common that

[97] According to Section 4 of Defamation Ordinance 2002, "Defamation actionable: The publication of defamatory matter is an actionable wrong without proof of special damage to the person defamed and where defamation is proved, damage shall be presumed."

[98] For example, Charles Fried notes, "Besides giving us control over the context in which we act, privacy has a more defensive role in protecting our liberty. We may wish to do or say things not forbidden by the restraints of morality, but which are nevertheless unpopular or unconventional. If we thought that our every word and deed were public, fear of disapproval or more tangible retaliation might keep us from doing or saying things which we would do or say if we could be sure of keeping them to ourselves or within a circle of those who we know approve or tolerate our tastes." Fried (1968), pp. 883–884. Reference omitted.

media and journalists take the freedom of speech defense. Whenever the defendant invokes such a defense, the court is required to undertake a balancing exercise and decide whether the interference was a justified interference or constituted a breach of plaintiff's privacy right.

A chief characteristic of the law proposed here should be the formulation of general principles of balancing the right to privacy with countervailing rights and public interest. As far as public interest is included in free speech, it is also connected to the people's right to know or to access to information they are legitimately interested in. The Defamation Ordinance 2002 provides "public interest" as one of the defences which a defendant can invoke.[99] The case law developed under the Defamation Ordinance 2002 establishes that the burden of proof in relation to the public interest defense would be on the shoulders of the defendant.[100]

Just like the right to privacy, public interest cannot be defined in an exhaustive manner. Nor is it possible to enumerate all the possible situations where the right to privacy could be outweighed by public interest. However, some guidelines should be provided by the legislature for the courts in order to introduce some level of certainty to cases where free speech and people's right to know are involved because these interests very often confront the right to privacy. No right should take an inherent precedence over the other. Within the framework set by the legislator the courts should use an *ad hoc* balancing exercise to determine which right must yield to another one. What constitutes a public interest in a given situation is a question of fact, where judges need to consider some basic factors.[101] For example, journalists may invoke the public interest defense if they are entitled to newsgathering and dissemination of content on all matters to which the public has a right to receive. However, they are not entitled to *overstep certain bounds* of associated legal obligation and responsibilities.[102] These responsibilities include showing respect to people's rights such as their privacy of home, private life and private information.

The jurisprudence of the ECtHR under Article 8 and Article 10 of ECHR provides a valuable guide in this regard. The Strasbourg Court has formulated six-point general criteria and has applied these during the balancing exercise of privacy

---

[99] Section 5 of Defamation Ordinance 2002, "Defences: In defamation proceedings a person has a defence if he shows that [. . .] (b) the matter commented on is fair and in the public interest and is an expression of opinion and not an assertion of fact and was published in good faith; (c) it is based on truth and was made for public good".

[100] Mudasser Iqbal Butt v Shaukat Wahab and others, PLD 2006 Lahore, 557: "Ground raised by the defendants by way of defence that news items were published impartially, without malice and in the public interest, was not substantiated by any investigation or probe undertaken by the defendants to establish the veracity of the news items in question; only if such probe had been made diligently and in good faith, defendants could have shown that they had acted without malice and in the public interest. [Defendants] having failed to do so, they must be held liable for defaming the plaintiff." See also: 2010 C L D 1175 [Lahore] Rao DIL JAN KHAN v DR. Muhammad Younis and another.

[101] The question of whether or not judiciary is qualified to undertake the balancing of countervailing rights has already been discussed.

[102] ECHR, *Kaboğlu and Oran v Turkey*, judgment of 30 October 2018. Application No. 36944/07. See also: Axel Springer AG v Germany [GC], para 79.

against freedom of expression.[103] According to this criteria, the court should consider the contribution of the media report to a debate of public interest, the status of the affected person in a given society,[104] the subject of media news report,[105] nature of its content,[106] the prior conduct of both the parties,[107] nature of the environment where the photo was taken or which is conveyed through text.[108] Such a detailed consideration of various factors opposes the general maxim of 'public interest is what the public is interested in', and emphasizes on a much nuanced approach.[109]

By determining "public interest" in the context of freedom of speech and of the media, one must remember, however, that there is also a public interest in the upholding of a person's privacy right. Viewed this way, public interest should not be construed merely in a strict sense of a collective right of society to know or to access information but should also consider the societal interest in protecting privacy. In other words, the infringement of someone's fundamental right is not in the public interest as per the case law of the Supreme Court of Pakistan.[110]

For a valid defense of public interest, the Defamation Ordinance of 2002 also imposes the conditions on the comments of the defendants to be *fair*, *an expression of opinion and not an assertion of fact* as well as the publication of comments must be in *good faith*. This rule is reasonable and could be applied *mutatis mutandi* to

[103] See Sect. 5.4.3 for details.

[104] Whether the person was absolute public figure such as a politician or relative public figure such as media celebrity or a common person with no standing in public affairs.

[105] It means the determination of the genre of the report, i.e. Whether it was related to some serious political debate (such as qualification of a person for public office, expenditure from public exchequer and so on) or merely an entertainment related publication, whether the focus is on a genuine area of public interest or it unduly magnifies an otherwise trivial matter.

[106] To consider, whether the content conveying an objective message, whether there is any kind of bias or prejudice apparent against a person or group of persons, does it show a consideration of all the relevant aspects and contexts, whether the language and terminology used in the report is temperate or undue exaggeration and so on, whether the defendant has considered all the possible effects the report possibly have on the rights and responsibilities of other people.

[107] Whether the affected person has himself played any role in the divulgence of his own private information, or has given consent to the media for publication or has ever talked in public on the *sub judice* issue. Whether the defendant media company or reporter focus on serious issues of public interest or they focus merely on celebrity gossips and light tittle-tattle.

[108] If the complaint is related to photos of the plaintiff, relevant factors are: the manner and context in which images have been captured, did the plaintiff gave consent or knew about photo-making activities, whether the method of obtaining photos was amounting to harassment, what kind of device used for making the photo (e.g. long lenses camera, secret camera such as pen camera). If the complaint is related to text, whether it describe the locations, conduct or interactions of the plaintiff from his or her intimate sphere, personal sphere, private sphere or public sphere.

[109] See an analysis of ECtHR's balancing approach in a popular media related case: Cariolou (2016), pp. 138–152.

[110] 2006 S C M R 1415 (Supreme Court of Pakistan) Abdul Majeed v Government of Pakistan, through Secretary, Establishment Division and others. "[T]he retirement of a person on whimsical grounds amount to deprive him from the legitimate right of earning which is part of fundamental rights to live in terms of Article 9 of the Constitution and is definitely not in the public interest."

privacy cases. The defendant must show that his interference into privacy was necessary in the public interest, which also means that it was not motivated by profit making. The public interest defense of the media will be weakened if it is apparent that the news report was meant to sensationalize the story for attracting audience.[111]

7.2.5 *Remedies for Breach of Privacy*

The review of the legal landscape in Pakistan highlights the main problem of the lack of punitive or remedial measures for the violations of the right to privacy. The new law must fill this gap in a comprehensive manner. It is not sufficient to articulate the concept of privacy and its functional value. An effective protection of privacy is possible only through codified remedial measures. Statutory remedies perform many functions in relation to realizing the objectives of fundamental rights. The existence of remedial mechanism would deter the potential violator at one hand and on the other hand, the aggrieved party can claim for restitution of her or his harm.[112] The statutory remedies will not only make the law effective, certain and predictable for both plaintiff and defendant, but will also enable the judges to take privacy violations as serious issues of rights and obligations.[113]

7.2.5.1 Injunctive Remedy

The primary purpose of the proposed law should be to prevent any damage to the person due to the breach of her privacy right. For that purpose, the proposed 'Protection of Personal Privacy Act' should expressly provide for injunctive relief,

[111] Mudasser Iqbal Butt v Shaukat Wahab and others, P L D 2006 Lahore 557: "There is no evidence to show that any investigation or probe was undertaken by the defendants to establish the veracity of the news items in question. Only if such probe had been made diligently and in good faith, could die defendants have shown that they had acted without malice and in the public interest. Having failed to do so they must be held liable for defaming the plaintiff. [. . . . .] Furthermore, we are of the view that the news items in question are prime examples of irresponsible journalism."

[112] Moreham (2018), p. 4: "Remedies make rights real in practice for plaintiffs. They can provide redress and solace, punish and condemn outrageous violations, potentially deter future harmful conduct, and vindicate interests that are of importance to individuals and society as a whole. On the flipside, they can impose heavy burdens on defendants, including heavy financial loss, reputational damage and potentially serious incursions upon liberty."

[113] Scholz (2019), pp. 653, 657. "Considering privacy rights alongside their remedies addresses the fear of over-enforcement of privacy rights due to their vagueness. Taking privacy remedies seriously contributes to (1) clear boundaries for the rights and (2) adequate protection of the rights when infringed upon. Privacy advocates cannot assume that merely conceptualizing a right to privacy can protect privacy interests, even if that right is enshrined in statutory law. Without remedies to deter infringement of privacy, and disgorge violators of rents, recognizing privacy rights at law is meaningless. And without predictable rules for the measurement of privacy remedies, courts will be loathe to rule in favor of recognizing privacy rights." Footnotes omitted.

whereby the plaintiff can apply to a court of law for different kinds of injunctions. Injunction means an order of the court to prevent someone from intrusion or disclosure of personal information if the plaintiff comes to know that the defendant intends to do that. The plaintiff can also apply for preventing the defendant from repetition or continuation of the infringement. A controversial form of injunction is also known as super-injunction, where the media is prevented even from reporting the existence of injunction about the *sub judice* matter.[114]

Law of injunctions is quite established in other fields of civil law, particularly under contract and property law. In civil disputes, the plaintiff applies for an interim or interlocutory injunction, such as requesting to retain the *status quo* related to immovable property or goods, unless the main dispute is settled. The purpose of such suit for interlocutory injunction is to prevent the potential harm, which might be ensued due to the violation of a legal right. In Pakistan, Specific Relief Act of 1877 regulates the claims for injunctions,[115] while the procedure to adjudicate such claims is provided under the Code of Civil Procedure 1908.[116]

---

[114] See for a detailed discussion: Eady (2010).

[115] Section 52 Preventive relief how granted: "Preventive relief is granted at the discretion of the Court by injunction, temporary or perpetual." Section 53 Temporary injunctions: "Temporary injunctions are such as are to continue until a specified time, or until the further order of the Court. They may be granted at any period of a suit, and are regulated by the Code of Civil Procedure, 1908"; "Perpetual injunctions: A perpetual injunction can only be granted by the decree made at the hearing and upon the merits of the suit: the defendant is thereby perpetually enjoined from the assertion of a right, or from the commission of an act, which would be contrary to the rights of the plaintiff." Section 54. Perpetual injunctions when granted: "Subject to the other provisions contained in, or referred to by, this Chapter, a perpetual injunction may be granted to pre vent the breach of an obligation existing in favour of the applicant, whether expressly or by implication. When such obligation arises from contract, the Court shall be guided by the rules and provisions contained in Chapter II of this Act. When the defendant invades or threatens to invade the plain tiff's right to, or enjoyment of, property, the Court may grant a perpetual injunction in the following cases (namely): (a) where the defendant is trustee of the property for the plaintiff ; (b) where there exists no standard for ascertaining the actual damage caused, or likely to be caused, by the invasion; (c) where the invasion is such that pecuniary compensation would not afford adequate relief; (d) where it is probable that pecuniary compensation cannot be got for the invasion; (e) where the injunction is necessary to prevent a multiplicity of judicial proceedings." Section 55. Mandatory injunction: "When, to prevent the breach of an obligation, it is necessary to compel the performance of certain acts which the Court is capable of enforcing, the Court may in its discretion grant an injunction to prevent the breach complained of, and also to compel performance of the requisite acts."

[116] Order 39 Rule 2 provides: "Injunction to restrain repetition or continuance of breach. (1) In any suit for restraining the defendant from committing a breach of contract or other injury of any kind, whether compensation is claimed in the suit or not, the plaintiff may, at any time after the commencement of the suit, and either before or after judgment, apply to the Court for a temporary injunction to restrain the defendant from committing the breach of contract or injury complained of, or any breach of contract or injury of a like kind arising out of the same contract or relating to the same property or right. (2) The Court may by order grant such injunction, on such terms as to the duration of the injunction, keeping an account, giving security or otherwise, as the Court thinks fit. (3) In case of disobedience, or of breach of any such terms, the Court granting an injunction may order the property of the person guilty of such disobedience or breach to be attached, and may also

The issuance of injunctions is not a straightforward matter for the courts where media is a defendant due to a number of reasons. Issuing orders to restrain the publication of facts, dissemination of information or preventing a scheduled interview are regarded as interferences in the right to freedom of speech of journalists. Secondly, time is the essence of many news stories and old news is not considered as "NEWS". Thirdly, there is also a cutthroat competition for breaking news among news media outlets and so any curb on one outlet can give an opportunity to another one to publish or on-air the story. However, the breach of privacy is also an irreparable loss, and the information once disclosed cannot be completely undone. It is easier to make something public but it is not possible to convert public into private. Therefore, the judges have to conduct an initial balancing based on the *prima facie* facts of the case.[117]

7.2.5.2 Damages

The proposed statute for the protection of personal privacy must expressly provide for damages in the form of monitory remedies if the tort of breach of privacy is established. The tort of privacy infringement is actionable *per se* which means that the defendant is liable for his act and it is not necessary for the establishment of a wrong to prove that the plaintiff has suffered any damage as a result of the alleged action.[118] The plaintiff in privacy infringement cases has the right to claim for general damage (compensation for act of the defendant) and special damages (compensation for the special harm such as loss of job etc.) as well as an account of the profit generated by the defendant as a result of violation of the right to privacy of the plaintiff.

---

order such person to be detained in prison for a term not exceeding six months, unless in the meantime the Court directs his release."

[117] Moreham (2018), p. 13: "The decision whether to grant an injunction to protect privacy implicates a complex web of interests and requires courts to strike a sometimes difficult balance between competing interests. The question of how to strike this balance is perhaps most difficult where plaintiffs seek to restrain the publication of information which they allege violates their privacy rights, especially where a so-called super-injunction is claimed; that is an injunction, a term of which is that the existence of the injunction and proceedings cannot be disclosed. Courts must, in making decisions about whether to grant such relief, consider not only the importance of protecting privacy, but also other fundamental interests including freedom of expression and open justice."

[118] See for Pakistani case law related to damages and principles of obligations Nasir Ahmad Sheikh v SLICP, 1990 MLD 2261, "The real significance or legal damage is illustrated by tow maxims namely *injuria sine damnum* and *damnum sine injuria*. By *damnum* is meant damage in the substantial sense of money, loss of comfort, service, hearth, or the like. By *injuria* is meant a tortious act; it need not be willful and malicious; for though it be accidental, if it be tortious, an action will lie. Any unauthorized interference, however trivial, with some absolute right conferred by law on a person, is an injury, e.g. the right of excluding others from one's house or garden."

Pakistani case law of legal obligations is consistent on the issue of calculation of the amount of damages or devising any hard and fast yardstick for the assessment of the quantum of damages. [119]

Compensation for mental agony is already in practice, though in a very limited manner. One can find case law where the plaintiffs have successfully initiated tort actions for malicious prosecution against the defendants. The courts have awarded monetary compensation for such non-material loss. Thus, the tort action under the proposed privacy law cannot create any kind of conceptual controversy. The functional arguments in favor of privacy show that it safeguards many crucial dignitarian interests, the right to autonomy and personality rights. A violation of the right to privacy may deprive the person in those areas of non-tangible nature. According to scholars, complexity in the nature of harm of privacy violation as well as its immensity validates the comprehensive compensatory measures. [120]

---

[119] For example, in a case of compensation for mental agony due to malicious prosecution, a superior court of Pakistan held that no yardstick existed for the measurement or assessment of actual quantum of damages related to mental torture sustained by plaintiff. It held, "In order to prove the expenditure incurred on such litigation, a party could place on record details of such expenditure, but in the present case no specific evidence was available on that point–Even if plaintiff failed to prove actual quantum of damages, her suit was not to be dismissed on that ground as Court itself was competent in circumstances to ascertain quantum of damages [. . . .because of the fact that] she had to face the agony of such frivolous litigation for a number of years before various Courts in order to vindicate and safeguard her right of property, family prestige and reputation". The Court awarded the plaintiff an amount of Rs. 10,00,000 as damages to be paid by defendant so that "ends of justice would meet". 2004 CLC 223.

[120] Moreham (2018), p. 136: "The idea that privacy damages should compensate loss of dignity – and that that is why it is necessary to compensate for the loss of privacy *per se* – is therefore consistent with the way privacy is understood by jurists, philosophers and social scientists. To use another person's private experience to further one's research, to make money, to titillate, to entertain, or to make a point is to treat that person as a means to your ends rather than respect that individual's inherent value as a person. And that lack of respect is inherent in breaches of privacy independent of any distress or other consequential harm suffered. Such harm will therefore be suffered – and should be compensated – whenever there is an actionable breach." [. . . .] Such individuals have a compensable right to be treated with respect – as an end and not a means – whether they get distressed by privacy interference or not. Conceiving of harm in dignitary terms also helps explain why a breach of privacy is compensable even when the claimant knew nothing about it at the time. A person who films you in the shower so that he or she can obtain sexual gratification or sell the footage on the Internet is treating you as a means to his or her ends whether you knew about it or not. Indeed, the surreptitiousness of his or her conduct makes the dignitary interference worse. Not only does the intruder prevent you from taking evasive action, he or she deliberately alters your conditions of action whilst concealing that fact from you. As Benn says, the subject might be in a 'fool's paradise or a fool's hell' but either way, the observer is 'making a fool of him'. The affront to an individual's dignity therefore begins as soon as the surreptitious privacy breach occurs and he or she should be compensated accordingly. Footnotes and references omitted. Moreham suggests that in all privacy cases, the courts should identify the different elements of the losses in a precise manner and try to consider even obscure nonmaterial costs of privacy interferences such as the loss of dignity and autonomy. p. 142.

7.3 Conclusion and Outlook: Safeguarding Privacy in a Globalized World

In a world marked by the rapid proliferation of digital technologies, the concept of privacy has become a paramount concern transcending geographical boundaries. "Comparative Perspectives on the Right to Privacy – Pakistani and European Experiences" has undertaken a rigorous exploration of the intricate landscape of privacy rights in Pakistan and Europe, dissecting their legal, cultural, and societal dimensions. This comparative study, encapsulated in seven chapters, has uncovered insights and revelations about the state of privacy in our interconnected world. As we conclude, we reflect upon the overarching lessons learned from this extensive investigation.

At the outset, we recognized the fundamental disparities in media landscapes between Pakistan and Europe. The contrasting environments set the stage for our examination of privacy rights. Europe boasted well-established legal frameworks and safeguards, while Pakistan grappled with a media culture rife with invasive practices, from sensationalized reporting of sexual violence to the exposure of women and children. This disparity underscored the urgency of addressing these issues through comprehensive privacy legislation.

The conceptual underpinnings of the right to privacy, dissected in Chap. 3, revealed the intricate tapestry of privacy's various dimensions. Privacy emerged as a multifaceted concept, encompassing negative liberty, control over personal information, and an aspect of human life with strong intrinsic value. This groundwork highlighted the need for a nuanced approach to harmonizing basic rights, recognizing that balancing privacy rights with the right to freedom of speech is essential.

The examination of the constitutional framework in Chap. 4 brought into focus the limitations of normative anchors in Pakistan, posing substantial challenges. Despite these challenges, instances of jurisprudential development offered glimpses of expanded privacy protection. This chapter emphasized the delicate equilibrium required to navigate the complex terrain of constitutional rights, particularly the interplay between privacy and freedom of expression.

Expanding our perspective, Chap. 5 scrutinized the European Convention on Human Rights (ECHR) as a model for privacy protection. It underscored the relevance of the ECHR and the pivotal role of the European Court of Human Rights (ECtHR). This chapter highlighted the intricate task of reconciling privacy with countervailing rights, emphasizing the complexities inherent in the judicial balancing of competing interests.

The case studies of Germany and the United Kingdom in Chap. 6 provided tangible insights into how these nations approached privacy rights within their legal frameworks as well as under the influence of the European Convention on Human Rights. Germany's commitment to privacy protection through the General Personality Right served as an exemplar, reflecting a strong dedication to safeguarding privacy. In contrast, the United Kingdom's reliance on the breach of confidence tort posed challenges in providing comprehensive privacy safeguards.

Finally, this chapter offered a roadmap for Pakistan. It advocated for the explicit recognition of the right to privacy through legislation, building upon extensive conceptual study and comparative analysis. These recommendations, while not exhaustive, served as a foundational step toward addressing nuanced privacy-related issues in the future.

In summation, "Comparative Perspectives on the Right to Privacy – Pakistani and European Experiences" has illuminated the intricate facets of privacy rights and underscored the universal importance of protecting this fundamental human right. While Pakistan and Europe may differ in their approaches and challenges, the book's resounding message is clear: privacy is an indispensable right that transcends borders and demands protection in an evolving digital landscape. As we move forward, nations, including Pakistan, must adapt their legal frameworks to safeguard privacy, recognizing its inherent value in preserving human dignity and individuality. This book stands as a testament to the critical need for privacy protection in our interconnected world, offering valuable insights and guidance for a future that respects and upholds privacy rights for all.

The rapid advancement of new technologies has presented us with a multitude of legal challenges that demand systematic examination to regulate corresponding rights and obligations effectively. High-speed computer processors and data storage devices have ushered in transformative changes that affect every facet of our lives. The ability to process vast amounts of personal data rapidly, with the assistance of artificial intelligence (AI), has become increasingly accessible. The deployment of AI for tasks once exclusive to humans raises constitutional dilemmas, particularly when these technologies intersect with human rights.

Moreover, the advent of big data, metadata, the Internet of Things, and the pervasive use of algorithms in tech-driven decision-making, alongside the expanding role of social media replacing traditional media (such as print and electronic media), demands a comprehensive research-based approach. This approach is essential for addressing challenges to human dignity, personal development, and the right to data protection. These developments challenge not only the conceptual foundations but also the existing mechanisms for enforcing fundamental rights, both in Pakistan and elsewhere.

As discussed earlier, Pakistan's legal and constitutional responses have lagged behind European jurisdictions in addressing key issues concerning privacy and the media. However, addressing this disparity necessitates specific research initiatives that delve into the regulatory challenges posed by every form of communication and technological advancement from a human rights perspective.

This research study has endeavored to propose a legal framework for safeguarding and enforcing a crucial human right, the right to privacy, within the jurisdiction of Pakistan. While this 'legal pathway' may not comprehensively cover all human rights issues associated with the development of information and communication technologies, as well as digital media, it represents a significant step forward. Through extensive conceptual exploration and comparative analysis, the explicit recognition of the right to privacy and its concretization via legislation can serve as a foundational starting point. It offers the potential to address more intricate and nuanced privacy-related issues within a human rights framework.

In summary, the rapid evolution of technology has ushered in an era where privacy rights face unprecedented challenges. Legal systems must adapt and evolve to ensure the protection of fundamental human rights. This book's exploration of the Pakistani and European experiences underscores the universality of the need to safeguard privacy in our increasingly interconnected and data-driven world. By embracing a human rights perspective and adopting legal measures that explicitly recognize and protect privacy, nations can navigate the complexities of the digital age while upholding the dignity and rights of their citizens. However, it is clear that the outlook for privacy in the age of IT and AI requires ongoing research and study, as these emerging challenges were beyond the scope of this book.

References

Bloustein EJ (1964) Privacy as an aspect of human dignity: an answer to Dean Prosser. N Y Univ Law Rev 39:962

Cariolou L (2016) The developing law of privacy and the limits to the public interest defence: the Grand Chamber judgment in Couderc and Hachette Filipacchi Associés v France. J Media Law 8(2):138–152

Cohen JE (2013) What privacy is for. Harv Law Rev 126:1904

Davis F (1959) What do we mean by right to privacy. South Dakota Law Rev 4:1

Eady D (1996) A statutory right to privacy. EHRLR 1996:243

Eady D (2010) Injunctions and the protection of privacy. C J Q 29:4/41

Emerson TI (1979) The right of privacy and freedom of the press. Harv CR-CLL Rev 14:329

Finn RL, Wright D, Friedewald M (2013) Seven types of privacy. In: Gutwirth S, Leenes R, De Hert P, Poullet Y (eds) European data protection: coming of age. Springer, Dordrecht

Gerety T (1977) Redefining privacy. Harv CR-CLL Rev 12:233

Fried C (1968) Privacy. Yale Law Journal 77:475

Kotzur M (2022) Privacy protection in the world wide web—legal perspectives on accomplishing a mission impossible. In: Personality and data protection rights on the internet: Brazilian and German approaches. Springer International Publishing, pp 17–34

Mance J (2009) Human rights, privacy and the public interest—who draws the line and where? Liverpool Law Rev 30:3/263

Moreham NA (2014) Protection against intrusion in English legislation. In: Witzleb N, Lindsay D, Paterson M, Rodrick S (eds) Emerging challenges in privacy law: comparative perspectives. Cambridge University Press

Moreham NA (2018) Remedies for breach of privacy. Hart Publishing

Nissenbaum H (2004) Privacy as contextual integrity. Wash Law Rev 79:119

Rolph D (2007) Preparing for a full-scale invasion? Truth, privacy and defamation. Commun Law Bull 25(3/4):5

Scholz LH (2019) Privacy remedies. Indiana Law J 94:2/653

Schwartz PM (1999) Privacy and democracy in cyberspace. Vand Law Review 52:1607

Solove DJ (2002) Conceptualizing privacy. Calif L Rev 90(1087):1092–1126

Solove DJ (2006) A taxonomy of privacy. Univ Pa Law Re 154:477

Solove D (2007) The future of reputation: gossip, rumor, and privacy on the internet. Yale University Press

Solove DJ (2008) Understanding privacy. Harvard University Press

Solove DJ, Schwartz PM (2012) Reworking information privacy law: a memorandum regarding future ALI projects about information privacy law
Taylor G (2000) Why is there no common law right of privacy. Monash Univ Law Rev 26:235/270
Tunick M (2015) Balancing privacy and free speech: unwanted attention in the age of social media. Routledge
Tzanou M (2013) Data protection as a fundamental right next to privacy? Reconstructing a not so new right. Int Data Privacy Law 3(2):88
Van der Sloot B (2015) Privacy as personality right: why the ECtHR's focus on ulterior interests might prove indispensable in the age of big data. Utrecht J Int Eur Law 31:25
Veit RD (2022) Safeguarding regional data protection rights on the global internet—the European approach under the GDPR. In: Personality and data protection rights on the internet: Brazilian and German approaches. Springer International Publishing, pp 445–484
Wacks R (2013) Privacy and media freedom. Oxford University Press